W9-DDS-145

BATTLEGROUND
BUSINESS

BATTLEGROUND

BUSINESS

VOLUME 2 (O–Z)

Edited by Michael Walden and Peg Thoms

GREENWOOD PRESS
Westport, Connecticut • London

Library of Congress Cataloging-in-Publication Data

Battleground : business / edited by Michael Walden and Peg Thoms.
p. cm.
Includes bibliographical references and index.
ISBN-13: 978–0–313–34065–9 (set : alk. paper)
ISBN-13: 978–0–313–34066–6 (v. 1 : alk. paper)
ISBN-13: 978–0–313–34067–3 (v. 2 : alk. paper)
1. Business. 2. Commerce. I. Walden, M. L. (Michael Leonard), 1951– II. Thoms, Peg, 1948–
HF1008.B38 2007
658—dc22 2007021681

British Library Cataloguing in Publication Data is available.

Library of Congress Catalog Card Number: 2007021681
ISBN-13: 978–0–313–34065–9 (set)
978–0–313–34066–6 (vol. 1)
978–0–313–34067–3 (vol. 2)

First published in 2007

Greenwood Press, 88 Post Road West, Westport, CT 06881
An imprint of Greenwood Publishing Group, Inc.
www.greenwood.com

Printed in the United States of America

The paper used in this book complies with the Permanent Paper Standard issued by the National Information Standards Organization (Z39.48–1984).

10 9 8 7 6 5 4 3 2 1

CONTENTS

GUIDE TO RELATED TOPICS

Following are the entries in this book arranged by broad topics:

MARKETING ISSUES

SALARY AND WELL-BEING ISSUES

O

OIL ECONOMICS AND BUSINESS

This is a good-news/bad-news entry. Since the nineteenth century, there has been both a regular and periodic concern that fossil fuel supplies will be inadequate to support and maintain the world's energy dependent economy and society. In the twentieth century, the most prominent advocate of the theory of impending trouble was the well-respected geologist and geophysicist M. King Hubbert, who predicted in 1956 that U.S. crude oil production would peak between 1965 and 1970. U.S. crude oil production did in fact peak in 1971. Hubbert further predicted in 1974 that global crude oil production would peak in 1995. However, world oil production has not yet peaked.

In the twenty-first century, there continues to be widespread concern and support for Hubbert's contention that the fossil fuel era would be of very short duration. Some analysts argue that Saudi Arabian oil production may have already peaked and may now be in decline. Saudi Arabia is the largest supplier of crude oil exports to the world market. Others argue that total world oil production, if it has not already peaked, will peak in a few years.

The first piece of good news is that world oil production has not yet peaked and may continue production at current, or higher, levels in the foreseeable future—decades or more. The second is that even if the pessimists are correct, it is likely that there will be cost-effective fossil fuel substitutes for oil that allow continued economic growth and improvement in living standards for the population of the world. There is no question that the fossil fuel content of the geology of the earth is finite.

What is the bad news? The bad news is that just as the world is now predominantly a fossil fuel economy, the world is likely to continue to be a predominantly fossil fuel economy for at least the balance of the twenty-first century.

When fossil fuels are used, they emit greenhouse gases. The 1997 Kyoto Protocol amended the international treaty on climate change to assign mandatory targets for the reduction of greenhouse gas emissions. If there are adequate fossil fuel resources to maintain or increase our global fossil fuel consumption, then there will be unavoidable tension between maintaining and improving our energy-dependent standard of living for the growing population of the world and curbing greenhouse gas emissions. "Unavoidable tension" is a polite way of saying a political catfight. And this is an international political catfight that may take decades to resolve.

THE CENTRALITY OF OIL

The primary source of energy used by the world economy comes in a variety of forms: petroleum (crude oil); natural gas; coal; and hydro, geothermal, solar, wind, biomass, and nuclear energy. Electricity is a derived form of energy that can be generated by any of the primary energy sources. Many energy sources have multiple uses. For example, wind can power turbines to generate electricity or propel sailing ships. Sunlight can generate electricity photovoltaically or directly provide space heating. Natural gas can be used for space heating and cooling or to generate electricity. Coal can be used for transportation (locomotives and steamships), space heating, or electricity generation. These energy sources compete with each other in the energy market, and this competition determines which source is the most cost effective and technically efficient alternative for each specific use.

There is, however, only one energy source that broadly competes with all other energy sources in all uses. This is petroleum. The competitive centrality of petroleum, in addition to petroleum's predominance as the largest single source of energy for the world economy, is why so much attention is focused on world crude oil supplies. Because of petroleum's worldwide competitive interconnectedness to the markets for all other sources of energy, when the world oil market sneezes, each of the markets for other types of energy at least sniffles.

THE FLOW OF OIL

The standard way that energy economists think about the amount of oil produced and consumed is in barrels per day. There is a good reason for this. Oil is always on the move. It flows in drill pipes from underground geological formations to the surface of the earth. There it is temporarily deposited in lease tanks before beginning another journey by pipeline to a refinery. A refinery is a vast network of pipes, pressure vessels, and storage tanks through which oil flows as it is converted from crude oil to refined products such as gasoline, jet fuel, and heating oil.

TECHNOLOGY CREATES RESOURCES

When I was a young graduate student in the early 1960s, I traveled through Louisiana, Texas, and Oklahoma, interviewing oil company exploration executives for background for my PhD dissertation. One interview still vividly stands out in my mind. Jim Finley was the exploration vice president for a consortium of major oil companies that was pioneering drilling on the outer continental shelf in the Gulf of Mexico. He very graciously spent an afternoon with me answering my (often naive) questions and explaining Gulf of Mexico outer continental shelf oil exploration and production.

Offshore oil production in the Gulf of Mexico actually began in the 1930s. In shallow water near to the shore, large wooden platforms were built on wooden pilings and drilling rigs and production facilities operated from these platforms. The platforms were connected to each other and to the shore by a network of docks and walkways.

After World War II, steel platform technology began to advance. This was complemented by advances in drill ship and drilling barge technologies and advances in undersea pipeline-laying techniques and technology. But compared to current industry offshore operations, exploration and production were still limited to relatively shallow water. I recall the pride, animation, and sense of adventure with which Jim Finley told me about what could then be accomplished with 1960s technology. Steel platforms could be set in 100 feet of water! Using directional drilling, drill bits could be turned (or "whipstocked") so that wells could be completed in water that was 300 feet deep. A deep well was a completion into a reservoir that lay 10,000 feet under the floor of the Gulf.

In 2006, the so-called Jack field in the deep waters of the central Gulf of Mexico was flow tested. The discovery well was drilled in 6,000 feet of water. The producing formation lies 25,000 feet under the floor of the Gulf of Mexico. The Jack field is part of a larger geologic formation that is estimated to contain 9–15 billion barrels of oil, a 50 percent increase in U.S. proved reserves. The seismic and geophysical technologies that allowed identification of the Jack field and the drilling and production technologies that allow development of the field are amazing. As late as the last quarter of the twentieth century, the Jack field might as well have been on Mars. For all practical purposes, the oil resources of the Jack field did not exist. New technologies create new resources.

Refined products leave the refinery and move to market through pipelines. Sometimes crude oil and refined products also move great distances around the world by ocean tanker. Since time is money, there are large economic incentives to minimize the amount of time that oil spends in storage tanks along its route from geological formation to refined-product customer.

The United States uses about 20 million barrels of oil a day. How much is that? An oil barrel is 42 gallons, so 20 million barrels a day equals 840 million gallons per day. And how much is this? Visualize a reddish-orange-and-yellow one-gallon gas can used to fill a lawn mower. Start at the Miami City limits and line up 42 of these one-gallon cans across the northbound lane of the interstate highway from Miami to Chicago. Repeat that lineup of cans across the interstate all the way to Chicago until the northbound lane is full of gas cans. That is 840 million gallons of oil.

Now, blink your eyes, and all the oil cans disappear (i.e., the oil is consumed). Tomorrow, blink your eyes again and all 840 million oil cans—full of oil—reappear. The vast production network of wells, pipelines, tankers, and refineries replaces yesterday's consumption with today's new production.

This is a logistic miracle. It happens every day, day in and day out, 365 days a year. It happens not only in the United States, but all over the world. And world production and consumption is 85 million barrels of oil a day.

The planning and implementation imperatives that this daily feat of logistics imposes upon the oil industry are the practical reasons why industry operators commonly measure production and consumption in millions of barrels a day. Oil, of course, is not the only source of energy. So it is useful to have a measure of energy that allows comparison across the various types of energy. That measure is the British thermal unit, or Btu. Production and consumption statistics are also kept on an annual basis. But beneath the annual numbers, energy is moving in a ceaseless hourly and daily flow.

THE PATTERNS OF ENERGY CONSUMPTION

The world used 444.3 quadrillion Btus of energy in 2004. A Btu, or British thermal unit, is the heat equal to 1/180 of the heat required to raise the temperature of one pound of water from a temperature of 32 degrees Fahrenheit to 212 degrees Fahrenheit at a constant pressure of one atmosphere. An atmosphere is the air pressure at sea level. A quadrillion is a million billion, or $10.^{15}$ This is a tremendous amount of energy. The word used to mean a quadrillion Btus is "quad."

Table O.1 shows the types and amounts of each type of energy consumed in 1980 and in 2004 on a worldwide basis and the increases in energy consumption over the 1980–2004 interval. Table O.2 shows the relative percentage shares of each type of energy for 1980 and 2004 and the 1980–2004 increase.

In each year, petroleum was the largest single source of energy (Table O.1). Petroleum accounted for 46.6 percent of total world energy consumption in 1980 and 38.7 percent in 2004 (Table O.2). Petroleum, however, was not the largest addition to world energy supplies over the 1980–2004 period. Although petroleum supplied 22.4 percent of the 163.1 quad increase of 2004 consumption relative to 1980 consumption, natural gas (30.3%) and coal (27.2%) supplied larger shares of the increment in production (Table O.2).

In 1980, as shown in Table O.2, the three fossil fuels (petroleum, natural gas, and coal) supplied 90.8 percent of all worldwide energy consumption. In 2004, the share of fossil fuels in total consumption was 86.7 percent. Fossil fuels accounted for 79.8 percent of the 58.0 percent increase in world energy consumption between 1980 and 2004.

On a worldwide basis, as shown in Table O.2, renewable sources of energy (hydro, geothermal, wind, solar, and biomass forms) accounted for 6.5 percent

Table O.1 World Consumption of Energy by Type of Energy (1980 and 2004).

Type of energy	Quadrillion Btu consumed 1980	2004	Increase	Percent Increase
Petroleum	131.0	167.5	36.5	27.9
Natural gas	54.0	103.4	49.4	91.5
Coal	70.2	114.5	44.3	63.1
Total fossil	255.2	385.4	130.2	51.0
Hydro	17.9	27.5	9.6	53.6
Geothermal, solar, wind, and biomass	0.5	3.9	3.4	680.0
Total renewable	18.4	31.4	13.0	70.7
Nuclear	7.6	27.5	19.9	361.8
World total	281.2	444.3	163.1	58.0

Note: Due to rounding, totals may not add up.
Source: U.S. Energy Information Administration. 2006. *Monthly Energy Review,* August.

Table O.2 Relative Contributions of Various Types of Energy to Total World Energy Consumption, Increase (1980, 2004, 1980–2004).

Type of energy	Percent contribution to total world consumption 1980	2004	1980–2004 Increase
Petroleum	46.6	38.7	22.4
Natural gas	19.2	23.3	30.3
Coal	25.0	25.8	27.2
Total fossil	90.8	86.7	79.8
Hydro	6.4	6.2	5.9
Geothermal, solar, wind and biomass	0.2	1.0	2.1
Total renewable	6.5	7.1	8.0
Nuclear	2.7	6.2	12.2
World total	100.0	100.0	100.0

Note: Due to rounding, totals may not add up.
Source: U.S. Energy Information Administration. 2006. *Monthly Energy Review,* August.

of total energy consumption in 1980 and 7.1 percent in 2004. Renewables accounted for 8.0 percent of the increase in world energy consumption between 1980 and 2004.

Renewables, however, had strong growth over the 1980–2004 interval (see Table O.1). The contribution to total world energy consumption made by the combination of geothermal, solar, wind and biomass forms increased by 680 percent, from 0.5 quads to 3.9 quads. Hydro grew 53.6 percent, from 17.9 quads to 27.5 quads. Overall, total renewable production and consumption grew by 70.7 percent, from 18.4 quads to 31.4 quads, as opposed to 51.0 percent growth for total fossil fuels, from 255.2 quads to 385.4 quads.

Nuclear power increased by 361.8 percent between 1980 and 2004, from 7.6 quads to 27.5 quads. Over the quarter century spanning 1980 through 2004, the fastest-growing sources of world energy consumption were nonhydro renewables and nuclear forms. Nevertheless, fossil fuels accounted for nearly 80 percent of the total growth in energy consumption over that same period.

Tables O.3 and O.4 mirror Tables O.1 and O.2, but the focus is the United States. Between 1980 and 2005, U.S. energy consumption increased 27.5 percent, from 78.3 quads to 99.8 quads (Table O.3). Fossil fuels supplied 89.4 percent of U.S. energy consumption in 1980 and 85.9 percent in 2005 (Table O.4). Fossil fuels also supplied 73.0 percent of the 21.5 quad increase in U.S. energy consumption over the 1980–2005 interval (Tables O.3 and O.4).

Between 1980 and 2005, the total renewable energy consumption in the United States increased 0.6 quads, or 10.9 percent. This net increase reflects a 0.8 quad increase for the combination of biomass, geothermal, solar, and wind forms that is partially offset by a 0.2 quad decrease in U.S. hydropower. In general, although the use of hydropower increased on a worldwide basis and decreased in the United States, the pattern of U.S. energy consumption is similar to the pattern for the world. Over the quarter century from 1980 to 2004/5, both the United States and the world increased total energy consumption. For both the United States and the world, by far the principal source of total energy consumption was fossil fuel. In relative terms, fossil fuels lost a few percentage points of market share. But for both the United States and the world, increased fossil fuel consumption accounted for over 70 percent of the total increase in energy consumption. Use of nuclear power increased in both absolute and relative

Table O.3 U.S. Consumption of Energy by Type of Energy (1980 and 2005).

	Quadriillion Btus consumed			
Type of energy	**1980**	**2005**	**Increase**	**Percent Increase**
Petroleum	34.2	40.4	6.2	18.1
Natural gas	20.4	22.5	2.1	10.3
Coal	15.4	22.8	7.4	48.1
Total fossil	**70.0**	**85.7**	**15.7**	**22.4**
Hydro	2.9	2.7	–0.2	–6.9
Biomass	2.5	2.8	0.3	12.0
Geothermal	0.1	0.4	0.3	300.0
Solar	NA	0.1	0.1	NA
Wind	NA	0.1	0.1	NA
Total renewable	**5.5**	**6.1**	**0.6**	**10.9**
Nuclear	2.7	8.1	5.4	200.0
U.S. total	**78.3**	**99.8**	**21.5**	**27.5**

Note: Due to rounding, totals may not add up.
Source: U.S. Energy Administration. 2006. *Monthly Energy Review,* August.

Table 0.4 Relative Contributions of Various Types of Energy to Total U.S. Energy Consumption (1980, 2005, and 1980–2005 Increase).

	Percent contribution to total U.S. consumption		
Type of energy	**1980**	**2005**	**1980–2005 Increase**
Petroleum	43.7	40.5	28.8
Natural gas	26.1	22.5	9.8
Coal	19.7	22.8	34.4
Total fossil	89.4	85.9	73.0
Hydro	3.7	2.7	–0.9
Biomass	3.2	2.8	1.4
Geothermal	0.1	0.4	1.4
Solar	NA	0.1	0.5
Wind	NA	0.1	0.5
Total renewable	7.0	6.1	2.8
Nuclear	3.4	8.1	25.1
U.S. total	100.0	100.0	100.0

Note: Due to rounding, totals may not add up.
Source: U.S. Energy Information Administration. 2006. *Monthly Energy Review*, August.

terms in the United States and worldwide. With the exception of hydropower outside the United States, renewable sources made relatively modest contributions to both absolute and relative energy consumption in the United States and on a worldwide basis.

OIL PRODUCTION: THE INTENSIVE MARGIN

Economists have long considered two general approaches to increasing or maintaining the production of output: the intensive margin of production and the extensive margin of production. Think of a tomato farmer. If the farmer wants to increase production, one way to accomplish this is by getting more output from her existing fields. This can be achieved by installing irrigation, applying fertilizer, hiring more labor to pick and cultivate more carefully, applying pesticides and herbicides, and the like. These production enhancement techniques are all examples of expanding output at the internal margin of production.

There is also an external margin of production—an alternative way the farmer could expand production. She could plant, cultivate, and harvest additional fields of tomatoes. She could manage the new fields in exactly the same way that she managed her original fields. If she were to follow this approach, the farmer would be expanding output at the external margin of production. Not surprisingly, if there are economic incentives to expand the output of some commodity, there are production responses at both the internal and external margins of production.

Terms of art in the oil and gas industry are "resource" and "proved reserves." Resources exist in nature. Proved reserves are an artifact of humans. Resources are the total global endowment of fossil fuels that nature has bestowed upon us. Resources exist whether they have been discovered or not. Proved reserves are the portion of a discovered resource that is recoverable (or producible) under existing technological and economic conditions.

In order to understand how the concept of the internal margin applies to oil production, it is necessary to review a little petroleum geology. Oil does not occur in huge underground lakes or pools. What is often called a pool of oil actually appears to the naked eye to be solid rock. The oil is contained in the microscopic pore spaces between the tiny grains of sand that make up the rock. Porous rock that contains oil is called reservoir rock. The reservoir rock of the Prudhoe Bay oil field on the North Slope of Alaska could be cut into thin slabs, polished up, and used as the facing on a bank building. Passers-by would be none the wiser.

Geologists speak of source rock, reservoir rock, and caprock. Source rock is the progenitor of fossil fuels. Eons ago in geologic time, plant and animal life lived and died and were deposited as organic material in sedimentary basins. The earth's crust moved and buckled and bent and folded over upon itself. This process rolled organic sedimentary material deep underground, where, over the course of geologic time, heat and pressure converted the organic sediments to fossil fuels—petroleum, natural gas, and coal.

Fossil fuels are solar fuels. The energy they contain derives from the energy of the sun. It is just that the production process that created them is much more roundabout—millions of years more roundabout—than the process that uses the energy of the sun to warm a solar water heater.

Oil formed in the source rock is pushed by underground pressures through various strata of permeable rock until it is trapped against a layer of impermeable rock—the caprock. The source of the pressure pushing the oil into the ultimate strata of reservoir rock is often water driven by a subterranean aquifer. If no caprock stops its pressure-driven journey, the oil escapes to the surface of the earth—on land or under the oceans. These are natural oil spills. One of the largest known deposits of oil in the world—the Athabasca Tar Sands in Alberta, Canada—is such a natural oil spill.

Nature abhors a vacuum. Nature also abhors a partial vacuum. Oil in a strata of reservoir rock is under great pressure, trapped between a water drive and the impermeable caprock. It requires tremendous pressure to force oil to flow through solid rock from the source rock to the caprock. When a well pierces the caprock and enters the reservoir rock, a partial vacuum is created. The great pressure differential between atmospheric pressure at the surface of the earth and the underground reservoir pressure causes the oil to flow to the well bore and then up through the well casing to the wellhead at the surface.

In the nineteenth century and the first half of the twentieth century, successful oil wells were often allowed to erupt as gushers and temporarily spew a fountain of oil from the drilling derrick. This is no longer the case. Reservoir pressure is precious and managed carefully. As natural reservoir pressure dissipates, less and less oil is forced through the reservoir rock to the well bore and daily production declines.

Not all the oil in place in a reservoir is produced. In the earliest days of the oil industry after Col. Edwin Drake drilled his discovery well in 1859 near Titusville, Pennsylvania, as little as 10 percent of the oil in place was produced before the natural reservoir pressure was exhausted and primary oil production ceased to flow. To offset the loss of production as primary output slowed, secondary production techniques were developed.

There are many different kinds of secondary production technology. The classic secondary production technique is the walking beam pump, which resembles a mechanized sawhorse bobbing up and down. Others include drilling injection wells and pumping water, natural gas, or carbon dioxide into the reservoir to maintain pressure. Secondary recovery shades into tertiary recovery such as injecting steam to make heavy oil flow more freely or injecting surfactant detergents to maintain reservoir pressure and to wash oil out of tight pore spaces and help it to flow to the well bore. From the inception of production, modern reservoir engineering now uses whatever techniques are cost effective to maintain reservoir pressure, improve flow, and increase the ultimate recovery of oil in place. The result has been a significant increase in the percent of oil in place that is recovered through production. In the twentieth century, 10 percent recovery became 30 percent recovery. Now it is often possible to achieve 50 percent or higher ultimate recovery of the oil in place. Higher prices for oil make application of expensive enhanced recovery technologies more cost effective and also encourage the development of new technologies.

A large fraction of the oil discovered from 1859 to 2006 remains unrecovered and in place in known reservoirs. At historical and current prices with historical and current technologies, it has not been cost effective to produce it. Most of the oil in place that has not qualified to be designated as proved reserves will likely never be recovered and produced. But if petroleum becomes more scarce relative to our desire to benefit from its use, its price (adjusted for inflation) will rise, perhaps dramatically. If, or when, that occurs, a variety of responses, interactions, and consequences will ensue. One of these responses will be at the intensive margins of production. New discoveries will be developed more intensively, and old oil fields will be intensively reworked.

FOSSIL FUEL PRODUCTION: THE EXTENSIVE MARGIN

The fossil fuels are all hydrocarbons. Petroleum is the most widely used fossil fuel with the largest market share of any energy source because transportation is such an important use. Liquid transportation fuels—for example, gasoline and jet fuel diesel—are easier, more convenient, and less costly to store, transport, distribute, and use than solid or gaseous fuels. However, the resource base for petroleum is smaller than that for coal and natural gas.

Engineers and scientists can convert the hydrocarbons in coal into liquid fuels. The Fischer-Tropsche process (named for two German chemists) is the best-known technology. It was used by Germany in World War II and by South

Africa during the apartheid embargo. A variation of the backend of the Fischer-Tropsch process can also be used to convert natural gas to liquid fuel. ExxonMobil is building a big gas-to-liquids (GTL) plant in West Africa. Qatar is building a very large GTL plant in the Persian Gulf to facilitate the marketing of its substantial natural gas reserves. The output of a GTL plant is equivalent to an environmentally friendly diesel fuel. We are on the cusp of extending the commercial production of liquid hydrocarbon fuels to natural gas. Higher oil prices will extend the commercial horizon to coal-based liquid hydrocarbon fuels.

The recent exploration activity focused upon the Lower Tertiary geologic formation in the deepwater Gulf of Mexico is another illustration of the relevance of the extensive margin. Two-thirds of the surface of the earth is covered by water.

CAN ETHANOL REPLACE GASOLINE?

Ethanol is a type of ethyl alcohol. Ethanol has been used as an additive for gasoline to oxygenate the fuel in order to reduce emissions and pollution. For this purpose, a common blend of ethanol and ordinary gasoline is a fuel called E15. E15 is 85 percent petroleum-based gasoline and 15 percent ethanol. A much more ethanol-intensive blend is E85. E85 is 85 percent ethanol and 15 percent gasoline.

The U.S. automobile industry produces many cars that are ethanol capable and can run on either 100 percent gasoline or fuels such as E15 and E85. E15 ethanol is used as a replacement for the chemical MTBE for purposes of oxygenation. E85 ethanol is used primarily as a replacement for gasoline itself. Ethanol contains only about 80 percent as many Btus of energy per gallon as does gasoline.

In the United States, most ethanol is made from corn. There are biofuels other than ethanol and biological feedstocks other than corn. The cultivation of alternative biofuel feedstocks—switchgrass for example—is apt to be less energy intensive than the cultivation of corn. But corn is currently a major U.S. crop. The conversion of corn to ethanol is a market-tested technology. So, for illustrative purposes, the focus here is upon corn-based ethanol.

The U.S. corn harvest averages about 11 billion bushels of corn per year. The principal use of corn is for animal feed. Between 1.5 and 4 billion bushels of corn are exported for this purpose. There are about 81 million acres of cropland planted for U.S. corn production. For the last decade, the average price of corn has been about $2.00 per bushel, although in 2006 corn was $2.50 per bushel. A bushel of corn is 60 pounds of corn.

The United States uses 144 billion gallons of gasoline per year. The conversion process of corn into ethanol yields slightly more than 2.7 gallons of ethanol per bushel of corn. If the entire 11 billion bushel current U.S. corn crop were converted into ethanol, about 20 percent of U.S. gasoline use could be replaced by ethanol.

Such a program would have many major consequences. Consider just two. First, U.S. demand for imported oil would be reduced. Second, the U.S. price of corn would increase dramatically. We would pay for the program at both the gas pump and the grocery store. There is a place for ethanol, but that is likely to be a small market as a substitute for MTBE rather than a broad market as a major replacement for gasoline.

There has been considerable exploration for and production of oil and natural gas on the great deltas of the shallow near-shore outer continental shelf—the North Sea, the Bight of Benin, the Gulf of Mexico, the South China Sea, and so on. Exploration and production in water depths up to 10,000 feet and at geologic horizons 25,000 feet beneath the ocean floor are now possible.

Vast new areas about which we now know relatively little have become accessible. Attractive prospects will not be limited to just the near-to-shore relatively shallow waters bordering the continents. New deepwater geologic horizons lie before us. A great adventure will continue. If the last 50 years of history in the Gulf of Mexico tell us anything, the technological limits will not long remain at 10,000 feet of water depth and 25,000 feet beneath the ocean floor. For liquid hydrocarbon fuels, Hubbert's peak lies before us—perhaps a long way before us.

PRICE VOLATILITY

Following World War II, oil prices were quite stable for a number of reasons. Prices spiked in the early middle 1970s following the Arab oil embargo. Prices spiked again at the end of the 1970s and in the early 1980s, coincident with the Iranian revolution. In the early 1990s, the first Gulf War was accompanied by another spike in prices. In 2006, due to supply dislocations in Alaska, Venezuela, Nigeria, and Iraq, prices spiked again and reached nearly $80 a barrel. We can learn a number of things from these price spikes.

First, short-run demand for and supply of oil are quite inflexible. Small dislocations on either side of the market can cause big swings in price. Second, volatility is a two-way street. What goes up often comes down. The price bust in the mid-1980s and the soft markets of the late 1990s and early 2000s illustrate such turnarounds. The big downward slide of prices from the 2006 highs punctuates the message. Third, economic recessions are often attributed to oil price spikes, but we should be cautious about such suggestions. In every instance, oil price spikes were accompanied by restrictive monetary policies applied by the sometimes draconian U.S. Federal Reserve restrictions. Fourth, there is upward pressure upon prices due to increasing demand for energy from the growing economies of India and China. This is good news. The world is a much better place with billions of Indians and Chinese participating in dynamic economies that are demanding more energy than it would be were these countries failed societies with stagnant demands.

There is a further general lesson in our experience of price volatility. As prices fluctuate, we adapt. The original Honda Civic and the SUV are classic examples of our response to higher and lower prices. In an important sense, $75 oil and $3 gasoline are a bargain. In terms of what oil (and, potentially, other liquid hydrocarbon fuels) does for us, and what we would have to give up without it, there are no readily available cost-effective substitutes.

In Europe, high fuel taxes cause gasoline prices to be more than $5 a gallon. But even at these prices, motor vehicle use in London has to be restricted in order to reduce congestion. As a hypothetical example, consider the effects of $5-a-gallon gasoline in the United States. If gasoline cost $5 a gallon because of long-term higher crude oil prices, this would be equivalent to a price of $125 a barrel for crude oil. Such prices would cause much pain, but after adjusting and adapting, it is unlikely the economy would suffer long-term collapse. Supply-side initiatives at all dimensions of the intensive and extensive margins, however, would be undertaken with incredible creativity and vigor. Demand-side responses would also be significant. In the short run, high-tech modern versions of the original Honda Civic would be widely adopted. In the long run, land-use patterns and building design and construction would change.

CONCLUSIONS

Fossil fuels are the workhorse of the world energy economy. Nuclear power is making a growing contribution to electricity generation. Outside the United States, new hydro facilities have also contributed to increased energy consumption. Nonhydro renewable energy use has grown rapidly from a small base. But these nonhydro renewable sources make a very modest contribution toward meeting increased energy demands or total energy use. It is likely that supplies of fossil fuel resources will be ample to meet growing energy demands for the foreseeable future.

Consumption of fossil fuels generates carbon dioxide. Many environmentalists believe that the greenhouse effect of increased atmospheric concentrations of carbon dioxide is the principal cause of global warming. In *The Skeptical Environmentalist,* Bjorn Lomborg expresses reservations about the extent of environmental degradation due to human activities and the linkage between carbon dioxide concentrations and global warming.

Nevertheless, serious people consider the links between human activity, fossil fuel use, increased carbon dioxide concentrations, and global warming to be very strong and regard the situation to be very serious. This is a big problem.

Modern societies and the global economy are built on fossil fuel use. There are now no cost-effective substitutes for fossil fuels. Reducing carbon dioxide emissions significantly will require dramatic changes in the way we organize our activities and live our lives. Many people, especially skeptics, will not make these sacrifices happily. If the skeptics are correct, we will incur great costs for few, if any, benefits. The resolution of these questions will become an increasingly important item on the global political agenda.

Further Reading: Lomborg, Bjorn. 2001. *The Skeptical Environmentalist,* Cambridge: Cambridge University Press.

Edward W. Erickson

ONLINE AUCTIONS

Online reverse auctions became popular in business in the mid-1990s. The promise of savings to businesses was great. Businesses may have seen the value to their own firms, but they did not consider the impact on the rest of the supply chain, long-standing relationships, or quality of the product purchased. What are the issues of online reverse auctions and should businesses implement this procurement tool in preference to other longstanding methods?

WHAT IS A REVERSE AUCTION?

In order to understand what a reverse auction is , we must first understand a forward auction, a process that is familiar to most of us.

We have all been to, or at least read about, estate auctions or barn auctions. At such an event, an auctioneer stands in front of the assembled bidders, speaks very quickly, attempts to build excitement in the bidding process, and tries to get the potential buyers to bid against each other, thus increasing the selling price of the item being auctioned. The auctioneer's goal is to obtain the highest possible price for the goods. Thus, a forward auction is one in which there is one seller and many buyers, as shown in Figure O.1, and the price the seller will pay is being increased in the process.

An example of an online forward auction is eBay. In 1998, most of the items on eBay were Beanie Babies. In 2003, *60 Minutes* reported that 50 million people were eBay users. By 2005, that number exceeded 125 million.

Opening bids on an item in an eBay auction may begin quite low—say $7 for a laptop computer—and rise to levels in line with the retail market at hundreds or even thousands of dollars. This strategy is certainly enticing to buyers and is an example of multiple bidders vying for the product and ultimately raising the price.

Reverse auctions, in contrast, involve one buyer and many sellers, as shown in Figure O.2. A potential buyer places a requirement, also known as a request for quotation, for a product. Potential sellers make the product available and participate in the reverse auction. In order to obtain the business, the sellers bid the price *down*. The lowest bidder wins the buyer's business. Thus, reverse

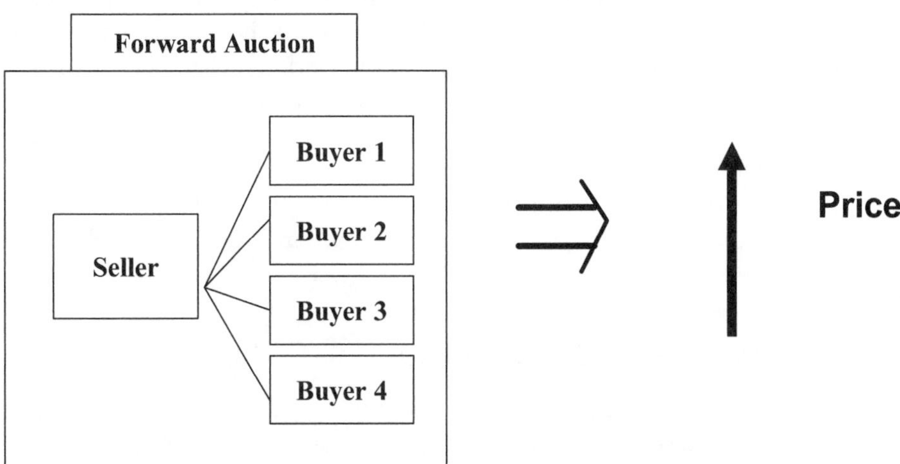

Figure O.1 Forward auction.

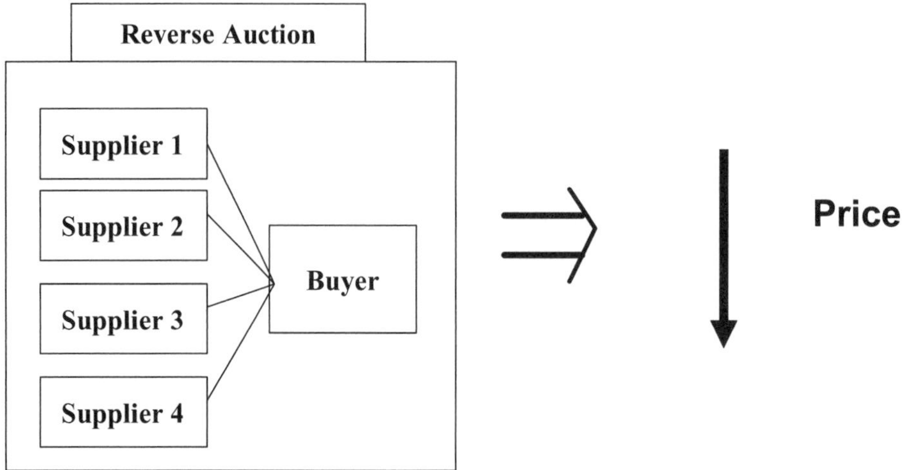

Figure 0.2 Reverse auction.

auctions are a tool for purchasing or procurement and are used with the objective of lowering the price to the buying firm.

WHO IS INVOLVED IN A REVERSE AUCTION AND WHY?

Over the past few decades, businesses have focused on supplier relationships, strategic sourcing, and even strategic alliances to ensure raw materials and services are available at the best price and quality. Both research and practice have stressed such strategic relationships in the purchasing function. The idea was that if both parties have a stake in the outcome, the critical factors of price, quality, and delivery are more likely to be achieved.

Online reverse auctions or procurement auctions have gained popularity due to an increasing emphasis on profitability and cost savings in business. The Internet has made a supplier's location and size inconsequential and, in some cases, unimportant. As long as the supplier can fulfill the contract, it can be located across the street or in another part of the world. The supplier may be a multinational corporation or a mom-and-pop shop. Therefore, the real competition is open to anyone who has access to the Internet and can, in theory, meet the buyer's requirements. In the earliest days of reverse auctions, suppliers were prequalified by the buyer. However, today, many auctions take place without an extensive prequalification process. The presumption is that the supplier will meet the requirements.

WHY IS A REVERSE AUCTION HELD?

Online reverse auctions are a tool for the purchasing or procurement function to buy raw materials or services. There is not a significant conceptual difference between an online reverse auction, sealed bids, and requests for quotation. They are all procurement tools.

The difference between an online reverse auction and other procurement tools is that the Internet makes the bidding process faster and places it in a more controlled environment since the buyer can open and close the auction at his or her discretion. It also enables suppliers from all over the world to participate. Suppliers may range from small to large firms.

Businesses are using online reverse auctions as another tool for the purchasing function with the hope of driving their costs down through the auction bidding.

A FIRM'S FIRST ENTRY INTO ONLINE REVERSE AUCTIONS

A major firm engaged in online reverse auctions several years ago primarily to determine the real impact of this novel tool on their business. One of their first documented auctions involved a standard product for which the last buy was $300,000. Over 20 suppliers were invited to the auction. One-third of the invitees never showed up (or logged in) for the auction, one-third came (i.e., logged in) to the auction and bid once, and one-third came to the auction and bid multiple times until a firm won the bid. The firm saved over $50,000, more than 15 percent, from the last purchase price.

The buyer (the firm that initiated the auction) was left wondering: Why did some suppliers not show up? Why did some suppliers show up and bid only once? When do auctions work? For which types of products? How about services? What happens next time this product is needed in the business? Where do the savings come from? Who won?

HOW IS AN ONLINE REVERSE AUCTION CONDUCTED?

Online reverse auctions are typically conducted either by the firm itself or through an auction house. In-house auctions are often run with software developed by the firm or purchased from an outside software vendor. Market makers such as Advanced Purchasing Technology offer to take on the sourcing function for firms and use auctions along with other techniques. They promise savings of 15–20 percent for the buyers. Some state that savings in commodity products have reached up to 90 percent.

There are also a variety of auction types. These include the English auction, the Dutch auction, the first-price sealed-bid auction, and the second-price sealed-bid auction.

English or increasing bid auctions begin with an opening bid from a seller. Bidding continues until only one bidder remains. A reserve price (below which the item will not be sold) may also be used. In a reverse English auction, a potential supplier opens the bidding, which then continues (downward) until one supplier is left.

A Dutch auction is one in which the seller starts at a high price and then continuously decreases the price. The first buyer who accepts the price wins the contract. In a reverse Dutch auction, the buyer begins at a low price and continuously increases the bids. The buyer purchases from the first supplier who is willing to meet the price.

In a first-price sealed-bid auction, independent (and confidential) bids are submitted by potential buyers. The contract is given to the buyer with the highest bid. In the reverse first-price sealed-bid auction, suppliers independently bid. The business is given to the supplier with the lowest bid.

In the second-price sealed-bid auction, each buyer submits a single bid and the contract is given to the buyer with the highest bid, but the price paid is that of the second-highest buyer's bid, or the second price. In the second-price sealed-bid reverse auction, each supplier submits a single bid and the contract is given to the supplier with the lowest bid at the second-lowest supplier's bid, or second price.

Millet et al. also describe online reverse auctions according to the degree of knowledge of bid rank and/or price. These auction types include one in which no information is revealed to other bidders (blind), only the rank of the bidder is revealed (rank only), only the low-bid amount is revealed (low bid), both the low-bid amount and the bidder's rank are revealed (low bid and rank), and whether the bidder was in the lead or not (lead/no lead). Their study determined that the most effective type of auction, was the rank-only auction.

In addition to type or format, overtime or extension of the bidding period is another attribute that may be implemented and may affect the results of the auction. Since many auctions announce a specific closing time, there may be endgame behavior by the bidders. Early bids are of no benefit to the bidder but reveal information to his or her rivals. Late bidding prevents competitors from seeing one's bid and undercutting it. Late bidding facilitates collusions and independent pricing and often produces prices well above those predicted by auction theory. Each of these auction types and practices affects the outcome of an online reverse auction.

HOW DO WE MEASURE SUCCESS?

How can firms engaging in online reverse auctions determine if they are successful? What is the measure of success?

In some firms, the quantifiable measure of an auction's success is the difference between the last purchase price and the winning bid from the auction. In other cases, it is the difference between the last contract price and the winning bid. In still others, it is the difference between the first bid of the auction and the final bid. In each of these cases, the measure is in price. There is little apparent regard for the quality, delivery, or flexibility of the orders. Many auction participants explain that it is a given that these criteria will be fulfilled. Therefore, price becomes a major factor and, in some cases, the only factor.

Other success measures include finding the optimal market price, a determinant that is ambiguous and difficult to measure, at best. Minimal transaction cost is also a measure used by some firms. While this is an interesting measure, it presumes that the price will be minimized by whatever means by which the purchase takes place. Finally, some firms measure the satisfaction of buyers and sellers of various procurement tools and judge success on that basis.

As with anything one does, there must be a reason for participating in an auction. Mostly firms engage in online reverse auctions in order to save money.

They may sell the idea to their management without fully investigating whether the price reduction in an auction will actually result in cost savings at the end of the purchase.

So while the implementation of the auction process may sound good from the outset, there may be instances in which the low bidder cannot fulfill the contract and does not actually obtain the business. These situations are not typically tracked, and the savings may be reported as if the low bidder is actually fulfilling the contract.

In any case, the measure of success of online auctions in a quantitative sense relies on capturing reliable measures of price, quantity, delivery, and performance both before and after the implementation of auctions. However, the post-implementation measure of performance is often colored by the need to justify participating in the auction in the first place.

WHAT IS THE ISSUE?

The issue is that once one link in the supply chain begins to squeeze one price, the rest of the links must also tighten up. The selling firm is now not as profitable since it was pressured into selling for a lower price. Look at the diagram in Figure O.3. The sizes of the boxes represent the relative profit of each of the firms. Firm 1 conducts an auction and firm 2 bids on the business. Firm 2 bids the lowest price and wins the business. If the winning bid is lower than the last price to the firm, at the very least the winning firm (firm 2) is making less profit on this transaction than it did before. In the worst case, firm 2 is actually losing money on the transaction.

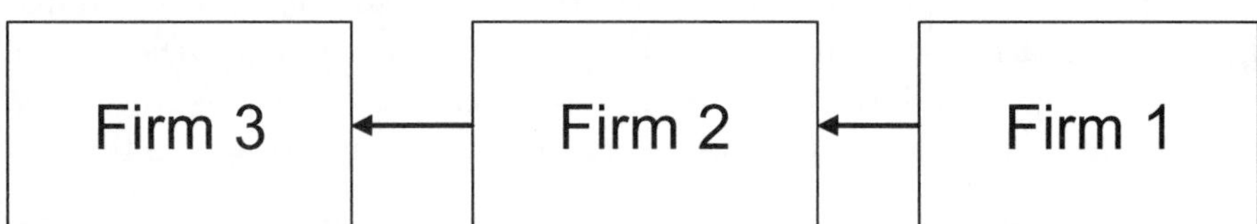

Figure O.3

In order to increase its profit, firm 2 then pushes firm 3 for lower prices, which may result in firm 2 holding an auction. Thus the *little guy* gets squeezed. The money or profit comes out of the supply chain specifically as shown in Figure O.4, where firm 2 has reduced profits from giving up price to firm 1. The pressure to reduce costs increases.

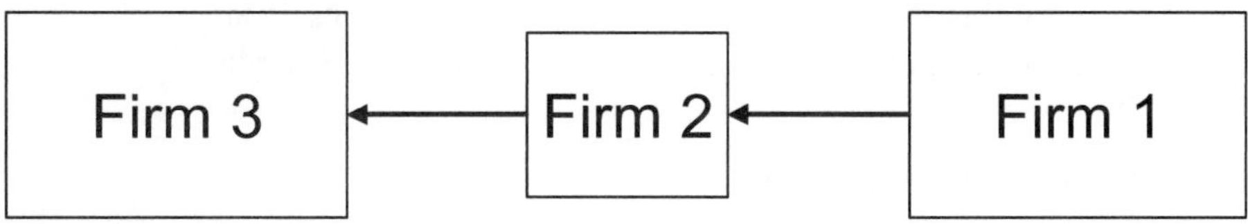

Figure O.4

Finally, firm 2 is under pressure and potentially moves toward the auction tool to obtain better prices for its raw materials and firm 3 is forced to reduce prices and profits, as shown in Figure O.5. In fact, some large firms actually encourage their suppliers to use auctions to squeeze even more price out of the chain.

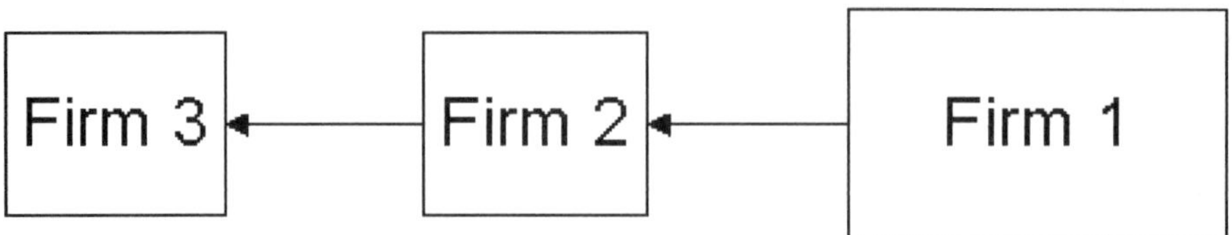

Figure O.5

Overall, firm 1 has sustained its profits while its upstream suppliers have reduced their prices and subsequently reduced profits. Firm 1 is often a large firm with plenty of buyer power, while firms 2 and 3 are generally smaller with little supplier power. In other words, if the larger firm says that the suppliers must participate in an auction in order to have any chance of being awarded the business, then the smaller firms have little choice but to participate.

WHY ARE REVERSE AUCTIONS CONTROVERSIAL?

After many years of suppliers and buyers cultivating relationships with each other and espousing strategic supplier relationships, the lure of auctions has become strong. The perceived savings of auctions have overtaken what many feel is the essence of good business: good business relationships. Buyers have stated that they consider factors other than price, including tangible and intangible factors, when awarding the business. However, auctions offer no cover because the lowest price (or second lowest in second-price sealed-bid reverse auctions) wins the auction.

Not only are there relationship issues to contend with, but the use of auctions can cause a great deal of damage to firms. Sometimes the selling firm is just not willing to drop the price further. It may choose to differentiate tits product or withdraw it from the sales floor until the price increases.

Finally, auctions can cause dramatic shifts in supplier profiles for a firm. For example, Robert Emiliani and Donald Stec of Pratt & Whitney relate that in order to implement the savings suggested by the auction tool, thousands of parts (out of 3,500 active parts) would need to be re-sourced in order to distribute their product. The overarching issue in this case is that things are not as good as they seem when we are looking at the implementation of reverse auctions. Relationships with suppliers, re-sourcing parts, quality, and other issues must be handled.

WHAT ARE THE OPTIONS?

The options depend on the players. A small supplier that does not hold specific leverage with its customer may be easily coerced into playing the auction game, while the larger participant in the relationship may be able to leverage some of its power into *not* participating.

ARE ONLINE REVERSE AUCTIONS A GOOD THING?

There are definitely two schools of thought on this. First, is the school that holds that online auctions are an automated procurement tool. Auctions provide a virtual place for buyers and sellers to meet. They are independent of place or sellers' locations. Auctions typically allow small or little-known sellers to compete on a level playing field with larger and more prestigious competitors. They also remove some of the costs from the final product and thus, some of the profit, from the value chain. This should result in a lower cost to the final consumer.

However, an alternate perspective holds that the removal of profit acts as a detriment to the smaller participants in the value chain and often drives them out of business. The larger competitors will be the survivors and ultimately will control the pricing and terms of sale. Competition, in this instance, will actually be reduced.

WHAT DO YOU NEED TO KNOW?

Look at the Total Costs

When the incumbent supplier wins a bid to provide a product to the buyer, there are a number of advantages. First, there is no prequalification, since that has already been done. The quality is known to be acceptable with the incumbent supplier and the delivery and terms of sale have already been proven with an existing supplier.

However, if the incumbent does not win the bid, there is a cost of changing suppliers. The costs may include the testing of the product within the buyer's operation, additional transportation, certification with key customers, administrative costs, and supplier training, among other things. The cost to switch to an alternate source is often high and is often overlooked by management in the quest to save money.

Look at the Strategic Relationships

Companies spend a good deal of time building relationships with both suppliers and customers. One must be careful that the online procurement auction does not become a price-only purchasing tool. If the auction process severely damages the relationship, one should look toward a higher commodity product to obtain more savings and less opportunity for problems in the future.

Suppliers should be strategic partners on whom one can count when there are raw material disruptions or market forces at work to negatively affect the business. If the product to be sourced is a strategic component, one should consider other means of procurement.

Understand the Purpose of the Specific Online Reverse Auction

One reason for buyers to engage in online reverse auctions is to reduce the supplier base. It is important to understand this rationale before engaging in an auction as a seller. One must determine if one is likely to be eliminated as a supplier, determine if this is an acceptable alternative, and then, and only then, decide if one wants to participate in the auction.

In order to make a good decision on participation, one must fully understand all costs associated with purchase of the product as well as the use and switching of suppliers.

TRUE COSTS OF A NON-INCUMBENT WINNING THE BID

All costs of changing to new supplier must be taken into account in order to fully realize the value of online procurement auctions. Products should be evaluated individually to determine the cost of switching suppliers. If the cost is high, a firm should think about sourcing other products using auctions.

Consider the following example:

The auction has been won by a new supplier. The savings is 15 percent of the unit price but the new supplier is farther away from the manufacturing facility and there will be incremental freight costs as well as a 5 percent import duty. Additionally, the costs of supplier training and certification as well as general administrative costs will be 10 percent of the product price for the next three years.

Table 0.5

	Incumbent	New supplier	
Unit costs	$100/unit	$85/unit	15% savings
Transportation	$10/unit	$15/unit	
Import duty		$ 4.25	5%
Supplier switching incremental costs		$8.50	10% for three years
Total costs	$110/unit	$112.75	

Assuming the supplier-switching costs remain constant for three years (not unlikely in a complex manufacturing environment), the actual cost is higher if the incumbent is not chosen in a product with high switching costs, even though the bid price is lower.

SUMMARY

One must be prepared and have a strategy in place in advance if one intends to participate in an online reverse auction. The bidding occurs quickly. One should not let the excitement of the bidding distract from the strategy to obtain (or even lose) the business. The time frame is reduced and face-to-face negotiation is nonexistent. It is important to understand the rules of the auction format and to be sure that the "heat of the battle" is not the first time one sees the bidding format.

Understand that right now, price appears to be the single criterion. However, as the tool evolves, it is possible that other factors (important to the buyer), such as reliability, quality, and delivery, will regain importance. The multidimensional purchasing criteria would require a more sophisticated automated auction tool. Buyers suggests that in the future, bots (automated robots) may allow buyers and sellers to bid on price as well as other criteria. The bots will place bids automatically without human intervention. Some bots will be intelligent in that they will make their bid according to a bidding strategy designed by the seller. That will be one more step for an automated procurement tool—the next evolution.

Further Reading: Dimitri, N., G. Piga, and G. Spagnolo. 2006. *Handbook of Procurement: Auctions, Contracting, Electronic Platforms and Other Current Trends.* Cambridge: Cambridge University Press; Neef, D. 2001. *e-Procurement: From Strategy to Implementation.* Upper Saddle River, NJ: Prentice Hall.

Diane H. Parente

OUTSOURCING AND OFFSHORING

Behaviors and perceptions sometimes disconnect. This is evident when the words "outsourcing" and "offshoring"—which mean the placement of U.S. jobs in foreign countries—raise the hackles of the public that appears to benefit from the lower consumer prices and mortgage rates occurring as a result of globalization. Consumers economize by buying the least expensive item that they believe meets their needs. Store owners recognize that and ask their suppliers to provide those items at the lowest cost. The wholesalers in turn seek out the least expensive producers for the given quality of the good in question. Since the 1960s, the least expensive producer has increasingly been overseas, and U.S. manufacturers have moved abroad. Meanwhile, foreign investors have supplied capital to U.S. capital markets and have helped keep interest rates lower than otherwise possible.

So, how does the same globalization phenomenon generate economy-wide benefits yet there are still winners and losers on an individual level? How do changes in the domestic economy interact with the patterns of globalization? Finally, why is there a disconnect between economic benefits and public perceptions?

MACRO BENEFITS AND MICRO WINNERS AND LOSERS IN A DYNAMIC ECONOMY

Economies grow and change over time. This growth increases the standard of living for a society, but not all participants benefit equally, and there are often losers in the process, as owners of once-valuable resources (e.g., real estate in the ghost towns of the West and riverfront mills in the industrial Northeast) find that the demand for those resources has declined. Yet the globalization of

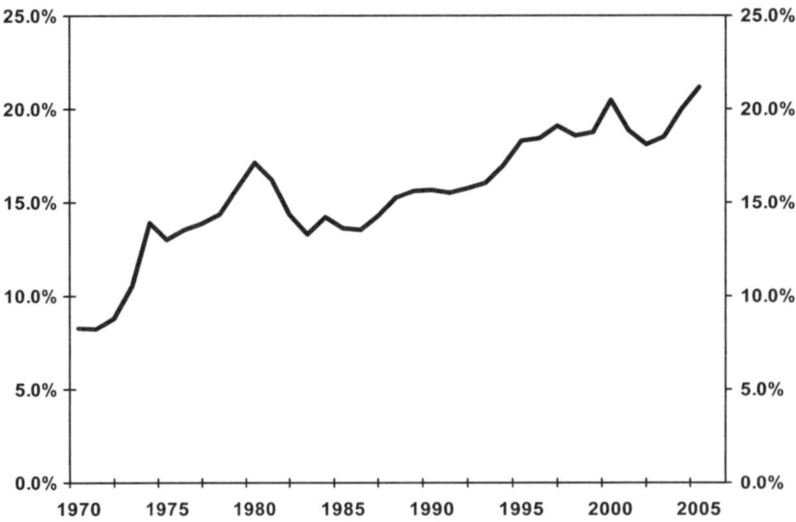

Figure O.6 Globalization: U.S. exports and imports as a percentage of nominal GDP.
Source: U.S. Department of Commerce.

the U.S. economy has been a long-term trend, as exhibited in Figure O.6, which shows combined exports and imports as a percentage of annual national income. Today this measure of globalization stands at 20 percent of the U.S. economy.

The theme underlying any effective Western economic system is that each consumer acts in her or his own interest to minimize costs, while each producer seeks to maximize profit. Consumers maximize their welfare subject to income limitations. Producers, meanwhile, act to offer the least expensive product that will meet the customer's needs. The boom in discount and Internet shopping over the past 10 years reflects the consumer's desire to minimize expense of dollars, time, or both. In response, producers have sought to minimize costs in order to maximize profit and thereby have an incentive to seek international sourcing of goods and services that many in the popular press call outsourcing.

GLOBAL LABOR MARKET

Trade allows for the division of labor across countries. This division of labor in turn allows for economies of scale and scope and the development of specialized skills. Specialization encourages innovation and promotes dynamism. Economies of scale, scope, and specialization allow production to be more efficient and therefore lower cost. Historically, we have seen the migration of production in this country in agriculture and textile production. The opening of the Midwest made New England farms high cost and led to a shift of major agricultural production from the Northeast to the Midwest. As for textile production, we have seen a migration from England to New England, then to the Southeast and then on to Mexico and China, and now to Vietnam. Over time, we have seen this industry move to locations where manufacturers can economize on their biggest cost—labor.

Geographical migration of production has benefited consumers by providing a greater supply of goods and services at a lower price. The lower prices mean that consumers have more real income to be spent elsewhere. In turn, we have seen an increase in the consumers' standard of living.

The shift in the locus of manufacturing production also means that there are gainers and losers in jobs and land values over time. Southern cities and low-skilled workers have benefited, while New England cities and higher-wage union workers have been the losers. The process of production relocation generally benefits society at large, as less expensive goods are produced for all consumers in the nation, while there is also a regional redistribution of jobs and wealth within the economy.

In recent years, there has been a global redistribution of production with lower-wage manufacturing jobs in textiles and apparel relocating to Asia. Meanwhile, states like North Carolina increased their exports of high-valued manufactures such as machinery, electrical machinery, and pharmaceutical products. Today these three sectors, along with vehicles and plastics, comprise the state's top five export industries. The globalization of product markets has lead to an expansion of world trade. Durable goods manufacturers, such as construction, farm, and industrial machinery, have seen a global increase in demand for their products. Yet as production has grown, there are many physical as well as practical barriers to labor mobility. Therefore, manufacturers who wish to be close to their customers are finding that they cannot source all production from their U.S. base and, as a result, must outsource production to other countries to remain competitive.

Trade does lead to both losses and gains of jobs—both directly in the affected community and indirectly in the surrounding community. As discussed below, policies encouraging the retraining of workers are more likely to be successful than those increasing the prices to consumers. On net, however, lower consumer prices provided by more efficient global production produce an increase in household purchasing power and a broader variety of goods and services for consumers in general. It is helpful to recall that the United States is the world's largest exporter as well as a major beneficiary of foreign direct investment, which provides jobs in this country. Witness, for example, this inflow of foreign capital in the form of a Japanese aircraft manufacturer in North Carolina and a German auto manufacturer in South Carolina.

Unfortunately, those who lose jobs due to trade are not necessarily the same people who get jobs created by trade. Short-run adjustments are painful and represent economic and social challenges. However, our focus should be on the worker, not the job.

Overall, trade has a small net effect on employment, and this trade effect on employment is overwhelmed by the normal massive turnover in the labor market (see Figure O.7). Rather than trade, it is population, education and training, labor force participation, institutions, and flexibility of the labor force that determine long-term employment growth. Labor markets evolve over time, and trade is just one of many influences. We do know that trade often leads to structural change in the labor markets with consequential effects on the mix of jobs across

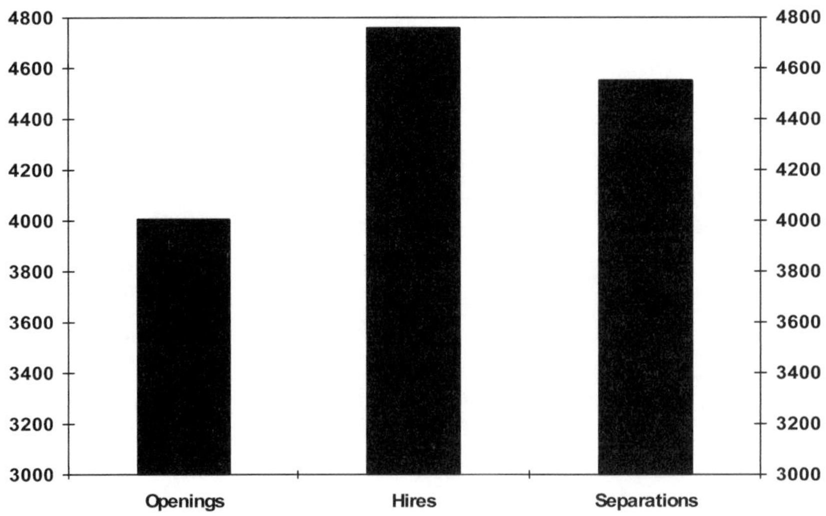

Figure 0.7 Job market dynamics (thousands of jobs) (June 2006).
Source: U.S. Department of Commerce.

industries, the skill levels required, and the ultimate locations of job growth. For example, in recent years lower transaction costs and improvements in international communications have led to a rising global demand for computerization and digitalization of business services, which has boosted the fortunes of U.S.-based software and hardware firms.

Meanwhile, the customer service of many of these software and hardware products and services has increased the global demand for educated English-speaking workers abroad in places such as Ireland and India. This demand for foreign workers is driven by the consumer who wants 24-hour service at the touch of a button. Therefore, companies are more likely to meet that demand at lower wages and benefit costs by hiring first-shift workers in India or Ireland than second- and third-shift workers in the United States.

In contrast, attempts to manipulate the economic theme of markets by tariffs, quotas, or labor regulations may temporarily slow job loss, but at the cost of higher prices to consumers, and a misallocation of resources toward inefficient production in the rest of society. In the past this inefficient production has been seen in subsidies to steel and textile industries or in the tariffs imposed in the nineteenth century to protect inefficient agriculture. In the end, the steel and textile mills still closed, and many Eastern and Southern farms became suburbs. Government interference in the economic process only increased short-term costs to the rest of the economy through higher prices. Moreover, over the long term, government interference frequently prevented the proper reallocation of resources to more productive uses. Protectionism on trade provoked retaliation from foreign governments and a retreat from competition. As a result, protectionism leads to bloated inefficient industries that decrease productivity and engender a lower standard of living.

INSOURCING SERVICES

Balanced discussions on trade issues are often interrupted by emotional outbursts or political grandstanding. While some manufacturing jobs are disappearing, many higher-paid service positions are being created here as foreigners increase their demand for U.S.-based services. These high-value services provided to users abroad include legal, financial, engineering, architectural, and software development services. This insourcing of professional services to the United States generates a surplus in the service component of our balance of payments accounts. The economic market-based system provides a wider array of goods and services at a lower cost than the alternatives. Greater global competition provides such benefits to society overall. There are costs of globalization that should be addressed, but by means other than preventing trade.

GLOBAL CAPITAL MARKETS: INFLOW OF CAPITAL TO THE UNITED STATES

Another variation on our theme is the pattern of global capital (financial) flows and the globalization of capital markets. In contrast to labor, capital crosses borders fairly easily. In sympathy with labor, the return of capital provides an incentive to allocate capital to its best use. We in the United States benefit from an inflow of capital that lowers the price of credit interest rates—relative to what they would be otherwise (this reduces the interest rates on home mortgages, for example).

In addition, global capital markets lead to the development of new financial instruments that provide greater liquidity to international investors. We see this in the development of instruments such as mortgage-backed and asset-backed securities. Globalization of product markets has meant the introduction of new brands and products from foreign countries into the U.S. consumer market in particular. With capital markets, globalization has meant that U.S. financial assets such as mortgage-backed securities are now available for sale across the globe, while foreign investors with excess cash can now direct that cash toward U.S. markets.

Globalization of products leads to an expansion of world trade. The globalization of capital markets is also leading to an expansion of financial markets. For the United States this means a broader demand for mortgages, car loans, and business credit, which thereby effectively lowers interest rates for the American consumer. In this case, the American consumer comes out the big winner from globalization. Consumers find that credit is more readily available at lower interest rates.

Foreign investors benefit by purchasing U.S. financial assets that are perceived to offer higher returns and lower risks than many foreign assets. This is particularly true when you view the benchmark interest rates between countries (Figure O.8).

Just as trade alters the global distribution of production, capital flows alter the global distribution of financial investment. Over recent years, we have seen

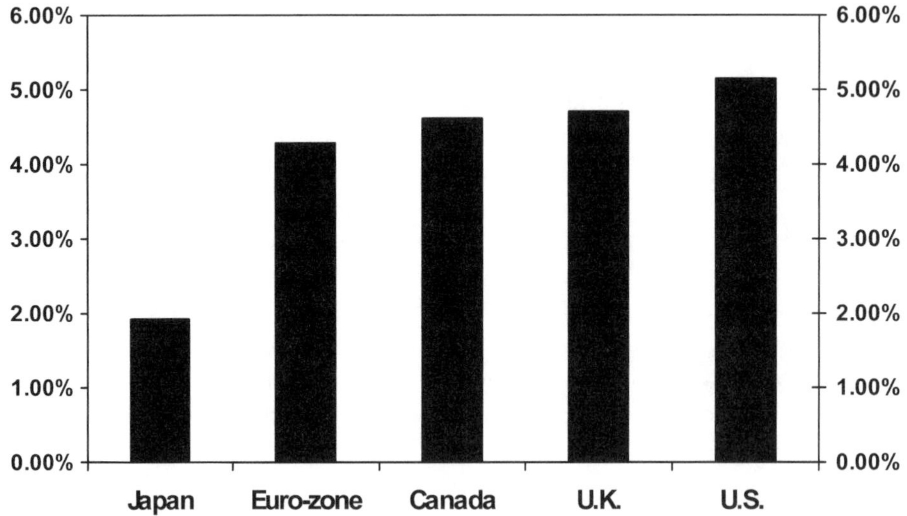

Figure O.8 10-year government bond rates (end of Q2 2006).
Source: Federal Reserve System.

a growth of U.S. financial instruments and market values. Therefore, the United States benefits from the globalization of financial markets. Global savings migrate to higher return U.S. investments (Figure O.9) and thereby raise output and incomes.

Public policy in the United States has promoted these capital flows by reducing taxes on dividend and capital gains, while also lowering barriers to

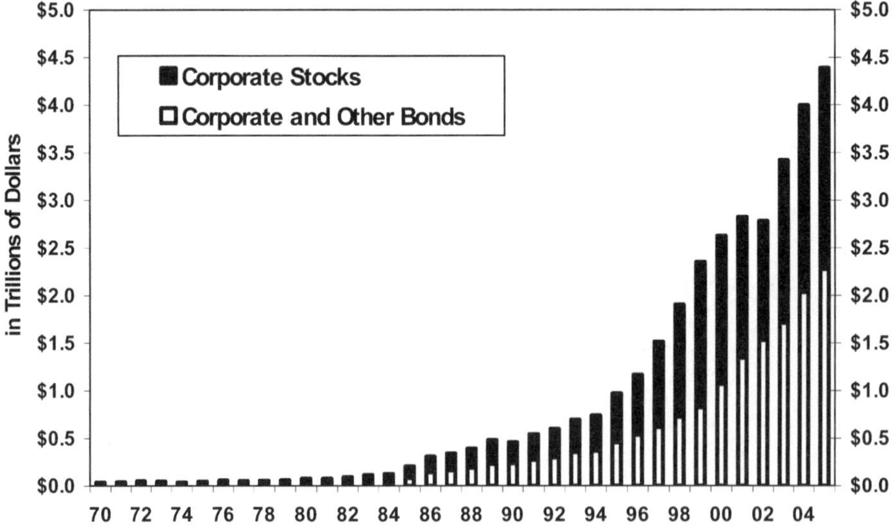

Figure O.8 U.S. securities held abroad.
Source: Federal Reserve System.

cross-border investment by foreign investors. This has helped promote capital flows into the United States, even while other nations limit capital flows into or out of their own nations.

WHAT SHOULD BE DONE ABOUT GLOBALIZATION?

Globalization is a product of economic incentives, not the result of some great conspiracy. Households have a limited budget and attempt to save money when they shop. Producers attempt to meet consumer demands by supplying products at a price that meets their budget. Meanwhile, many U.S. firms cannot meet their global demand by production solely in the United States and thereby locate production facilities near their customers. On the financial side, the globalization of capital markets has lead to an increase in financial flows to the United States and has thereby increased the availability of credit and lowered interest rates. Lower rates mean that more families are able to purchase homes and businesses can finance expansion. This process is unlikely to stop.

Policy makers and voters need to recognize the dislocation costs associated with the global reallocation of production and financial flows along with the benefits that derive from such reallocation. For American workers, the cost disincentives of retaining labor in many facilities in the United States may be too large to retain the old jobs in the old facilities. This may be particularly true for labor-intensive manufacturing and service jobs that require low- or semiskilled workers. In U.S. history, we have seen the migration of jobs before, from the agricultural work forces in rural areas to the manufacturing facilities of the pre–World War II era. Technological and communication changes have made many low-skilled jobs obsolete and therefore not viable economically over the long run. Certainly many workers can no longer build careers upon these jobs. Recall that consumer preferences have also shifted, with more consumer dollars going toward services—eating out—as opposed to buying groceries for all the household's meals at the store.

While jobs may go, workers remain, and this should be our focus. Public and private programs need to be directed at worker retraining—not factory retention—in cases where the economics are clear. Labor markets are becoming increasingly flexible so that jobs are more likely to come and go, but the workers remain. Public policy is better served by the improvement of the skills of workers rather than the preservation of specific jobs. In many states, we have seen the emergence of many programs at community colleges with a dedicated focus on worker retraining. Of course, it is incumbent upon the worker to recognize that there is a responsibility to develop those skills and to be willing to move or change jobs more in the future than was necessary in the past.

As for manufacturing, it is important to note that many public policy decisions are aimed at discouraging production in the United States. Whatever their intentions may be, many communities simply do not want a factory in their backyard. As a result, firms are outsourcing production abroad simply because they cannot produce the gasoline, plastics, rubber, metals, textiles, and the like in this country.

On the other hand, large capital inflows into the United States also offer a solution by which incentives can be directed to foreign firms to allocate capital to areas where there is a viable workforce. We have seen this in many states where incentives are offered to locate firms in certain communities.

Offshoring creates value for the U.S. economy by passing on the efficiency that results in lower costs of goods and services to the U.S. consumer. This consumer then takes the extra money saved at the store and spends it elsewhere. U.S. companies benefit by being able to meet consumer demand by supplying the goods or services at a lower cost. Economic resources can be used then for more value-added products and services. Redeployed labor and capital to other manufacturing and service-sector activities will be more productive and have a longer economic life than those production activities and jobs in declining industries. U.S. workers and consumers benefit from specialization. Final assembly can often occur in the United States while component production takes place around the globe. Production of goods and services is not carried on for its own sake but is undertaken to serve the demands of the consumer. Therefore, the value of any product is determined by consumers and then works its way down into the factors of production. It is impossible to governmentally control trade and consumer choice without distorting economic activity.

When a less costly way to make a good is discovered, the value of all factors used in making that good also changes. The national standard of living cannot rise when states attempt to force up the price of some factors so that the owners of those factors used in production gain an artificial advantage that results in the inefficient allocation of scarce resources in the economy. Globalization reflects the demands of the consumer. Attempts to alter that trend will only diminish the welfare of the average consumer.

Further Reading: Ricardo, David. 1817. *On the Principle of Political Economy and Taxation,* London: John Murray; Smith, Adam. *Wealth and Nations.* 1776. Available at http://www.econlib.org/library/Smith/smWn.html

John Silvia

P

PENSIONS

A pension is a regular payment given to retired employees. Pensions are only one part of a retiree's income, however. Other income sources include Social Security, income from personal retirement savings, and earnings. Many older people continue to work during retirement, especially in the early years of retirement. So consumers planning for retirement need to think about all four sources of income.

Pension benefits are usually paid monthly. People use the terms "pension plans," "retirement plans," or "superannualtion plans" to mean the same thing—the term "pension plan" is used here. Pension plans are divided into two broad types: defined benefit and defined contribution plans.

According to a study by the Employee Benefits Research Institute, in 2006, 67 percent of workers age 16 and over worked for an employer that sponsored a retirement or pension plan. Of these, about half (51%) participated in their employer's retirement plan. Most (54%) were in a defined contribution plan; 27 percent were in a defined benefit plan, and 18 percent were in both defined contribution and defined benefit plans. In addition, more than half of all workers (55%) had either a pension plan or other retirement savings in their own IRA (individual retirement account) or Keogh plans. Data from the 2004 Survey of Consumer Finances show that 57 percent of workers and retirees have a pension or retirement savings in an IRA or Keogh.

DEFINED BENEFIT PLANS

Defined benefit plans are an older form of pension plans. Defined benefit plans define the amount of the pension benefit that will be paid to employees at retirement, and then the employer sets aside funds to pay that future benefit.

Suppose Ann is 25 years old. Her boss tells her that she will pay Ann $12,000 a year in retirement when Ann is 65. Ann's boss must set aside enough money now to make those $12,000-a-year payments 40 years from now. Ann's boss will need to estimate what investment return she can earn on the funds and how many payments she will need to make (i.e., how long Ann will be retired).

In some cases, instead of a fixed amount, the pension benefit amount is calculated based on a formula—for example, a combination of worker's earnings and years of work. Suppose the formula for Sam's company pension is 1 percent of the average of his earnings for the last three years times the number of years he has worked for the company. Sam's earnings for the last three years were $40,000, $50,000, and $60,000 (the average is $50,000), and he retired after 30 years of work. The formula is: 1% × 50,000 × 30 = $15,000

Again, Sam's boss must set aside enough money now to make those $15,000-a-year payments 30 years from now. In addition to estimating the investment return she can earn on the funds and how long Sam will be retired, she will need to estimate how long Sam will work for her and what Sam's salary will be in his last 3 years of work.

With a defined benefit plan, employers are responsible—and bear the risk—for having enough money in the fund to be able to pay for the pension. The actual cost of the defined benefits plan to the employer is uncertain. The cost is only an estimate because the formula depends upon a number of variables, such as the average retirement age, the life spans of employees, the returns earned by any of the pension's investments, and any additional taxes.

Up until the 1980s, defined benefit plans were the most common type of pension plan. But these plans lost popularity due to their cost and changes in the laws that cover pensions. Also, as workers changed jobs more often, there was a need to have a pension plan that was more portable and could move with the employee from one employer to another.

HOW LONG WILL THE MONEY LAST?

Depending on the payout option chosen, most pensions will annuitize benefits at retirement and pay workers a steady stream of payments throughout their lifetime. The IRS has minimum withdrawal rules based on the ages of the retiree and any beneficiary. But when it comes to "dissaving" out of other retirement savings, most workers have to figure out on their own how much to withdraw each year. Table P.1 shows how long money will last, depending on the interest rate earned and the percent of principal withdrawn. For example, suppose Alan has $100,000 in an investment account at 65 when he retires, and it's earning 6 percent. If he withdraws 10 percent ($10,000) per year, his IRA funds will last about 15 years, or until he's 80.

Table P.1 How Long Will the Money Last?

Interest rate earned	Percent of principal withdrawn (payout rate)													
	2%	3%	4%	5%	6%	7%	8%	9%	10%	11%	12%	13%	14%	15%
1%	69	40	28	22	18	15	13	11	10	9	8	7	6	5
2%		55	35	25	20	16	14	12	11	10	8	8	7	6
3%			46	30	23	18	15	13	12	10	10	9	9	8
4%				41	28	21	17	14	13	11	10	9	9	8
5%					36	25	20	16	15	13	12	10	9	9
6%						34	24	18	15	13	12	10	9	9
7%							31	22	17	15	13	11	10	9
8%								29	21	16	14	12	11	10
9%									27	20	16	13	12	10
10%										26	19	15	13	11
11%											24	18	14	12
12%												23	17	14
13%													22	16
14%														21

Money withdrawn at these rates will never be depleted. At these rates, only interest is being withdrawn; the principal remains intact.

Note: Numbers indicate the number of years it will take to deplete principal and accrued interest.

DEFINED CONTRIBUTION PLANS

In contrast to a defined benefit plan that defines the benefit to be paid in the future in retirement, a defined contribution plan defines the amount an employer will contribute into an account for each employee. Employees may be able to choose how the contributions to their own accounts are invested—choices can include mutual funds, stocks or other investments, and securities. The returns on the investments, either gains or losses, are credited to the individual employee's account.

At retirement, the amount of money in the account is used to create the series of payments the retired worker will receive in retirement. With a defined contribution plan, employees—not the employer—bear responsibility for having enough money in the pension account for retirement. If employers contribute enough and make good investment choices, the investments grow and employees will have a large amount in their accounts to use in retirement; if employers make poor choices, employees won't have as much money in retirement.

For example, suppose Ben's employer tells Ben he will put $1,000 a year into a defined contribution plan. At the end of 30 years, Ben's employer will have paid $30,000 into Ben's account. If Ben's employer chooses an investment that pays 2 percent per year, at the end of 30 years Ben will have $1,217,042 in his account. If he takes out $5,000 per month, his money will last about 30 years. On the other hand, if Ben's employer chooses an investment that pays 5 percent, at the end of 30 years he would have $1,993,165—or nearly $776,000 more. He could take out $10,700 a month—more than double—and his money would still last 30 years.

Employers can easily calculate the cost of a defined contribution plan, in contrast to the defined benefit plan. Once employees are vested (eligible to receive money) in the plan, most plans are portable—as workers change jobs, they can take their funds with them or roll them over into an individual retirement account (an IRA).

CASH BALANCE PLANS

There is a third type of pension plan—the cash balance plan. Cash balance plans are defined benefit plans, but the benefit that is defined is an account balance, not a monthly benefit. For example, instead of promising workers a pension of $12,000 a year, a cash balance plan would promise a nest egg of $100,000 at retirement. When workers reach retirement, they have a choice of taking a series of monthly payments (an annuity) or taking the entire cash balance as a lump sum. Most traditional defined benefit pension plans do not offer this lump sum payout feature.

HOW ARE PENSION BENEFITS PAID OUT?

Most pensions give retirees a choice of how to receive benefits—and how much they receive depends on which option they choose, as some options pay more per month than others. As with the cash balance plan, one option may be to take a lump sum from the plan. Retirees could then invest this amount in an account and then withdraw interest and principal from the account.

Employees may have a choice of how much their monthly benefits will be. Usually, the option that pays the most per month is a single life annuity option. In this payout plan, pension benefits are paid out based on the retiree's life expectancy. Because women tend to live longer than men, the payout for men is usually higher than for women. Another option is a joint and survivor annuity. The benefits are based on the life expectancy of the retiree and the joint beneficiary of the pension—usually the husband or wife of the retiree. The monthly benefits for a joint and survivor annuity are generally lower than the single life annuity option because the pension plan has to pay out benefits over the combined life expectancy of two people, which is usually a longer period of time.

Some pension plans provide for benefits to be paid out for a guaranteed number of years, regardless of how long the retiree lives. For example, employees may be able to choose a 20-year certain single life annuity. If an employee retired at age 65 and chose this option, he would receive benefits throughout the rest of his life, even if he lived to be 100. If he only lived until age 75, the remaining 10 years of the 20-year certain payouts would go to a designated beneficiary. The payouts for this option depend on the number of years of guaranteed payouts and are generally lower than the those for the single life annuity, but higher than payouts for the joint and survivor annuity.

Not all pensions adjust to accommodate cost-of-living increases—an important feature to consider in planning for retirement income. Suppose a pension paid out $1,000 a month, with no cost-of-living adjustment. If prices rise 10 percent over 5 years, it would take $1,100 to buy the same goods and services that once cost $1,000, but the pension stays at $1,000. Retirees would need to have some other source of funds, such as other retirement savings or IRAs, to maintain their purchasing power.

CONSUMER PROTECTIONS IN PENSION PLANS

The major federal law that provides consumers rights and consumer protections for their pensions is the Employee Retirement Income Security Act (ERISA). For example, ERISA sets out the maximum vesting period—how long employees need to work for an employer before they have a right to a pension that cannot be taken away. There are two vesting options for pension plans. The first option, called cliff vesting, provides employees with 100 percent of their benefits after 5 years of service. If an employee leaves after only 4 years of work, he will have no pension.

The second option provides for graduated vesting; employees earn a right to 20 percent of their benefits after 3 years, and then increases of 20 percent per year (40% after 4 years, 60% after 5 years, 80% after 6 years), so that after the seventh year, employees have rights to 100 percent of their benefits.

What happens if the company goes out of business—and the pension that workers were counting on goes away? ERISA also created the Pension Benefit Guaranty Corporation (www.pbgc.gov), which ensures pension benefits for workers. The drawback is that the benefit amounts retirees receive from the PBGC may be less than the pension benefits they were expecting—so they have less money in retirement.

ERISA also requires that if a retiree chooses a single life annuity option, the spouse must co-sign the benefit selection form. This provision came about because many retirees were choosing single life annuity options, which paid more while the retiree was alive but left their spouses with no pension income. In an era when many women were not employed outside the home, this made a lot of sense—without a pension, many widows had to survive only on Social Security.

401(K), 403(B), AND 457 PLANS

A 401(k), 403(b), or 457 plan is an employer-sponsored retirement plan that allows employees to set aside some of their current earnings as personal savings for retirement. Employees don't pay taxes on these earnings until they withdraw them in retirement, when their tax rate may be lower. The numbers refer to the sections in the Internal Revenue Service tax code that apply. The 401(k) applies to most workers, while a 403(b) plan covers workers in educational institutions, religious organizations, public schools, and nonprofit organizations; 457 plans cover employees of state and local governments and certain tax-exempt entities.

Neither benefits nor contributions to these plans are defined. Employees choose how much to contribute (up to limits set by the IRS), and how to invest the money. Workers over age 50 can contribute extra money into a catch-up fund for retirement. If employees move to a different job, they can roll over the money into an individual retirement account or they may be able to move the assets into the new employer's new 401(k) plan.

Employers may match worker contributions—an important benefit to think about when one is looking for a job. Consider Matt and John. Both work for Mega Corporation, which provides a match of up to 5 percent in the company 401(k). Both make $40,000 a year. Matt does not participate in Mega's 401(k), so his taxable salary and total compensation are $40,000. John, on the other hand, contributes 5 percent to his 401(k). His pay is reduced by $2,000, so his taxable salary is $38,000 instead of $40,000. But Mega Corp. adds a matching 5 percent—$2,000—to his 401(k) fund. So John's total compensation is his $38,000 pay plus the $2,000 he puts into his 401(k) plan plus Mega's $2,000 contribution to his 401(k)—or a total of $42,000.

Some employers have "opt-in" 401(k) plans while others have "opt-out" or automatic enrollment plans. For automatic enrollment plans, employers set an initial contribution rate and investment option. In either case, employees can choose how much to contribute and how to invest the money to tailor it to their specific needs.

IRAS, SEP IRAS, AND KEOGH PLANS

Individual retirement accounts (IRAs) are self-directed retirement accounts—workers choose how much to contribute and how to invest the money. Money contributed to an IRA must come from earnings, although spouses not employed outside the home are allowed to put money into an IRA as well. There are three kinds of IRAs: pre-tax IRAs, post-tax IRAs, and Roth IRAs.

Contributions to a pre-tax IRA are restricted to people without other pensions and are subject to income limits set by the IRS. Taxes on the money put into the account and taxes on any interest or gains are deferred until retirees withdraw the money.

Almost anyone can set aside money in a post-tax IRA, again subject to IRS limits for annual contributions. When retirees withdraw the money, they pay taxes on the earnings but not on the principal.

A Roth IRA is a special kind of post-tax IRA; contributions are limited by income but all withdrawals are tax-free. Money invested in any of theses types of IRAs is usually put into securities, particularly stocks, bonds, and mutual funds.

SEP IRAs, Simplified Employee Pension plans, are usually used by small businesses that want to provide their employees with some retirement funding. Employees set up their own IRAs and employers can contribute to these accounts.

Keogh plans are for self-employed individuals and their employees. These plans receive special tax treatment like a tax deferral on contributions and earnings until workers retire and start receiving benefits.

The Internal Revenue Service has special rules about money in IRAs, which it enumerates in IRS Publication 590 (available at http://www.irs.gov/pub/irs-pdf/p590.pdf). If workers withdraw money before age 59½, they have to pay taxes on that money as well as a 10 percent penalty. Also, workers must start withdrawing funds by age 70½, and there are specific minimum withdrawals required under tax law.

IT'S YOUR RESPONSIBILITY

There are more options, and therefore more choices, for retirement planning today than in the past. The days of working without having to worry about retirement are long gone—indeed, if they ever existed in the first place! Especially as more people change jobs over the course of their careers, options for accumulating funds for retirement become even more important.

Ultimately, it's the worker's responsibility to learn about the various retirement plans and choose the one or ones that best fit their situation. Employers, friends, and the government can help provide information, but in the end the worker has to decide on the plan and provide the discipline to implement the plan for his or her financial well-being in retirement.

Further Reading: Choose to Save. 2005. *Ballpark Estimate for Retirement Savings.* Available at http://www.choosetosave.org/ballpark; Copeland, Craig. 2006. *Individual Account Retirement Plans: An Analysis of the 2004 Survey of Consumer Finances.* EBRI Issue Brief, No. 293. Available at http://www.ebri.org/pdf/briefspdf/EBRI_IB_05_3-20061.pdf; Copeland, Craig. 2006. *Retirement Plan Participation and Retiree's Perception of Their Standard of Living.* EBRI Issue Brief, No. 289. Available at http://www.ebri.org/pdf/briefspdf/EBRI_IB_01-20061.pdf; Internal Revenue Service. 2005. *Individual Retirement Accounts.* IRS Publication 590. Available at http://www.irs.gov/pub/irs-pdf/p590.pdf; U.S. Department of Labor. n.d. *Savings Fitness: A Guide to Your Money and Your Financial Future.* Available at http://www.dol.gov/ebsa/pdf/savingsfitness.pdf; U.S. Department of Labor. 2003. *What You Should Know about Your Retirement Plan.* Available at http://www.dol.gov/ebsa/publications/wyskapr.html; VanDerhei, Jack, Craig Copeland, and Dallas Salisbury. 2006. *Retirement Security in the United States: Current Sources, Future Prospects, and Likely Outcomes of Current Trends.* Washington, DC: Employee Benefit Research Institute. Available at http://www.ebri.org/pdf/publications/books/ebri_rsus.pdf.

Jeanne M. Hogarth

PERSONAL SUCCESS WITHOUT SELLING YOUR SOUL

It's an age-old question: Can you be yourself and still do well in the workplace? Or does winning in the real world require one to make compromises? To get ahead and reach performance expectations, is it necessary, from time to time, to do things that don't smell good, behave in ways that don't feel right, or choose to do things that don't resonate with one's deeply held values and beliefs? Do you have to sell your soul to succeed? A variety of opinions exists.

On one side of the fence are the compromisers. They might stretch the truth to get their way, choose work that they hate because it pays handsomely, or act in phony ways just to please others and get what they want. Faustian bargains don't trouble them. They willingly do whatever it takes to accomplish their purposes. While these people may find compromise-demanding situations troubling, ultimately they give in. They turn a blind eye to those principles and standards that underlie authenticity and integrity. These people are compromisers because they measure their worth as humans in terms of the positions they occupy, the accomplishments they have achieved, and the material rewards they have earned. And when it is all said and done, many of these people get what they set out to attain. They move ahead in organizations precisely because they are effective at doing what their organizations want them to do. They can earn handsome pay packages when they produce outstanding results, despite their methods. While they may earn the outward measures of success, every compromise they make has the potential to diminish their self-respect, the admiration others might otherwise have for them, and their sense of lasting fulfillment.

On the other side of the fence are the non-compromisers. These are the people who are willing to stand and fight for what they truly believe. They are strong-willed and rigid individuals. These sturdy souls will not bend under pressure. They are impervious to intimidation. They cannot be bought or persuaded into going against their values. They insist on being who they see themselves as being, and there is no changing that. Non-compromisers derive considerable satisfaction from knowing that they are authentic and highly principled. But with this knowledge, they can easily grow smug and self-righteous. Moreover, in many ways, large and small, they can irritate others, who usually view non-compromisers as being arrogantly critical of those who are not like them. Non-compromisers may even become unmanageable and uncooperative nuisances. Some of them turn into tyrannical bosses.

One reason these people are unbending is that their certainty of the correctness of their actions and habits gives them self-confidence and enables them to define who and what they are as individuals. Hence their rigidity—they are not about to allow the slightest slipup to damage their spotless reputations or lead them into disingenuousness. Being a person of character is of utmost importance to them. In truth, they are more concerned with their own authenticity and integrity than they are with the larger purposes of their organizations.

Clearly, a number of opinions exists as to whether it is advisable to disregard or go against what one claims to believe to get what one wants. At one time or another each of us is bound to face this basic question: Can I succeed at work without having to sell my soul?

WHAT IS SOUL?

Every bit as much as humans are physical beings endowed with powers of intellect and emotion, they are also spiritual beings. Each has a soul, a capacity to be influenced by spiritual forces, eternal truths. It is spiritual forces that urge people to use and perfect their intellect and to acknowledge and appreciate their emotions. The desire to create, to improve, to serve purposes larger than self-interest, to cooperate with others, to strive for excellence, and to act responsibly are examples of spiritual forces that act on the soul. An unhealthy soul is one that is unresponsive to spiritual forces and eternal truths. A healthy soul is quickened and guided by them.

Soul is what and who a person truly is. It is a person's humanity. It is a person's uniqueness. It is a person's core values and beliefs as revealed by how that person thinks, makes choices, and acts. It is a person's capacity to be influenced by spiritual values, beyond things worldly and material. But there is much more to what soul is than these things alone. In truth, the soul will always have mysterious depths that range deeper than our competency to understand permit. Regardless, we can gain valuable insights about what we believe to be healthy souls by looking at the lives of those we most admire for their qualities of character and unique achievements. When we think of Mother Teresa, who followed her calling to minister to the lowest of the lowly in the worst slums of Calcutta, we realize that soul involves reverencing forces greater than oneself and serving a great calling.

When we study the life of Jane Goodall, who became fascinated with chimpanzees and spent most of her life studying these creatures in their natural habitat in remote sections of Africa, pioneering a new method of research, we see other aspects of soul. We see that it involves creativity and boldness and dedication. When we consider Jack Welch, who oversaw one of the greatest business success stories in the history of the United States as leader of General Electric for 20 years and instilled a dedication to quality and ongoing improvement throughout the organization, we may conclude that soul involves commitments to excellence and learning through one's experiences. When we think of Meriwether Lewis, who led the greatest expedition ever undertaken across the North American continent, we see soul. Lewis's soul guided his intense desire to discover the wonders of the West and the integrity to follow scrupulously the scientific methods he learned from the best minds of his time to record it. Georgia O'Keefe showed soul as she painted what her imagination created, breaking the limiting conventions of what was thought to be acceptable art in her time.

It would be a mistake to conclude that a person who exhibits attributes of soul in one dimension of his or her life lives with soul in all other dimensions—no one is that fully awakened spiritually and flawless in all regards. Our everyday encounters with others and our understanding of self tell us that each normal mortal life exhibits spots of the good and exemplary and admirable interspersed with areas of darkness and the despicable. Indeed, humans are complex creatures—and they have souls that can be awakened and enriched by spiritual forces.

Even though our understanding of what soul involves is limited and our ability to define it is crude at best, it is, nonetheless, possible to identify various ways in which spiritual forces have made people attractive and successful by examining the lives and actions of those we admire and think of as persons who live their lives above the ordinary:

1. They heard their voice from within speaking to them, and it led them to what they were created to do. Eager to make a significant contribution, they said yes to their calling and it felt right. They followed heir callings.

2. They expressed their uniqueness by doing what they were created to do. They acted on their urge to create.
3. They followed their callings with unhesitating boldness. They risked failure by taking paths their hearts told them to take.
4. They let events shape them, choosing to pursue those opportunities that struck a reverberating chord for them. They accomplished much because they chose to be empowered, not victimized, by their circumstances. They had a way of turning their life experiences into valuable lessons.
5. They had substance at their core. They believed in something worth giving their lives to. They saw the consequences of their ambitions as being far more important than their own ambitions. To put it simply, they lived by ideals. They had integrity.
6. They were thoroughly authentic with themselves and others, especially with others. Their friendship was motivated by the simple desire to share intimacy, and they didn't fear it.
7. They regarded their calling as far larger than themselves, far more important than their own comfort, security, and ego. They worked to serve that cause, doing whatever needed do be done. They were unconcerned with who received the credit and rewards; knowledge of the success of their cause was reward enough.
8. They reverenced realities and forces far greater than themselves—eternal truths, ideals of civilization, beauty, the creator of life. Forces beyond the worldly animated them. They freed themselves from the addictive consumptive patterns brought on by the same pestering appetites that make otherwise good and likeable people small, miserable, and boring.

CHALLENGES TO LIVING WITH SOUL IN THE WORKPLACE

Anyone who has tasted the realities of the workplace knows that there are very real and powerful forces in organizations that are inhospitable to the well-being of soul, to being one's authentic self. The never-ending stream of demands does not permit the soul time to think, to reflect, to savor the moment, to find places to apply our God-given talents. The heavy emphasis on competition and efficiency makes people act in ways they cannot admire, leading them to be less the kind of person they would prefer to be. Individuals are frequently asked to perform work that they don't fully believe in or value, and sometimes this includes doing things that they do not feel proud of doing. The emphasis that's placed on material rewards and all the status and power that seem to go along with having things mislead people into craving money and possessions that appear important but turn out to matter very little. These are things that do not give them the happiness and peace of mind they thought they might bring. Business operates in a competitive atmosphere where there are only a few winners, causing many to feel sometimes that they have less value than they would prefer to think. This atmosphere can often make people feel that their coworkers are potential enemies, not real friends, and antagonisms are aroused.

CHALLENGES TO LIVING WITH SOUL WITHIN OURSELVES

The essence of what soul involves might well be captured in one word—authenticity. A person with soul is authentic. This is a person who lives her beliefs, a person who hears and follows his heart's deepest desires and freely expresses them, a person who marches to her own drumbeat, a person who is his own man. Firm beliefs and strength of character are the main elements of soul, and each one demands struggle.

Why is it that many people, perhaps most people, at least once in their lives yield to the pressures found in the workplace? Which tendencies and inclinations are most responsible for keeping them from being authentic human beings with soul, and exhibiting those qualities that make them truly human? Thoughtful observation will reveal three major obstacles: (1) an overpowering concern for self, (2) an acceptance of what's known as relativism, and (3) an inability or unwillingness to commit themselves to things spiritual, beyond the prosaic.

Overconcern with Self

The bumper sticker that proclaims, "He who dies with the most toys wins," captures the widespread belief that happiness is found in possession. And how does one go about securing this happiness? The answers are found in popular self-help books: Looking Out for Number One; How to Work the Competition into the Ground and Have Fun Doing It; Cashing in on the American Dream: You Can Have It All; and The Art of Winning the Money Game and Living a Life of Joy. Money becomes many people's life report card. Their primary aim becomes one of loading up on loot and doing whatever it takes to get it. A well-adjusted person does have a certain amount of self-awareness and is moderately self-conscious. She is careful in exercising self-control and she masters her desires and directs them wisely. She develops her abilities. To respect and love oneself, but not excessively, is healthy. Eric Fromm, the psychologist whose writings tell us that we must love ourselves if we are ever to be able to love others, also shows that excessive self-concern is rooted in inner self-hatred. People who feel worthless often become very selfish and self-centered (Fromm 1956).

Compromisers buy into the belief that happiness is found in having things. Consequently, they generally strive single-mindedly to possess those things that are commonly thought to be indicators of success—wealth, power, and prestige. Those who live with soul see success as being something different. They define it as doing good things with whatever abilities one has and feeling good about oneself for having mastered and thoughtfully utilized one's human capabilities, not from feeling safe and secure in material objects and not from feelings of smugness and importance from one's accomplishments and from having secured the approval of others. An unusually talented person with the gift of intellect and sharp wit may do better in terms of pay and rank than someone of only average intellect and verbal ability. Yet the latter person may actually struggle more gallantly with issues of right and wrong, be more authentic in his or her interactions with others, be regarded as more trustworthy than most, and come up with more creative approaches to improving the quality of work, although only in small ways, than his or her more gifted counterpart. There are givers and takers in our world; there are those who lift others up and there are those who lean on others for support. The person who reaches out to others and gives time to bettering the world and those who struggle with problems is a human who has risen above the debilitating curse of excessive self-concern.

Acceptance of Relativism

Many people are affected by the idea of openness, which holds up the ideal of being open to and accepting of all standards and beliefs. Many people believe that if everyone were open minded and accepting of differing beliefs, it would follow that we would all be more tolerant and conflict and discord would disappear. This primitive notion of tolerance embraces a line of thinking that goes something like this: (1) There really is no certainty as to which standard of conduct is correct and best; (2) It is supremely important to accept others and be accepted by them—we ought not offend others by suggesting that we believe our ways and beliefs are superior to theirs; and (3) We need to accept the idea that any standard or point of view is just as good as any other one. It's all relative. These three elements are the basis of relativism, which is seen by many as a virtue because it is thought to be a reflection of one's tolerance.

What relativists fail to grasp is that the fact that a person firmly believes that a particular standard or ideal or point of view is best or true or most correct does not mean that he or she is intolerant of others who see things differently. It does not mean that the person with deeply held convictions cannot coexist harmoniously with those who believe differently.

Relativism can be destructive because it tends to seduce people into doing whatever they feel like doing. They grasp for whatever they most want and try to hold on to it by any means they have at their disposal. Afterward, they defend their actions by creating nice-sounding reasons to justify their purposes and methods. While these individuals might exercise a fair measure of creative thought in concocting excuses and explanations for their motives and actions, they never really exercise their minds in matters of graver importance, matters of right and wrong, good and evil, truth and fiction. The person who accepts everything as equally good or correct may consider him- or herself tolerant and open minded, but the sad fact is that this person really never thinks at all. What the relativist considers to be tolerance is really a form of closed-mindedness—he or she never opens his or her mind to struggle with difficult questions having to do with how one ought to live, choose, and behave.

Neglect of Things Spiritual

Those who live with soul tend to be as much concerned with things intangible as they are with things tangible. These people recognize things spiritual have greater potential than things material to make lives richer or poorer. Of course humans need to eat. They must be protected from illness and kept safe from dangers. They must be housed and clothed. But what accounts more for their overall well-being are not things material but things unseen. These unseen forces are quite real—being loved and loving, and having a sense of self and a driving purpose in life, a sense of proportion, the self-confidence to stand on one's own two feet and make decisions, the capacity to be an authentic human being doing significant things that make a difference in the world.

In the minds of those with soul, success lies in the character of one's actions, not in the tangible results one's actions produce. Here is an illustration of this idea. After he left the presidency, John Quincy Adams returned to Congress, where he spoke out against slavery, despite the gag rule designed to prevent people from doing so. When asked why he persisted in what appeared to be a hopeless cause, Adams said, "Duty is ours, results are God's." This quotation captures the essence of what those who live with soul mean by success. The fly fisherman does not measure his success in terms of the fish he catches so much as he does in the way he fishes—how well he reads a stream, ties knots, selects the right flies, casts, presents the floating fly, and lands his catch. Catching fish is thrilling, but it isn't all there is to fishing. The enjoyment the furniture maker experiences from the praises others give for the beauty and quality of his pieces is not equal to that he derives from knowing how to design tables, chairs, and bureaus. Having a finished product to enjoy does not compare to the satisfaction he derives from selecting the right woods to use, and then shaping, carving, and finishing them. The way to a soulful life requires using one's God-given capacities to the fullest possible extent.

HEARING YOUR INNER VOICE: FOLLOWING YOUR CALLING

Every human has an inner voice that quietly but persistently begs for attention. It comes from the soul and speaks in the language of desires, impulses, intuitions, insights, and imagination. This inner voice calls us to realize our unique talents, aptitudes, and passions. By heeding its calls, people make better choices and ultimately find the greatest levels of satisfaction. The inner voice nudges each of us gently, calling us to choose wisely, to find and follow our dreams, to live well. Yet many people never pay attention to this powerful force coming from within. Instead, they are captivated by other callings from without, worldly pressures, and desires.

Hearing one's inner voice requires one to overcome deafening forces such as being overly concerned with reaching career goals that blind one from seeing new possibilities, being too busy to stop and reflect on what's in one's heart, and becoming satisfied with tired-out and easy-to-accomplish aims instead of attempting what's new and challenging. With all the pressures of family life, demands from higher-ups at work, and personal desires for having fun, little time is available for quiet reflection on a daily basis. The pace of life is fast and unrelenting. And when we do have a spare moment, we feel too tired to do anything but curl up and sleep.

This is compounded by the fact that in an age of high parental expectations, many youngsters sign on to career paths that may impress others but not truly reflect their individuality and aptitudes. They follow these paths largely to please and impress others. Yet these paths don't feel right. I once had a student come into my office for help scheduling courses. She seemed bothered by something, and I encouraged her to talk about her classes and what she liked and disliked. As she began telling me what she found interesting and not so exciting, I got the sense that she really didn't like her business courses at all. I said, "It doesn't seem to me that you enjoy your business courses. Are you sure you are pursuing the right major?" That caught her a bit off guard, but she took the opportunity to express her true feelings. With a sigh of relief, she said to me, "To tell you the truth, no. I'd much rather study something else." As we talked more she said that her mother, who was an accountant, and her father, who was an attorney, wanted her to study business. They believed that she needed to major in a subject that would lead to a high-paying income. But this student was not finding much enjoyment in studying business. She was made differently as a person and her heart (her inner voice) was quietly, yet persistently, telling her that business was not for her. She went on to explain how much she had enjoyed her job the previous summer working with children and how much they loved her and she loved them. She was clearly a person who had interests other than business.

Readers wanting to find ways of liberating themselves from unfulfilling work will find useful advice in two books. The first is Do What You Love, the Money Will Follow, by Marsha Sinetar. This volume offers a step-by-step guide for finding work that expresses and fulfills one's needs, talents, and passions. Sinetar give readers a spiritual yet practical approach to following their hearts and making a living by explaining how they can tune into their inner world of talent, banish outmoded networks telling them what they should be doing, and liberate themselves from unfulfilling jobs.

The other book is titled Passion at Work: How to Find Work You Love and Live the Time of Your Life, by Lawler Kang. According to Stewart Friedman, director of the Work/Life Integration Program at the Wharton School, "Kang's engaging book offers really useful ideas for how to live in a way that aligns your actions with your values. Doing so brings passion to your work and to the rest of your life" (Kang 2005).

CONCLUSION

One of the more important things one can do to retain one's authenticity is to place oneself in situations in which compromises are minimized. Those who make the mistake of trying to succeed in fields for which they are ill suited doom themselves to a miserable existence. The conflicts to be found there will be simply too great to ignore or tolerate. Selecting the type of work and the employer that match one's values, interests, and abilities is far better for a person's well-being than is entering workplaces that do not. Even when one does find a good match between the type of work and the nature of the employing organization and themselves, conflict is bound to arise. Being unbending, steadfastly refusing to be anything other than 100 percent true to oneself, is generally a fair sign that an individual is more interested in him- or herself than anything else, an orientation that has never been found to be admirable or healthy.

BECOMING YOUR AUTHENTIC SELF AND WORKING WITH OTHERS EFFECTIVELY

When he was CEO of Super Valu Stores, Mike Wright told me, "All of us should worry about whether our egos have gotten out of control. I think more problems result from an imbalance of the ego. It can destroy companies, families, and individuals. As you get higher in an organization, you worry whether people are telling you the truth. I think you can change by being at the top, and you won't know it. People won't tell you because they are scared to. So, you've got to keep asking yourself, 'What am I doing to be a jerk around here?'"

There can be little doubt that effectiveness in the workplace depends on getting along well with others, working harmoniously and productively in teams, and cooperating. These conditions are impossible to achieve in the absence of spiritual forces—honesty, sincerity, neighborliness, and cheerfulness—that are easily neglected or harmed when people become overly consumed with getting what they want, acting with vain pretentiousness, and pursuing their own interests by whatever means necessary.

Strong, productive relationships in the workplace require respect and helpfulness. Employees who interact with others without guile or obstructing pretenses make for good teammates. When he ran Lockheed, Roy Anderson told me, "In this company it's pretty well known that those who try to push themselves up are going to run into difficulty because in trying to do that, they damage others. We look for the types of people who just by pure talent and effort and dedication have the respect of their peers."

The DuPont Corporation follows a practice they call the flower principle, which they use when assessing managers. The thinking behind it goes something like this: flowers look good from the top down but are not as beautiful when seen from below, looking up. So, when they assess their managers for promotion potential, upper management goes to those who work for the manager under examination and asks for their opinions. They sometimes find that some of the managers who look good to upper management from above are not seen as good by those who work under them.

References

Fromm, Erich. 1956. *The Art of Loving.* New York: Harper.

Kang, Lawler. 2005. *Passion at Work: How to Find Work You Love and Live the Time of Your Life.* Upper Saddle River, NJ: Prentice Hall.

Further Readings: Kang, Lawler. 2005. *Passion at Work: How to Find Work You Love and Live the Time of Your Life.* Upper Saddle River, NJ: Prentice Hall; Sinetar, Marsha. 1989. *Do What You Love, The Money Will Follow: Discovering Your Right Livelihood.* New York: Dell; Watson, Charles E. 1999. *What Smart People Do When Dumb Things Happen at Work.* Franklin Lakes, NJ: Career Press.

Charles E. Watson

POVERTY AND RACE

Hurricane Katrina's devastation of the city of New Orleans and other Gulf Coast communities in 2005 refocused the nation's attention on the relationship between race and poverty in America. The people most adversely affected by this catastrophic event and its aftermath were overwhelmingly black, and overwhelmingly poor. A common reaction to the media's dramatic images of disaster victims in New Orleans, especially those seeking refuge in the attics of flooded homes, building rooftops, and the Superdome, was: "I didn't think the problem of race and poverty was still with us."

As this entry shows, the attention to poverty and race brought about by Katrina is yet another phase in the race/poverty discourse in America, which has shifted sharply several times over the past 50 years. In this entry, we will show how the face of poverty in the United States has changed over the past 40 years in response to antipoverty policies and structural changes in the economy.

BACKGROUND AND CONTEXT

Concerns about America's poor ebbed and flowed throughout the twentieth century. After receiving limited public policy attention prior to World War II, concern about America's poverty problem abated after the war, and it did not become a priority policy issue again until the early 1960s.

Since the early 1960s, public policies implemented to alleviate poverty in America have ranged from the very liberal to the extremely conservative. Reflecting this state of affairs, the absolute and relative size of the poor population in the United States has fluctuated widely over the last 40 years. Table P.2 shows the poverty status of the U.S. population for selected years between 1960 and 2003.

The Poor and Efforts to Alleviate Poverty in America

Political attitudes toward America's poor were decidedly liberal during the 1960s. In both political and policy circles, the prevailing view was that poverty was a structural problem characterized by racial discrimination and systematic exclusion of racial minorities in all walks of American life. This view led to the first major federal effort after World War II to address America's poverty problem: the war on poverty and the Great Society programs launched by President Johnson.

Table P.2 Poverty Status of the U.S. Population, Selected Years (1960–2003).

Year	All people	Poor people	Percent poor
1960	179,503	39,851	22.2
1970	202,183	25,272	12.6
1980	225,027	29,272	13.0
1990	248,644	33,585	13.5
2000	278,944	31,581	11.3
2003	287,699	35,861	12.5

Source: U.S. Bureau of the Census, Current Population Survey. Annual Demographic Supplements, Poverty and Health Statistics Branch/HHES Division. Available at http://www.census.gov/hhes/poverty/histpov. Accessed May 13, 2006.

Before the war on poverty, the U.S. poor totaled 39.8 million, 22.4 percent of the nation's population in 1960 (Table P.2). As a consequence of the Johnson administration's antipoverty programs, which sought to redress the systematic inequities in American society, the incidence of poverty was reduced by 36 percent during the 1960s. By 1970, only 25.4 million people (12.6% of the U.S. population) were poor.

But the war on poverty was short lived, as the Vietnam War assumed center stage during the early 1970s, resulting in a redirection of federal resources away from efforts to eradicate poverty in America. Moreover, with the election of President Nixon, attitudes toward the poor became more conservative: the prevailing view held that poverty was a function of human or personal failings rather than a structural problem. As a consequence of these developments, the assault on America's poverty problem was substantially curtailed just as economic stagflation and a deep recession occurred, resulting in an increase—absolute and relative—in the size of the nation's poor population. During the 1970s, the U.S. poor grew from 25.4 million to 29.2 million, increasing from 12.6 percent to 13 percent of the total population by 1980 (Table P.2).

Political attitudes toward the poor became even more conservative during the 1980s. Instead of acknowledging the short duration of the nation's official war on poverty, both the Reagan and Bush administrations of the 1980s argued that America's persistent poverty problem, especially the resurgence of growth during the 1970s, was a product of 1960s-era liberal policy making. In their eyes, the federal welfare program—Aid to Families with Dependent Children (AFDC), in particular—was the culprit.

AFDC, they contended, destroyed the work ethic, bred long-term dependency, and encouraged a range of other anti-social or dysfunctional behaviors, including out-of-wedlock pregnancy, family disruption, and even illegal activities revolving around gangs and drug dealing, especially in the nation's cities. The problem, they asserted, was not material poverty, but, rather, moral poverty. They also believed that the antipoverty programs of Johnson's Great Society slowed the economy by sapping taxes from productive investments that would otherwise spur economic growth and job creation.

To combat these problems and behaviors, the Reagan and Bush administrations waged what some characterize as a war on the poor, drastically cutting federal spending on social programs (especially AFDC) and eliminating government regulations viewed as crippling industry and private enterprise. These policies, especially efforts to create a deregulated business environment, drastically altered the structure of economic opportunity for the nation's most disadvantaged citizens, in particular the large number of African Americans concentrated in urban ghettoes.

Specifically, the business policies accelerated the decline of highly unionized, high-wage, central-city manufacturing employment—a process referred to as deindustrialization—and accelerated capital flight away from U.S. cities and toward third world countries—a process referred to as employment deconcentration—leaving behind a substantial population that became the jobless or under-employed poor. In part as a function of these business policy impacts and partly as a consequence of cuts in a host of 1960s-era social programs, the poor population continued to increase during the 1980s, reaching 33.5 million, or 13.5 percent of the total U.S. population, by 1990.

During the 1990s, the poor population declined for the first time since the 1960s—from 33.5 million (13.5% of the total population) at the beginning of the decade to 31.5 million (11.3% of the total population) at the end. It should be noted that this decline occurred despite prognostications that poverty would increase substantially after the enactment of the most sweeping welfare reform

DUELING MEASURES OF POVERTY

Although poverty might seem like a simple concept, it isn't. Measuring poverty requires specific calculations, which means poverty must be precisely defined.

The official definition of poverty used by the U.S. Census Bureau is over 40 years old. Developed in 1965, the formulation of the definition involved several steps. First, the spending necessary for a household to consume nutritious yet frugal meals was calculated. This spending was different for households of different sizes. Second, this food spending was multiplied by a factor—roughly three—to equal the spending necessary to afford an adequate amount of all consumer goods and services. This, then, was the poverty threshold. Finally, if a household's income from working was below the poverty threshold for its size, then the household was classified as poor. Each year the poverty thresholds are adjusted upward to account for the general increase in the cost of living.

There are many issues with the official measure of poverty, but two in particular stand out. One is whether simply multiplying food spending by three is adequate to produce an income that would allow one to afford all necessary goods and services. What if prices and costs for some services, like health care, are increasing much faster now than in the past? Wouldn't this mean the poverty thresholds are too low?

Second is whether the values of various kinds of public assistance received by households should be included before it is decided if a household is poor. For example, many households receive assistance through programs like Food Stamps and Medicaid. Many households also receive direct cash assistance through temporary welfare payments and payments from the government if they are working and their earnings fall below a certain level (the name of this program is the earned income tax credit). If the objective of measuring poverty is to see how many people are poor after government-provided help is accounted for, then the value of these government programs should be included in a household's income.

The U.S. Census Bureau calculates poverty rates based on these two concerns. An alternative poverty rate includes the cost of medical services in the poverty thresholds. When this is done, the poverty rate (percentage of people who are designated poor) increases approximately 1 percent from the official rate. Another alternative poverty rate is calculated after the values of government antipoverty programs in a household's income are included. These poverty rates are approximately four percentage points below the official rate.

The conclusion is that how much poverty exists depends on how poverty is defined and measured.

legislation since the war on poverty was launched in the mid-1960s—the Personal Responsibility and Work Opportunity Reconciliation Act of 1996 (PRWORA).

In an effort to respond to past criticisms of the social welfare system, especially those advanced by conservative social policy analysts, the 1996 PRWORA sought to reduce dependency by imposing time limits on welfare. Reflecting liberal views about the underlying causes of poverty, it also provided a range of supports designed to encourage and facilitate former welfare recipients' transition to work. Thus, in contrast to the liberal policies of the 1960s and the conservative policies of the 1980s, this legislation was decidedly centrist, as it represented a "carrots" (work incentives and supports) and "sticks" (welfare time limits) approach to poverty alleviation in America.

The successful implementation of the reforms inherent in the 1996 legislation was aided tremendously by the decade-long economic boom, which created a large number of entry-level jobs that matched the skill levels of the long-term welfare-dependent population. But the recent economic downturn has adversely affected the federal government's effort to move former welfare recipients to the world of work as well as the structure of employment opportunities in the U.S. economy more generally, especially for low-skilled workers. Due to the massive layoffs spawned by corporate scandals and business failures, the U.S. poor population increased by 4.3 million after 2000, bringing the total to 35.9 million in 2003. As a result of this absolute increase, the share of the U.S. population that was poor increased from 11.3 percent in 2000 to 12.5 percent in 2003.

Uneven Impacts of Past Poverty Alleviation Programs

Notwithstanding the fluctuations in the absolute and relative size of the U.S. poverty population over the last 40 years, there were, according to the Census Bureau, almost 4 million fewer poor people in the United States in 2003 than there were in 1960. And it should be noted this absolute decline occurred in the midst of a 60 percent increase in the total U.S. population—from 179.5 million in 1960 to 287.7 million in 2003 (see Table P.2).

But past efforts to alleviate poverty in the United States have been unevenly distributed, resulting in a significant shift in both the demographic composition and the geographical distribution of the poor. Figure P.1 provides insight into where significant inroads have been made in the alleviation of poverty and where major challenges remain. Figures P.2 through P.5 illustrate how the face of poverty in the United States has changed over the last 40 years as a consequence of the uneven distributional impacts of past poverty alleviation efforts.

In 2003, as Figure P.1 shows, there were 9.2 million fewer poor people living in families, 0.6 million fewer poor families, 7.6 million fewer poor whites, 1.8 million fewer poor blacks, 4.9 million fewer poor children, 1.9 million fewer poor elderly people, 4.6 million fewer poor Southerners, and 14.3 million fewer rural poor in the United States than there were 40 years earlier. However, there were 5.0 million more poor people in female-headed households, 5.0 million more poor unrelated individuals, 1.6 million more poor female-headed families, 6.6 million more poor Hispanics, 3.0 million more poor working-age individuals

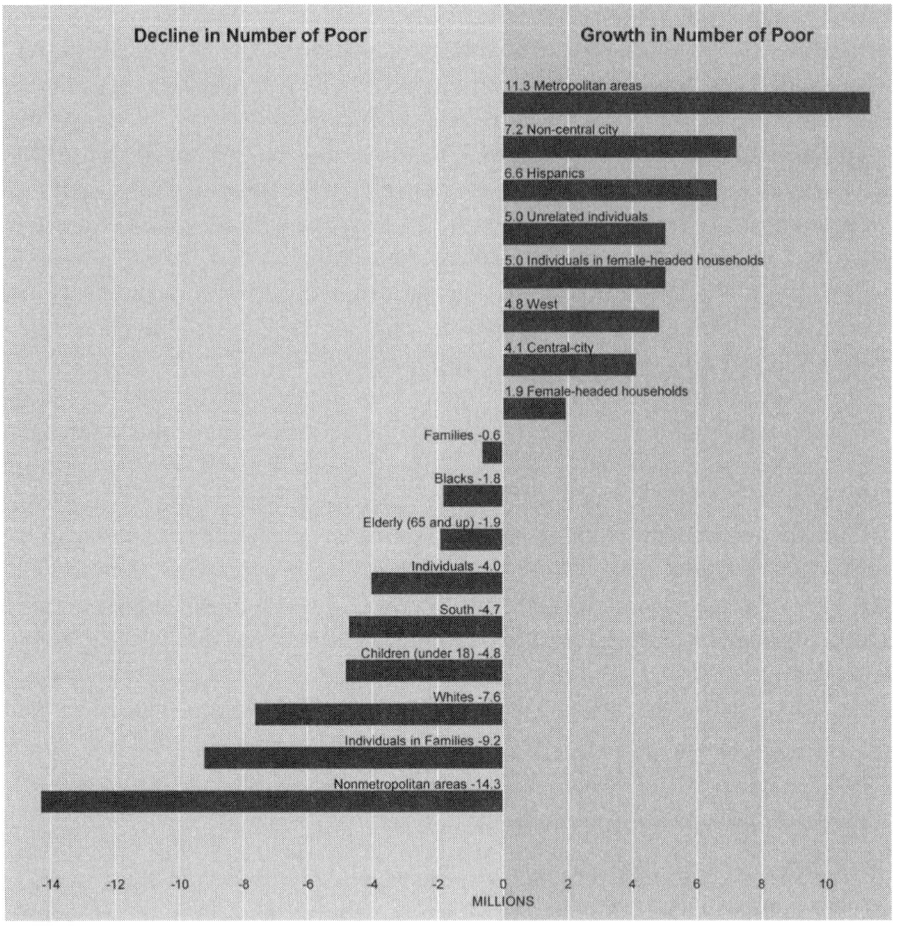

Figure P.1 The changing profile of the U.S. poor (1960–2003).
Source: U.S. Census Bureau. Available at www.census.gov.

(18–64 years old), 11.3 million more poor people living in metropolitan areas (4.1 million in central cities and 7.2 million outside central cities), and 4.8 million more poor people in the western region of the United States than there were in 1960.

Undergirding these statistics are five noteworthy shifts that have transformed the face of poverty in the United States over the last 40 years: shifts in regional distribution and place of residence, as well as changes in the age, family status, and racial/ethnic composition of the nation's poor.

As Figure P.2 shows, the decline of the South's share of the U.S. poor and the concomitant increase in the West's share is one of these shifts. In the early 1970s, close to half of the nation's poor was concentrated in the South. Thirty years later the South's share of U.S. poverty had decreased to 40 percent. Paralleling the South's declining share, the West's share of the nation's poor increased from 16 percent in 1971 to 24 percent in 2003. As shown below, this shift is

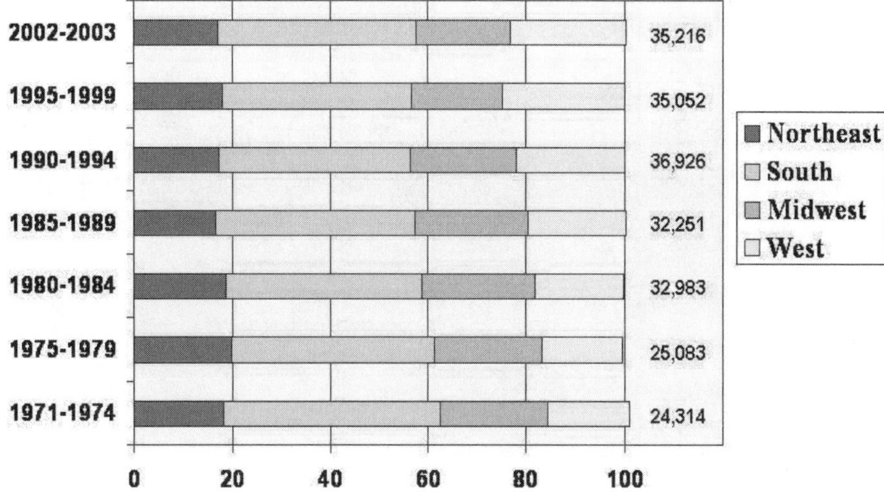

Figure P.2 Distribution of U.S. poor by region (1971–2003).

Source: U.S. Bureau of the Census. 2004. Current Population Survey, Annual Demographic Supplements. Poverty and Health Statistics Branch / HHES Division. Available at http://www.census.gov/hhes/poverty/histpov. Accessed June 1, 2006.

due in part to the influx of poor Hispanic immigrants into the United States over the last three decades, most of who settled—at least initially—in the Southwest. Throughout this period, as Figure P.2 shows, the Northeast's and Midwest's shares of the nation's poor remained relatively stable—in the 17–20 percent range in both regions.

Changes in the types of communities in which the nation's poor reside constitute a second major shift. As the United States has become more urbanized, so has the poor population. In the mid-1960s, as Figure P.3 shows, almost half of the nation's poor resided in rural areas. By 2003, only 21 percent resided in such areas. Today, a majority of the U.S. poor lives in metropolitan areas, with significant concentrations both inside and outside central cities.

Over the past 40 years, the age composition of the poor also has changed; this constitutes the third major shift. In general, the shares of the U.S. poor under age 18 and over age 65 decreased, while the 18–64 share increased sharply (see Figure P.4). Historically, poverty among working-age individuals (18–64) was due primarily to detachment from the labor market (i.e., jobless poverty). However, as the American economy was structurally transformed from goods production to service provision, a growing contingent of the labor force became what is referred to as the working poor. Due to skills deficits or other types of constraints (e.g., lack of affordable child care, inferior public school education, lack of economic opportunities in close proximity, and employer bias), these individuals have been relegated to part-time jobs they don't want—mainly in the service sector of the U.S. economy—or full-time jobs that pay below poverty-level wages, provide few (if any) benefits, and offer no prospects for career mobility (see Table P.3).

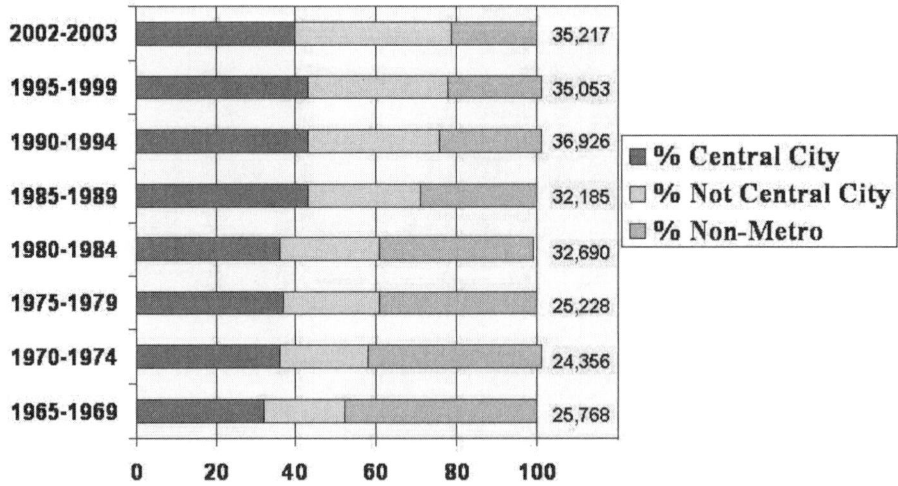

Figure P.3 Distribution of U.S. poor by place of residence (1965–2003).

Source: U.S. Bureau of the Census. 2004. Current Population Survey, Annual Demographic Supplements. Poverty and Health Statistics Branch / HHES Division. Available at http://www.census.gov/hhes/poverty/histpov. Accessed June 12, 2006.

The family context in which the poor find themselves is the fourth major shift. Poverty among all families declined by 18 percent over the last four decades. But, as Figure P.5 shows, poverty has become less concentrated in married-couple families and significantly more concentrated in female-headed families. Female-headed families accounted for over half of all families in poverty in 2003. This shift has been termed the feminization of poverty.

Change in the racial and ethnic composition of the nation's poor population is the fifth major shift. Heightened immigration—legal and illegal—from Mexico, other parts of Latin America, and Southeast Asia is principally responsible for the increasing diversity of the nation's poor. The white share of the U.S. poor declined from 70 percent in the mid-1960s to 44.3 percent in 2002–2003. During this period, the African American share declined from 30 percent to 25 percent. These declines have been offset by increases among the immigrant groups, especially Hispanics. Since the early 1970s, the Hispanic share of the nation's poor has grown from 11 percent to nearly a quarter of the total. This shift explains, at least in part, the growing concentration of the nation's poor in the West.

CONCLUSION

A range of public policies spanning the political ideological spectrum have been implemented to address America's poverty problem since the 1960s. Whether because of these policies—which were based on varying assumptions about the causes of poverty—or because of fundamental shifts in the American economy, fewer Americans live in poverty today than 45 years ago, even though the total population grew by 60 percent over this period.

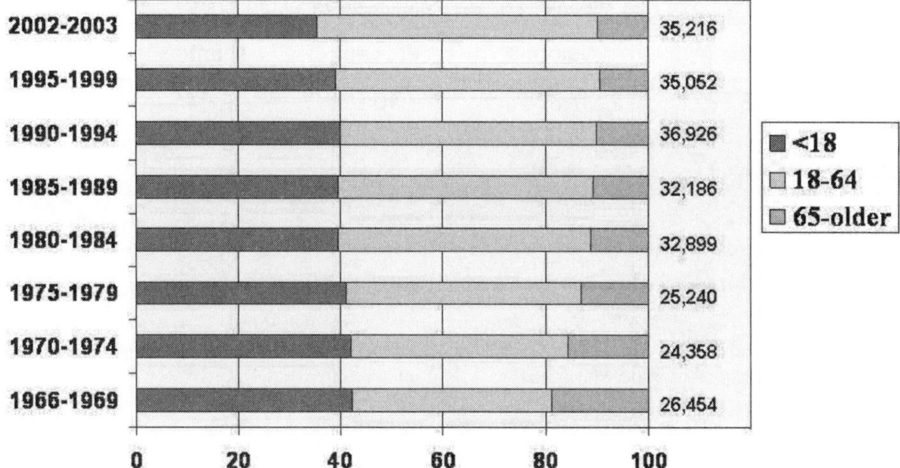

Figure P.4 Distribution of U.S. poor by age (1966–2003).

Source: U.S. Bureau of the Census. 2004. Current Population Survey, Annual Demographic Supplements. Poverty and Health Statistics Branch / HHES Division. Available at http://www.census.gov/hhes/poverty/histpov. Accessed June 12, 2006.

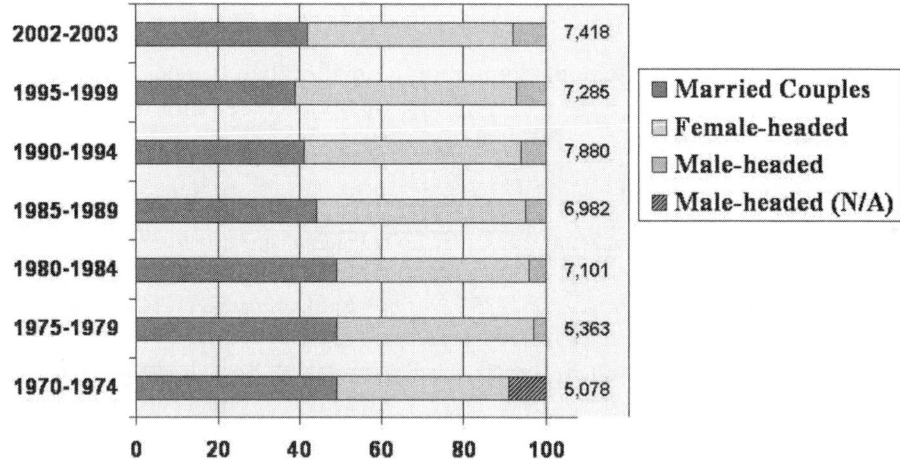

Figure P.5 Distribution of U.S. poor by family type (1970–2003).

Source: U.S. Bureau of the Census. 2004. Current Population Survey, Annual Demographic Supplements. Poverty and Health Statistics Branch / HHES Division. Available at http://www.census.gov/hhes/poverty/histpov. Accessed June 12, 2006.

While many of the social and economic conditions associated with poverty in the 1960s persist, immigration, combined with regional and global shifts in job growth, changed the face of poverty in America in several ways.

- Poverty in the South declined significantly, but there was a substantial increase in the West as the proportion of Hispanics living in poverty more than doubled.

Table P.3 Work Status of Poor People, 16 Years and Over, Selected Years (1980–2003)

Year	Total	Number	Percent	Number	Percent
1980	18,892	7,674	40.6	1,644	8.7
1985	21,243	9,008	42.4	1,972	9.3
1990	21,242	8,716	41.0	2,076	9.8
1995	23,077	9,484	41.1	2,418	10.5
2000	21,080	8,511	40.4	2,439	11.6
2003	24,266	8,820	36.3	2,636	10.9

Source: U.S. Bureau of the Census. Current Population Survey, Annual Demographic Supplements, Poverty and Health Statistics Branch/HHES Division. Available at http://www.census.gov/hhes/poverty/histpov. Accessed May 15, 2006.

- Rural poverty declined while urban poverty grew.
- Poverty among the elderly and children declined while poverty among working-age adults increased sharply. Today, the working poor account for a higher proportion of Americans in poverty than the jobless poor.
- Poverty increased in female-headed, single-parent households as the number and proportion of these families grew, especially among African Americans.

Although the size of the poor population is smaller than it was in the 1960s, Hurricane Katrina served as a vivid reminder that poverty remains a substantial problem in America.

See also: Immigrant Workers in the United States

Further Reading: Abramovitz, Mimi. 1992. "The New Paternalism." *The Nation,* 255: 368–71; Amarota, Steven A. 2002. "Immigrants in the United States—2002: A Snapshot of America's Foreign Born Population." *CIS Backgrounder.* Washington, DC: Center for Immigration Studies; Bawden, D. L., and J. L. Palmer. 1984. "Social Policy: Challenging the Welfare State." In *The Reagan Record,* ed., J. L. Palmer and I. V. Sawhill. Washington, DC: Urban Institute; Bennet, W. J., J. J. DiIulio Jr., and J. P. Walters. 1996. *Body Count: Moral Poverty . . . and How to Win America's War Against Crime and Drugs.* New York: Simon & Schuster; Bluestone, Barry, and Bennett Harrison. 1982. *The Deindustrialization of America.* New York: Basic Books; Boger, John Charles. 1996. "Afterward: A Debate Over the National Future." In *Race, Poverty, and American Cities,* ed., John Charles Boger and Judith Welch Wegner. Chapel Hill: University of North Carolina Press; Boger, John Charles. 1996. "Race and the American City: The Kerner Commission Report in Retrospect." In *Race, Poverty, and American Cities,* ed., John Charles Boger and Judith Welch Wegner, 3–76. Chapel Hill: University of North Carolina Press; Brooks, Michael P. 1964. *The Dimensions of Poverty in North Carolina.* Durham: North Carolina Fund; Danziger, Sheldon. 2002. "Welfare Reform: A Fix for All Seasons." *Milken Institute Review* 4:24–33; Eberstadt, Nicholas. 2006. "The Mismeasure of Poverty." *Policy Review* 138; Fitzgerald, Joan, and Allan McGregor. 1993. "Labor-Community Initiatives in Worker Training." *Economic Development Quarterly* 7:160–71; Garfinkel, Irwin, and Sara McLanahan. 1986. *Single Mother and Their Children: A New American Dilemma.* Washington, DC: Urban Institute; Gillespie, Ed, and Bob Schellhas, eds. 1994. *Contract with America: The*

Bold Plan by Rep. Newt Gingrich, Rep. Dick Armey and the House Republicans to Change the Nation. New York: Times Books; Grant, David, and James H. Johnson Jr. 1995. "Conservative Policymaking and Growing Urban Inequality in the 1980s." In *Research in Politics and Society,* ed., R. Ratcliff, M. Oliver, and T. Shapiro, 127–59. Greenwich, CT: JAI Press; Harrington, Michael. 1962. *The Other America: Poverty in the United States.* New York: McMillan; Haveman, Robert H., ed. 1977. *A Decade of Federal Antipoverty Programs: Achievements, Failures, and Lessons.* New York: Academic Press; Housing and Household Economic Statistics Division. 2006. *The Effects of Government Taxes and Transfers on Income and Poverty: 2004.* Washington, DC: U.S. Census Bureau; ; Jencks, Christopher, and Paul Peterson. 1991. *The Urban Underclass.* Washington, DC: Brookings Institution; Johnson, James H., Jr., and Melvin L. Oliver. 1992. "Economic Restructuring and Black Male Joblessness: A Reassessment." In *Urban Labor Markets and Job Opportunity,* ed., G. Peterson and W. Vroman. Washington, DC: Urban Institute Press; Johnson, James H., Jr., Elisa Jane Bienenstock, and Walter C. Farrell Jr. 1999. "Bridging Social Networks and Female Labor Force Participation in a Multi-Ethnic Metropolis." *Urban Geography* 20:3–30; Johnson, James H., Jr., Walter C. Farrell Jr., and Jennifer A. Stoloff. 2000. "An Empirical Assessment of Four Perspectives on the Declining Fortunes of the African American Male." *Urban Affairs Review* 35:695–716; Johnson, James H., Jr., and Walter C. Farrell, Jr. 1998. "Growing Income Inequality in American Society: A Political Economy Perspective." In *The Inequality Paradox: Growing Income Disparity,* ed., J. A. Auerbach and R. S. Belos, 133–80. Washington, DC: National Policy Association; Johnson, James H., Jr., Karen Johnson-Webb, and Walter C. Farrell Jr. 1999. "A Profile of Hispanic Newcomers to North Carolina." *Popular Government* 65:2–12; Johnson, James H., Jr., Karen Johnson-Webb, and Walter C. Farrell Jr. 1999. "Newly Emerging Hispanic Communities in the U.S.: A Spatial Analysis of Settlement Patterns, In-Migration Fields, and Social Receptivity." In *Immigration and Opportunity: Race, Ethnicity, and Employment in the United States,* ed., F. D. Bean and S. Bell-Rose, 263–310. New York: Russell Sage Foundation; Katz, Michael. 1986. *In the Shadow of the Poor House: A Social History of Welfare in America.* New York: Basic Books; Kirkpatrick, C. D. 2002. "Poverty's Grasp on Families Threatens Children's Futures." *Herald-Sun,* September 22; Lemann, Nicholas. 1991. *The Promised Land.* New York: Knopf; Mead, Lawrence. 1986. *Beyond Entitlement: The Social Obligations of Citizenship.* New York: Free Press; Mead, Lawrence. 1992. *The New Politics of Poverty.* New York: Basic Books; Murray, Charles. 1984. *Losing Ground.* New York: Basic Books; Murray, Charles. 1995. "Reducing Poverty and Reducing the Underclass: Different Problems, Different Solutions." In *Reducing Poverty in America: Views and Approaches,* ed., Michael Darby, 82–110. Thousand Oaks, CA: Sage; Newman, Katherine S. 1999. *No Shame in My Game.* New York: Russell Sage Foundation; Our View, 2003. "Slippery Slope." *Raleigh News & Observer,* January 15; Palmer, J. L., and I. V. Sawhill, eds. 1984. *The Reagan Record.* Washington, DC: Urban Institute; Patterson, James T. 1986. *American's Struggle Against Poverty: 1900–1985.* New York: Basic Books; Pear, Robert. 2002. "Number of People Living in Poverty Increases in U.S." *New York Times,* September 25; Phillips, Kevin. 1990. *The Politics of Rich and Poor: Wealth and the American Electorate in the Reagan Aftermath.* New York: Random House; Piven, Frances Fox, and Richard A. Cloward. 1971. *Regulating the Poor: The Functions of Social Welfare.* New York: Vintage Books; Plotnick, Robert D., and Felicity Skidmore. 1975. *Progress Against Poverty: A Review of the 1964–74 Decade.* New York: Academic Press; Proctor, Bernadette, and Joseph Dalaker. 2003. *Poverty in the United States: 2002.* Current Population Reports, P60–222. Washington, DC: U.S. Census Bureau; Squires, Gregory D. 1982. "Runaway Plants, Capital Mobility, and Black Economic Rights." In *Community and Capital in Conflict: Plant Closings and Job Loss,* ed., J. C. Raines, Lenora

E. Berson, and David McI. Gracie. Philadelphia: Temple University Press; U.S. Department of Health and Human Services. 1999. *Fact Sheet: The Personal Responsibility and Work Opportunity Reconciliation Act of 1996.* Washington, DC: Author; Wilson, William Julius. 1987. *The Truly Disadvantaged.* Chicago: University of Chicago Press.

James H. Johnson Jr. and Allan M. Parnell

PRICE GOUGING

An accusation of price gouging is essentially an accusation that a seller is charging a price that is too high. In general, a claim that a price is too high is troubling, as it presumes that there is some other price that is the right one. When price gouging is charged, "too high" is usually taken to mean that the price cannot be justified by the seller's costs. The seller will make a profit on the transaction, a profit that is deemed, by someone, to be unreasonable, a windfall, or unnecessary.

The problem with the accusation is that firms in a market economy are not required to price at cost, or at cost plus some set margin. In fact, one of the things that allows a market economy to function is that businesses move resources into areas of the economy where there are profits to be made. By doing so, these businesses increase the availability of goods that are comparatively scarce. Over time, those actions force prices down and erode profits.

In recent years, natural disasters and oil price fluctuations seem to be the circumstances that prompt most of the charges of price gouging. Each of these events offers lessons about how markets work in response to various kinds of external shocks to the economy.

The approach of a hurricane is a good example. As a storm gains strength and tracks in our direction, we become students of meteorology. Suddenly, the workings of weather systems hold our attention, as fronts and steering systems and pressure differences are matters of consequence. With somewhat less drama, the aftermath of a hurricane can teach us something about economics. Now the social systems that ordinarily work mostly unnoticed to provide the things we take for granted are called upon to deliver very different bundles of goods and services and to do so quickly and under adverse circumstances.

Except in the most severe cases, almost as soon as hurricane conditions have ended, the goods and services necessary for recovery begin to be delivered to the affected areas. Some of these will be brought by state and local government agencies and some will be provided by charitable organizations. Much will be provided by the public utilities. But a very large share of the resources that will be required to restore normal life and repair damaged property will be provided by private parties—businesses small and large that will offer for sale a great volume of goods and services that ordinarily are provided on a scale that is miniscule by comparison—food, water, chainsaws, blowers, tarps, garbage bags, plywood sheets, roofing materials, rakes, batteries, propane, ice, gasoline, window glass, framing lumber, roofers, tree cutting services, cleaning services, and on and on. All these must arrive quickly to avert the immediate crisis and begin to bring life back to normal. Most of this is provided—sold to eager buyers by eager sellers.

Like the private economy that serves us in normal times, much of this crisis economy has no central coordinating authority that makes it all work. Typically, even before the storm has moved on, trucks are on their way to the affected area from scores of different sources with hundreds of different goods. Stores that are stripped clean of emergency goods before the storm hits will reopen with restocked shelves not long after the storm is over. An army of private actors puts this all in process. How this all happens offers lessons in basic economics.

The recovery period offers attractive opportunities to these private actors. Some companies see it as an opportunity to burnish their reputations, to introduce themselves to new customers, or to cement their relationships with current customers. Many companies see an opportunity to sell larger volumes of the goods they normally sell. Others see an opportunity to sell things that they do not—perhaps cannot—ordinarily sell. It isn't just profit opportunities that motivate these private actors—they may also act out of concern for others or a sense of community obligation, or to enhance their own positions in their communities. But the opportunity to profit plays a large role even in emergency circumstances.

In economic terms, during a recovery period some goods are subject to dramatically increased demand (plywood, tree cutting services), some are subject to dramatically reduced supply (clean water, fuel), and others may be subject to both. Either of these conditions—increases in demand or decreases in supply—tend to increase prices. It is into this mix that we typically hear allegations of price gouging.

Price gouging has no precise definition in economics. There is also no federal statute that defines or prohibits price gouging. State legislatures, responding to public dissatisfaction with high prices, have struggled to define price gouging. Twenty-nine states have price-gouging statutes, but the definitions used in these statutes vary widely. Most state statutes are effective only when a state of emergency has been declared by the federal, state, or local government. Many use subjective terms such as "exorbitant," "unconscionably excessive," or "unjustified" to define price gouging. As it is commonly used, the phrase "price gouging" simply means that a seller has sold or offered to sell a good at a price that someone else thinks is too high. Most often, price gouging is alleged when a price has increased by a large amount in a small amount of time.

Allegations of price gouging are not confined to the aftermath of hurricanes, of course, but such claims are often associated with some kind of dislocation or disaster. War or the threat of war has often brought increased prices for gasoline and with it a raft of price-gouging claims. Earthquakes, blizzards, heat waves, and floods can also raise prices and prompt charges of price gouging. Certainly claims about price gouging can be made when increases in demand or decreases in supply are more gradual, but for the most part, such claims are confined to circumstances in which price increases occur abruptly.

In ordinary situations, a price adjusts so that the available supplies of a good match the amount that consumers would like to purchase. Such price adjustments are what coordinate production and consumption in a market economy.

Price is a signal that tells producers whether the goods that they can produce will be worth more in the economy than the cost of producing them. Price also is a signal to consumers that indicates the costs that they impose on other members of society by consuming a good—how valuable the good is elsewhere in the economy.

This perspective helps explain why it is difficult to provide a definition of price gouging that captures the intended meaning—charging a price that is just too high. As some of the examples below demonstrate, almost any price, regardless of how high it is, performs the important function of adjusting the quantities that producers produce and consumers consume. Particularly during times of economic dislocation, the agility of unconstrained markets in coordinating economic activity is an important advantage.

For the purpose of the following discussion, let's define price gouging as charging a price that is just too high to provide any social function other than transferring wealth from the seller to the buyer. That provisional definition will let us examine several claimed instances of price gouging.

PRICE ADJUSTMENT IN CRISIS

When supplies of some good are dramatically reduced or demands are dramatically increased, prices increase, sometimes quite dramatically. Such a result is the ordinary working of supply and demand, the most fundamental and best-tested framework in economics. That said, we might well ask, How does the price adjustment actually happen?

When it becomes evident to at least some people that the quantities of some good that are available will not be adequate to satisfy the demand at the current price, participants in the market begin to adjust the price. In some instances, consumers offer sellers higher prices in order to get the quantities they want. More often, it is suppliers who initiate the price adjustment by increasing their posted prices. At some point it becomes clear to them that they will quickly sell out of their inventories at the current price, and that even if they raise prices they can still sell everything they have in stock or have available to them. They face an easy choice: they can sell everything they have at a low price, or they can sell everything they have at a higher price. A few sellers may initiate the price change and may even see their sales slow for a short time, while those who are slow to raise prices sell out. Some sellers raise prices in a more passive way, simply by holding back inventories of goods, then selling them when the price has gone up.

In economists' terminology, the price increase brings about a new equilibrium equating supply and demand. The higher price performs the function of rationing the available supplies. At the new price, consumers can obtain what they want at the available price, although what they will want to purchase is less than they would have purchased at the old price.

All that said, many people, maybe even most people, are offended by price increases in these circumstances. Aren't sellers benefiting from other people's misfortunes? Couldn't they afford to at least sell out their current inventories at their old prices? The answers to these questions are yes and yes, but the questions and their answers are largely irrelevant. The important issue is whether the price increases have a good effect overall. And the answer to that question—perhaps surprising to most readers—is yes! Price increases in these circumstances do two things, both very important. First, they allocate the available supplies to the most crucial uses. Second, they draw more supply into the affected area.

Again, hurricanes provide a useful example. In the aftermath of a hurricane, a common problem is often removing fallen and leaning trees—most immediately from the tops of houses, but also from roads, driveways, parking lots, and yards. In the immediate wake of the hurricane, people who have the skills and equipment to remove trees are able to charge prices that are considerably more than their usual rates. At these high prices, only the most urgent jobs get done. Trees on houses come off, while trees on driveways can wait a day or two, and trees in parking lots and yards a bit longer. People planning regular maintenance or landscape work want to wait until prices go back to their normal levels. Meanwhile, the high prices for these services draw tree removers from outside the area or draw people with tree-removal skills from other activities. For example, attracted by the opportunity to earn high wages, crews may travel from West Virginia into Florida, and motorcycle mechanics may help out with tree removal for a few days.

Suppose that tree cutters were prevented by law from charging prices above those in use before the storm hit? What harm would that do? For one thing, there would be no reason for suppliers to seek out the most urgent recovery work, since the rate caps would have the effect of imposing a uniform price for all kinds of work. Why seek out the most urgently needed jobs? Why do the risky and difficult work of removing a tree from the roof of a house when safer and more routine landscape work pays the same rates, the rates charged before the storm? Why not focus on putting one's own life in order rather than doing work for other people, particularly when the same wages will be available next month? Why drive a truck 600 miles to the disaster area and stay in a motel when the same rates are available back home? Why work longer days than usual when only the usual rates are offered?

Of course, these principles apply to more than tree removal. Recovery from a hurricane requires the services of carpenters, roofers, glaziers, masons, electricians, and so on. And it's not just services that are needed after a recovery. Plywood, framing lumber, plasterboard, and roofing materials are in great demand. Again, higher prices increase the amounts of these products that are available in the recovery area and allocate available supplies to the projects that are needed right away: making surviving structures weather tight to prevent further damage, making those structures habitable where possible, and eventually replacing structures that have been destroyed. New back decks and remodeled family rooms should wait, and they do, as people put off such projects until prices return to normal.

If prices of some goods are not allowed to rise in the face of dramatic decreases in supply or increases in demand, then the amounts of goods that people would like to buy exceed the available supply. The difference is a shortage, and that shortage must be managed somehow. Sometimes, particularly when the price is high, we say that price rations the available supply. When price doesn't rise, the available supply is still rationed, but by other means. Businesses of various types take care of their regular customers first. Locals may get preference over visitors or newcomers. Long waits in lines may ration short supplies. In that case, the monetary price is only a part of the cost of obtaining the rationed good. People also pay a price in time costs—the value of the time they spend waiting in line or otherwise jockeying to obtain some good. This time cost then becomes the means by which the good is rationed. Of course, a high time price for a scarce good does nothing to encourage suppliers to increase the quantities available. The time that people spend obtaining the good is just a transactions cost—it is a valuable resource that is used up by the process of transacting. Time that could be spent on putting things right is instead spent standing around or trying to get people on the phone.

In times of crisis, high prices for certain essential goods do perform a vital social function by increasing supplies and moderating demands so that available goods go to the most essential uses. In comparison to various types of (non-price) rationing, price adjustment coordinates supplies and demands without using large amounts of people's time that could otherwise be put to better uses. For these reasons, increases, even large increases, in the prevailing prices of goods sold openly in the market cannot be considered price gouging, at least by the provisional definition offered above.

What about gasoline prices of $5 or more along the evacuation routes leading out of New Orleans just before Hurricane Katrina? The prices were roughly double the prevailing prices just before the approach of the storm. Might this be an example of price gouging that meets the definition offered above—serving no useful function, but merely an example of opportunistic behavior by the owner of the gasoline station?

Although the station owner may not have had anything better in mind, even these high prices serve a valuable social function, possibly even a lifesaving one. Here again, the high price served to allocate the limited quantities available to the most important uses. At ordinary prices, even people with half a tank of gasoline or more might be inclined to fill up just to be sure that they'd have enough for the trip. People with near-empty tanks who were stopping would certainly want to fill their cars up with gasoline. Since there wasn't enough gasoline available for everyone to leave New Orleans with full tanks, the limited supply would soon be exhausted. But at $5 a gallon, people who already had a half a tank of gas or more were encouraged to drive 100 miles or so up the road, spreading the demand for gasoline over a wider area and leaving some behind for people who might otherwise run out of gas. Similarly, people pulling in to gas stations were encouraged to limit their purchases, again leaving some behind for other people who would come along later. Had they been facing only the normal prices, the same prices that they would find farther up the road, they would have had no incentive to curtail their purchases. The high price confronted people with an important reality—gasoline would be very valuable to people who came along after them—and prompted people to behave in a very cooperative way by taking what they really needed and leaving the rest for other people.

ORDINARY PRICE FLUCTUATIONS

What about price increases in less extreme circumstances? For example, what about gasoline prices, which seem to go up significantly with threats of war in the Middle East or forecasts of bad weather. Can such price increases be justified? After all, those events don't actually increase the amount of gasoline that people are consuming or disrupt deliveries of gasoline or crude oil. Isn't that price gouging?

The price increases that result from potential or actual supply disruptions reflect the anticipation that fuel supplies might be very limited at some time in the future. When such disruptions become a realistic possibility, it would be desirable for consumers to reduce consumption for awhile, so that inventories can be built up as a precaution. If price is free to adjust, that is precisely what will happen. Suppliers of gasoline and other oil products know that if supplies are disrupted, scarce supplies will become very valuable; we would face emergency circumstances like those in the previous sections. Faced with that possibility, some parties—mostly companies—would have an incentive to accumulate inventories. As they do this by reducing the amounts available to consumers, prices rise. This prompts consumers to reduce consumption, allowing buildup of precautionary inventories. Here again, we see that price adjustments serve an important purpose. In effect, such price increases shift resources from the present, where they are relatively abundant, to a future in which they might be quite scarce.

Sometimes it is suggested that intermediaries such as wholesalers or retailers should not be able to increase prices so long as they are selling products that they bought at an old (lower) price. The logic is that the owners of these inventories would enjoy a windfall gain, a profit that they did nothing to earn, if they were allowed to raise their prices. But if companies that hold inventories cannot gain from price increases yet must accept losses from price decreases, the ordinary margins that they earn would have to increase to compensate for the expected losses, so the average price to consumers would not be any lower. But worse than that, wholesalers and retailers would have every incentive to keep inventories as low as possible, which would have the undesirable effect of making us all more vulnerable to fluctuations in demand or disruptions of supply.

What about a rule that said, in effect, that you can't raise prices of old inventory when prevailing prices have gone up, but you don't have to lower prices of old inventory when prevailing prices fall? Such a rule would seem to be fair, but it would be no help to a firm holding an inventory of gasoline when prices fall. Customers could simply go elsewhere, leaving the firm with a lot of old expensive gas that they couldn't sell at the old prices. Consumers would buy from suppliers who had not been caught with big inventories and were therefore already charging lower prices. All suppliers would have to cut prices, in spite of the rule, in order to compete. The rule therefore would provide no escape from the problem and would leave wholesalers and retailers with an incentive to maintain smaller inventories than they would in the absence of these pricing rules.

Also, policies aimed at preventing people from profiting from increases in inventory values are inconsistent with the way that we treat the gains from other assets. Homeowners, for example, are not expected to sell their houses for what they paid, or for a fixed amount above what they paid. Similarly, people who own stocks are permitted to sell their stock for whatever the market price is when they are ready to sell.

A price increase is seldom welcomed by consumers, but price really is just the bearer of some bad news. The actual bad news is that there is a reduced availability of the good, relative to the amounts that people would like to consume.

FRAUD, DURESS, AND PRICE-FIXING

Does the argument above mean that there are no objectionable prices? Does it mean that all price increases contribute to the overall efficiency of the economy? Not quite. Some prices changes transfer wealth to sellers without helping to coordinate resource allocation thus meeting the provisional definition of price gouging we established for this discussion.

As noted above, most of the state statutes that specifically address price gouging are quite vague and the statutes seem to prompt little prosecution. There are, however, legal doctrines and statutes that do address specific actions or particular circumstances, including emergencies. These doctrines are concerned with fraud, duress, and price-fixing.

Fraud involves some misrepresentation by one of the parties to a contract. Usually, we think of fraud as sellers making misrepresentations, for example making false statements regarding the quality of a product, its origins, or how it was acquired. Another kind of fraud would be a misrepresentation about prevailing prices for a particular good or service. A seller who is offering to sell a common vase for $100 that commonly sells for $20 but falsely claims that "these commonly sell for more than that, one just like this sold for $150 just last month" is committing fraud.

Emergency circumstances may make people particularly vulnerable to fraud. Suppose a tree removal company charged $8,000 to remove a tree from the roof of a house when the going price for such a difficult job, even at elevated recovery prices, is $2,500. Any assurance given that such a price is the going rate or what everybody is getting would probably constitute fraud. A seller charging such a price would be unlikely to quote it openly as an offer to sell services and, on the contrary, might make efforts to conceal the details of the transaction. Such an "off-market" price is unlikely to provide useful information to market participants—encouraging suppliers to enter the market or demanders to manage their demand. Such a transaction is likely to occur only when market information is extremely poor, and particularly when buyers are in a position that makes it very costly to delay entering an agreement in order to determine actual market prices.

Antifraud statutes may be used to address certain instances of alleged price gouging. Rules against misrepresentation reduce the incentive to mislead. Generally, we expect that voluntary agreements leave both parties better off than they would be without the transaction, but when one of the parties to an agreement deliberately misleads the other, that presumption is mistaken. Thus prohibitions against fraud are unlikely to interfere with many beneficial agreements. Still, antifraud statutes apply only to limited instances of alleged price gouging. Prices that are openly posted or announced and that result in multiple voluntary transactions by informed parties are unlikely to be addressed by antifraud statutes and can generally be presumed to be beneficial to both parties.

The law of duress addresses circumstances in which people face serious personal injury or significant loss of property. In such a circumstance, the law provides some relief to people who have agreed to extremely high prices. A person who is facing possible loss of life is entitled to trespass, or to take needed goods, and pay only the damages that he imposes on another party. The courts are unlikely to enforce an agreed-upon price under circumstances in which the buyer was under duress.

One element of duress is that the endangered party faces pure monopoly (one seller with no competitors), which allows the seller-rescuer to extract almost anything from a buyer who otherwise faces loss of life, or the full value of any property that would otherwise be lost. The doctrine therefore is properly quite limited. When several competing sellers offer the required goods or services, and particularly when these are offered to multiple buyers who are similarly situated, it is unlikely that sellers could negotiate prices that are abusive or unconscionable.

Price-fixing is a conspiracy among sellers to charge a particular price, typically a price that is higher than the price that would emerge under competition. In short, it is an agreement not to compete. When a price-fixing agreement is completely successful, the conspirators charge the monopoly price. Such an agreement does interfere with the efficient allocation of resources.

Economists note that price-fixing agreements tend to break down—they contain the seeds of their own destruction. The problem for such agreements is that while all the conspirators would like the agreement to survive, each one of them individually has an incentive to cut his or her price slightly under the agreed-upon price in order to attract customers at the expense of other participants. Still, price-fixing agreements do sometimes survive, at least for a time.

Explicit price-fixing agreements are illegal under U.S. antitrust law (Section 1 of the Sherman Act). Occasionally charges of price gouging incorporate an explicit charge of price-fixing. Far more often, the price-fixing charge is implicit, as when people claim that Big Oil decided to raise prices, or that the big oil companies act uncompetitively. Where there is reason to believe that price-fixing is the source of a price elevation, there are steps that federal and state authorities can take under the law. In fact, charges of price gouging often do lead to such investigations. More often than not, when price-gouging charges do result in antitrust investigation, the price elevation is found to be the result of ordinary market forces, not an illegal conspiracy.

For example, the Federal Trade Commission conducted an investigation of gasoline prices in the aftermath of hurricanes Rita and Katrina. Their general conclusion was that there was no evidence of a price-fixing conspiracy at the refining, transportation, wholesale, or retail levels. For example, one section of their report concludes that the FTC "Staff found no evidence of anticompetitive behavior in its review of national and regional gasoline pricing after the hurricanes."

The legal rules of fraud, duress, and price-fixing are, as discussed above, quite narrowly defined doctrines. So defined, these legal principles find some economic support: fraud supports transactions that may not result in gains from trade. Further, in a legal regime in which fraud cannot be punished under law, potential traders must be wary and consequently transactions become more costly. In a legal regime in which rescuers could extract enormous prices, potential rescuers would have an incentive to withhold help until circumstances become dire. And price-fixing results in inefficient monopoly prices.

In contrast, vague laws against prices that just seem too high are troublesome from both legal and economic perspectives. From a legal perspective, without clear definitions of what is legal, it is difficult for sellers to know what prices they can charge. Further, without clear boundaries, prosecutors can use the law for political or other objectives. From an economic point of view, price-gouging statutes can interfere with price adjustments that are important for coordinating the economy. Coordination is particularly important during a crisis.

Further Reading: Federal Trade Commission. *Investigation of Gasoline Price Manipulation and Post-Katrina Gasoline Price Increases.* Washington, DC, Spring 2006.

Steve Margolis

PSYCHOLOGICAL AND HONESTY TESTING IN THE WORKPLACE

Employment tests have been around for a long time. In fact, as early as 2200 B.C., the Chinese emperor tested government officials every three years to determine their fitness for remaining in office. There is also evidence that in 1115 B.C., candidates for government posts were examined for their proficiency in several areas, including music, archery, horsemanship, writing, arithmetic, and the rites and ceremonies of public life (Bohlander and Snell 2007). Some authors claim that such testing represents the origins of the current U.S. civil service system, which uses tests for hiring because of the legal requirement to make personnel decisions based on merit.

Currently, employers use tests in lots of different ways, and there many different kinds of tests from which to choose, including ability tests, skills tests, psychological tests, honesty tests, drug tests, and even handwriting tests. These tests are typically used for preemployment screening—to determine whether an applicant will be a good employee—but some employers also use testing to assess employees' potential for promotion or advancement in the organization, or their need for additional training.

This entry will discuss personality tests, which can be divided into two groups—psychological tests (also called personality assessments, profiles, or inventories) and integrity tests (also called honesty tests). Psychological tests attempt to identify general personality characteristics. Integrity tests attempt to determine the trustworthiness of the test taker. Both forms of personality tests are currently used by employers for employment decisions. Yet this kind of employment testing is controversial for a couple of reasons. First of all, testing is an unregulated industry, meaning that anyone could create a test and offer it for use without conducting the appropriate reliability and validity studies on that test. The result could be that the test doesn't do a good job of testing what it claims to test and/or the test isn't a good predictor of actual job performance. Thus, employers who rely on the test results in hiring may be making choices based on faulty data.

Legal issues also make employment tests controversial. Even if an employment test is validated, it may adversely affect minorities or women—that is, it may screen out more minority or female applicants than white men—and be perceived as discriminatory. Thus, many companies may avoid testing because of the fear of legal problems associated with it.

So, the debate over personality testing in the workplace centers around two questions: Does personality testing help employers make better employment decisions? And is personality testing worth the potential legal problems associated with it?

HISTORY OF EMPLOYMENT LAW AND TESTING

An examination of the history of employment law in the United States will help us address the second question posed above. Title VII of the federal Civil Rights Act of 1964 banned employment decisions that unfairly discriminate against a person on the basis of race, color, religion, sex, or national origin. A federal agency, the Equal Employment Opportunity Commission, was created to enforce Title VII, and it has issued several sets of guidelines on employee selection procedures over time as definitions of discrimination and equal employment opportunity evolved through court cases.

In the 1960s, the U.S. court system tended to interpret employment laws according to a doctrine known as disparate treatment. This meant that the plaintiff—the job applicant or employee bringing the lawsuit—had to prove that an employer's hiring processes intentionally treated him or her differently because of his or her race, color, religion, sex, or national origin. But a landmark decision by the U.S. Supreme Court in 1971, Griggs v. Duke Power, changed employment law dramatically. In this case, Duke Power required job applicants to have a high school diploma, but the court found that a diploma was not required for doing the job in question. In addition, the high school diploma requirement effectively screened out a disproportionately large number of black applicants. So, even though the practice was unintentional, the court found that Duke Power had violated Title VII because of its adverse impact on minority applicants. This decision was groundbreaking because it was the first to be based on a disparate impact definition of discrimination: regardless of intent, any employment procedure (such as a test) that results in discrimination against a protected class (meaning those who are protected from discrimination under Title VII) is unlawful unless the employer can demonstrate that the practice is either job related or a "business necessity." Thus, this disparate impact approach shifted the burden of proof from the plaintiff (the applicant) to the defendant (the employer). This meant that if a company wanted to use selection tests, it would need validity data—proof that the test was related to the job—in order to prevail in court (Lee 1988).

As a result of Griggs v. Duke Power, attorneys advised employers to either conduct formal validation studies of their tests or discontinue testing in order to avoid discrimination charges. Because validity studies were complex, time consuming, and expensive, many employers eliminated their testing programs. (Psychological Services Inc., a leading test publisher at the time, reported that it lost half of its business when the Griggs decision was made; Lee 1988.) Thus, the 1970s are characterized as a rather egalitarian period during which many employers chose to avoid potential legal problems by using selection methods that didn't include testing.

The 1980s, however, showed a renewal of interest in testing by firms, in part because of methodological advancements in the field of industrial psychology that made it easier to demonstrate the validity of tests. These advances drastically reduced the cost for an assessment firm to create and validate a firm-specific or job-specific test battery—one that would stand up in court. But economic conditions also prompted firms to resume testing in the 1980s. The increased emphasis on improving productivity and competitiveness in American businesses made companies aware of the high cost of poor hiring decisions, and more willing to use testing to avoid those costs. Val Arnold, vice president of individual assessment at Personnel Decisions Inc., an assessment and consulting firm in Minneapolis in 1988, said, "Companies are more concerned with competitiveness. If you're a manufacturer and you've got a new plant with self-managed work teams, you'll want to do a real careful job of screening employees. It's tough to be competitive when workers aren't competent, aren't a good job fit, or aren't working together" (Lee 1988).

Thus, toward the end of the 1980s and into the 1990s, we saw a significant increase in the number of companies that used testing for employee selection. When Congress outlawed most polygraph tests (the so-called lie detector tests) in 1988, it spurred even more interest in honesty and personality testing. By 1994, more than 5,000 U.S. employers were estimated to be using personality testing as part of their hiring process, with more firms adopting testing each year (O'Meara 1994). According to the Association of Test Publishers, the growth rate in employment testing in the United States was 10–15 percent annually from 2002 through 2004 (Association of Test Publishers n.d.). A recent online Google search for "personality tests and employment" resulted in over 1.1 million hits, providing evidence of the prevalence of personality tests in employment today.

RESULTS OF GOOGLE SEARCHES

Search Terms	*Results—Number of Hits*
Personality tests and employment	about 1,170,000
Honesty tests and employment	about 1,030,000
Psychological tests and employment	about 1,130,000
Employment testing company	about 14,100,000

Currently, federal employment law is still based on Title VII and subsequent EEOC and other court cases throughout the years, and discrimination cases continue to be based on the principles of disparate treatment and disparate impact. In addition, many states have passed laws that affect employment practices, and several have passed laws that severely restrict or outlaw various personality tests. For example, Massachusetts has passed a law that prohibits employers from requiring an applicant to take a written examination to determine honesty.

It appears that state laws limiting personality tests have been prompted by state legislators' beliefs that such tests are ineffective and discriminatory. So, to protect employers from wasting their time and effort on tests that don't work, and from potential discrimination charges, and to protect job applicants from discrimination, legislatures have found it easier to prohibit employment testing than to try to regulate the testing industry. However, some personality tests are quite effective as selection tools.

EFFECTIVENESS OF PERSONALITY TESTS—RELIABILITY AND VALIDITY

There are two basic measures of effectiveness for a test—reliability and validity. Reliability refers to the ability of a test to provide similar results or scores over time, or on repeated testing. For example, if a test is reliable, when an individual takes that test more than once, he or she would earn similar scores each time.

While it is important for a test to provide reliable information, the test must also provide valid information regarding that person's suitability for a job. "Validity" refers to what the test is measuring and how well it is measuring it. Practically speaking, validity indicates how well the test results predict job performance. Thus, a valid test helps identify better applicants for a job and also satisfies Equal Employment Opportunity regulations.

The extent to which a psychological test or honesty test is correlated with or predictive of actual work behavior is called criterion-related validity. For each job there are certain criteria that best measure success in that job. If a personality test shows a high correlation with those success criteria, it is considered to have criterion-related validity. This type of validity also comes in two different forms—concurrent validity and predictive validity.

Concurrent validity means that criterion data from current employees are compared with scores on a test taken around the same time by the same employees. For example, a supervisor would rate his employees on their honesty or integrity and then give the same employees an integrity test. Then, the supervisor's ratings and the test scores would be compared for each employee. High concurrent validity would mean that there was a high correlation between the two scores. In other words, employees with high supervisor ratings on integrity also received high test scores, and low-rated employees got low test scores.

Predictive validity, however, is determined by testing job applicants and collecting job performance data (criterion data) after the applicants have been hired and working for a period of time. For example, job applicants for a sales position would take a personality assessment. After these people have been hired and have worked for six months, their job performance would be rated by their supervisor. Then, the supervisor's ratings and the personality test scores would be compared for each employee. High predictive validity would mean that there was a high correlation between the two scores. For example, if applicants who received high scores in extroversion on the personality assessment subsequently turned out to be those employees who performed best on the job and therefore received the highest supervisor's ratings, then the test would be considered to have predictive validity. From an employer's perspective, predictive validity is the most important type of validity because it means that the preemployment test (the personality assessment, in this case) actually helps predict future performance of job applicants.

To be complete and accurate, both concurrent validity and predictive validity studies should be verified through cross-validation. This entails giving the test to a different sample of individuals, but drawn from the same population, in order to verify the results from the original validation study. For example, to cross-validate the predictive validity of the preemployment personality assessment mentioned above, the test would be given to another set of applicants for the same job. Then, after the applicants had been hired and had worked for six months, their supervisor would rate their performance, and their test scores would be compared with the supervisor's ratings, just as was done in the first study. If the results of this second study are consistent with the results of the first study, then this cross-validation confirms or verifies the predictive validity of the personality assessment.

Test validity is typically assessed using the statistical method known as correlation analysis, which measures the relationship between test scores and performance criterion data. A statistical formula is used to calculate a coefficient of correlation, which in validity studies is referred to as a validity coefficient. The full range of correlation coefficients is from −1.00 to +1.00. A validity coefficient of zero indicates that there is no direct (linear) relationship between the test score and the performance criterion measure. This would mean that the test is not related to the job performance measured. A negative validity coefficient means that there is an inverse relationship between the test score and the criterion. This means that a high test score would be related to a low criterion score (supervisor's rating of job performance) and vice versa. Likewise, a positive validity coefficient means that there is a direct relationship between the test score and the criterion score. Obviously, this means that higher positive validity coefficients indicate greater test validity.

Considerable research has been conducted on the validity of employment tests in general, and personality tests in particular. When employment tests of all kinds are validated against a single job performance criterion, such as supervisor's rating, the maximum validity coefficients typically average around +0.35 (Landy 1992). However, when used alone, personality assessments have very low predictive ability. Additional research has shown that higher validities can be obtained by combining a personality assessment with other predictors (Boudreau, Sturman, and Judge 1994).

On the other hand, honesty tests have been shown to be valid predictors of job performance, as well as other disruptive behaviors such as disciplinary problems, absenteeism, and theft. A major study that examined 25 leading integrity tests, and over 180 research studies, found the estimated average predictive validity coefficient of integrity tests for predicting supervisory ratings of job performance to be 0.41. The study also showed that integrity tests predict the general category of disruptive behaviors better than they predict theft alone (Ones, Viswesvaran, and Schmidt 1993).

CREATING VALID TESTS FOR EMPLOYMENT PURPOSES

Practically speaking, if an employment test has a high validity coefficient, it should mean that the test does a better job of predicting future job performance, and that use of the test increases the probability of selecting a good employee. Unfortunately, this isn't necessarily true. First of all, the job performance criterion used for the validity study must be representative of the actual job for which the test is being used. So one of the first steps in good test construction is to carefully analyze the job in question and identify the major duties and responsibilities of the job. Then, the employer must identify the essential knowledge, skills, abilities, or characteristics that are necessary to perform the job. This process is called job analysis and is often done by human resource department specialists within the organization or external experts who are hired for this purpose. Next, an appropriate way to measure those necessary abilities or characteristics must be identified. These measurements, such as a supervisor's rating, can then be used as the performance criterion for the validity study.

From a technical perspective, the best tests are those that have been specifically created to test those characteristics or abilities that have been identified (through job analysis) as critical for a specific job within a specific organization. (Again, there are many professional assessment/consulting firms that offer this kind of service for a fee.) Once the test has been created for a specific job, a criterion-validation study should be conducted to confirm the validity of the test.

This all sounds pretty straightforward—do a good job analysis, then hire a consulting firm to create a test, and you can be sure that your test will help weed out the undesirables and identify the winners from your applicant pool. But Robert Hogan, an organizational psychologist and president of Hogan Assessments Inc., says that's not necessarily the case. "Of the 2,500 test publishers out there, only three or four are legitimate," says Hogan. "Most of these people are selling snake oil" (Emmett 2004). Hogan and other experts cite a host of problems with personality tests, including poor test construction, bad validation techniques, and misapplication of tests.

Another problem is that the human resources personnel in many organizations don't have the necessary skills to discern a good test from a bad one. "Lots of people are selling tests and lots of people in human resources don't know what they're looking at," says Glenn DeBasi, an industrial psychologist and corporate vice president of human resources at Alex Lee Inc., a $2.4 billion food company in North Carolina. Regarding personality tests, he says, "While many human resources folks lack the background in statistics or research methodology to evaluate the tests, if you look behind the scenes, most test publishers themselves haven't done a good job of demonstrating that the tests predict anything of value" (Emmett 2004).

GUIDELINES FOR EMPLOYERS

So, what's an employer to do? Well, there are some guidelines for employers to follow that can help ensure that their personality testing program will help choose good employees. First of all, employers should recognize that testing alone is not enough. Personality tests should always be used in conjunction with other selection procedures, such as thorough background checks and structured behavioral interviews. If other tests are being used, employers should make sure that the tests are appropriately validated for the particular job in question. Work-sample tests or performance tests, where an applicant is asked to demonstrate or perform one or more job tasks that would be required in the job, are also good predictors. Test takers generally view these tests as fairer than other tests (Steiner and Gilliland 1996), and these tests are less likely to have an adverse impact on employee relationships with employers than general ability tests.

With respect to personality assessments, a host of research studies have shown that there are five identifiable dimensions of personality, typically referred to as the "Big Five" by psychologists. These five personality dimensions are neuroticism, extroversion, openness to new experience, agreeableness, and conscientiousness. Conscientiousness is the degree to which a person is organized, responsible, careful, hard working, achievement oriented, and thorough. Not surprisingly, research has confirmed that individual differences in conscientiousness appear to be consistently related to job performance, almost regardless of the job (Tett, Jackson, and Rothstein 1991). Some studies have also shown that extroversion is related to performance in specific jobs, such as sales. However, as mentioned earlier, personality tests have very low predictive ability when used alone. Only when used in combination with other tests or selection procedures have they been shown to predict job performance. Furthermore, using a personality assessment alone may subject the employer to potential legal liability if it has an adverse impact on minorities or women and/or has not been validated for the specific job.

Although honesty tests have been shown to predict disruptive behaviors such as disciplinary problems, absenteeism, and theft when appropriately designed, there is still potential legal liability in using them. To minimize this liability, if an employer chooses to use an honesty test to select people for a particular job, he or she should document the business necessity of such a test, including an assessment of the consequences of hiring a dishonest individual. Additionally, it is recommended that an honesty test be used in combination with other selection tools in order to make informed, legally defensible hiring decisions. It is also generally recommended that honesty tests only be used for pre-selection screening, since administering them to current employees could create serious morale problems.

In order to make better employment decisions, employers should implement a system that starts with a thorough job analysis that identifies the critical duties and responsibilities of the job and the corresponding knowledge, skills, abilities, and characteristics desired in individuals applying for that job. Then, they should use a combination of techniques to assess the applicants' fit for that job. These should include a background check, a structured interview that uses behavioral questions, and tests that are predictive of performance in the job.

When choosing a test or a testing firm, employers should choose carefully. For tests, they should review the available literature to make sure that the test has been validated and is appropriate for predicting performance in that job. If the employer's human resource personnel don't have the appropriate background to choose and administer tests, it probably makes more sense to hire a professional testing company to do testing. Again, choosing the testing firm should be done carefully. The employer should get a list of the testing firm's previous clients and contact those clients regarding their satisfaction with and results obtained from the testing firm's service. The employer should also be wary of testing firms that simply use an existing test and claim that it will be predictive for the employer's situation. The employer should insist on seeing the results of previous validation studies for any existing test that the testing company intends to use and insist that the testing company do validation studies for any new tests created for the employer.

Once all these procedures have been carried out, the employer should use all the results to do an overall assessment of the applicant's suitability for the job in question. By using a combination of assessment techniques, including personality testing, employers can do a good job of selecting the best potential employees from the applicant pool.

So what are the answers to our original questions? To the first question—Does personality testing help employers make better employment decisions?—we can say, with some certainty, "It can help." Whether it actually does help depends on what tests are used, and how they are used.

To the second question—Is personality testing worth the potential legal problems associated with it?—we can respond with a guarded yes. If personality testing is conducted appropriately, with validated tests, it can actually minimize the legal liability of the organization.

See also: Drug Testing in the Workplace

References

Association of Test Publishers. n.d. Available at www.testpublishers.org. Accessed February 2, 2007.

Bohlander, George, and Scott Snell. 2007. *Managing Human Resources.* 14th ed. Mason, OH: Thompson South-Western.

Boudreau, J. W., M. C. Sturman, and M. A. Judge. 1994. "Utility Analysis: What Are the Black Boxes, and Do They Effect Decisions?" In *Assessment and Selection in Organizations: Methods and Practice for Recruitment and Appraisal,* edited by N. Anderson and P. Harriot, 77–96. New York: Wiley; Murphy, Kevin R., and Ann Harris Shiarella. 1997. "Implications of the Multidimensional Nature of Job Performance for the Validity of Selection Tests: Multivariate Frameworks for Studying Test Validity." *Personnel Psychology* 50:823–54.

Emmett, Arielle. 2004. "Snake Oil or Science? That's the Raging Debate on Personality Testing." *Workforce Management* 83 (10): 90–92.

Landy, Frank J. 1992. "Test Validity Yearbook." *Journal of Business Psychology* 7 (2): 111–257; Hunter, J. E., and R. H. Hunter. 1984. "Validity and Utility of Alternative Predictors of Job Performance." *Psychological Bulletin* 96: 72–98; Robertson, Ivan, and Mike Smith. 2001. "Personnel Selection." *Journal of Occupational and Organizational Psychology* 74 (4): 441–72.

Lee, Chris. 1988. "Training Makes a Comeback." *Training* 25 (12): 49–59.

O'Meara, Daniel P. 1994. "Personality Tests Raise Questions of Legality and Effectiveness." *HR Magazine* 39 (1): 97–100.

Ones, D. S., C. Viswesvaran, and F. L. Schmidt. 1993. "Comprehensive Meta-Analysis of Integrity Test Validities: Findings and Implications for Personnel Selection and Theories of Job Performance." *Journal of Applied Psychology* 78:679–703.

Steiner, Dirk D., and Stephen W. Gilliland. 1996. "Fairness Reactions to Personnel Selection Techniques in France and the United States." *Journal of Applied Psychology* 81 (2): 134–41.

Tett, R. P., D. N. Jackson, and M. Rothstein. 1991. "Personality Measures as Predictors of Job Performance: A Meta-Analytic Review." *Personnel Psychology* 44: 703–45.

Further Reading: Barrick, M. R., and M. K. Mount. 1991. "The Big Five Personality Dimensions and Job Performance: A Meta-Analysis." *Personnel Psychology* 44:1–26; Mount, M. K., and M. R. Barrick. 1995. "The Big Five Personality Dimensions: Implications for Research and Practice in Human Resource Management." In *Research in Personnel and Human Resource Management,* edited by G. Ferris, 13:153–200. Greenwich, CT: JAI; Schmidt, F. L., D. O. Ones, and J. E. Hunter. 1992. "Personnel Selection." *Annual Review of Psychology* 43:627–70.

Randy C. Brown

PUBLIC RELATIONS AND REPUTATION MANAGEMENT

HOW DO PR PROFESSIONALS SPEAK OF REPUTATION MANAGEMENT?

The Public Relations Society of America has developed a short definition of PR:

> Public relations helps an organization and its publics mutually adapt to each other.

A common textbook definition is:

> Public relations is a management function that seeks to identify, build, and maintain mutually beneficial relationships between an organization and all of the publics on whom its success or failure depends (Cottip, Center, and Broom 2001).

The expression "mutually adapt" in the Public Relations Society of America's definition suggests that a PR professional seeks to adapt, influence, and change not only the perception of many "publics" but also the behavior of the organization and its management. This is notable because it suggests that perception is not quite everything.

Good PR does help to shape the perception of the buying public. The PRSA further explains that PR provides a "conning tower" for identifying new markets and products and paves the way for the sale of products and services. It can help to integrate and enhance efforts in related functions like sales, advertising, promotion, and marketing.

Good PR can help manage the "employee public" by building morale and enhancing productivity and team spirit. It also helps to create an organizational self-image that improves recruitment and retention of good employees.

Good PR can provide an early warning system for social and political change and help protect the present position of the organization from surprise attack. It can manage the perception of the general public, the media, and legislators by communicating the organization's position and lobbying for its success.

Good PR can also help to manage organizational change by guiding smooth transitions. It can reduce executive isolation by being the eyes and ears of management. And it can sponsor organizational efforts in social responsibility, creating social value that is genuine, not merely a managed perception (Public Relations Society of America n.d.).

TRUST

Arguing that companies that can develop strategies to convince stakeholders to trust them will have a major competitive advantage over those that cannot, W. Michael Hoffman of the Center for Business Ethics at Bentley College in Waltham, Massachusetts, says, "We are in an economic environment in which trust is at a premium. It's like air: When it's present, you don't think about it. When it's not present, you think about it all the time" (Gilbert 2003).

BEST FOOT FORWARD VERSUS HONESTY?

Is there a conflict here? The phrase "reputation management" implies that one manages the reputation instead of simply letting the reputation happen. It suggests the positive communication of a position, something well beyond letting actions speak for themselves. It suggests the deliberate building of an image, an image probably more attractive than simple accuracy and truthfulness would present. It may involve, as a component of good PR, internal efforts to live up to that attractive image and thus make the image true. But if the image is significantly more attractive than the truth, is it dishonest in some sense? Is it unfair? How far should the best-foot-forward approach be pushed?

The Interview

Everyone advises that a job interview is a time for to put one's best foot forward—on the resume, in dress, and in speech and manner. Don't lie on the resume, but don't include an explanation of why you were fired. Dress formally in your best outfit even if the employer's environment is casual. Don't slouch or yawn even if it's boring. Be sure to mention all your good points, and learn to turn each questionable aspect into a plus. Everyone gives this advice, and it seems fair. The interviewer expects your best-foot-forward approach, expects to have to probe for flaws, expects to get less than the full story, and would probably be stunned and dismayed by brutal honesty. Under these circumstances would anyone suppose that best foot forward is in any sense dishonest? Should reputation management be handled like an interview?

The Party

Let's say you've been invited to a party where you'll meet many new people. You've been given no dress code, but you're sure it's informal. You've heard that first impressions count and that you should make a good impression. You hope people will like you, and you've been told to be yourself. Is being oneself honest?

- What to wear. Are a blazer and tie too much? Does being yourself mean blue jeans? If you want to make a good impression, you probably should shower and perhaps use cologne. Heavy cologne?
- The entrance. Do you rent a limo or drive the pickup? Either one will make an impression. What kind of impression does a three-year-old Camry make?
- The style. Do you strut and let them know how classy you are? Or do you find a comfortable quiet corner and interact only as necessary?

Most of us seek a moderate approach. In fact, common behavior usually defines moderate. We'll wear neat, casual clothing, drive the Camry, and mix into the crowd. It's not quite best foot forward, and it doesn't make a big impression, but it's the moderate way of making personal choices to manage a personal image. Should reputation management by an organization be handled in a similarly moderate way?

The Lawsuit

Suppose you are an attorney presenting a defendant's case, and in response to the plaintiff attorney's attack on the defendant, you say, "Well, that's a good point! I guess you're right about that," and you offer no rejoinder. The jury would probably be surprised, even confused, and the judge would wake up. You were expected to deny, object, distract attention to something else, and resume attacking the weaknesses in the case. In fact, you are being paid to do that. It is a fully accepted principle that legal cases have partisan, one-sided arguments on each side, that each side will do its best-foot-forward presentation of the case, and that the judge and jury will somehow discern the truth as it squeezes out from between two clashing positions.

The PR Campaign

Let's say a company is preparing for the release of a new product. The competition is also planning to release a similar product, better in some ways, worse in others. In affirming the positive aspects of your company's reputation, would you overstate the positives? Would you, directly or by implication, refer to any weaknesses in your competitor's reputation? In positioning the product, would you overstate its advantages over the competitor's? Would you try to manipulate the consuming public to keep any comparison discussion focused on those features where your product is better and avoid comparison in areas where the competitor's product is better? Would you ever bring up those features where the competitor's has an advantage? How much should the best-foot-forward approach be pushed and the lame foot hidden?

Most of us have come to expect a PR and advertising campaign to be entirely best foot forward and possibly to overstate. As much as we might manage our personal reputations (e.g., at an informal party) in a moderate way, we assume that people in competitive situations push the pluses. As interviewers, we may expect the interviewee to perform, to dance, and to present a partisan, one-side-only view. As consumers, we may expect advertisers and sellers to perform similarly. As jurors, we fully expect a forcefully presented one-sided position. As voters, we may want the plain truth from a political campaign, but we settle for a carefully spun message from the candidate.

The PR Recovery Effort

Suppose that you are trying to manage the reputation of a company that has been selling a less-than-optimal product. The product has some problems that tend to emerge after initial purchase and use, sometimes causing inconvenience, additional expense, or even danger. Since in most cases the product works as intended, would you emphasize its positive aspects? Would you acknowledge the difficulty? Would you openly, freely, and proactively alert all users of potential problems, even if no regulatory agency were requiring a recall? What do customers expect?

Any acknowledgement is potentially damaging to the company's reputation, especially an acknowledgement proactively communicated to all users. The reputation is already suffering, and the choice is whether to quietly stop the bleeding with a Band-Aid or to publicly clean the wound. A best-foot-forward instinct may lean toward offering denial and a Band-Aid. It is probably a common instinct in such circumstances, and the decision is one that must be faced frequently.

Business history is littered with stories of decisions on both sides of the choice. There is the classic story of Johnson and Johnson's immediate removal of Tylenol, its leading moneymaker, from all shelves because someone poisoned several bottles. It cost the company untold millions but preserved its long-developed reputation of putting customers' interests above all other interests, including those of investors, and ultimately enabled the return of Tylenol in new bottles and the enhancement of the Johnson and Johnson reputation. A classic story at the other end of the spectrum is Ford's resistance to fixing the Pinto, deciding instead, after cost-benefit analyses determined that the average settlement for wrongful death would be one million dollars per human life, that it was cheaper to pay for the deaths than to recall and fix the Pintos. Years later, Ford made similar choices in reputation management when faced with the Ford Explorer/Firestone tire spat. Reputation management is often a short-term decision with a long-term effect.

WHAT ABOUT TRUTH, HONESTY, AND TRUST?

Reputation management is mostly about trust. It would seem that honesty and truth telling lead to trust. Honesty and truth telling are essential in ethical behavior. But even if a PR professional is not driven primarily by a desire to behave ethically but by a need to enhance an organization's reputation in any way possible, it would seem that honesty and truth telling would be effective techniques. So, whether the primary driver is ethics or effectiveness, practicing honesty and truth telling is the right thing to do. They lead to trust, which is at the heart of reputation management.

SELLING TRUST

The multibillion-dollar accounting frauds of WorldCom, a telecommunications giant, were among the corporate scandals of 2002. Chris Atkins of Ketchum, a public relations firm, says, "It's going to take years before people stop thinking of WorldCom as an unethical institution. On the other hand, I'm often surprised by how short America's memory really is." Jonathan Crane, a WorldCom executive, notes the changes the company has made and the company's new commitment to integrity and says, "It is something salespeople want to make sure they get on the table" (Gilbert 2003).

Trust is fundamental to business effectiveness. Business ethicists, PR professionals, and marketers alike know that trust is essential, because the lack of it usually disables business sales or transactions. It's so much riskier to do business with someone we don't trust that if there's an alternative, we'll do business with someone else instead. In general, the business community cannot function smoothly without trust. And most transactions involve trust, even if legal contracts accompany the transactions. Trust is the air in the business climate.

Honesty is something that characterizes the sender of a message, while trust is something the receiver of a message has. So these are different things, usually connected, but potentially separate. Can trust happen without truth or honesty? Can truth and honesty happen without producing trust? In both cases, it seems the answer is yes. Trust is in the receiver. Trust is, in this sense, a perception. Reputation, like trust, might seem to be attached to the sender, to the organization, but it is mostly in the receiver or one of the publics toward which PR is addressed. Is reputation management then about managing the trust and the perception of the publics?

THE PUBLIC—DO THEY EXPECT SPIN?

We the public might like to think that we want truth in all things. We may think that as consumers, employees, voters, and investors, we should all have a commitment to the truth and should be offended by every lapse in preventing it. We should find it unethical to overstate the quality of products and services, the solvency of a company, or the attractiveness of a political candidate. We may imagine that, in the face of increasingly sophisticated PR and advertising, we are responding with a growing hunger for the truth. Maybe so. Maybe not.

Contemporary U.S. culture is at the vanguard of social experimentation in playing with the truth and in consuming messages. Through more media than ever before, we are constantly bombarded with ever-more sophisticated and subtly manipulative messages. And as a public, we may have come to expect it, to demand it, to "pull" it from those whose job it is to "push" products, services, and points of view. We rank as the foremost consumer society in human history, raising consumerism to the ideological level of, some say, religion. According to this view, we define ourselves through the products and services we buy. As aggressive consumers, we may be "pulling" not just products but also the PR and marketing messages. We may be watching and listening from this stance: Sweet talk me into your product/service/candidate, please. Give it your best shot!

STRAIGHTFORWARD REPUTATION MANAGEMENT

How feasible is it to commit to a long-term straightforward approach to reputation management? Some have succeeded. Johnson and Johnson is an example. Merck has been an example—but will it weather the Vioxx problem? Volvo was an example—but can it weather the purchase by Ford? Jim Collins's bestseller Good to Great studies how some companies have managed transformations from good companies to great companies through long-term disciplined commitment. While he does not directly address PR approaches, he finds in these great companies cultures that would be compatible with a straightforward PR approach. These cultures confront brutal facts and make long-term commitments to quiet, disciplined, gradual, and steady change. Their transformations have no tag lines or spectacular launch events. Their leaders are not high-profile celebrities with big personalities, but self-effacing, quiet, reserved, humble, and committed to the organization's long-term success (Collins 2001). A PR professional who believes in a straightforward approach would probably find these companies and others like them very hospitable environments.

What if the various publics with whom an organization is trying to do reputation management—the consumers, employees, legislators, and voters—are not ready for honesty in communications? What if we have become so jaded and cynical about advertising, PR, and campaign messages that we can't handle the truth? What if the contemporary culture that surrounds us is so packed with overstatement and spin that we consistently expect it? What if we have come to assume that no PR-related message is honest, even when it is actually honest? Then how would someone with an honest message get through and convince us of its truthfulness?

It's not hard to imagine that, as publics in contemporary society, this is where we are. Part of growing up and becoming a functioning member of society is developing a defensive cynicism. Children's TV programming is more heavily regulated against false and misleading advertising, because children are just developing that defensive cynicism and are still vulnerable. Adults are somewhat protected by regulations, but because any regulations impinge further on commercial free speech, we are reluctant to fully protect consumers. We take social Darwinism to a more subtle level and say, "If you're gullible enough to believe that stuff, you deserve to lose your money!" The rest of us protect ourselves. We resist trusting.

Consider again the expectations we have of interviewees, of political candidates, of attorneys, of CEOs, of salespeople, and of spinners. We expect them to put their best foot forward and to hide the problem. We expect partisanship, hype, and spin, but not too much. We may even admire their style when it seems confident, focused, and smooth but not oily. They may gain our trust more easily than someone whose honesty and forthrightness make them occasionally hesitant, faltering in certainty, non-spinning, and humble. So, if this is true, do we, the public, expect spin?

If we expect spin, then the approach for PR professionals and others involved in reputation management begins to crystallize. If our defensive cynicism is best penetrated by just the right style, just the right kind and amount of spin, then PR people might think they must step up to the challenge. If honesty doesn't cut it, then it seems they must push it to the next levels. But is this as honest as we might like it to be? Is it ethical?

ETHICAL REPUTATION MANAGEMENT—HONESTY OR SPIN?

Given that PR seeks to build trust while many of its publics expect best foot forward and maybe some spin, there are choices to be made about what approaches to take. It may be helpful to array these choices in approaches on a continuum from brutal honesty to snake oil (Figure P.6). We can divide that continuum into five levels and discuss those levels in terms of ethics, public relations, and public expectations

- The extremes. Levels I and V rarely work. Only small portions of any public respond favorably in any circumstances to either a voluntary brutal honesty approach or an unabashed snake oil approach. It is conceivable that either approach might sometimes work, but a PR professional would be well advised to avoid them.

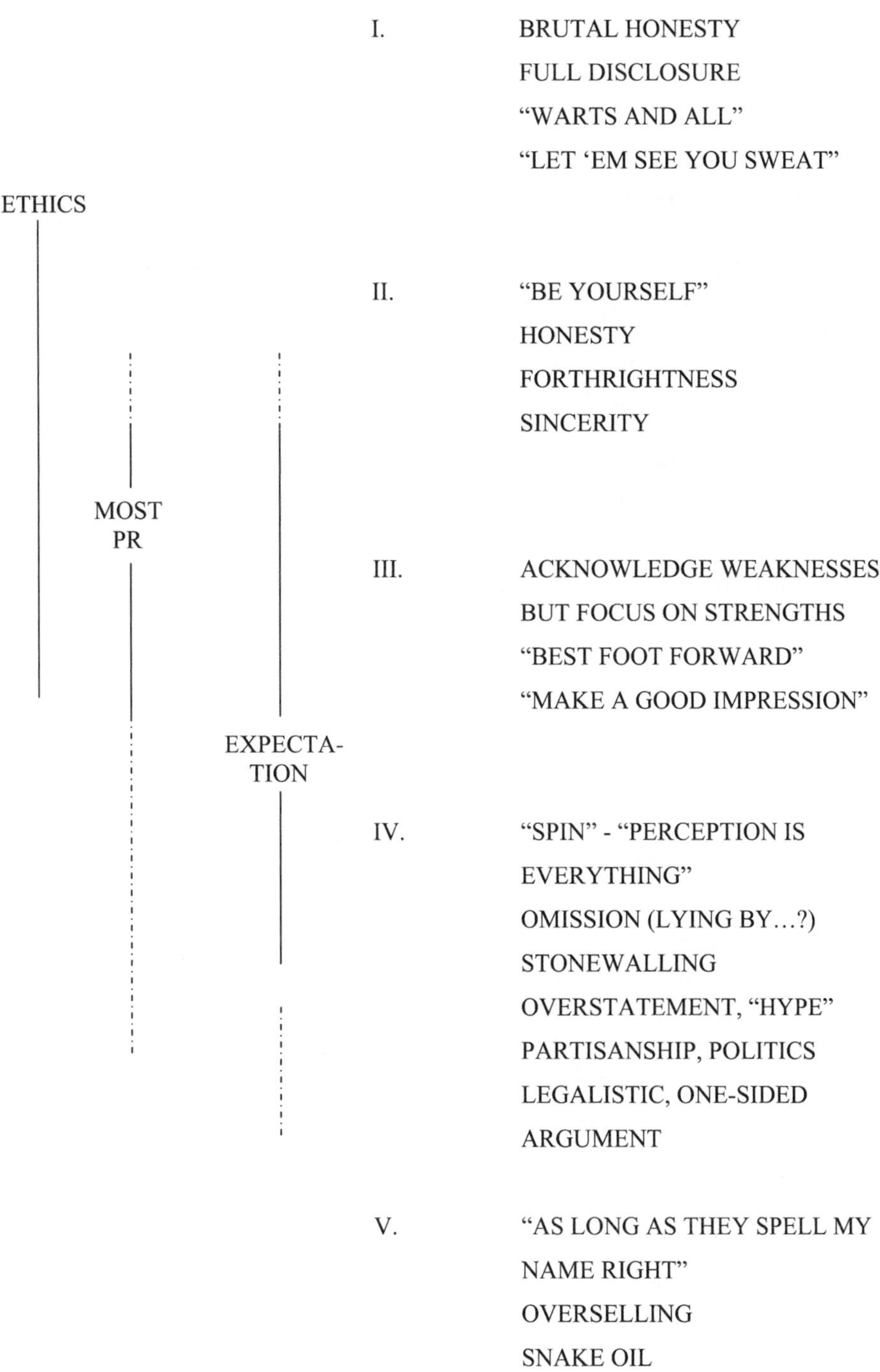

Figure P.6 Approaches in reputation management.

- Ethics. Levels I, II, and III are clearly ethical. Level I is ethical but ineffective. Level II is clearly ethical, but in many circumstances people don't expect it and might not respect it. Level III, given the challenges of PR, seems ethically respectable. Why not put one's best foot forward when it is expected? Level IV, however, goes too far and presents challenges to ethical justification.

- Public relations. Levels II, III, and IV all include postures common to PR. Responsible PR professionals want to think they are working in levels II and III, venturing into level IV only when they feel they must—for example, stonewalling when there is an open legal case or spinning when unfairly attacked by the media. In fact, level II is such a PR challenge that it is difficult to maintain, and level IV is so tempting in challenging circumstances that PR activity often slides into it.
- Expectation. We the public might like to think that we respect level II and would prefer it. But our schooled cynicism hinders our respect for level II, and our appreciation of the best-foot-forward dance makes us respect level III. Our schooled cynicism should give us defenses against level IV, but, ironically, we may be so battered with level-IV approaches that only more of the same approaches have a chance of getting through to us.

WHAT SHOULD A GOOD PUBLIC RELATIONS PERSON DO? IT DEPENDS

If Figure P.6 is accurate, it appears that the PR professional should try to work at level III. It works on all counts. It's ethically respectable and respected by the public as a best-foot-forward approach.

Level II—honesty and forthrightness—would be ideal from an ethical perspective and possibly a pleasure to do PR business in if the organization has the strength, will, and discipline to maintain it. Some PR professionals feel it is the optimal approach, because they have confidence that the public will eventually come to see that the honest messages are, in fact, true. The publics' defensive cynicism will ultimately yield to a consistent and patient long-term approach. These PR professionals feel that even putting one's best foot a little too far forward risks invoking that cynicism. The approach requires great discipline in PR and, of course, in the organization's culture and leadership. This approach sounds like this: businesses should focus on doing their business as well as possible with the confidence that their customers and the public will ultimately respect them for their straightforward efforts.

While some business leaders and some PR professionals believe in this approach and are willing to commit themselves to it, many leaders and PR professionals are more cynical and believe that even if they commit themselves to it, the public won't believe them. So, from this point of view, the decision on approach depends on one's public.

Level IV—spin and hype—falls in the realm the public has come to expect, and it showcases some of the skills often associated with PR, promotion, and advertising. It stretches the ethical dimension. Some of the behavior is not clearly ethical, and some is clearly not ethical. These approaches are full of risk, not just to the PR professional and the company reputation, but to the public as well. So, should the good PR professional use these approaches? It depends on the circumstances:

- The risk to health and safety. The worst reputation-destroying events are those that occur when a company has knowingly overstated the safety of a product, has been discovered, and continues an overstated PR recovery effort. Consumers and workers in a complex society need protection because they cannot know enough to avoid all dangers. They ultimately get that protection through governmental agencies, a judicial system, and media scrutiny. The system is not perfect, and it leaves tempting loopholes, especially with new products and services. Playing fast and loose with health and safety issues can cause disastrous reputation damage. On the other hand, if the product or service does not specifically affect health and safety, there is less scrutiny, less public disgust, and probably less reputation damage.
- The risk of major financial loss. Recent corporate scandals have highlighted the growing temptations to overstate financial conditions to the point of committing accounting and auditing fraud. Investors expect some general hype about a company's condition and its prospects, but they expect and deserve clarity and accuracy in accounting. The temptation to carry hype into the books and to do what Enron did must be compelling. But the consequences are a disaster to the company, not just its reputation. On the other hand, if there are no significant financial consequences, the public, including the investment public, may be more forgiving of hype gone bad.
- The aggressiveness of competitors. If the industry in which a company operates is generally civil and competitors are fairly straightforward, then a PR decision to push the approach up a notch (level IV) constitutes a form of attack. When a competitor attacks, or when an entire industry is PR-aggressive, it seems only sensible to counter with more aggressive PR. It may be a competitive necessity.
- The legal situation. If there is pending legal action involving a company, there may be no realistic PR choice other than stonewalling and simply reiterating the company's legal (possibly one-sided) position.
- The aggressiveness of activist or media attacks. It's difficult to maintain a moderate approach if an attack is loud and extreme. But a moderate approach may work well in winning the public's trust if the opposition is so offensively loud and extreme that people don't like them. On the other hand, if the attack is cleverly aggressive and controlled, a more aggressive PR response might be necessary.

In summary, then, the short answer to our primary question is that the straightforward approach is ideal if you can do it. A qualified best-foot-forward approach is respectable and is in the mainstream of responsible reputation management. And the perception-is-everything approach is common and sometimes justifiable depending on the circumstances, but dangerous.

References

Collins, Jim. 2001. *Good to Great.* New York: Harper Business.

Cutlip, Scott, Allen Center, and Glen Broom. 2001. *Effective Public Relations.* Upper Saddle River, NJ: Prentice Hall.

Gilbert, Jennifer. 2003. "A Matter of Trust." *Sales and Marketing Management,* March, pp. 30–35.

Public Relations Society of America. n.d. *The Public Relations Profession*. Available at www.prsa.org/Resources/profession/index. Accessed May 9, 2006.

Further Reading: Cross, Gary. 2000. *All-Consuming Century: Why Commercialism Won in Modern America.* New York: Columbia University Press; Seitel, Fraser. *The Practice of Public Relations.* Upper Saddle River, NJ: Prentice Hall; Van Hook, Steven R. *All About Public Relations*. Available at http://aboutpublicrelations.net/toolkit.htm.

Philip K. Iobst

R

RICH COUNTRY/POOR COUNTRY

Anyone who has traveled outside the United States knows firsthand that people in other countries live their lives quite differently from Americans. From country to country, huge differences exist in the kinds of foods people eat, the kinds of homes in which they live, the leisure activities in which they engage, and what they do for a living. One very fundamental reason for these differences—the one that is most amenable to examination by economists—is cross-country differences in economic well-being.

Why some countries are wealthy while others are poor is an issue that has occupied the attention of economists for hundreds of years. In this article we will explore some of the reasons why incomes per person vary from country to country. While there are obviously other important elements to how well off we might judge individuals to be in a particular society, income is clearly a very critical indicator of social welfare.

IS INCOME THE BEST MEASURE OF HOW WELL OFF PEOPLE ARE?

"I've been rich and I've been poor. Believe me, rich is better."

—Mae West

When it comes to measuring how well off people are, economists tend to use income as their indicator of choice. But is this the best measure? We know, after all, that there are many things that contribute to an individual's sense of well-being that are not directly purchased with the income that that individual earns. Some of these are public goods that are not traded in markets and as such cannot be directly purchased—for example, an unpolluted environment. Others things, like good schools and roads, are provided by governments. While people pay for these things through taxes on income and property, they generally are provided to all residents regardless of how much they earn (and how much they pay in taxes).

Social scientists—especially researchers from disciplines other than economics—have devoted considerable energy to exploring alternatives to income per capita as indicators of well-being. Typically, these efforts involve a variety of social development indicators related to individuals' access to basic human needs. Not surprisingly, different researchers have different ideas of what constitutes a basic human need. But most include access to minimal levels of nutrition, health, clothing, shelter, and opportunities for individual freedom and self-improvement.

Table R.1 presents data reported by the World Bank on different social development indicators for different countries, ranging from poorest to richest. A striking feature of these data is that they indicate that, on average, good things like life expectancy and access to safe water improve as per capita incomes increase, while bad things like infant mortality and child malnutrition decrease. So there appears to be a rough correspondence between income per capita and other measures of human well-being.

Table R.1 Social Indicators for Various Levels of Income per Capita in the 1990s.

Indicator	**Less than**			**More than**	
	$1,000	**$1,000–2,000**	**$1,000–2,000**	**$1,000–2,000**	**$10,000**
Infant deaths per 1,000 live births	107	73	33	30	6
Life Expectancy at birth (years)	49	57	68	69	76
Number of physicians per 1,000 inhabitants	33	88	161	181	231
Access to safe drinking water (percent of population)	35	54	72	81	95
Energy Consumption per Capita (kg of Oil Equivalents)	46	189	977	2029	4857
Malnourished children under five years old (percent of total)	35	30	16	12	2
Adult literacy (percent of total)	52	60	85	83	96

Source: World Bank. World Development Indicators. CD-ROM

But there is substantial variation in various social indicators within income classes as well. For example, a country may score well on adult literacy but poorly on child mortality. In order to facilitate comparisons, a number of indices that seek to combine various individual measures of a country's social development indicators exist. All such indices are somewhat arbitrary, since they depend on which particular indicators are chosen as components. The best known of these is the United Nations Development Program's Human Development Index (HDI). Reported annually, the HDI combines measures of life expectancy, educational attainment, and income per capita into an index ranging from 0 to 1, with higher numbers indicating better performance.

Figure R.1 presents the HDI values from 1998 for 37 countries, along with the per capita income figures for those same countries. Again, a strong correlation between income per capita—the economists' indicator of choice—and the broader HDI is evident. Also observable, however, is the fact the correlation is by no means perfect. For example, the HDI values suggest that Sri Lanka has roughly the same level of social development as Brazil, despite the fact that the average Sri Lankan earns only about one-third the amount of the average Brazilian.

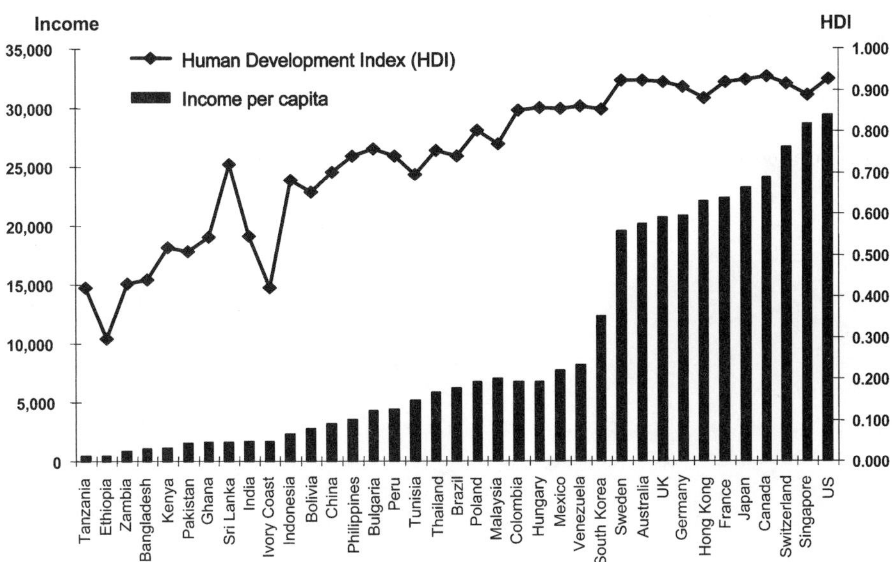

Figure R.1 Comparing different measures of well-being.

HOW BIG ARE THE DIFFERENCES ACROSS COUNTRIES?

Table R.2, which lists the average annual income per person for 37 nations in 1998, provides a glimpse of just how varied the economic performance of different countries around the world is. To facilitate comparison, all figures are reported in U.S. dollars and have been adjusted to account for differences in the cost of living among the different countries.

Several things are striking about this list. First and foremost is just how big the gap between the poorest and richest countries is. The income of the average

Table R.2 Income per Capita for Selected Countries (1998).

	Income per capita (in U.S. dollars)	Location
Low-income countries		
Tanzania	$490	Sub-Saharan Africa
Ethiopia	$500	Sub-Saharan Africa
Zambia	$860	Sub-Saharan Africa
Bangladesh	$1,100	South Asia
Kenya	$1,130	Sub-Saharan Africa
Pakistan	$1,560	South Asia
Ghana	$1,610	Sub-Saharan Africa
Sri Lanka	$1,610	South Asia
India	$1,700	South Asia
Ivory Coast	$1,730	Sub-Saharan Africa
Indonesia	$2,290	Southeast Asia
Bolivia	$2,820	Latin America
Middle-income dountries		
China	$3,220	Asia
Philippines	$3,540	Asia
Bulgaria	$4,280	Eastern Europe
Peru	$4,410	Latin America
Tunisia	$5,160	North Africa
Thailand	$5,840	Southeast Asia
Brazil	$6,160	Latin America
Poland	$6,740	Eastern Europe
Malaysia	$6,990	Southeast Asia
Colombia	$6,720	Latin America
Hungary	$6,730	Eastern Europe
Mexico	$7,660	Latin America
Venezuela	$8,130	Latin America
High-income countries		
South Korea	$12,270	Asia
Sweden	$19,480	Western Europe
Australia	$20,130	Australia
United Kingdom	$20,640	Western Europe
Germany	$20,810	Western Europe
Hong Kong	$22,000	Asia
France	$22,320	Western Europe
Japan	$23,180	Asia
Canada	$24,050	North America
Switzerland	$26,620	Western Europe
Singapore	$28,620	Asia
United States	$29,340	North America

Source: Dwight, Steven Radelet, Donald Snodgrass, Malcolm Gillis, and Michael Roemer. 2001. *Economics of Development.* 5th ed. New York: Norton.

American is roughly 60 times greater than the income of the average person living in the East African nation of Tanzania. Remember that the figures have been adjusted to reflect the different costs of living in each country. So the average American can afford to purchase 60 times the amount of goods and services that an average Tanzanian can!

The second striking aspect of the figures in Table R.2 is the distinct regional differences in economic well-being of different countries. The poorest countries tend to be found in sub-Saharan Africa and South Asia, while the richest countries are generally those of Europe, North America, and Australia. Countries in Latin America, Eastern Europe, and Asia (outside the Indian subcontinent) tend to occupy a middle area—richer than the poorest countries, but poorer than the rich countries of North America and Western Europe.

EXPLAINING THE DIFFERENCES

There is no simple explanation for why one country is richer than another at any given point in time. Instead, a number of factors tend to interact in complex ways. In very general terms, the main drivers of intercountry differences in economic well-being may be grouped into five categories: natural resources, human resources, geography, government, and history.

Natural Resources

Some countries are blessed with abundant natural resources. These include mineral resources like oil, coal and iron, as well as land that is productive in agricultural uses (including forestry uses). Some mineral resources, like iron, are fundamental inputs into key productive activities like manufacturing. Others, like coal and oil, are converted into energy needed to fuel productive processes. Agricultural resources support the production of food that people eat, the wood people use to build homes, and the fibers that people convert into cloth.

All else being equal, countries that are well endowed with natural resources have an advantage over countries with poorer resource bases. The oil-rich nations of the Arabian peninsula are a prime example of countries that would be much less well off (not to mention less important geopolitically) were it not for their staggering deposits of oil.

But an abundance of natural resources by no means guarantees that a country will be rich. There are a number of countries that are very poor despite having lots of natural resources. For example, Nigeria is an oil-rich country whose citizens earned, on average, less than $1,200 in 1998. The central African nation of the Congo (formerly Zaire) has massive deposits of copper, diamonds, gold, and other precious metals, yet its citizens are among the poorest on the planet. On the other side of the coin, a number of highly developed countries—of which Japan is a prime example—have relatively little natural resource wealth. Clearly, then, abundant natural resources are not a sure ticket to economic well-being, nor does a lack of natural resource wealth inevitably doom a country to a low standard of living.

Human Resources

The creation of wealth is a human endeavor that depends critically on the skill of the people involved in productive activities. People provide the labor resources necessary to transform raw products into more useful ones, or to supply services that are either consumed directly or used to facilitate the production of other goods and services. People also engage in activities to develop new, improved ways of producing things more efficiently. As such, the abilities and aptitudes of a nation's population—not to mention such intangibles as a national work ethic—are key determinants of a country's overall economic performance.

Economists often use the term "human capital" in discussing the overall quality of an economy's human resource base. One highly important element in the formation of human capital is education. This is particularly true today, since an ever-growing share of modern economic activity requires workers engaged in productive endeavors to possessive sophisticated knowledge and problem-solving abilities.

It is hardly surprising, then, that countries with well-educated citizens—as indicated by high levels of literacy or many years of schooling—tend to perform much better economically than countries with more poorly educated workforces. In recognition of this fact, the World Bank and other international organizations place an extremely high priority on promoting education in less developed countries as a way of encouraging economic growth in those countries.

Geography and Trade

We hear much these days about globalization and the growing interconnectedness of national economies through international trade. But countries have been trading with each other for a very long time, and economists have long recognized that trade is a highly important element of the overall economic performance of a country (and hence the well-being of its citizens). The basic reason is that different countries are endowed with different resources, both natural and human, and trade allows individual countries to specialize in the kinds of productive activities that take best advantage of their particular strengths, or comparative advantages. The same applies to trade between regions within countries.

Geography is important in this regard because where a country is located affects how costly it is for that country to engage in trade. A landlocked country with no ports—like Bolivia or Afghanistan—has less access to international markets than a country that has a long coastline. Likewise, in geographically large countries—especially those with formidable natural barriers like mountain ranges or deserts—the costs of internal transportation can be high, which in turn dampens the prospects for trade between different regions within the country.

Government and Policy

The activities and policies pursued by governments play an important role in the overall functioning of economies. In very simplistic terms, governments collect money from the people and spend that money on various kinds of activities. The kinds of things that governments spend money on may or may not be beneficial to the functioning of the economy. Investments in roads, communications infrastructure, educational systems, and the like can have enormous positive effects by facilitating production and trade. On the other hand, other kinds of expenditures—for example, money spent on ill-conceived military adventures—can have disastrous consequences.

Equally important, governments establish and maintain legal and social institutions that ensure individual property rights and personal security. When such institutions are effective, they have a remarkably positive impact on economic activity. Conversely, where property rights are uncertain, individuals and businesses tend to reduce the amount of economic activity they engage in: consumers are relatively more uncertain that they will receive the goods that they purchase, and producers face larger probability that they will not receive all the profits that they have coming to them.

The ways that governments collect money are important too. Taxes can have important effects on citizens' incentives to work and businesses' incentives to earn profits. Both the fraction of earnings that are taxed and the degree to which different members of a society are taxed play a role in the overall amount of economic activity within that society's economy. Finally, and very importantly, government corruption represents a powerful negative force that adversely affects overall economic performance in many countries. Some of the poorest countries in the world are run by some of the world's richest men! In these countries, a substantial fraction of total national output finds its way into the foreign bank accounts of a very few powerful individuals—much to the detriment of the economy as a whole.

History

One very striking feature that jumps out when one considers the economic performance of different countries is that the poorest countries tend to be ones that were colonies of European countries well into the twentieth century. In many important ways, the relatively lower level of economic well-being of these third world countries appears to be a remnant of their colonial past: those countries are still relatively young, and many are still struggling to effectively marshal their natural and human resources and establish the social institutions necessary to promote sustained economic growth.

History matters because events that happen and policies that are pursued at one moment in time have effects that persist through time. Investments and policies may pay dividends that grow more or less rapidly over time. Negative events like wars and natural disasters may have bad consequences that dissipate quickly or slowly, depending on the various factors that have been discussed above—natural and human resources, geography, and government.

Of course, some of the world's richest countries—the United States, Australia, and New Zealand—were also colonies at one time, although they gained their independence quite some time ago (and it would probably be more accurate to

ECONOMIC GROWTH

It is interesting to note how differently economies have fared over time. Table R.3 provides the average incomes of 17 advanced economies in 1870 and 1985. In 1870, Great Britain and New Zealand were the second- and third-richest countries on the list—and, in fact, in the entire world. In contrast, they were the two poorest of the 17 sampled countries in 1985

Table R.3 Income per Capita in 1870 and 1985 for Selected Countries.

	1870		1985	
Country	**Income per capita**	**Rank**	**Income per capita**	**Rank**
Australia	$3,192	1	$18,386	7
United Kingdom	$2,740	2	$15,787	17
New Zealand	$2,615	3	$16,122	16
Belgium	$2,216	4	$16,987	12
Netherlands	$2,216	5	$16,767	13
United States	$2,063	6	$23,619	1
Switzerland	$1,823	7	$23,267	2
Denmark	$1,618	8	$20,163	4
Germany	$1,606	9	$17,161	11
Austria	$1,574	10	$16,747	14
France	$1,560	11	$17,257	10
Sweden	$1,397	12	$18,710	6
Canada	$1,360	13	$20,704	3
Italy	$1,231	14	$16,359	15
Norway	$1,094	15	$19,253	5
Finland	$929	16	$17,365	9
Japan	$622	17	$17,779	8

Note: All income figures in 1985 U.S. dollars.
Source: Heston, Alan, Robert Summers, and Bettina Aten. 2002. *Penn World Table Version 6.1.* Philadelphia: Center for International Comparisons at the University of Pennsylvania.

The economic impacts of important actions and events tend to grow exponentially in much the same way that interest earned on a bank account grows exponentially. Even small differences in a country's economic growth rate will, if it is sustained over a period of decades, lead to striking outcomes.

In the introduction to their book *Economic Growth,* Harvard University economists Robert Barro and Xavier Sala-i-Martin provide an insightful example of this phenomenon. They note that between 1870 and 1990 the United States' economy grew by approximately 1.75 percent per year. Had the U.S. economy only grown by 0.75 percent over that same time period—roughly the rate at which the economies of Pakistan, the Philippines, and India have grown over the last century or so—the average American would have earned 70 percent less in 1990 ! Put another way, if growth had been one percentage point lower since 1870, the average American's income in 1990 would have been roughly equivalent to that of the average Mexican.

call them satellite outposts of the colonizing countries even at the time of their independence). Moreover, some less developed countries have registered phenomenal rates of economic growth over the past few decades. Notable in this regard are the so-called Asian Tigers—South Korea, Taiwan, and Singapore and Hong Kong. The success of these countries is widely attributed to shrewd outward-looking government policies aimed at stimulating industrialization and facilitating the export of manufactured goods—policies that may well serve as a model for other poor nations looking to facilitate sustained economic growth now and in the future.

SUMMARY

Very large gaps in economic well-being exist between the world's richest and poorest countries. In this article, we have discussed a number of factors that figure into these differences—natural resources, human resources, geography, government, and history. As we have seen, though, there is tremendous variability in the relative importance of any one of these factors to economic performance. How well off a country is at a particular point in time reflects a combination of the resources it possesses, the policies and institutions that its government has pursued, and its unique historical circumstances.

It is an inescapable fact of economic life that the income earned by the citizens of a country increases only if overall economic activity grows faster than the population. Thus, in discussions on how poor countries can become richer, steps needed to foster economic growth are usually the main focus. Of course, this is not to say that material wealth is the only standard of how well off a nation's citizens are: there are lots of things that money can't buy! But to the extent that material well-being translates into overall social welfare, there is ample scope for all governments—of rich and poor countries alike—to take actions to facilitate economic activity.

Further Reading: Barro, Robert J., and Xavier Sala-i-Martin. 1995. *Economic Growth.* New York: McGraw-Hill; Maddison, Angus. 2003. *The World Economy: Historical Statistics.* Paris: OECD; Perkins, Dwight, Steven Radelet, Donald Snodgrass, Malcolm Gillis, and Michael Roemer. 2001. *Economics of Development.* 5th ed. New York: Norton.

Mitch Renkow

S

SALARY DISPARITY

Salary disparity refers to the practice of paying individuals with different demographic characteristics a different wage for work of equal value. Often this refers to gender differences, but the term is also used for pay differences based on race, disabilities, age, and other demographic differences.

The concept of salary disparity in the United States has been a source of heated debate for decades. The controversy is not over whether it exists, but rather why it exists and whether or not anything can or should be done to correct it. Salary disparity can be discussed in regard to a variety of demographics, such as gender, race, disability, and age. Although not an exhaustive list, these characteristics seem to receive the most attention in regards to research and policy.

GENDER

The most current data show that women who are working full time throughout the year are earning approximately 76 percent as much as men (see the Feminist Majority Foundation, www feministcampus.org). This number reflects an upward trend since the 1970s, when the wage ratio between men and women reached a low of 57 percent in 1973 (Sorensen 1994). Although the wage gap has slowly continued to decline, many people argue that there is no real reason why a wage gap should exist at all today. In earlier decades, when women had less education, experience, and time to spend in the workforce, a wage gap was justifiable. Today however, these reasons no longer apply. So why does such a large wage gap still exist?

A look at the history of women in the workplace can shed some light on this question. Before World War II, women of European descent typically only participated in the labor force before they were married. During this era, white men typically earned a family wage (i.e., enough money to support a family). The common culture of the time dictated that after marriage women would only work in the home, taking care of the domestic responsibilities, while men would support the family with the wages earned outside the home. During World War II, however, women started participating in the labor force in great numbers. Due to the shortage of men, businesses were forced to hire women to do many of the necessary wartime jobs that ordinarily only men would be responsible for. In addition, because middle-class women of European descent were never considered to be the wage providers for their families, it became acceptable for businesses to pay them less than what the men would have earned for the same type of work. Minority women, who often did have to work, were paid less because they were both minorities and women.

After the war, many white women continued to participate in the labor force, but now only in jobs that were deemed suitable, such as the nursing and clerical professions. In addition, women were found working mostly in areas that were considered extensions of what they did at home, like child care. Over time, jobs became separated into what was called women's work and men's work. Because men were responsible for supporting the family, it was considered acceptable for women to be paid a lower overall wage consistent with their role as a second wage earner—that is, a wage that was only meant to supplement the man's wage, not support an entire family. It is argued that over time, this occupational segregation created a culture that has allowed salary disparity between men and women to continue into the twenty-first century.

Although the passage of the Equal Pay Act in 1963 prohibited unequal pay for equal work and the Civil Rights Act of 1964 prohibited employment discrimination based on race, color, religion, sex, or national origin, these two pieces of federal legislation did little to correct the wage gap between men and women. The female-to-male earnings ratio for full-time workers actually fell from 61 percent in 1960 to 59 percent in 1975 (Figart and Mutari 2002). Although this legislation did allow women to fight for equal pay for essentially the same work, it did not address the portion of the wage gap that is attributable to the underevaluation of female-dominated jobs.

The controversy over salary disparity remained an important topic for policy makers during the 1970s and 1980s, when a new movement involving the concept known as comparable worth began to take shape. Comparable worth is the idea that women and men should be paid equal wages for jobs that have been judged to require similar responsibilities; levels of education, skills, and training; and job conditions. Comparable-worth polices have been implemented in a number of U.S. states. These policies are based on a job evaluation plan that is constructed to determine the relative worth of a job and is subsequently used as a factor in wage determination. Only the state of Minnesota has found success using comparable-worth policies, which in one case increased their female-to-male pay ratio from 72 to 80.5 percent (Sorensen 1994). Other states that have implemented comparable-worth policies have not had the same kind of success. This is undoubtedly due to the various ways in which comparable worth can be implemented. Nevertheless, comparable-worth advocates claim that because women are segregated into certain occupations that pay considerably less than occupations that are predominately male, women cannot achieve pay equity without some type of intervention.

In order to fully understand the current debate over salary disparity between men and women, it is important to distinguish between the most popular explanations for its existence. The human capital theory focuses on labor supply, relying on the preferences or voluntary choices of women, while the discrimination explanation focuses on labor demand, relying on job-related variables such as the preferences of employers and the restrictions faced by female employees (Anker 2001).

Human capital explanations suggest that wage gaps exist because of productivity differences between the sexes. According to this theory, in the past, women invested less in education and training due to their anticipated responsibilities to the family. In addition, because women expected to spend fewer years than men in the labor force, women concentrated in educational specialties that were less economically rewarding than those chosen by men (Jacobs 1995).

Compared to men, women were also more likely to find themselves leaving and reentering the workforce and therefore preferred jobs that do not require skill accumulation. In addition to this, married women were (and continue to be) responsible for a large portion of the household duties. In particular, child care can cause women to have less energy to expend in the workplace, and hence less effort may be put forth on the job. Over time, less education and experience resulted in salary disparity between men and women.

The second explanation for the wage gap focuses on job-related variables. This explanation, sometimes referred to as occupational segregation, deals predominately with the issue of discrimination. Before the passage of the Civil Rights Act in 1964, women were excluded from many jobs due to discrimination practiced by employers, male employees, or customers. This discrimination gave women limited access to a small number of "female-oriented" occupations that were deemed less valuable than those held by men and hence resulted in lower wages. It has been argued that over time it became a cultural norm for female-dominated occupations to be undervalued in terms of wages, compared to those jobs performed predominately by men. It is here that comparable-worth policies have strived to make an impact.

Given that women have made great strides in the human capital aspect of the wage gap, it seems that policy makers should direct their attention more toward the issue of discrimination. In fact, the most recent legislation dealing with salary disparity between men and women seems to be doing just that. This legislation, known as the Fair Pay Act, would prohibit pay discrimination on the basis of race and national origin, as well as sex. The bill would therefore expand the standard in the Equal Pay Act of 1963 by prohibiting "discrimination between workers performing dissimilar work in equivalent jobs, rather than just prohibiting sex discrimination between workers performing substantially the *same* jobs as outlined" in the Equal Pay Act.

RACE

When looking at salary disparity in terms of race, researchers have found that the wage ratio of African American men to white men is 78 percent. African American women face an even larger wage differential, earning only 63 percent as much as white males (see the Feminist Majority Foundation, www feministcampus.org).

The arguments regarding the causes of salary disparity between African Americans and white males are very similar to those used to explain the causes for wage differentials between the sexes. In fact, the Civil Rights Act of 1964 was just as important for African Americans as it was for white females when it comes to the outlawing of employment discrimination. So how does the discussion on salary disparity differ when it comes to race? Really the only difference is the way in which discrimination is defined. There are two types of discrimination with regards to race. The first deals with racial prejudice, and the second deals with what is called statistical discrimination.

In general, prejudice is defined as a hostile attitude toward a person because he or she belongs to a particular group that is presumed to have objectionable qualities. It has been shown that wage gaps between whites and African Americans are at least partly due to the personal prejudice of employers against African Americans. Statistical discrimination deals with the issue of incomplete or imperfect information about worker productivity. Here, discrimination is caused by racial stereotypes, which leads employers to pay black workers less because they think that African Americans are less productive or because employers have inaccurate information about their productivity.

A brief history of African Americans in the workplace will prove useful in understanding the various policies enacted to combat racial discrimination and the resulting wage gap. The plight of African Americans in the labor force was similar to that of women prior to World War II and during the years that followed. African Americans were segregated into low-wage jobs, which for the most part were agricultural. Entire industries and categories of employment were segregated by race. For example, in grocery and department stores, clerks were white and janitors and elevator operators were black (see Affirmitive Action Review at http:// womenhistory.about.com). Generations of African Americans were confined to low-paying jobs and would never have the opportunity to move up the ladder.

Prior to the Civil Rights of 1964, the ability to obtain human capital through education was also restricted for African Americans, as most were limited to attending only predominantly black colleges. African Americans were often restricted in the types of classes they could take, and few—if any—received any type of professional education.

One of the first major attempts to alleviate discrimination in education and the workforce was undertaken by President John F. Kennedy, who created the Committee on Equal Employment Opportunity in 1961. It was then that the term "affirmative action" was first used to refer to measures designed to achieve nondiscrimination. However, it wasn't until the passage of the Equal Economic Opportunity Act of 1972 that affirmative action became a law "whereby employers, labor unions, employment agencies, and labor-management apprenticeship programs were required to actively seek to eliminate discrimination against and increase employment of women and minorities."

From the beginning, affirmative action was perceived as a temporary remedy that would end once a level playing field for all Americans was achieved. However, by the late 1970s, it became apparent that certain aspects of the policy were flawed. In the 1980s and 1990s a backlash against affirmative action was mounted and the debate regarding its implementation became more complex. Opponents of affirmative action claimed that although the system opened the door for jobs, promotions, and education to minorities, it shut the door on whites. In addition, some people even argued that unqualified minorities were getting a free ride on the American system, which created disincentives for hard work to the overall majority. The opinions of the Supreme Court justices have been divided in affirmative action cases, partially because of opposing political ideologies, but also because each case is unique to its specific circumstances.

Affirmative action policies today focus mainly on education and employment and require measures to be taken to ensure equal opportunities for minorities in the areas of career advancement, salary increases, school admissions, scholarships, and financial aid. One of the most important rulings on the issue in 25 years involved a case in 2003 that dealt with the University of Michigan's affirmative action policies. The Supreme Court decisively upheld the use of affirmative action in higher education, ruling that "although affirmative action was no longer justified as a way of redressing past oppression and injustice, it promoted a 'compelling state interest' in diversity at all levels of society" (see Law Center at www.cnn.com).

Nearly all researchers agree that the government antidiscrimination programs beginning in 1964 after the passage of the Civil Rights Act contributed to the improved income of African Americans. However, drawing conclusions about which specific antidiscrimination programs were most effective is rather difficult. The numbers show that before the Civil Rights Act of 1964, the median black male worker earned only about 60 percent as much as the median white male worker; by 1993, the median black male earned 74 percent as much as the median white male; and by 2004, the median black male earned 78 percent as much as the median white male (see U.S.Census Bureau at www.census.gov).

The controversy over salary disparity between races seems to stem mostly from the policies enacted to correct the discrimination that causes it. In particular, opponents of affirmative action are especially vocal about the disincentives created by the policy itself. For example, critics argue that affirmative action policies lead to the hiring of unqualified minority workers, which constitutes unfair reverse discrimination and causes inefficient production while at the same time reducing incentives for minority workers to become qualified. On the other hand, supporters of affirmative action claim that the hiring of minority workers will lead to the availability of better information on their productivity, which will break down stereotypes and encouraging formerly excluded workers to invest in job skills.

TIME LINE OF THE IMPORTANT EVENTS IN THE HISTORY OF SALARY DISPARITY

Fair Labor Standards Act of 1938

The Fair Labor Standards Act of 1938, as amended, is published in law in sections 201–19 of title 29, United States Code. "The Act provides for minimum standards for both wages and overtime entitlement, and spells out administrative procedures by which covered work time must be compensated. Included in the Act are provisions related to child labor, equal pay, and portal-to-portal activities. In addition, the Act exempts specified employees or groups of employees from the application of certain of its provisions."

World War II (1939–1945)

By necessity, minorities began entering the workforce in great numbers during the war. This is believed to have been a crucial turning point in the structuring of the American labor force.

Equal Pay Act of 1963

The Equal Pay Act, which is part of the Fair Labor Standards Act of 1938, as amended, and is administered and enforced by the Equal Employment Opportunity Commission, prohibits "sex-based wage discrimination between men and women in the same establishment who are performing under similar working conditions."

Title VII of the Civil Rights Act of 1964

Title VII prohibits "employment discrimination based on race, color, religion, sex and national origin."

Age Discrimination in Employment Act of 1967

The Age Discrimination in Employment Act prohibits "employment discrimination against persons 40 years of age or older."

Schultz v. Wheaton Glass Company (1970)

"A U.S. Court of Appeals rules that jobs held by men and women need to be 'substantially equal' but not 'identical' to fall under the protection of the Equal Pay Act. An employer cannot, for example, change the job titles of women workers in order to pay them less than men."

Rehabilitation Act of 1973

The Rehabilitation Act prohibits employment discrimination against individuals with disabilities in the federal sector and contains provisions governing remedies and attorney's fees. Key language in the Rehabilitation Act, found in Section 504, states: "No otherwise qualified handicapped individual in the United States, shall, solely by reason of his handicap, be excluded from the participation in, be denied the benefits of, or be subjected to discrimination under any program or activity receiving federal financial assistance."

Regents of the University of California v. Bakke (1978)

The Supreme Court ruling in this case imposed limitations on affirmative action "to ensure that providing greater opportunities for minorities did not come at the expense of the rights of the majority—affirmative action was unfair if it led to reverse discrimination."

Americans with Disabilities Act of 1990

The Americans with Disabilities Act was closely modeled after the Civil Rights Act and is the most sweeping disability rights legislation in history. It mandated that local, state and federal governments and programs be accessible, that businesses with more than 15 employees make "reasonable accommodations" for disabled workers and that public accommodations such as restaurants and stores make "reasonable modifications" to ensure access for disabled members of the public. The act also mandated access in public transportation, communication, and in other areas of public life.

University of Michigan's Affirmative Action Policies (2003)

In *Grutter v. Bollinger,* the Supreme Court (5–4) upheld the University of Michigan Law School's affirmative action policy, ruling that race can be one of many factors considered by colleges when they select their students because it furthers "a compelling interest in obtaining the educational benefits that flow from a diverse student body."

Fair Pay Act of 2003 (Current Proposed Legislation)

"The major provision of the Fair Pay Act prohibits wage discrimination based on sex, race, or national origin among employees for work in 'equivalent jobs.' Equivalent jobs are those whose composite of skill, effort, responsibility, and working conditions are equivalent in value, even if the jobs are dissimilar. The Act is a natural extension of the 1963 Equal Pay Act, which is limited to sex-based discrimination in the same jobs. For enforcement purposes, the Fair Pay Act allows class action lawsuits to be filed and provides for compensatory and punitive damages."

Smith v. City of Jackson, Mississippi, No. 03–1160, 544 U.S. (2005)

"The Supreme Court ruled that workers over 40 years old could sue under the ADEA when an employer's action has a 'disparate impact' on their age group and the employer's action was not 'reasonable.' In other words, the employees are not required to prove that the employer intended to discriminate against older workers in a disparate impact case."

DISABILITY

A disability is defined as a lack of ability to perform an activity in the manner or within the range considered normal (Berkowitz and Hill 1986). Differences in earnings between the disabled and nondisabled can be partly explained by the fact that fewer people with disabilities work. In addition, people with disabilities are generally less educated and are employed in occupations requiring fewer skills than are the nondisabled. However, it is has been shown that even after education and type of work are taken into consideration, disabled workers still receive lower wages on average than the nondisabled workforce.

Although it is well established that disabled individuals face a disadvantaged relative economic position, it is much less clear what factors are contributing to this outcome. Health problems can potentially limit the productivity of disabled workers and often have a negative impact on their employment status. In addition, disabled workers may also face lower wage and employment levels due to employer prejudice or discrimination due to employers' misconceptions or lack of information, as was the case with African Americans.

Discrimination due to lack of information or employers' misconceptions may cause wage differentials because employers believe that disabled workers are, on average, less productive than other workers. Under these circumstances, employers often use education level, job history, and preemployment test scores to measure the productivity of disabled individuals instead of actually observing their work. Some studies have found that discrimination accounts for between 30 and 50 percent of the wage differential between disabled and nondisabled workers and also leads to lower labor force participation among the disabled (Johnson and Lambrinos 1985). A more recent study, however, has found that from 1984 to 1993, only 3.7 percent of the earnings differential was due to discrimination against disabled workers (DeLeire 2001).

Even though the actual numbers in terms of percentage are substantially different, studies consistently seem to show that discrimination is a factor in wage differentials among disabled and nondisabled workers. In response to these findings, federal legislation has been enacted with the intention of eliminating discrimination against disabled workers. For example, the Rehabilitation Act of 1973 was the first major piece of federal legislation establishing employment protection for disabled employees of the federal government or those working for federal contractors. Although the Rehabilitation Act applied only to federal employees, it is considered the beginning of a shift in disability policy. The focus went from implementing transfers to disabled individuals who were presumed unable to work to creating access to jobs through the establishment of antidiscrimination rights and accommodations (see National Council on Disability at www.ncd.gov; Yelin 1997).

More recently, Congress passed the Americans with Disabilities Act (ADA) in 1990 "to provide a clear and comprehensive national mandate for the elimination of discrimination against individuals with disabilities." The ADA established provisions that promoted equal access and opportunity to employment in the public and private sectors for individuals with disabilities. The ADA also mandated the provision of reasonable accommodation of disabilities by employers that encompasses both physical barriers to facilities as well as job restructuring with respect to the scheduling, pace, or flow of work.

The ADA has received serious criticism, most notably from the business sector. From a business perspective, the hiring of a disabled worker could impose additional costs in terms of the cost of an accommodation necessary for access. Hence, the provisions of the ADA that require employers to incur additional costs to accommodate the disabled may have the unintended consequence of reducing the employment of disabled workers rather than increasing it.

Some researchers have suggested a wage subsidy (payments made by the government to workers) for disabled workers to encourage them to remain in or reenter the workplace after becoming disabled (DeLeire 2000). It is argued that this wage subsidy would reduce the cost of hiring and accommodating disabled workers, which would subsequently increase the firms' incentives to hire them.

AGE

Salary disparity among older and younger workers can be difficult to measure due to a variety of factors that come into play. Some of these factors may be the result of unjust perceptions that employers have of older workers, while some might prove to be real and justifiable. For example, some employers may have negative perceptions of older workers' productivity given their inability (or unwillingness) to learn new skills and possible decreases in stamina. Other employers may fear higher costs associated with hiring older workers due to a possible increase in health premiums and the increased possibility that work-limiting health problems may arise. Whether real or perceived, these factors contribute to the unfair treatment of older workers in the workplace.

It is often difficult to discern whether wage gaps between younger and older workers is the result of real differences in productivity or age discrimination. The fact that there is little evidence documenting the impact of discrimination against older workers in the workplace is in part due to the fact that older workers have higher incomes and lower unemployment rates than younger workers. In addition, productivity becomes hard to measure in such cases because there are conflicting factors at work. On one hand, older workers have more experience, which should increase productivity, but on the other hand, at some point in certain jobs, age could be detrimental to skills and hence cause productivity to decrease.

Researchers have described three possible explanations for the wage differential between older and younger workers (Herz and Rones 1989). First, as mentioned earlier, the human capital theory predicts lower productivity of older workers due to underinvestment in training to acquire upgraded skills. Second, older workers tend to want more leisure time, which would account for fewer hours spent working and hence lower incomes. Finally, employers may offer lower wages to older workers due to the older workers' decreased ability to find comparable alternative employment. It should be noted, however, that labor unions have advocated seniority as the only fair way to discriminate in terms of pay, so older workers may make more than younger workers doing more difficult work.

Stories of hostile work environments, demotions, or forced retirement eventually brought the issue of age discrimination under great scrutiny. Concerns by policy makers over these types of reoccurring incidents prompted Congress to pass the Age Discrimination in Employment Act of 1967, which outlawed discrimination against workers between the ages of 40 and 65 (Johnson and Neumark 1997). The Age Discrimination in Employment Act prohibits employers from using age as a factor in human resources practices, including compensation and benefits.

The baby boom generation (people born between 1946 and 1964) has and will continue to play a major role in the issue of salary disparity in the years to come. As the workforce becomes more and more saturated with people approaching retirement age, age discrimination could become more prevalent due to the sheer volume of older workers in the labor market.

CONCLUSION

A common theme among the four demographics described above dealing with salary disparity is the issue of discrimination. Although it is not easy to measure, research consistently shows that it exists and that it plays a role in the wage differentials we see today. Policies enacted to correct it will always stir up debate concerning the nature of its existence. Although we may never see it completely disappear, as a society, everyone can play a role in trying to diminish its presence by becoming more educated on the topic and by encouraging policy makers to make sound judgments regarding the ways in which it is handled.

See also: Glass Ceiling

References

Anker, Richard. 2001. *What Is Equality and How Do We Get There? Women, Gender, and Work.* Edited by Martha Fetherolf Loutfi. Geneva: International Labour Office.

Berkowitz, Monroe, and M. Anne Hill, eds. 1986. *Disability and the Labor Market.* Ithaca, NY: ILR Press, Cornell University.

DeLeire, T. 2000. "The Unintended Consequences of the Americans with Disabilities Act." *Regulation* 23 (1): 21–24.

DeLeire, T. 2001. "Changes in Wage Discrimination against People with Disabilities: 1984–1993." *Journal of Human Resources* 36 (1): 145–58.

Figart, Deborah M., and Ellen Mutari, eds. 2002. *Living Wages, Equal Wages: Gender and Labor Market Policies in the United States.* London: Routledge.

Herz, D. E., and P. L. Rones. 1989. "Institutional Barriers to Employment of Older Workers." *Monthly Labor Review* 112 (4): 14–21.

Jacobs, Jerry A., ed. 1995. *Gender Inequality at Work.* Thousand Oaks, CA: Sage.

Johnson, W. G., and J. Lambrinos. 1985. "Wage Discrimination against Handicapped Men and Women." *Journal of Human Resources* 20 (2): 264–77; Baldwin, M., and W. Johnson. 1994. "Labor Market Discrimination against Workers with Disabilities." *Journal of Human Resources* 29 (1): 1–19.

Johnson, R. W., and D. Neumark. 1997. "Age Discrimination, Job separation, and Employment Status of Older Workers: Evidence from Self-Reports." *Journal of Human Resources* 32 (4): 779–811.

Sorensen, Elaine. 1994. *Comparable Worth: Is It a Worthy Policy?* Princeton, NJ: Princeton University Press.

Yelin, E. H. 1997. "The Employment of People with and without Disabilities in an Age of Insecurity." *Annals of the American Academy of Political and Social Sciences* 549 (1): 117–28.

Further Reading: Murphy, Evelyn, and E. J. Graff. 2005. *Getting Even: Why Women Don't Get Paid Like Men—and What to Do about It.* New York: Simon & Schuster; Segrave, Kerry. 2001. *Age Discrimination by Employers.* Jefferson, NC: McFarland; Thomason, Terry, John F. Burton Jr., and Douglas E. Hyatt, eds. 1998. *New Approaches to Disability in the Workplace.* Madison, WI: Industrial Relations Research Association.

Kerry A. King

SAME-SEX PARTNER BENEFITS

The controversy over providing employee benefits for same-sex partners is really one of contrasting values and beliefs in American society and is one issue in the so-called culture war in America that involves issues ranging from abortion to gay rights. The arguments on both sides of this controversy are fairly predictable. Proponents say that extending the same benefits to all is an equitable way to treat all employees, regardless of their sexual orientation or marital status, and that it helps attract and retain good employees. The opponents argue that extending benefits to same-sex partners conflicts with the sanctity of marriage, and that only an opposite-sex partner should be entitled to partner benefits.

On this issue, corporate America has been ahead of the curve and has increasingly recognized that offering the same benefits to all employees is just good business, in that it allows firms to attract, hire, and retain good employees. In today's corporate environment, these policies are one yardstick by which employees measure the company's commitment to diversity in their workforce.

The sentiment in America's general population is quite different, though, as evidenced by the majority of states now passing either "defense of marriage" legislation or state constitutional amendments that ban same-sex marriages and/or civil unions between same-sex partners. These acts and amendments are intended to prohibit recognition of same-sex marriages or civil unions and to prevent employees' same-sex domestic partners from receiving benefits that would be offered to them if they were heterosexual.

LOTUS DEVELOPMENT CORPORATION—THE PIONEER IN SPOUSAL-EQUIVALENT EMPLOYEE BENEFITS

In corporate America, Lotus Development Corporation, the developer of 1-2-3 spreadsheet software, was the first publicly traded corporation to offer benefits to the same-sex partners of their employees. From the time of its founding in 1982, Lotus had a corporate culture that was quite unique. This included a human resources function that was broadly integrated with other business functions and championed workplace diversity. When a new vice president of human resources was hired in 1989, he found that there were widespread inequities in pay and benefits across the company. Furthermore, because of its inability to hire and retain women and minorities, Lotus was attracting government attention concerning discriminatory employment practices (Grant 1995).

In response to these issues, Lotus formed a diversity advisory group to investigate the changing demographics in the workplace, design Lotus's response to these changes, and write an annual diversity report to summarize the diversity efforts at the company. At this time in the software industry, there was strong competition for employees, so the HR department was very interested in attracting and retaining women and minorities, both to enhance the firm's competitive position and to prevent any government action (Grant 1995).

About this same time, three lesbian employees at Lotus created the Extended Benefits Task Force to work on a proposal to "extend Lotus employee benefits to non-married 'spouse-equivalents' of Lotus employees in the same manner as benefits are routinely extended to legal spouses now" (Grant 1995). When the task force began looking for current models for such benefits at other firms, they found that a few small private-sector companies offered spousal-equivalent benefits (e.g., the *Village Voice,* Ben & Jerry's Homemade), along with several West Coast cities, but no publicly traded companies had such a policy.

There were several other issues for HR to consider, too. One issue was the cost of extending spousal-equivalent benefits. Since few insurance companies offered such coverage, there was little actuarial data on which to base the risks, and therefore the costs, of providing this coverage. Tax issues were also a concern, since Lotus's current flexible benefits program was tax qualified under the federal Internal Revenue Service Code. However, the IRS Code only recognized a dependent spouse for coverage and did not recognize spousal equivalents. So, if Lotus extended benefits to ineligible dependents, Lotus's whole plan could be disqualified for preferential tax treatment. If disqualified, this would mean that all employees' premium payments would be paid after taxes, not with the pretax earnings, and they also would have to pay federal taxes on the benefits they received (i.e., the portion of insurance premiums paid by Lotus; Grant 1995).

Lotus was concerned about creating a benefit program that was equitable to all employees—one that offered the same benefits to lesbian and gay employees as those offered to married heterosexual employees. Since heterosexual couples could choose to marry and get dependent-spouse benefits, and homosexuals could not legally marry at that time, Lotus chose to consider offering spousal-equivalent benefits only to gay and lesbian couples in committed long-term relationships. Accordingly, Lotus was thinking about requiring some sort of documentation or affidavit verifying the length of the relationships of gay and lesbian employees seeking benefits for their partners (Grant 1995).

There were potential legal issues, too. Since heterosexual couples in long-term relationships were not going to be offered spousal-equivalent benefits,

EMPLOYERS OFFERING DOMESTIC PARTNER BENEFITS

Overall

	Respondents	*Yes*	*No*	*Plan to*
Opposite sex	454	34%	65%	1%
Same sex	458	27%	71%	2%

By Size

	Small	*Medium*	*Large*
Opposite sex	31%	32%	44%
Same sex	22%	25%	36%

By Year

	2001	*2002*	*2003*	*2004*
Opposite sex	26%	31%	31%	34%
Same sex	16%	23%	23%	27%

Source: Society for Human Resource Management. 2005. *Benefits Survey Report, 2004.* Alexandria, VA: Author.

they could file suit against the company claiming that the new policy was discriminatory. Likewise, since heterosexual couples were not required to provide documentation of their marriages, gay and lesbian couples could claim that the new policy was discriminatory in that they were required to provide documentation of their long-term relationships that wasn't required of heterosexual couples.

Finally, all these issues were addressed, and in September 1991, more than two-and-a-half years after the formation of the Extended Benefits Task Force, Lotus announced its spousal-equivalents benefits policy to its employees and invited them to a forum to discuss the new policy. Three days later, the *Boston Globe* ran a front-page story about the policy, which stirred considerable controversy across the country. According to the vice president of human resources, Lotus was deluged with letters, but the "responses were 80% positive to 20% negative; people called and wrote to congratulate Lotus on its leadership, and to condemn the company for falling prey to everything from the forces of Satan to the pressures of political correctness and liberalism run amok" (Grant 1994).

TWO DECADES OF CHANGE

While Lotus, introducing its policy in 1991, was the first publicly traded corporation to offer benefits to same-sex partners, it is the *Village Voice,* a New York City weekly—which introduced its policy in 1982—that has the distinction of

EMPLOYERS OFFERING DOMESTIC PARTNER BENEFITS BY INDUSTRY

	Finance	*Govern-ment*	*Health*	*High Tech*	*Manufac-turing*	*Services*	*Wholesale/ Retail Trade*
Opposite sex	31%	26%	30%	46%	44%	66%	49%
Same sex	25%	12%	26%	36%	24%	46%	43%

Source: Society for Human Resource Management. 2005. Benefits Survey Report, 2004. Alexandria, VA: Author.

being the first U.S. employer to offer health insurance benefits for their employees' same-sex partners. Since Lotus introduced their spousal-equivalents coverage, more employers each year have offered benefits to employees' same-sex partners, with most the rapid change occurring in the last decade. By sthe end of 2003, 67 of *Fortune*'s 100 "Best Companies to Work For" provided benefits for same-sex partners, according to the Lesbian and Gay Journalists Association. The Human Rights Campaign reported that by the end of 2003, 36 counties and 91 cities across the United States offered some type of benefits to domestic partners, and by the end of 2005, a total of 9,370 private employers, state and local governments, government agencies, and colleges and universities provided health insurance coverage to employees' domestic partners. By the end of 2006, the majority (254) of the Fortune 500 provided equal benefits to same-sex couples (Human Rights Campaign 2006).

In spite of controversy and IRS headaches, many companies, like Lotus, have added domestic-partner coverage because they want to offer equitable benefits across their employee base, to support diversity in the workplace, and to recruit and retain talented employees. However, not all firms share that view. John Haslinger, the New England health and welfare practice leader for Mellon's Human Resources & Investor Solutions in Boston, says that based on Mellon's client population, approximately 10 to 15 percent of employers are comfortable offering domestic-partner benefits (same-sex) and view it as a civil rights issue. A similar percentage is on the opposite side of the issue, finding it "morally reprehensible," according to Haslinger (Geisel 2004).

A 2005 Hewitt Associates study indicated that the primary reason most companies offer domestic-partner benefits is to attract and retain employees (Hewitt Associates 2005). The Employee Benefit Research Institute also found that those employers with a benefits package that appeals to a diverse workforce have a recruiting advantage and demonstrate that they value diversity. In addition, employee morale and productivity improve in work environments where employees believe that their employer demonstrates that it values its employees (Employee Benefit Research Institute 2005).

ADDITIONAL CONTROVERSY IN THE WORKPLACE: SAME-SEX MARRIAGES

The advent of same-sex marriages being allowed in some states created even more controversy and issues for employers with respect to employee benefits. A

FORTUNE 500 COMPANIES THAT OFFER DOMESTIC PARTNER HEALTH BENEFITS, 1999–2006

Year	*1999*	*2000*	*2001*	*2002*	*2003*	*2004*	*2005*	*2006*
# of Firms	96	124	158	175	199	219	246	254
% of Firms	19.2%	24.8%	31.6%	35.0%	39.8%	43.8%	49.2%	50.8%

Source: Human Rights Campaign. 2006. The State of the Workplace for Gay, Lesbian, Bisexual and Transgender Americans. Washington, DC: Author.

civil marriage between a man and a woman in the United States confers many rights to the married couple under federal law, including federal laws that govern employee benefits. For example, the value of the health insurance coverage for a spouse is usually considered a nontaxable benefit for the worker under federal law. Likewise, other employer-provided privileges and benefits, like family leave and bereavement leave, are only offered with respect to an employee's spouse. In addition, under federal pension law, the Employee Retirement Income Security Act (ERISA) regulates employers' self-insured pension plans. ERISA does not require employers to establish pension plans, but for those employees who have chosen such coverage, ERISA does require employers to provide joint and survivor annuities that provide for continuing benefits to a surviving spouse. In addition, one important amendment to ERISA, the Consolidated Omnibus Budget Reconciliation Act of 1985 (better known as COBRA), provides some workers and their families with the right to continue their health coverage for a limited time after certain events, such as the loss of a job (Travinski 2006).

Because of the specific rights that are granted spouses under current law, when states began to allow same-sex couples to marry, the idea of extending marriage rights to same-sex couples became a political issue in the United States. It began in 1993, when the Supreme Court of Hawaii ruled that refusing to grant marriage licenses—and the associated privileges—to same-sex couples was sex discrimination under the state constitution. This ruling provided impetus for those opposed to same-sex marriage to rally support across the country to try to prevent similar rulings in other states. By 1996, the there was enough political pressure to get the federal Defense of Marriage Act (DOMA) passed by Congress. DOMA defines marriage as a union only between a man and a woman and denies federal recognition of same-sex marriages. Thus, under DOMA, benefits to which married partners are entitled do not have to be provided to partners in same-sex marriages. Effectively, DOMA means that employers do not have to provide benefits to married same-sex partners, but they can choose to do so. However, if employers do provide benefits to employees' same-sex partners, preferential treatment under federal laws that are afforded to opposite-sex spouses would not be available to same-sex spouses (Travinski 2006).

In 1998, Hawaii voters passed the very first "defense of marriage" amendment to their state constitution, and the state legislature exercised its power to ban same-sex marriage. Over the next five years, since it was clear that same-sex marriage would not take place in Hawaii, and it was generally believed that same-sex marriages would not be legalized, only three other states proposed and passed defense of marriage amendments.

However, in November 2003, the Massachusetts Supreme Court, in Goodridge v. Department of Public Health, ruled that same-sex marriages were legal in the state. Fearing that their own state supreme courts would issue similar rulings in the future, social and religious conservatives across the nation proposed defense of marriage amendments at the state level (often referred to now as mini-DOMAs). Some of these state constitutional amendments go further than DOMA by forbidding a state from recognizing even nonmarital civil unions and domestic partnerships between same-sex partners, while others allow for same-sex unions that are not called marriages. By November 2006, 27 states had approved defense of marriage amendments.

There have been several significant court cases that challenged these amendments. Chief among them was a chief judge's ruling in the United States District Court for the District of Nebraska in May 2005 that the state constitutional amendment violates the United States Constitution, stating that "the intent and purpose of the amendment is based on animus against this class (gay, lesbian, and homosexual couples)" (*Citizens for Equal Protection v. Bruning* 2005). This was the first state constitutional provision banning same-sex marriage to be ruled unconstitutional.

HOW FIRMS ARE HANDLING SAME-SEX MARRIAGES

The responses by firms to the legalization of same-sex marriages have been mixed with respect to employee benefits. Some firms simply decided that since same-sex marriages were now legal, employees in same-sex marriages would be eligible for the same benefits as their counterparts in heterosexual marriages. In those states where same-sex marriages were allowed, this meant that state and federal laws were inconsistent, because DOMA still existed at the federal level. Thus, benefits offered to same-sex partners were afforded different tax treatment at the state and federal levels. Since under federal DOMA, same-sex marriages were not recognized, the value of benefits provided to a same-sex partner (e.g., employer-paid premiums for health insurance) was subject to taxation as imputed income, and in addition, premiums had to be paid with after-tax income. Some firms that had a strong commitment to providing equitable benefits for all employees have gone so far as to "gross up" the pay of a gay or lesbian employee whose partner was receiving benefits. This grossed-up additional income is meant to equalize the tax penalties faced by gay and lesbian couples whose marriages aren't recognized by the IRS. Other firms have chosen to offer same-sex partner benefits, but the couple has to bear the additional tax burden of the benefit.

Other organizations have responded by removing their spousal-equivalent benefits, arguing that these benefits were originally offered to same-sex couples because they couldn't get married and get the same benefits as married couples. Now that same-sex couples had the same opportunity to marry as heterosexual couples, these firms decided to offer benefits only to married couples—same sex or opposite sex. Since same-sex marriages became legal in Massachusetts in May 2004, several companies have rescinded their domestic-partner benefit plans in Massachusetts. Those companies include the New York Times; Armonk, New York–based IBM; Waltham, Massachusetts-based Raytheon Corp.; and the National Fire Protection Association, Boston Medical Center, and Emerson College, all in Boston (Greenwald 2005).

According to IBM's vice president of global workforce diversity, when IBM introduced same-sex domestic partner benefits in 1996, it did so with the provision that the policy would end once the state in which the employees lived recognized same-sex marriages. Then, when Vermont recognized civil unions between same-sex couples, which gave them rights similar to those held by married couples, IBM amended its policy to say that domestic-partner benefits would end when a state recognizes their same-sex marriage "or creates a comparable status" to reflect the situation in that state. IBM's new policy in Massachusetts affected fewer than 12 Massachusetts employees, who were given until January 2006 to marry in order to retain their domestic partner benefits (Greenwald 2005).

A spokesperson for Emerson College said, "Now that gay couples can marry, they're on the same footing as heterosexuals." Only six employees out of several hundred at Emerson were affected by the policy change. Three got married, two lost coverage, and one switched to his partner's primary coverage plan (Greenwald 2005).

However, some employees in the gay community were not pleased by firms' decisions to drop their same-sex partner benefits. Some homosexual couples complained that by removing spousal-equivalent benefits, employers were essentially forcing them to get married in order to continue to receive the benefits that they had been receiving. This was perceived as discriminatory. One gay worker who had been in a committed relationship for 24 years put it this way: "It seems like you make progress being accepted and then, all of a sudden, they try to take it away" (Lyman 2005).

Other employers have introduced domestic-partner benefits covering same-sex and opposite-sex couples for the first time. National Grid USA, a large utility company based in Massachusetts, had been exploring how to encourage greater diversity in its workforce when gay marriage was legalized in Massachusetts. Both factors motivated its national introduction of a domestic-partner benefits program for both same-sex and heterosexual couples (Greenwald 2005).

THE CURRENT LANDSCAPE

It should be obvious from the preceding sections that there is still great diversity of opinion across organizations in the United States regarding the issue of providing benefits for same-sex partners of employees. The three key reasons that organizations don't offer domestic-partner benefits seem to be that no employees have asked for them, the perceived costs are too high, and there is opposition to them based on "moral" reasons. The first of these is understandable; why offer a benefit if none of your employees want it? The second rationale—high costs—hasn't been found to be true for most organizations offering such benefits (except for small employers, whose preemployment benefits costs tend to be considerably higher, anyway). For large employers, the costs have been found to range from less than 1 percent to about 2 percent of total benefits costs for the organization. And some companies that offer benefits to both same-sex and opposite-sex partners have reported that their costs are lower among the same-sex domestic partners (Institute of Management and Administration 2004).

The third reason—so-called moral grounds—simply reflects the widely held belief in the United States that a homosexual lifestyle is morally wrong, and consequently, those who live it should not have the same privileges and benefits that heterosexuals are provided. Such strongly held beliefs are, in large part, faith based and have been the primary impetus behind DOMA and state legislation prohibiting same-sex marriage.

The major reasons that many employers are offering benefits to same-sex partners of employees are a desire to treat all employees equally and equitably, attract and retain the best employees possible, and increase the diversity in their workforces. In an increasingly competitive labor market, the first two of these reasons seem rather obvious and make good business sense. Many firms are also finding that greater workforce diversity has contributed to greater innovation, better employee morale, and improved productivity.

So, the current controversy tends to be based more on contrasting values and beliefs in American society than one based on differing strategic or management philosophies of business. Amid the controversy, more firms each year are making the business decision to offer domestic partner benefits. In addition, a growing number of firms have recently joined the Business Coalition for Benefits Tax Equity, organized by the Human Rights Campaign. The coalition's members support legislation to equalize tax treatment of employee benefits so that gay and lesbian couples receive the same tax breaks that married couples enjoy. One company that has joined the coalition is the Chubb Corporation, a property and casualty insurer. About the coalition's efforts, Chubb's chief diversity officer says, "These firms are trying to work with legislators to move society the way the workplace is moving" (Elswick 2006).

At the same time, opponents of gay rights and same-sex marriage are continuing their efforts to prohibit recognition of same-sex marriages and are now supporting the Federal Marriage Amendment, which would prohibit states from recognizing such unions by amending the United States Constitution to define marriage as a union between one man and one woman. Some political analysts believe that this is also an attempt to prohibit same-sex partner benefits from being legally offered across the nation.

With the political landscape in flux over same-sex marriage, the future is uncertain with respect to same-sex partner benefits. It appears that employers will continue to do what is best for them in a competitive labor environment, while lobbying for legislative change. And the opponents of gay rights will continue to lobby for restrictions on those rights. We should also expect to see lawsuits from the gay and lesbian community challenging the constitutionality of both state laws and the federal DOMA. It should make for an interesting future, complete with heated debate, legislative agendas at both the state and federal levels, and precedent-setting judicial decisions.

References

Citizens for Equal Protection v. Bruning. 2005. Available at http://www.nebar.com/pdfs/DCOpinPDFs/4–03cv3155.pdf. Accessed Junen 10, 2006.

Elswick, Jill. 2006. "Employer Coalition Seeks Benefits Tax Equity for Domestic Partners." *Employee Benefit News,* January 1, p. 1.

Employee Benefit Research Institute. 2005. *Finances of Employee Benefits: Health Costs Drive Changing Trends.* Washington, DC: Author.

Geisel, Roseanne White. 2004. "Responding to Changing Ideas of Family." *HR Magazine* 49 (8): 94.

Grant, Sarah B. 1994. *Lotus Development Corporation: Spousal Equivalents (B).* Harvard Business School case 9-394-201. Boston: Harvard Business School Publishing.

Grant, Sarah B. 1995. *Lotus Development Corporation: Spousal Equivalents (A).* Harvard Business School case 9-394-197. Boston: Harvard Business School Publishing.

Greenwald, Judy. 2005. "Advent of Gay Marriage Alters Massachusetts Partner Benefits." *Business Insurance* 39 (3): 4–5.

Hewitt Associates. 2005. *Benefit Programs for Domestic Partners & Same Sex Spouses.* Washington, DC: Kenneth McDonnell.

Human Rights Campaign Foundation. 2006. *The State of the Workplace for Gay, Lesbian, Bisexual and Transgender Americans.* Washington, DC: Author.

Institute of Management and Administration. 2004. "Is It Time to Consider Same-Sex Benefits at Your Co.?" *IOMA's Report on Managing Benefits Plans* 4 (8): 1–14.

Lyman, Rick. 2005. "Gay Couples File Suit After Michigan Denies Benefits." *New York Times,* April 4.

Travinski, Michael S. 2006. "Employee Benefits for Domestic Partners and Same-Sex Spouses." *Journal of Pension Benefits* 13 (2): 29–38.

Further Reading: Ashton, Judith, and Gary M. Feldman. 2004. "The Massachusetts Same-Sex Marriage Ruling: Groundbreaking Issues in the American Workplace." *Employee Relations Law Journal* 30 (3): 3–13; Clarkson-Freeman, Pamela A. 2004. "The Defense of Marriage Act (DOMA): Its Impact on Those Seeking Same-Sex Marriages." *Journal of Homosexuality* 48 (2): 1–19; Haslinger, John A. 2004. "Same-Sex Marriage: Benefits Design, Policy and Administration." *Workspan* 47 (7): 16–24; Kratzke, William P. 2005. "The Defense of Marriage Act (DOMA) Is Bad Income Tax Policy." *University of Memphis Law Review* 35 (3): 399–445; Schelberg, Neal S., and Carrie L. Mitnick. 2004. "Same-Sex Marriage—Implications for Employee Benefit Plans." *Employee Benefits Journal* 29 (2): 46–51.

Randy C. Brown

SARBANES-OXLEY ACT

Sarbanes-Oxley Act (also called the Public Company Accounting Reform and Investor Protection Act of 2002) is a federal law passed by both houses of

Congress in 2002. President George W. Bush signed the Sarbanes-Oxley into law on July 30, 2002, and stated that this was the most far-reaching reform of American business practices since the time of Franklin D. Roosevelt. The president also warned, "This law says to every dishonest corporate leader: you will be exposed and punished; the era of low standards and false profits is over; no boardroom in America is above and or beyond the law" (White House 2002).

Sarbanes-Oxley deals with the various aspects of corporate governance. The term "corporate governance" refers to the way a corporation is managed, administered, and controlled by various interested parties such as shareholders, boards of directors, and managers. This law has raised a firestorm of controversy in the United States and also internationally. Why should a law that deals with corporate governance become controversial? To answer this question, we need to understand the nature of a corporation and the place of corporate governance in a corporation.

NATURE OF A CORPORATION

Today in the United States and across the world, the economic landscape is dominated by corporations; many of them are global in nature and can rival governments in terms of budgets and power. The corporate form for conducting a business has gained international popularity. Why? The simple reason is that the corporate form of business offers limited liability to the owners of a corporation. For example, if the owners put $100 in the corporation (buy shares) and the corporation goes bankrupt, then the owners only lose $100. However, if the business is run as a proprietary or partnership, then the owner may be responsible for all debts of the company and may even lose his or her personal assets such as houses and cars. This legal protection offered by the limited liability concept resulted in risk taking and innovation. Today's corporations are owned by thousands of investors who pool their money together and are run by professional managers. The people invest, and managers manage, and if they are successful, both of them reap rewards.

However, as owners generally have no direct hand in running a corporation, there is the possibility of mismanagement by the managers. What is to stop the managers from running the company for their benefit? The history of laws designed to prevent such frauds makes fascinating reading. The corporate form of business has been abused by the managers many times, and a host of laws have been passed as a result. The stock market crash of 1929 was partly caused by management fraud. Consequently, the Securities Act of 1933 and the Securities Exchange Act of 1934 were passed by the Congress.

HISTORY OF SARBANES-OXLEY ACT

In 2000, as the stock market nose-dived and the Internet bubble burst, there was a general discontent among investors regarding corporate governance. The following years saw a succession of corporate scandals that shocked the public.

Table S.1 History of Legislation to Prevent Corporate Fraud.

Legislation	Reason
Owens-Glass Act of 1913: This act provides rules for financial reporting and reserve requirements for banks. Glass-Stegall Act of 1933: This act separated commercial and investment banking.	This act was enacted due to bank failures caused by inadequate or nonexistent reserves. There was a conflict of interest in banks that conducted commercial and investment operations, which resulted in massive banking frauds.
Securities Act of 1933: This act requires disclosure of all important information before securities (shares) are registered.	Shares were issued by many corporations who provided false and misleading information to the public.
Securities Exchange Act of 1934: This act requires that all companies listed on stock exchanges should file quarterly and annual audited reports with the Securities and Exchange Commission.	Many corporations issued unaudited fraudulent financial reports and manipulated their stock price for the benefit of top management.
Investment Company Act of 1940: This act established financial responsibilities for directors and trustees of investment companies (the companies that invest in stock markets). It also made disclosure of financial and managerial structures mandatory.	Investment companies abused the funds provided by the investors by investing in related companies and manipulating stock prices.
Foreign Corrupt Practices Act of 1977: This act made proper design, maintenance, and documentation of internal control systems a requirement for the U.S. companies.	U.S. corporations were bribing foreign officials for business and also made banned political contributions in United States.
FIDCA Improvement Act of 1991: This act mandated reports by managers on internal controls and also compliance with federal law.	There was a massive failure of savings and loan type institutions due to fraud and conflict of interest among officers and directors.
Private Securities Litigation Reform Act of 1995: This act requires auditors and lawyers to inform the Securities and Exchange Commission of any allegations of wrongdoing (including financial wrongdoing) by the corporation.	This act is intended to prevent frivolous litigation against public companies.
Sarbanes-Oxley Act of 2002:	The act was prompted by a series of corporate frauds and failures that involved blue-chip companies in the United States.

Source: Rockness, H., and Rockness, J. 2005. "Legislated Ethics: From Enron to Sarbanes-Oxley, the Impact on Corporate America." *Journal of Business Ethics* 57:31–54.

Table S.2 Time Line for Sarbanes-Oxley Act of 2002.

Time	Event
2000	The stock market begins to cool off.
2001	Enron scandal comes to light; billions of dollars of market value vanishes.
2002	Many well-known companies, such as AOL, Adelphia, Global Crossing, Kmart, Lucent Technologies, Merck, Tyco International, and Waste Management, are found to be culpable of committing fraud.
June 15, 2002	Arthur Andersen, the Enron auditor, is indicted and criminally convicted.
July 9, 2002	President George Bush gives a speech about accounting scandals.
July, 2002	WorldCom files for bankruptcy—the largest corporate bankruptcy ever; a major financial fraud underlies the demise of the company.
July 30, 2002	The Sarbanes-Oxley Act is passed.

Corporate scandals involve unethical behavior on the part of the top managers and generally result in a fraud that involves manipulating the accounting results of the company. The accounting rules in the United States (and in the rest of the world) are flexible and can be interpreted in a variety of ways. Many times these rules are bent illegally by the top management to portray the company in a positive light. Eventually, if the fraud comes out, then the stock price of the company crashes and frequently the company goes bankrupt.

In 2001 and 2002, many prominent U.S. companies were found to be manipulating their financial statements. The biggest fraud involved a company called Enron. This company, based in Houston, Texas, dealt in electricity, natural gas, paper, and communications and claimed revenues of approximately $100 billion in 2000. At the time, the company employed approximately 20,000 people and was considered one of the most innovative companies. The performance of the company was revealed to be a fraud primarily sustained by accounting gimmicks rather than real performance. The company went bankrupt in 2001 and investors and employees sustained billions of dollars of losses. Arthur Andersen, the external auditors of the company, and a leading accounting firm, also went bankrupt with Enron (Enron Fraud InfoCenter 2006).

The public outrage fueled by the Enron scandal forced Congress to take steps that resulted in Sarbanes-Oxley. The act is named after sponsors Senator Paul Sarbanes (D-MD) and Representative Michael Oxley (R-OH) and was overwhelmingly approved by both houses. This act contains 11 titles (sections) that deal with various aspects of corporate governance. Issues such as responsibility of managers, independence of external auditors, and increased financial disclosure are covered by the different titles. This act also moved the responsibility to set the auditing rules and standards from the private sector (the American Institute of Certified Public Accountants set the rules earlier) to the public sector (Public Company Accounting Oversight Board now has the authority to set the auditing rules).

REQUIREMENTS OF SARBANES-OXLEY

A major thread that runs through corporate frauds is the concentration of power in the hands of top management. Such concentration enables top management to operate over and above internal controls in the corporation. Internal control is a system of checks and balances in the company. Such checks and balances prevent and detect errors and fraud. However, internal controls do not guarantee absence of errors and fraud. A good system of internal controls and corporate governance prevents top executives from exercising unbridled power. Sarbanes-Oxley introduced many new requirements to prevent such concentration and abuse of executive power. The major provisions are summarized below (Sarbanes-Oxley Act n.d.).

Responsibilities of the Managers

Sarbanes-Oxley imposed a number of new responsibilities, obligations, and prohibitions on senior management, including the certification of the accuracy of financial reports, the creation of internal control reports, and restrictions on personal loans and stock sales. The act also stipulates heavier penalties for criminal behavior.

Public corporations are required to issue an annual report containing financial statements, management discussion of operating results, and the auditor's report. Sarbanes-Oxley now requires the chief executive officer and chief financial officer to certify that financial reports accurately reflect the company's real performance. In the past, top executives accused of fraud often pleaded ignorance of accounting matters and tried to shift blame onto accountants. This certification closes such loopholes.

Managers are also required to issue an internal control report with each annual report. The internal control report states that establishing and maintaining internal controls is the responsibility of the management. It also assesses the existing internal control systems' strengths and weaknesses. External auditors then attest to the veracity of that report. Auditors cannot check every transaction in the company since modern corporations have trillions of transactions; as such, they rely on internal controls to evaluate the financial position of the company. If top management is negligent in establishing and enforcing internal controls, audits are ineffective. The internal controls report issued by management compels top management to pay attention to internal controls.

Sarbanes-Oxley also bans corporations from offering personal loans to their executive officers and directors. For example, former WorldCom CEO Bernard Ebbers received approximately $300 million dollars in personal loans from the company. Many such instances of personal loans came to light in 2001 and 2002. Sarbanes-Oxley put an end to such practices.

Many top managers are granted stock options or stock of the company. Since the top managers have better information about the company than the average public, they can time the sale of stock to reap maximum profits. Sarbanes-Oxley does not ban this kind of insider trading outright (except under certain conditions) but requires that such sales be reported quickly for the benefit of all investors.

Compensation for CEOs and CFOs is required to be disclosed publicly. Such disclosure was required before Sarbanes-Oxley; however, now the information is easy to find and more transparent. Also, top managers are required to return bonuses awarded for financial performance later found to be based on faulty accounting.

Criminal and civil penalties for violation of securities laws and misstating financial statements are more severe under the new law. In the past, laws dealing with financial fraud were lenient and courts tended to award light sentences, and rarely any jail time, to top managers. Sarbanes-Oxley now provides long jail sentences and stiff fines for the managers who knowingly and willfully misstate financial statements.

Responsibilities of the Auditors

Auditors are expected to be independent from their clients. In the past auditing contracts were often made on the basis of friendships and business relationships, which compromised auditors' independence from the companies whose books they examined. Sarbanes-Oxley contains various provisions to strengthen auditor independence.

Auditors are banned from providing other fee-based services that could lead to a conflict of interest and undermine their independence from companies they have been hired to audit. Before Sarbanes-Oxley, auditors were allowed to provide certain consulting services such as advice for hiring personnel, internal auditing, and designing financial information systems. Sarbanes-Oxley provides a long list of services that can no longer be performed by auditors. Such a ban is designed to prevent a business relationship between the auditor and the client. It is believed that these other, possibly more profitable, contracts compromise auditors' independence and undermine their willingness to adhere strictly to auditing guidelines.

Sarbanes-Oxley also aims to prevent auditors from becoming too cozy with their clients. The audit partner supervising the audit should be rotated every five years, which, it is hoped, will encourage professional, as opposed to personal, relationships between the partner and the top management.

Furthermore, a person employed by an audit firm is barred from assuming a top managerial position with the client company for at least one year after leaving the auditing firm. This provision prevents what used to be called revolving doors between the audit firms and client companies.

Finally, the newly established Public Company Accounting Oversight Board now has the power to investigate auditing firms and penalize them for noncompliance with the law.

Responsibility of the Board of Directors

In the corporate form of business, a company's owners, or shareholders, appoint members to a board of directors. The board of directors, in turn, is supposed to see to it that the company is run with the best interests of the owners, not top management, in mind. In the real world, the CEO often chooses board members from among friends and acquaintances, leading many shareholders to believe their interests are given lower priority than management's. In an attempt to remedy this cronyism, Sarbanes-Oxley contains provisions to strengthen the independence of the members of the board of directors from management. The audit committee (a committee of directors that deals with financial matters) of the board of directors should have people on the audit committee who do not serve (and get money from) the company in any other capacity and should not work for a subsidiary of the company. The audit committee should keep track of complaints received regarding financial improprieties and problems with internal controls. If necessary, the audit committee can hire independent counsel to investigate important matters.

Responsibility of the SEC

The SEC (Securities and Exchange Commission) is the federal agency whose duties include the administration of the Sarbanes-Oxley Act. The SEC has been granted new powers and an expanded budget to supervise compliance with the new law and can:

- Set standards of professional conduct for lawyers who practice before the SEC
- Prohibit a person from serving as a director or an officer of a public company
- Freeze payments to officers or managers of the company if it suspects that securities laws have been violated

These provisions in the Sarbanes-Oxley seem to be straightforward and appropriate for proper corporate conduct. However, the enactment and implementation of this act raises a host of ethical and operational questions that are still being debated.

PROBLEMS WITH SARBANES-OXLEY

The objections raised against Sarbanes-Oxley are philosophical and operational in nature. The primary problem in any legislation designed to prevent corporate fraud is the price paid by many for the mistakes of a few. The question that has been repeatedly asked is, can you legislate ethics and honesty? Can you make a law that makes top executive behave in the interests of investors? These questions become more pertinent when we understand that the majority of top managers are ethical and honest. The mistakes of a few cause problems for all businesses since compliance with new laws costs a lot of money and effort, which distracts businesses from doing business. On the other hand, a few top executives have caused enormous damage to the integrity of the capitalist system and ruined thousands of lives. There are arguments on both the sides and no clear answers have emerged.

Romano raises a compelling philosophical argument against Sarbanes-Oxley (Romano 2005). Romano argues that Sarbanes-Oxley demands substantive corporate governance mandates. This means that the act specifies how a business should be conducted and is intrusive in nature. The earlier laws required complete disclosure of all information but not the directives on how to conduct business. Romano evaluates the academic literature related to corporate governance requirements mandated by Sarbanes-Oxley and concludes that such a far-reaching law is not required. Gifford and Howe argue that the requirements of the act that deal with the conduct of business (as opposed to the disclosure of information) may result in corporations foregoing promising business opportunities (Gifford and Howe 2004). Thus, the act may in fact be detrimental to business. The crux of the argument is that the government mandates do not allow more efficient and effective private-sector solutions to bubble up. However, conclusive evidence for or against these arguments may not come for a long period of time.

Sarbanes-Oxley also applies to foreign corporations listed on the U.S. stock exchanges. The requirements of the act apply to 1,300 foreign companies, and none of these companies was involved in any corporate scandal (Falencki 2004). Since Sarbanes-Oxley requirements often supersede the home country regulations for these companies, there were angry protests from the United Kingdom, Germany, and Japan. These countries argued that Sarbanes-Oxley is not conducive to the smooth operation of global business. A few foreign corporations have already removed themselves from the U.S. stock exchanges because they do not wish to comply with Sarbanes-Oxley.

Sarbanes-Oxley also creates operational problems for the businesses. These are discussed now.

Costs of Compliance: The major complaint of many executives that it is taking a lot of money to comply with the requirements of the act. The costs of compliance primarily stem from Section 404 of the act. This section requires that the internal controls be maintained and documented by all public corporations. Many corporations have found that it takes a great deal of time to document the controls. Many top managers have spent a considerable amount of time making sure that their departments and companies complied with Sarbanes-Oxley. This time spent has distracted these executives from their business duties. The estimates of the cost range from 5 to 10 percent of profits to thousands of dollars per employee (Cocheo 2005).

Section 404 has also raised many other concerns. Will this section result in outsourcing and offshoring of accounting and finance jobs? Will this section cause public companies to go private? There are many software packages helping companies cope with Section 404. What is the liability in case software packages do not function as advertised?

Small Publicly Listed Companies: Many small public companies do not have the resources of large corporations. Such companies will find it very difficult to comply with the act, particularly Section 404, and may have to delist and go private. Additionally, this act may pose problems for companies wishing to go public. If the act applies to nonprofit organizations, then it will cause major problems for such organizations.

Table S.3 Section 404: A Four-Letter Word?

Section 404: Management Assessment of Internal Controls

(a) Rules required.—The Commission shall prescribe rules requiring each annual report required by section 13(a) or 15(d) of the Securities Exchange Act of 1934 (15 U.S.C. 78m or 78o(d)) to contain an internal control report, which shall—

(1) state the responsibility of management for establishing and maintaining an adequate internal control structure and procedures for financial reporting; and

(2) contain an assessment, as of the end of the most recent fiscal year of the issuer, of the effectiveness of the internal control structure and procedures of the issuer for financial reporting.

(b) Internal Control Evaluation and Reporting.—With respect to the internal control assessment required by subsection (a), each registered public accounting firm that prepares or issues the audit report for the issuer shall attest to, and report on, the assessment made by the management of the issuer. An attestation made under this subsection shall be made in accordance with standards for attestation engagements issued or adopted by the Board. Any such attestation shall not be the subject of a separate engagement.

Source: Sarbanes-Oxley Act. Available at http://frwebgate.access.gpo.gov/cgi-bin/getdoc.cgi?dbname=107_cong_bills&docid=f:h3763enr.txt.pdf. Accessed July 1, 2006

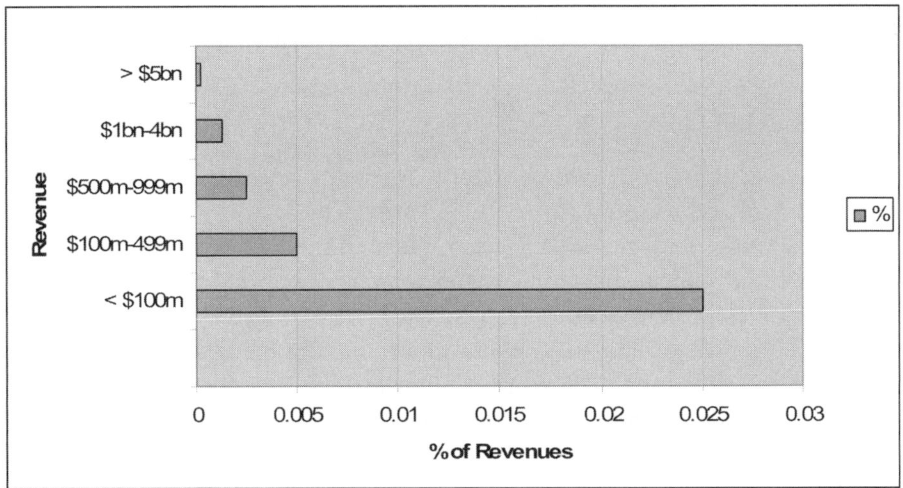

Figure S.1 Compliance costs vs. revenues.

Source: "A Price Worth Paying?" 2005. Economist. May 19. Available at http://www.economist.com/business/displayStory.cfm?story_id=3984019. Accessed June 17, 2006.

Impact on Directors and Managers: The new requirements make it hard for companies to hire directors on their board. The insurance rates for directors and officers are skyrocketing.

Audit Fees: Since the auditor's responsibilities have increased considerably due to the act, there is much more audit work. The audit fees increased considerably after the act.

The Auditor and the Management: The auditor was earlier used as a resource by the management and was sometimes a partner in strategic thinking. However due to the act, most of the auditors do not participate in any strategic and operational decision making. This has affected communication between the auditors and management.

Costs of Independence: The consulting services provided by the auditors enhanced their business knowledge of the client. The auditor is now not allowed to perform these services for the client. Such a ban lowers the knowledge base of the auditor regarding client businesses and may adversely affect the auditing process.

Costs of New Accounting Infrastructure: Since auditing rule-making is shifted from the private sector to the public sector, the future of the existing mechanisms have become uncertain. The existing investment in the standard-setting institutions may be wasted. Additionally, the investment in the public sector and design of new rule-making mechanisms may cost additional money.

A review of the literature indicates that there have been many complaints regarding Sarbanes-Oxley, particularly by small companies and managers. This is not unexpected, since the act has far-reaching implications not only for internal controls and financial reporting but also for corporate governance. The question now is: are there any benefits to the act? Interestingly, new findings have begun to find benefits. Also, many corporations have taken the provisions of the act and creatively used those to control costs and increase competitiveness.

THE BENEFITS OF SARBANES-OXLEY

The costs of complying with new law are generally high since it involves initial investment and learning curve effects; Sarbanes-Oxley is no exception. The costs are also tangible, quantifiable, and incurred immediately. The benefits of compliance and operational improvements are diffuse, long term, and harder to quantify. Michael Oxley counters his critics, saying: "How can you measure the value of knowing that company books are sounder than they were before?" He also adds that these costs are in reality investments for the future. Moody's, a credit-rating firm, believes that companies are strengthening their accounting controls and investing in infrastructure required to support quality financial reporting. Huron, a consulting firm, says that companies are relying on themselves to sort out complex financial issues and not blindly following the auditor's advice. Dennis Nally, the chairman of PWC, believes that over time America will see fewer incidents of accounting fraud ("A Price Worth Paying". 2005).

Concrete empirical evidence to support various claims may take time and may not be conclusive. However, a study conducted by the Institute of Internal

Auditors Research Foundation points out the operational benefits due to Sarbanes-Oxley. The top ten areas are described below (Rittenberg and Muller 2005).

- The control environment in the company is now closely assessed and scrutinized by the board, audit committee, and management.
- The controls are regularly monitored and evaluated by the management.
- The closing of books and year-end adjusting entries is more structured. In the past, some fraud has slipped at this stage.
- The antifraud policies and procedures are in place and responsibilities are clearly defined. In the case of Enron, concerns raised by lower-level accountants went unheeded.
- The risks associated with information technology and computers are better understood and proper controls are being put in place.
- The documentation of controls has resulted in proper training of employees and better understanding of risks.
- The relationship between controls and risk is better understood in different corporations.
- The operating personnel and management understand their responsibility for controls and do not view controls as an accounting problem.
- The audit trail—connections between people, transactions, and documents—is improved. Such improved audit trail is useful in pinpointing responsibility.
- The basic controls such separating duties so that no one person controls the entire transaction (such as collecting, recording, and depositing cash) are being implemented and are no longer being neglected.

The benefits of Sarbanes-Oxley may accrue over the next few years or perhaps a decade. A quick quantification of costs and benefits is not possible. Sarbanes-Oxley is not intended to be a short-term fix but rather a long-term solution for many vexing problems encountered in accounting and finance. The accounting processes will be streamlined due to new procedures and the benefits may flow over the many years (White 2005). At this point, the studies are basically capturing one aspect of corporate governance and do not illuminate the entire picture.

SUMMARY

Sarbanes-Oxley is the latest salvo in an unending war against corporate fraud and wrongdoings; the difference is that the act ventures into areas not explored before. The act came into being as a reaction to the bankruptcy of Enron—an extremely powerful global corporation in its heyday. The act requires that many aspects of corporate governance, which were earlier left to management's discretion, now must conform to new legal mandates. The big question is, will this law really help reduce corporate fraud in America? If the answer is yes, then the costs to implement the law are really investments. But if not, this law may impair the competitiveness of U.S. business. Any statements beyond the obvious will be speculations.

Many powerful forces—for example, global corporations, top managers, big accounting firms, politicians, and lobbyists—fight when accounting rules are set. These groups have competing agendas and different motives, and these do not always coincide with the public interest. However, sometimes momentous events such as a series of corporate frauds and bankruptcies converge to create the need for the passage of sweeping legislation. Sarbanes-Oxley is one such piece of legislation, and finding objective opinions and studies that deal with the effects of this law is very difficult.

Already lobbying efforts have begun to eliminate or dilute the requirements of Sarbanes-Oxley. It is not clear what provisions of the act will be standing when the dust settles. The biggest test of Sarbanes-Oxley will probably come when another major corporate fraud is discovered within a company that has passed Sarbanes-Oxley's requirements. The eternal chase between the law and the outlaws will, however, keep on going.

References

Cocheo, S. 2005. "SOX Gone Silly: Sarbanes-Oxley Issues That Make CEOs Mad." *ABA Banking Journal* 97 (8): 50–54.

Enron Fraud InfoCenter. Available at http://www.enronfraudinfocenter.com. Accessed May 29, 2006.

Falencki, C. 2004. "Sarbanes-Oxley: Ignoring the Presumption against Extraterritoriality." *George Washington International Law Review* 36 (5): 1211–38.

Gifford, R., and H. Howe. 2004. "Regulation and Unintended Consequences: Thoughts on Sarbanes-Oxley." *CPA Journal*. Available at http://www.nysscpa.org/cpajournal/2004/604/perspectives/p6.htm. Accessed July 9, 2006.

"A Price Worth Paying?" 2005. *The Economist,* May 19. Available at http://www.economist.com/business/displayStory.cfm?story_id=3984019. Accessed June 4, 2006.

Rittenberg, L., and P. Miller. 2005. *Sarbanes-Oxley Section 404: Looking at the Benefits.* Altamonte Springs, FL: IIA Research Foundation. Available at www.theiia.org/download.cfm?file=343. Accessed July 6, 2006.

Romano, R. 2005. "The Sarbanes-Oxley Act and the Making of Quack Corporate Governance." *Yale Law Journal* 114 (7): 1521–611.

Sarbanes-Oxley Act Provisions. Available at http://frwebgate.access.gpo.gov/cgi-bin/getdoc.cgi?dbname=107_cong_bills&docid=f:h3763enr.txt.pdf.

White, B. 2005. "Sarbanes-Oxley Section 404: First Year Lessons." *Mortgage Banking* 66 (3): 15–16.

White House, Office of the Press Secretary. 2002. *President Bush Signs Corporation Corruption Bill.* Available at http://www.whitehouse.gov/news/releases/2002/07/20020730html. Accessed May 29, 2006.

Further Reading: Lucci, John Paul. 2003. "Enron: The Bankruptcy Heard Round the World and the International Richochet of Sarbanes-Oxley." *Alb. Law Review,* 67: 211; Sarbanes-Oxley Implementation Central. n.d. *Center for Audit Quality.* Available at.http://www.aicpa.org/sarbanes/index.asp.

Ash Deshmukh

SAVING

Very generally speaking, "saving" refers to income that is set aside, and not consumed, in the period when the income is earned. Current saving can be crucially important to the future welfare of individual households and to society. First, savings accumulated in the past is used to sustain consumption during periods of economic distress and in retirement. Second, saving sustained over long periods of time tends to increase future income and the standard of living.

Note the difference between "saving" and "savings" in the previous paragraph. Saving is an activity performed during a particular period of time: it is the act of setting aside income for future use. Savings, on the other hand, refers to the accumulated stock of dollars saved over many periods. For example, suppose a worker's saving is $1,000 each year for 10 years and earns 5 percent interest per year. The total accumulation of savings at the end of the tenth year is $13,208.80. Thus, saving is an addition to the accumulated stock of savings.

An individual household's saving is important because accumulated savings can be used to shore up consumption should a household member become unemployed or too ill to work. Additionally, household saving contributes to future asset income and can determine individuals' living standards in retirement.

Corporate saving is important because it provides a considerable fraction of funds firms use to finance investment in capital, such as plants and equipment, research and development, and patents. As a result, corporate saving tends to increase firms' future capacities to generate profits.

Government saving is important because it can augment or diminish the level of national saving. National saving is the sum of household, corporate, and government saving. National saving is important in the short run because changes in saving can affect production, employment, and prices. It is important in the long run because the level of saving affects the standard of living.

For example, in the short run, temporary changes in the level of national saving can affect firms' incentives to produce output, the rate of unemployment, and the rate at which prices change. These changes can have substantial effects on economic welfare. Some economic historians believe that an unusually large increase in household saving near the beginning of the Great Depression reduced output and increased unemployment in the early 1930s. In the long run, the level of saving determines the size of the nation's capital stock. The size of the capital stock is important because capital is the source of all income in the long run; thus, if used efficiently, saving contributes to the long run standard of living. Some economists believe saving also can affect an economy's long-run growth rate. In this case, relatively small changes in national saving, sustained over many periods, can have enormous impacts on living standards.

However, in order to have these beneficent effects, saving must be used efficiently. Whether saving is employed efficiently depends on a nation's level of financial development. The fundamental economic purpose of the financial system is the transfer of funds from savers to borrowers. The financial system provides two mechanisms that can be used to initiate the transfer of funds. First, savers can put their saving to work by purchasing stocks or bonds in financial markets. Second, savers can deposit funds in financial intermediaries, such as commercial banks, pension funds, and insurance companies. Borrowers finance capital investments by selling stocks or bonds in the financial markets, or by borrowing funds from financial intermediaries.

Efficient funds transfer, from savers to borrowers who wish to undertake productive capital investment, is crucial to the economic vitality of a nation. If the financial system fails to transfer saving efficiently, the saved funds tend to end up being wasted in unproductive uses, or they may not be used at all. In this case, the nation's capital stock can stagnate, and growth in the standard of living can fall behind or diminish.

HOW IS SAVING MEASURED?

Because of its importance, government agencies spend substantial resources measuring saving. The U.S. Bureau of Economic Analysis (BEA) reports measurements of saving. The BEA reports gross and net saving. As capital is used to produce commodities, it wears out or becomes obsolete. In either case, old capital loses value over time: that is, capital depreciates. Net saving is gross saving after adjustment for capital depreciation. Economists focus on net saving because net saving represents growth in the stock of capital available for production.

The BEA uses the terms "personal saving" and "household saving" interchangeably. The BEA defines net personal saving as personal income minus taxes and personal spending. Personal income includes worker salaries plus income earned by small businesses, such as proprietors, as well as income earned by some nonprofit institutions serving individuals, like charitable organizations. Personal income also includes interest and dividends earned by households and small businesses. Personal spending includes spending on commodities and interest paid on household debt. In dollars, net personal saving in the United States in 2004 was $159.3 billion. The net personal saving rate, as a fraction of national income, was about 1.4 percent.

The BEA defines undistributed corporate profits as corporate income remaining in corporate treasuries after dividend distributions to shareholders. Undistributed corporate profit represents corporate saving. In 2004, the dollar value of U.S. net corporate saving was $343.0 billion. The net corporate saving rate was about 2.9 percent of national income.

Government saving includes saving by federal, state, and local governments. In dollar terms, net government saving in the United States in 2004 was –$394.9 billion. The net government saving rate was about –3.4 percent of national income. Government saving is negative when government spending exceeds tax collections. Governments finance the difference between spending and taxes by borrowing funds in the market for bonds. Therefore, in 2004, the government borrowed a substantial fraction of funds saved by households and firms. There is no legal restriction on the amount of funds the federal government can borrow in a year. In contrast, state and local governments often are legally bound to balance the budgets they use to finance day-to-day expenses (e.g., salaries). It is not uncommon for states and local governments to have positive net saving in a year. Saving at the state and local level helps finance federal government borrowing. Some federal government borrowing is financed by savers in foreign countries.

Therefore, the net value of U.S. national saving was $107.4 billion in 2004, or 0.9 percent of national income. The BEA revises its income and saving measures on a regular basis as more information becomes available. Therefore, these estimates are likely to change in the future. Nevertheless, they are not expected to change by amounts that will alter the picture drawn here.

Measuring saving is not as simple as the above discussion may make it appear. There are difficult conceptual issues. For example, putting aside income to pay for education is an important form of saving. However, the BEA treats education funding as consumption (spending), not saving. Thus, an increase in education spending tends to reduce saving reported by the BEA.

WHAT DETERMINES HOW MUCH A NATION SAVES?

As a result of saving's important effects on household and social welfare, a substantial amount of research has been conducted to learn what determines saving and the effects government policies have on saving.

Economic theory and empirical evidence suggest consumers adjust saving to avoid large jumps and declines in consumption. For example, households benefiting from an unexpected temporary jump in income spend only a fraction of the windfall when it's received: they save the remaining fraction for the future. Unexpected shortfalls in household income tend to reduce saving. As well, higher corporate income contributes directly to corporate saving. In general, saving tends to rise with income.

In contrast, an increase in expected future income, current income held constant, can lead to more borrowing and less saving. For example, professional students and young families in newly formed households often spend more than their incomes with the expectation that higher future income will be sufficient to repay the debt.

A perhaps substantial fraction of household saving is put aside to finance retirement spending. The more a household saves when young, the higher the household's standard of living tends to be in retirement. Households that expect to be retired a relatively long time tend to save more. Therefore, the higher the fraction of the population that is in the labor force is, and the longer these workers expect to live, the higher individual and national saving tends to be.

The interest rate is the economic reward for saving. Saved funds earn interest when deposited in saving accounts, mutual funds, or pension funds. Or, if the saved funds are used to purchase corporate stocks or bonds, they earn dividends or capital gains. Everything else constant, the higher the interest rate, the more households are willing to save. Tax policies have had substantial effects on after-tax interest rates. This is discussed further below.

Some households appear to be more willing than others to forego current consumption and to save. These households are said to be more patient.

Countries with a relatively high fraction of patient households tend to save more than countries where households are impatient. A possible explanation of Japan's high saving rate is that the Japanese appear to be more patient than people in other countries.

The risk that future wage income will turn out to be less than expected, or that future expenses will turn out to be more than expected, leads to saving as a precaution against economic distress. Precautionary saving is a form of self-insurance against disappointing wages or unanticipated expenses.

Government policy has substantial effects on household, corporate, and national saving. As currently structured, the corporate income tax reduces the incentive for firms to invest in capital and the level of corporate savings available to spend on capital. Income taxes reduce after-tax interest rates, which tends to discourage saving. Some economists argue that a carefully implemented consumption tax would not tax income generated by new investments, so it would not discourage saving. Economists have used computer models to compare the effects of income and consumption taxes. Several studies indicate that a shift from income taxes to consumption taxes is capable of producing long-run increases in the capital stock and the standard of living.

Under certain circumstances, government borrowing could lower national saving. To see this, suppose, for the moment, that taxes do not affect the incentive to save. Suppose the government balances its budget this year, taking in tax collections just equal to spending. Now suppose the government reduces taxes next year but does not reduce government spending. The government must borrow to pay next year's difference between taxes and spending: this is a deficit-financed tax cut. Everything else constant, deficit-financed tax cuts mean the government is saving less. Lower government saving could cause a decline in national saving. The effect on national saving depends on the way households respond to the tax cut. If they save the tax cut, then household saving will increase by an amount sufficient to offset the decline in government saving: in this case, the deficit-financed tax cut would not reduce national saving. However, if households spend some or all of the tax cut, national saving would decline. In this case, the deficit-financed tax cut reduces national saving. Households working when the tax cut is implemented benefit from higher after-tax income. Future generations are worse off, because they inherit a smaller capital stock. In this case, the deficit-financed tax cut transfers wealth from future generations to current households.

The effect of federal government budget deficits on national saving is an important but unresolved issue. Some economists, like Robert Barro and his followers, argue that deficit-financed tax cuts are as likely to increase national saving as decrease it. First, households alive when a deficit-financed tax cut is first implemented may respond by saving the tax cut, because they are reluctant to benefit at the expense of future generations. In this case, national saving would not be affected. Second, the tax decrease alters incentives and could encourage higher household saving. For example, the income-tax cut reduces the tax penalty on interest income. Also, households may respond to the tax cut by working more or opening new businesses, thus, earning higher income, part of which will be saved. Empirical research has not provided decisive evidence on the saving effects of deficit-financed tax cuts.

The Social Security program in the United States is a pay-as-you-go system. That is, the Social Security Administration collects payroll taxes from current workers and transfers the funds to current retirees. Some economists argue that pay-as-you-go Social Security reduces national saving. Household saving may decline when pay-as-you-go Social Security is introduced, if current workers expect that after they retire their Social Security benefits will be fully financed by others. If, as a result, current workers do not reduce their consumption to pay their Social Security taxes, household saving declines. In this case, the introduction of pay-as-you-go Social Security reduces national saving. Retirees and workers living at the time pay-as-you-go Social Security is introduced benefit at the expense of future generations, receiving benefits they have not paid for. Future generations inherit a smaller capital stock. This is similar to the transfer of wealth potentially generated by deficit-financed tax cuts.

On the other hand, it can be argued that Social Security is unlikely to reduce national saving for the same reason that deficit-financed tax cuts do not: young workers may not decrease saving when Social Security is introduced because they are unwilling to benefit at the expense of future generations.

Economic research suggests one cannot fully appreciate the importance of saving without understanding the economic role of the financial system. A major achievement of modern finance is the ability to transfer funds from savers to borrowers in ways that reduce risk. Risk reduction has resulted from financial innovations that improve risk assessment and improve lenders' abilities to identify investments having the greatest potential for success. Thus, financial development increases social welfare by fostering the creation of new production processes that improve worker productivity and provide new products that consumers value.

The financial system's ability to allocate saving to productive uses may be as important to society as the amount saved. For example, the fraction of income saved in Japan tends to be much larger than in the United Kingdom. Nonetheless, the United Kingdom appears, on average, to be more innovative and productive. The difference stems, at least in part, from the fact that the highly developed and transparent financial system in the United Kingdom is more proficient at directing savings to productive investments. Although Japan saves a larger fraction of its income, a smaller fraction may end up in uses that provide economic benefits to Japanese citizens. This example indicates that it is possible for economies with relatively low saving rates, but highly developed financial systems, to be more productive and enjoy higher standards of living than economies with higher saving rates, but undeveloped financial sectors. As well, societies with outmoded financial systems tend to discourage borrowing. In this case, households must save to purchase expensive items, such as cars and homes. Saving tends to be high, but the high saving is a manifestation of the outmoded financial system, not efficient transfer of funds to socially useful investments.

DOES THE HOUSING BOOM EXPLAIN LOW SAVING RATES?

Could the housing boom be the cause of the recent low rate of saving by American households? The logic is as follows. Households consider all forms of saving when evaluating how much they need to put aside for the future. Included in this consideration are financial savings like stocks and bonds, mutual funds, and CDs (certificates of deposit). But also included are the wealth that households have in various kinds of assets. And the biggest household asset—of course—is their homes.

So if home values rise, households know they can convert those values to cash either by selling the home or by borrowing against the value in the form of home equity loans. The point is that increases in home values can be a substitute for saving out of current income. Thus, as the appreciation in home values has gone up, we would expect to see saving rates go down.

Do the data support this proposition? Look at the figure. It compares the personal saving rate with the rate of increase in home values since 1980. From 1980 to the mid-1990s there appears to be no relationship between the two rates. Both the saving rate and the home appreciation rate fell on trend. Yet there is a clear relationship since the mid-1990s: the saving rate fell and the home appreciation rate rose.

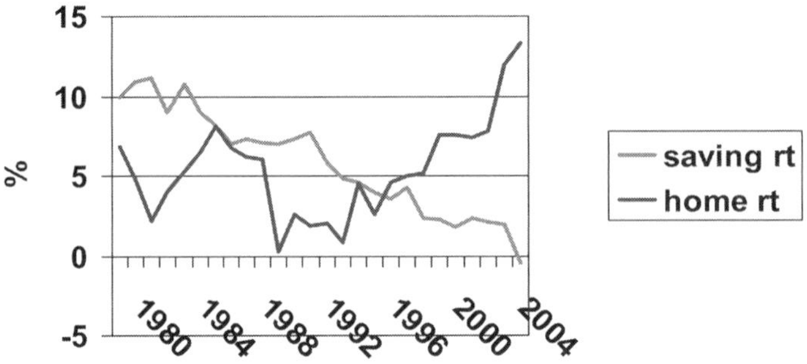

Figure S.2 U.S. personal saving rate, in percent.

Source: U.S. Department of Commerce. Available at www.commerce.gov.

So what does that mean? Is there a tie between the saving rate and the home appreciation rate or not? The answer is that there does appear to be a link, but only since the mid-1990s, for a couple of reasons. First, a higher percentage of U.S. households (close to 70%) have owned homes in the last decade than in previous times. Therefore, more households have recently benefited from rising home values.

Second, tax changes in the last decade have both decreased the taxes on home equity values and made it financially more lucrative for households to access those values via home equity loans. These tax changes have caused more homeowners to pay attention to their home values and consider those values a source of saving.

IS THE UNITED STATES PERSONAL SAVINGS RATE TOO LOW?

Some economists and policy makers express concern that U.S. personal saving is too low. To understand this concern, it is useful to distinguish saving and the saving rate.

"Saving" refers to the number of dollars of income saved. "Saving rate" refers to the fraction of income saved, the ratio of saving to income. In fact, saving and the saving rate sometimes move in opposite directions. To understand this, recall that gross saving includes capital depreciation. In 1983, the U.S. gross saving rate, as a fraction of gross domestic product, or the value of all production in the country, was 17.2 percent: by 2004, the rate had dropped to 13.2 percent. Nevertheless, after adjusting for inflation, gross saving rose from $976.6 billion to $1,424.0 billion during the period. Some are concerned about the low saving rate because, holding income constant, a lower saving rate means smaller additions to accumulated savings, which could slow growth in the standard of living. Nevertheless, the saving rate is a ratio of saving to income, so the saving rate could decline even while saving is rising, if income rises faster. That sort of saving rate decline may not be such a bad thing.

Is the U.S. saving rate too low? The question arises, at least in part, as a result of figures showing that the U.S. personal after-tax saving rate, as a fraction of after-tax personal disposable income, has declined steadily since the early 1980s (see Figure S.3). In 2005 the personal saving rate was negative for the first time since the Great Depression. Saving rates in other developed economies also have declined. For example, the personal saving rate was nearly 14 percent in the late 1980s in both Germany and Japan and declined, respectively, to about 10 percent and 7 percent in 2005. However, the U.S. saving rate was lower to begin with and has declined by a larger amount than the saving rates in these countries.

The personal saving rate clearly has declined substantially from its early 1980s high. Has it become too low? Several factors must be considered to answer this question. First, the saving rate may have been higher than desirable in the early

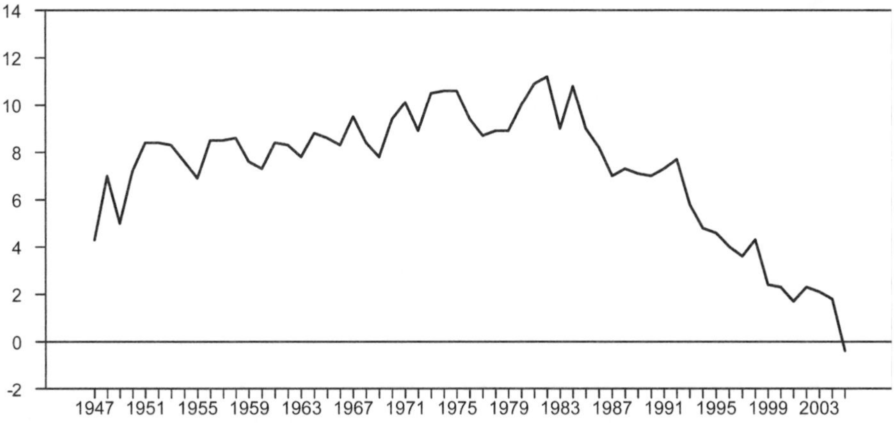

Figure S.3 Saving rate vs. increase in home values.

Source: U.S. Department of Commerce, Office of Federal Housing Enterprise Oversight. Available at www.commerce.gov

1980s. After all, the saving rate was also lower before the 1980s. The saving rate may not have to return to early 1980s levels to meet society's economic goals. Second, at least part of the saving rate decline may be more apparent than real if the rate is not measured in the most economically meaningful way. Third, some changes in the economic environment can make a decline in the saving rate economically reasonable. Fourth, and more ominous, the declining saving rate may be the result of bad choices that could prevent households and society from achieving their future economic goals. Finally, several of these possibilities may simultaneously be responsible for the decline in the saving rate.

The decline in the personal saving rate could result from the way it is measured, especially if all forms of saving aren't considered. Increases in the market value of assets permit increases in consumption, so they are an important part of economic income. The past two decades have seen enormous increases in the market value of household assets, like equity in homes. However, the BEA does not include capital gains income when it measures household income. If capital gains income were included, measured income and, therefore, the reported saving rate would be higher. Exacerbating this problem, BEA subtracts taxes on capital gains income from measured income, and this reduces the reported saving rate.

To finance education and research and development today, society must forego current consumption. As is the case for capital in general, accumulated technical knowledge and skills produce income. Therefore, spending on education and research and development is an important forms of saving. However, the BEA treats education and research and development as current consumption, which lowers the reported saving rate. Because research and development and education have increased as shares of the U.S. economy during the past two decades, this treatment has reduced the reported saving rate. This tends to give a misleading picture of the nation's true ability to produce future income.

The saving rate is the ratio of saving to income. If income rises rapidly, everything else constant, the saving rate tends to decline. Average incomes have increased relatively rapidly during the past two decades, and this has tended to reduce the saving rate.

Net national saving is gross national saving minus depreciation. Everything else constant, faster depreciation tends to reduce measured net saving. For example, U.S. gross saving increased 153.0 percent between 1983 and 2004. Depreciation increased 223.0 percent. The relative increase in deprecation has contributed to the decline in the net national saving rate. Faster depreciation results, in part, from relatively high rates of innovation because the introduction of new types of capital makes old capital less valuable. Thus, part of the decline in the net national saving rate results from welfare improving increases in technology.

So, one can conclude that the true personal saving rate almost certainly has not declined by as much as the reported saving rate. Nevertheless, the size of the decline in the reported figures suggests the true saving rate has declined, even after measurement problems are accounted for.

The decline in the saving rate may have resulted in part from changes in the economic environment that make a lower saving rate economically reasonable.

First, financial innovation has improved lenders' abilities to assess risk. Risk-reducing financial innovations appear to have encouraged lenders to increase loans to households and small business borrowers that previously had been shut out of loan markets. If borrowers who benefit in this way were inclined to borrow before the innovations took place but were constrained against doing so, the increase in borrowing makes them better off. However, the higher borrowing rate reduces the reported saving rate.

Second, growth in the global economy has been rapid during the past two decades. As developing countries become richer, they tend to save more (China is a good example today, and Japan and South Korea are examples from previous decades). Advanced economies with highly efficient financial markets are relatively safe places for rapidly developing countries to invest. The resulting global increase in saving tends to reduce the interest rate, which tends to discourage saving and encourage borrowing in more advanced economies such as the United States. In part, the lower U.S. saving rate tends to reflect higher global savings.

Also, during the past two decades there has been a continuation of the trend away from manufacturing production and toward services production. Service jobs are less physically demanding than most manufacturing jobs. In addition, advances in medical and telecommunications technologies have improved the health and mobility of senior members of households, as well as the ability of less mobile members to contribute to the workforce from remote locations. Thus, modern workers can hold jobs later in life than workers of past generations; thus workers will not have to save as much to meet their retirement consumption goals. However the secular increase in longevity tends to have an opposite effect on saving. The net effect on the saving rate could be negative, but the evidence is not yet in on this question.

More ominously, the decline in the saving rate may have resulted from changes in behavior that will make it harder for households to meet future consumption goals. U.S. households may have become less concerned about risks of economic distress. Or they may simply have become less willing to put off consumption to the future. And the increase in the number of U.S. retirees relative to workers has tended to reduce national saving. If these changes result from poor risk evaluation or short-sighted planning, the decline in the saving rate may be a harbinger of economic disappointment in the future.

GOVERNMENT PROGRAMS DESIGNED TO INCREASE SAVING

During the past 50 years or so, economists have learned a great deal about what determines a nation's standard of living, and what determines how fast economies grow. Saving is a crucial ingredient. These advances in understanding the importance of saving, together with declining saving rates, have led to the development of policies designed to increase saving. Most policies provide tax breaks for saving.

The U.S. federal government and many state governments have created a large number of tax-favored saving plans. Contributions to employer-provided pension plans are excluded from taxable income. Individual retirement accounts and college saving plans postpone taxes on income from savings. These plans reduce the tax on income earned in particular types of saving. It is hoped that the resulting increase in after-tax capital income would encourage households to save more.

A difficulty with tax-favored saving plans is that savers can shift preexisting savings from ineligible to tax-favored types of saving. A saving shift could occur even if the level of saving does not change or falls. If this happens, it would defeat the purpose the plan was designed to serve. Economists Glenn Hubbard and Jonathan Skinner studied the way savers respond to tax-favored saving plans and conclude that about 26 cents of every dollar in these plans represents new saving. The other 74 cents in these plans is preexisting saving shifted from elsewhere. Thus, nearly 75 percent of funds that were taxable before they were shifted are no longer taxable. This opens up a possibility that tax collections could decline if saving shifts were to occur on a broad enough scale. In that case, other taxes, such as the income tax, may have to be increased. But doing so could discourage saving in general.

Except in unusual circumstances, such as when life and limb are at risk, in order for a policy to successfully address a social problem, the cause of the problem must first be ascertained. Economists and policy makers do not fully understand the causes of the decline in the U.S. saving rate, or how serious a problem it is. Thus, policies designed to increase saving could be counterproductive.

SUMMARY

National saving is the sum of household, corporate, and government saving. Temporary changes in the level of national saving can affect firms' incentives to produce output, the rate of unemployment, and the rate at which prices change over time and can have substantial effects on economic welfare in the short run. In the long run, the level of national saving is important because the saved funds determine the size of the nation's stock of capital and the nation's standard of living.

Economic research indicates that the following factors tend to increase national saving: unexpected current income, expected declines in future income, more workers and longer retirements, higher interest rates, household patience, uncertainty about future wage income and future expenses, and lower income-tax rates.

Government policy may have substantial effects on saving. As currently structured, the corporate income tax reduces the incentive for firms to save and invest in future productive technology, equipment, and buildings. The personal income tax tends to reduce the incentive to save. Additionally, government budget deficits and Social Security have a potential to reduce national saving.

As the financial system becomes more efficient at its essential task—the transfer of funds from savers to borrowers—each saved dollar becomes a more powerful vehicle of investment and productivity. Economies with relatively low saving rates but highly developed financial systems can be more productive than economies with higher saving rates but undeveloped financial sectors. The way saving is used could be as important as its level.

The Bureau of Economic Analysis reports measurements of U.S. national saving and its components. The U.S. net personal saving rate has declined for more than two decades. The decline could prove to be harmful if it is caused by shortsighted planning, or unrealistic assessments of risk. Is the U.S. saving rate too low? The answer to this question is not as clear as the previous figure makes it appear. In and of itself, the decline in the personal saving rate may suggest the answer is yes. However, many features of reported saving rates and the modern U.S. economy suggest that more information is needed before we have a definitive answer. Sound economic policy would determine the causes of the saving rate decline before policies are designed to offset it. Otherwise, saving policy can produce unintended, and sometimes undesirable, consequences.

Further Reading: Altig, David, Alan J. Auerbach, Laurence J. Kotlikoff, Kent A. Smetters, and Jan Walliser. 2001. "Simulating Fundamental Tax Reform in the United States." *American Economic Review* 91:574–95; Auerbach, Alan J., and Laurence J. Kotlikoff. 1987. *Dynamic Fiscal Policy.* Cambridge: Cambridge University Press; Barro, Robert, J. 1974. "Are Government Bonds Net Wealth?" *Journal of Political Economy* 82:1095–117; Bureau of Economic Analysis. 1997. *A Guide to the NIPA's.* Methodology Papers Series. Washington, DC: U.S. Government Printing Office; Feldstein, Martin S. 1974. "Social Security, Induced Retirement, and Aggregate Capital Accumulation." *Journal of Political Economy* 85:905–26; Friedman, Milton. 1957. *A Theory of the Consumption Function.* Princeton, NJ: Princeton University Press; Garner, C. Alan. 2006. "Should the Decline in the Personal Saving Rate Be a Cause for Concern?" *Economic Review, Federal Reserve of Kansas City* 91:5–28; Hayashi, Fumio. 1986. "Why Is Japan's Saving Rate So Apparently High?" *NBER Macroeconomics Annual,* 147–210; Hubbard, Glenn R., and Jonathan S. Skinner. 1996. "Assessing the Effectiveness of Saving Incentives." *Journal of Economic Perspectives* 10:73–90; King, Robert, and Ross Levine. 1993. "Finance, Entrepreneurship, and Growth: Theory and Evidence." *Journal of Monetary Economics* 32:513–42; Maddison, Angus. 1992. "A Long-Run Perspective on Saving." *Scandinavian Journal of Economics* 94 (2): 181–96; Milken, Michael. 2006. "Seventh Decade." *Wall Street Journal,* September 19; Modigliani, Franco, and Richard Brumberg. 1954. "Utility Analysis and the Consumption Function: An Interpretation of Cross-Section Data." In *Post-Keynesian Economics,* ed., Kenneth K. Kurihara, 388–436. New Brunswick, NJ: Rutgers University Press; Summers, Lawrence. 1981. "Capital Taxation and Accumulation in a Life Cycle Growth Model." *American Economic Review* 71:533–44.

Benjamin Russo

SEX AND ADVERTISING

Jean Kilbourne contends, "These days, graphic sexual images seem more extreme, more pervasive, and more perverse than ever before. Images that used to belong to the world of pornography are now commonplace in family magazines and newspapers, in TV commercials, on billboards, and online" (Kilbourne 2005).

Consider the words from "Shake That," the popular song by Eminem and Nate Dogg that hit the pop 100 charts, peaking at number 6 in 2006 (Billboard 2007).

> There she goes shaking that ass on the floor
> Bumping and grinding that pole
> The way she's grindin that pole
> I think I'm losing control (Eminiem 2007).

The lyrics sound more like two men conversing at a strip club or a scene from a pornographic movie rather than an opening verse to a pop song. U.S. culture is awash in sexually explicit content, and the music industry is just one example. All forms of the media are caught up into the sex craze. We live in what appears to be a sex-obsessed society, with rude language, nudity, and eroticism oozing all around us. What was once the unexpected (in terms of acceptable content or language) has become the expected, and the expected has now become the norm. It is no longer necessary to read Penthouse or Playboy to see sexual imagery. Just turn on the TV, go to the movie theater, take a look at what teens are wearing, or watch commercials and look at print advertising.

Although the emergence of sex in advertising is not new, some of the controversies regarding it are. There are two basic issues surrounding sex in advertising: Does sex appeal work? In other words, does it really sell products and services? And has the use of sex in advertising gone too far? Should organizations limit their use of sexual images to sell their products and services, even if it does work? This chapter will explore both of these controversies.

DOES SEX APPEAL WORK?

Yes

The use of sex appeals is not a new phenomenon in marketing. The blatantly sexual images depicted on walls in ancient Pompeii suggest that sex was used in public places to advertise various products ranging from food to baths to prostitution. (This is reminiscent of the explicit catalogs of "services available" that are distributed by hand and found in display cases along the streets of Las Vegas every night.) In ancient times, these public advertisements were not limited to "sin cities" like Pompeii, nor to just "sin services."

As early as Victorian 1850, marketers were using the opposite sex as eye-catching images to promote their products and services.[4] According to Goodrum and Dalrymple, "Full female nudity was introduced with a photograph . . . to illustrate a Woodbury Soap ad in 1936" (Goodrum and Dalrymple 1990). Prior to that time, advertisers used sexual innuendos in copy by barely hinting at sexual images. Take, for instance, an advertisement for Iron Clad Hosiery from 1927. An attractive woman dressed in what today would be considered not very revealing undergarments seems to be caressing her "Iron Clad" ankle with an air of sensuality that is barely perceptible. The image is accompanied by the slogan "The kind of beauty that thrills." In addition, the print in the ad notes the "mysterious quality which glorifies the wearer's own shapeliness and grace" that the hosiery offers. It can be seen that the image is less sexually suggestive than the copy of the advertisement (Goodrum and Dalrymple 1990).

Sexual appeal has been defined as "the degree of nudity or sexual explicitness found in visual, audio, and/or verbal elements of advertisements" (Gould 1994; Reichert and Carpenter 2004). It has long been accepted that sex appeals have stopping power encouraging readers and viewers to stop, look, and listen. The "wow" factor of sexual appeals attracts attention to promotional messages, encouraging readers to notice specific messages out of the media clutter or barrage of stimuli to which they are exposed.

Nowhere has the stopping power of sex been used with more success than in the retailing industry. Consider Abercrombie and Fitch and its former quarterly publication called by many a "magalog." Although the company contended the publication was a catalog to showcase and sell its merchandise, most of the models in the magazine were nude or nearly nude. It should have made even the casual viewer wonder, "How can a retailer expect to sell clothes from a catalog when none of the models are wearing any?" The company and its magazine sparked public outcry with their depiction of teenage boys and girls scantily clothed (if at all) in very suggestive poses. According to critics, "Not only did the magazine target teens, it did so in a sexual way . . . evident in the way the individual images in the magazine were staged" (Spurgin 2006).

ABERCROMBIE AND FITCH

Picture a long slender figure in the background of a very dark room. As you look you notice that what you see is a male body with no clothing on. You begin to wonder, "Did I pick up the wrong magazine?" In order not to draw attention to yourself, you slowly peer over the cover page and notice that indeed you were still looking at a catalog, a clothing catalog, yet no one has clothes on!

The depiction is one that many young people have seen in the Abercrombie and Fitch quarterly catalog. Since the catalog's debut in 1997, its content has drawn regular protests. Items such as thongs for children with the words "eye candy" on it are just the beginning of the problems. In an effort to curb public criticism, the store placed the catalog in plastic bags and only distributed them through their online shop to consumers age 18 and older. Although their efforts were applauded, they decided in the winter of 2003 to pull the catalog from circulation.

Abercrombie and Fitch's financial state has been in jeopardy for some time. Market positioning and segmentation issues have plagued the company because of its racy appeal. Although racy appeal is commonplace in today's culture, the decline in profits for Abercrombie and Fitch brings about the question, Is it the racy content that the consumer is avoiding or the products themselves?

Source: "Abercrombie to Kill Catalog After Protests Over Racy Content." 2003. Wall Street Journal, December 10; DeMarco, Donna. 2002. "Abercrombie & Fitch Pulls Children's Thong." Knight Rider Tribune Business News, May 23.

No

Sexual imagery can also create problems and be counterproductive for marketers. While it is widely accepted that sex appeal attracts attention, studies show that is rarely encourages actual purchase behavior. Specifically, sexual images attract consumers to the ad but don't enhance the profitability of the brand or product. In some cases, sexual appeal has been shown to distract the audience from the main message of the marketer and interfere with comprehension, especially when there is complex information to be processed.

If marketers are going to use sexual images in ads, it is imperative that they know their audience, because several individual difference variables have been shown to play a role in the effectiveness of sexual appeals. For example, sex appeal seems to work differently for men and women and affect message comprehension and recall. Studies show that men often become so aroused by nudity used in ads that they have a hard time remembering components of the actual message or what the ad was about (Schiffman and Kanuk 2007). Women tend to be attracted to ads that use elements of fantasy, love, and romance, whereas men are more attracted to appeals that use nudity (Anne 1971). In addition, age seems to be related to whether a viewer responds favorably or unfavorably to sexual appeals (Maciejwski 2004). Younger audiences are usually less offended by sexual images, although this too may differ by gender. In a study of college-age consumers, researchers found that men and women differ significantly in their assessments of sexual appeals. Advertisers must take care when using sexual imagery (especially featuring women) in ads targeted to female college-age consumers (Maciejwski 2004). What one person finds erotic, another person may find offensive.

The bottom line for marketers is synergy. Sex ads don't work for all products. Sexually oriented appeals may be a poor promotional choice if the product, the ad, the target audience, and the sexual images themselves don't all fit and complement each other (i.e., when the sexual images are unrelated to product claims, such as scantily clad women selling products for a hardware store).

HAS THE USE OF SEX IN ADVERTISING GONE TOO FAR?

Most people agree that "the sexual ads that have drawn the most protest are those that exploit women as sex objects and those that use underage models in suggestive ways" (Duncan 2002). With the use of sexually oriented advertising comes scrutiny and protests by parents, legislators, and consumer activists—just to name a few groups. Consider the public furor over the FCUK brand from French Connection, or the Janet Jackson and Justin Timberlake incident during the half-time show at the 2004 Super Bowl when Jackson's left nipple was exposed to the American public. This so-called wardrobe malfunction resulted in months of debate about American core values and the role of the Federal Trade Commission (which is only one of several federal agencies that has jurisdiction over the monitoring of one or more aspects of advertising and marketing communication in the United States) in regulating live television programs (Elliot 2005). In the wake of this incident a time delay has been placed on all live television programs.

FCUK

"FCUK like a bunny." Wait, was that . . . oh no, it's just the latest French Connection United Kingdom T-shirt. Since the creation of the acronym FCUK, French Connection has come under a plethora of scrutiny. The parallels between their acronym and the word many find offensive is easily seen, but the use of this type of marketing tool is becoming more common. FCUK has been heavily criticized publicly for the use of its label, and profits have fallen. In mid-2006 FCUK shares almost hit a three-year low.

Public sensitivity to the controversial nature of the FCUK label has grown. The negative reaction of public watchdog groups has influenced consumers not to buy FCUK's products. However, governmental agencies don't see anything wrong with the label FCUK. In 2005 the UK patent office upheld the use of the French Connection acronym with arguments by lawyers that it is "completely mainstream." Although FCUK as an organization may be under financial constraints from consumers, it seems that this type of explicit language is commonly accepted as a functional aspect of culture.

Source: Adapted from Lea, Robert. 2006. "Under-Pressure FCUK Kisses Ad Man Goodbye." Knight Ridder Tribune Business News, July 7; Rossiter, James. 2005. "Patent Office Decides That FCUK Doesn't Spell Trouble." Knight Ridder Tribune Business News, December 21.

People still talk about the Calvin Klein controversy of the mid-1990s, when the designer used young-looking models (albeit over 18) to star in his controversial jean ads. While many critics rated these ads as outright "kiddie pornography," others contended that any PR is good PR (Lippe 1995). Some commentators compared these ads to the bare-bottomed toddler girl in the classic Coppertone ads, which are now viewed in a different way due to the current spotlight on pedophilia. The question remains: Was Klein just a wise businessman capitalizing on America's craving for sex? Are sexual images in advertising today just good marketing? On one side of the argument is the belief that "the chief aim of marketing is to sell more things, to more people more often for more money" (Danziger 2002). The bottom line is profit, and therefore, the sole obligation of the firm is to do whatever is necessary, within legal parameters, to maximize return on shareholder equity.

So, if sex sells more products, then sex in advertising is good for business. It sure has been good for a coffee stand in Seattle, Washington (Brady 1995). The owner has developed a special niche for his retail store, and business couldn't be better! He uses gorgeous women barely dressed in bras and panties to lean out the window to take orders and deliver coffee and sweet treats. According to the owner, anything is fair game as long as his employees' breasts and buttocks are covered so they aren't breaking the law. The business owners report few complaints other than long drive-thru lines!

The alternative point of view says that organizations must look beyond the specific profit interests of the firm and consider their greater social responsibility. Is sex in advertising going against moral and ethical standards? Is it exploiting women? Has it turned "sex into a dirty joke" (Kilbourne 2005)? Are sexually oriented ads just outright distasteful and wrong? Or do they just reflect a culture in which "the heat level has risen, the whole stimulation level is up" (Brady 1995)? An additional concern is that the more sexual images that are used in the media and advertising, the more acceptable the extent of the sexuality that will become in future advertising. In other words, sexual images are now an expectation in the advertising of clothing, perfume, body lotions, and hair products. The laws regarding sexual harassment indicate that acceptable behavior should be defined by what a "reasonable woman" would consider acceptable behavior. As we become socialized toward sexual innuendo and images, reasonable women will become more and more accepting of lewd behavior and images. This may up the ante for advertisers who feel continuously pressured to increase the "wow" factor and therefore increase the amount of sexual imagery they use.

As stated above, the unexpected in terms of sex appeal in advertising has become the expected, and now it has also become the norm. But the larger question is: Does that make it right? What are these graphic images teaching our youths? "That women are sexually desirable only if they are young, thin, carefully polished and groomed, made up, depilated, sprayed and scented" (Kilbourne 2005). At the opposite end of this spectrum, however, are new approaches to advertising, including the Dove theme suggesting that all women, regardless of their body type, are beautiful and desirable. Many advertisers are now using larger women as models. It has yet to be seen if this is an improvement or simply an extension of the use of sexual imagery. In other words, if large and less traditionally attractive women are also presented as sexual objects, some might say that we are going backwards instead of forwards.

The women's movement has spent decades fighting for an equal place at the table (i.e., equal pay for equal work, fair treatment, and the elimination of the glass ceiling). Has the women's rights movement been a waste of time if we are still reducing women to nothing more than sex objects? We are teaching our youths (both boys and girls) to devalue the mental and spiritual aspects of a woman and focus exclusively on the physical.

For thousands of years, advertisers have used women as eye-catching images in their ads. At the start of the twenty-first century, this strategy continues full speed ahead. By modern standards, the images are raunchier, more explicit, and more widely employed. As a society, we get to decide where to draw the line. Therein lies another controversy—in a complex culture, which ones of us will make the decision? Will we turn off the TV, decide not to buy a product, or refuse to shop at a retail store that uses sexually explicit images in its advertisements? Regardless of our opinions about the use of sex in advertising, we ought to be concerned that private companies and their advertising agencies appear to be making those decisions now. We need to ponder the long-term effects on our culture.

References

Anne, C. 1971. "Sexual Promotion Can Motivate, Distract, Alienate, or Liberate." *Advertising and Sales Promotion* 19 (10): 52.

Associated Press. 2007. "Coffee Shops Show a Little Skin to Compete," *KOMO-TV- Seattle, Washington-News,* January 9. Available at http://www.komotv.com/news/ 5402241.html. Accessed May 17, 2006.

Billboard. 2007. *Artist Chart History: Eminem.* Available at http://www.billboard.com/bbcom/retrieve_chart_history.do?model.vnuArtistId=315925&model.vnuAlbumId=752754. Accessed June 10, 2006.

Brady, James. 1995. "Fueling, Feeling the Heat." *Advertising Age,* September 4, pp. 1, 34.

Danziger, Pamela N. 2002. *Why People Buy Things They Don't Need.* New York: Paramount Market Publishing.

Duncan, Thomas R. 2002. "Social, Ethical and Legal Issues." *IMC: Using Advertising and Promotion to Build Brands.* New York: McGraw-Hill.

Elliot, Stuart. 2005. "Emphasizing Taste, and Not Just in Beer, at Super Bowl." *New York Times,* January 26.

Eminiem. 2007. "Shake That." *Rap Basement Lyrics.* Available at http://lyrics.rapbasement.com/index.php?sec=listing&id=959. Accessed June 8, 2006.

Goodrum, Charles, and Helen Dalrymple. 1990. *Advertising in America: The First 200 Years.* New York: Harry N. Abrams.

Gould, Stephen. 1994. "Sexuality and Ethics in Advertising: A Research Agenda and Policy Guideline Perspective." *Journal of Advertising* 23 (3): 73–81.

Kilbourne, Jean. 2005. "What Else Does Sex Sell?" *International Journal of Advertising* 24 (1): 119–22.

Lippe, Dan. 1995. "Readers Rate Klein 'Porn' Campaign." *Advertising Age,* September 4, p. 34.

Maciejwski, Jeffrey J. 2004. "Is the Use of Sexual and Fear Appeals Ethical? A Moral Evaluation by Generation Y College Students." *Journal of Current Issues and Research in Advertising* 26 (2): 97–105.

Reichert, T., and C. Carpenter. 2004. "An Update on Sex in Magazine Advertising: 1983 to 2003." *Journalism and Mass Communication Quarterly* 81 (4): 823–37.

Schiffman, Leon G., and Leslie Lazar Kanuk. 2007. *Consumer Behavior.* 9th ed. Upper Saddle River, NJ: Pearson Education.

Spurgin, Earl W. 2006. "What Was Wrong with Abercrombie and Fitch's 'Magalog'?" *Business and Society Review* 111 (4): 387–408.

Further Reading: Danziger, Pamela N. 2002. *Why People Buy Things They Don't Need.* New York: Paramount Market Publishing; Schiffman, Leon G., and Leslie Lazar Kanuk. 2007. *Consumer Behavior.* 9th ed. Upper Saddle River, NJ: Pearson Education.

Mary Beth Pinto and John D. Crane

SEXUAL HARASSMENT

Sexual harassment is not a new phenomenon. It is safe to say that as long as men and women have been working together, incidences of sexual harassment have occurred. However, before the 1960s, sexual harassment was not considered a problem. In fact, there was no definition for sexual harassment at all. As more women entered the workforce, discrimination became evident. Many women's rights groups fought for equality at work, and sexual harassment became a pressing issue in the workplace. High-profile media cases of harassment, such as that of for Supreme Court nominee Clarence Thomas and Anita Hill or President Bill Clinton and Paula Jones, and films like Disclosure (1993) and North Country (2005), continue to bring sexual harassment to the forefront of people's minds and public discussion. Many question what sexual harassment is and why it matters. Researchers have begun to look at the prevalence of sexual harassment and its affect on victims and the workplace.

Currently, about 15,000 cases of sexual harassment are reported every year (EEOC n.d.). Generally, sexual harassment is considered unwanted sexual attention or demands for sexual favors in a workplace. However, sexual harassment is much more complicated. Despite common assumptions, sexual harassment affects both men and women, in and out of the workplace.

SEXUAL HARASSMENT LAWS

Sexual harassment laws were created during the civil rights and women's rights movements. In 1964, the U.S. government attempted to eradicate discrimination in American society, work, schools, voting, and housing by passing the Civil Rights Act of 1964. Within the Civil Rights Act of 1964, a specific section, Title VII, explicitly prohibited discrimination based on race, color, national origin, sex, or religion. This later was expanded to include prohibiting discrimination based on age, ethnicity, disability and sexual orientation.

The Civil Rights Act created the Equal Employment Opportunity Commission (EEOC). The purpose of the EEOC is to address any discrimination in the workplace and to provide fair and equal employment opportunities for every person. Any complaints of workplace discrimination are directed to the EEOC. When the EEOC was first established, they expected their office would deal primarily with complaints of racial discrimination in response to Title VII. However, the EEOC soon found that sex discrimination comprised one-third of their complaints. Complaints of sex discrimination originally related to the hiring practices of women and gendered classification of jobs. Women were often not hired if they had small children or were fired if they became pregnant. Many jobs at the time were classified as strictly male or female, and a person of the opposite sex would not be permitted to apply.

The EEOC's mounting number of complaints of sex discrimination and harassment prompted laws related specifically to sexual harassment to be developed in the 1970s. The Supreme Court first recognized sexual harassment as a problem in 1974 (Williams v. Saxbe). It declared that sexual harassment was a significant problem and a form of sex discrimination. In 1980, the EEOC issued guidelines forbidding sexual harassment as a form of sex discrimination.

In 1986, the Supreme Court recognized that sexual harassment was indeed a violation of Title VII of the Civil Rights Act and established standards for whether conduct was welcome or unwelcome and when employers were liable for sexual harassment (Meritor Savings Bank v. Vinson). Sexual harassment law was further defined in 1993, when courts stated that plaintiffs could bring sexual harassment claims forth without showing that psychological harm occurred because of the harassment (Harris v. Forklift Systems). Today, sexual harassment laws are still being molded as new cases and issues are introduced into the court systems.

WHAT IS SEXUAL HARASSMENT?

According to Webster's Dictionary, to harass is to annoy persistently or to create an unpleasant or hostile situation. Sexual harassment is not as easy to define. While the courts have decided that sexual harassment is an important legal issue in workplaces, the definition of sexual harassment is complex.

Typically, people believe sexual harassment happens when a male boss suggests or demands sexual acts by a female subordinate, yet this is only one example of sexual harassment. The law clarifies sexual harassment by defining two types: quid pro quo and hostile environment. Under these categories, sexual harassment can encompass physical, verbal, nonverbal, or visual forms of harassment.

Physical harassment includes any unwanted or offensive physical contact between two individuals, such as inappropriate touching, kissing, or fondling. Verbal harassment includes derogatory, sexual, or offensive language or jokes, while nonverbal harassment can include behaviors such as staring or leering. Visual forms of harassment can include any printed item, media, or gesture that is pornographic or offensive.

Quid pro quo harassment is sexual harassment that occurs when one's employment or specific conditions of employment, such as promotions, raises, or benefits, are dependent on sexual favors. Any unwanted sexual advances or propositions are included in the EEOC's definition of quid pro quo harassment. Because of the explicit nature of quid pro quo harassment, the nature of the harassment is typically verbal and physical.

Since quid pro quo harassment must affect one's job directly, such as job status or other tangible benefits, the perpetrator of this type of harassment must have some power over a victim's employment status or benefits or assessment of job performance. Refusing quid pro quo harassment could mean actual or potential economic losses for an employee. An employee could lose a job or a deserved promotion, be transferred to a different job, or receive poor performance ratings.

Quid pro quo harassment only has to occur one time in order for a victim to be able to press charges. For example, a supervisor only has to request a sexual favor in exchange for a promotion once in order for the situation to be considered sexual harassment. Another type of harassment, hostile environment harassment, accounts for harassment that occurs repeatedly, but often in less obvious ways.

Hostile environment harassment can include any verbal, nonverbal, visual, or physical conduct that is sexual or derogatory in nature and interferes with an employee's work. This type of harassment can create a hostile, offensive, or intimidating work environment. Hostile environment harassment can be perpetrated by anyone in a working environment: supervisors, coworkers, subordinates, or even customers. It can be committed by groups of people or individuals. Job benefits or other conditions of employment are not contingent in hostile environment harassment.

Hostile environment harassment can occur in a variety of ways. A clear example of creating a hostile environment is bullying or teasing an individual about his or her gender or sexuality. More subtle situations can be considered to create a hostile environment as well, such as explicitly discussing sexual matters, telling offensive jokes, and viewing or displaying pornography or other offensive materials. Often, these more subtle behaviors are not directed at one particular individual but can create a hostile and uncomfortable working environment.

Both quid pro quo and hostile environment harassment can be damaging. For a business, sexual harassment can be very negative and costly. In cases of quid pro harassment, employers are held liable. If hostile environment harassment occurs, employers are liable unless they can prove that they attempted to correct or prevent the harassment. Despite efforts to prevent all kinds of sexual harassment, it does occur. Many researchers have questioned why sexual harassment occurs, and competing theories have been developed to try to explain the cause of harassment.

WHAT SEXUAL HARASSMENT IS NOT

Many men in work organizations worry about what they can and cannot say and do. Some feel that behaviors like offering a compliment on a coworker's new outfit or telling a joke could lead to a charge of sexual harassment. Still others believe that their right to free speech is being violated. Office romances are also an area of concern for both employers and employees.

Some see the prevalence of sexual harassment cases in the news as daunting. Some workers, particularly men, are afraid that being overly friendly or making jokes around the office could get them in trouble with employers or even charged with sexual harassment. Friendly compliments and non-offensive jokes are perfectly appropriate in an work setting. For example, a male complimenting a female coworker on a new haircut is appropriate. However, commenting on a coworker's outfit in a way that could be perceived as sexual or unwelcome is not appropriate. Often sensitivity is key when working with others and being aware of how they are receiving compliments or jokes. Of course, sexual or derogatory jokes are never appropriate in an office.

Some argue that concern with sexual harassment has gone too far. They believe that people are too sensitive and politically correct, which may infringe on the right to free speech. Censoring the types of language and behaviors allowed in offices may seem extreme or unfair to some, but it is important to remember that a work environment must be welcoming and nonthreatening to all workers.

Workers also are concerned about an employer's right to dictate with whom they can and cannot have a romantic relationship. With an increasing number of women and men working together, office romances have become another concern for employers. Some employers forbid all office romances for fear that they will distract from work or could lead to claims of sexual harassment. Others believe that employers do not have the right to restrict whom one chooses to date or possibly marry. The large amounts of time Americans spend at work provide ample opportunities to befriend coworkers and possibly start romantic relationships.

WHY DOES SEXUAL HARASSMENT OCCUR?

Sexual harassment is detrimental to victims, so why does it occur? Several competing theories try to explain sexual harassment. The main theories explaining sexual harassment are natural or biological, feminist, sociocultural, organizational, and individual difference theories (Tangri and Hayes 1997).

Natural/Biological Theory

A natural or biological theoretical explanation of sexual harassment states that sex and aggression are both human drives rooted in biology. Natural evolution and individual hormones can cause people to act on their aggressive and sexual drives. Natural/biological theory argues that men are more aggressive and sexual by nature and are more likely to struggle with these drives. Also, men have a strong drive to reproduce. All these factors cause men to act out on women.

Feminist Theory

For feminist scholars, sexual harassment is an expression of power, not of sex. Catharine MacKinnon states that sexual harassment is an expression of men's power over women (MacKinnon 1979). The feminist perspective asserts that power is at the root of sexual harassment and sexual harassment is a way in which men maintain and reaffirm their dominance in society. Furthermore, feminist theorists argue that sexual harassment is used to exploit and victimize women.

Sociocultural Theory

Borrowing from feminist theory, sociocultural theory aims to explain the complex influences that society and socialization have on individuals. Sociocultural theory argues that society creates strong gender stereotypes that are ingrained in individuals and that these stereotypes are coupled with differing gender statuses. These societal stereotypes and statuses are brought into the workplace and shape experiences. Sexual harassment is an extension of what society has taught individuals about appropriate gender roles in heterosexual family and dating settings.

Organizational Theory

The organizational theory of sexual harassment posits that the model of organization in a workplace can make it easier or harder for sexual harassment to occur. The type of power an organization utilizes can encourage sexual harassment. Formal hierarchal organizations are more likely to experience sexual harassment because men are more likely to hold higher positions in organizations. Men have more formal power and therefore harass women more. In addition, in predominantly male workplaces, females are more likely to be harassed.

According to organizational theorists, society can influence sexual harassment as well. Gender roles in society can encourage sexual harassment. The more differentiated gender roles are in a society, the more likely those roles will spill over into the work environment, encouraging sexual harassment.

Individual Difference Theory

Individual difference theory focuses on personal qualities or the personalities of individuals to try to explain sexual harassment. This theory often focuses on what makes a person a harasser and what characteristics harassers share. Research finds that people who are most likely to harass also have a high likelihood to rape, hold negative gender-role stereotypes, have less feminist attitudes, and have difficulty being empathetic.

Many theories aim to explain why sexual harassment occurs. A consensus has not been developed. However, clear themes arise within each theory. Sexual harassment may be the result of many factors working together, and the different types of harassment, quid pro quo and hostile environment, may be better explained by different theories.

WHO ARE THE VICTIMS AND WHAT ARE THE EFFECTS OF SEXUAL HARASSMENT?

Being a victim of sexual harassment can simply be aggravating or annoying, but more serious consequences ranging from economic losses to psychological problems can arise. At work, harassment can cause victims to decrease work performance, increase absenteeism, or even leave or lose their jobs. A stigma can also be attached to those who file sexual harassment complaints. Their lives and experiences become public knowledge, which is stressful.

Experiencing sexual harassment can lead to physical and psychological consequences. Victims report physical problems like headaches, stomachaches, sleeping disorders, and eating disorders (Gutek 1985). Psychological problems such as depression, anxiety, and post-traumatic stress disorder can also be consequences of sexual harassment (Avina and O'Donohue 2002). If sexual harassment continues, it can have the same affects on victims as rape or sexual abuse (Koss 1987). Victims of sexual harassment can even become suicidal.

Sexual harassment is commonly believed only to be perpetrated by men against women, but sexual harassment can affect either sex. While women are overwhelmingly more likely to experience sexual harassment, approximately 15 percent of all sexual harassment cases reported to the EEOC are filed by men.

Despite a higher percentage of sexual harassment complaints filed against men, it is hard to gauge how many men are sexually harassed. Often men and women respond to similar harassing behaviors in different ways. Certain comments or actions may be seen as offensive by women but not by men. Men report being less threatened or offended by behaviors that women find harassing (Berhdahl, Magley, and Waldo 1996). Behaviors and remarks can carry different meanings for different individuals, especially across genders. Additionally, men may be forced to conform to ideas of masculinity and either ignore or not report sexual harassment.

Male-to-female and female-to-male harassment are not the only directions of sexual harassment. It is also possible for same-sex harassment to occur. In 1998,

---

MYTHS ABOUT SEXUAL HARASSMENT

Myth: Some people invite sexual harassment by dressing provocatively or behaving in certain ways.

Reality: Sexual harassment does not occur because of how a person dresses or behaves. Victims vary by a number of characteristics, from age, sex, marital status, and occupation to dress, appearance, and behavior.

Myth: Most behaviors classified as sexual harassment are harmless, natural, and normal flirtations and behaviors. The seriousness of sexual harassment is overstated.

Reality: Sexual harassment has real and damaging consequences, including economic loss, physical illness, and psychological problems. Most harassment has nothing to do with flirting but is a demonstration of power used to intimidate, scare, or insult victims.

Myth: Most charges of sexual harassment are false.

Reality: Less than 1 percent of sexual harassment claims are false. Filing a sexual harassment charge can be challenging because it brings attention to the victim, makes him or her relive the harassment, and opens up the victim's life for investigation. Because of this, women rarely file complaints even when sexual harassment has occurred.

Myth: Women in predominately male environments should expect and accept sexual comments, jokes, and behaviors. Women in these situations are not being treated any differently from how men treat each other.

Reality: Women in predominately male environments are much more likely to experience sexual harassment. Harassment can be threatening and intimidating, creating a hostile working environment. These situations can also escalate, causing women to leave their jobs or be fearful of work.

Myth: If you ignore sexual harassment, it will stop.

Reality: Ignoring sexual harassment will not make it go away. Ignoring harassment may aggravate the situation, thus increasing harassment, or be interpreted as an act of compliance or agreement with the behavior.

Myth: Sexual harassment is rare.

Reality: Sexual harassment is extremely common. Between 40 and 60 percent of working women and female college students experience sexual harassment. Sexual harassment also happens to men, with as many as 15 percent of sexual harassment cases filed by men.

---

the Supreme Court recognized same-sex harassment to be a problem (Onclave v. Sundowner Offshore Services). Same-sex harassment can be perpetrated by someone who is homosexual, bisexual, or heterosexual. For example, a group of heterosexual males may bully another heterosexual male because of his lack of sexual experience, creating a hostile environment.

In theory, sexual harassment can be committed by anyone and can affect anyone; but who is most likely to experience sexual harassment? According to an extensive study of federal workplaces by Merit Systems Protection Board in 1981, women are most likely to experience sexual harassment (Merit Systems Protection Board 1981). Women who are younger than 45 and single and hold college degrees are the most likely to file complaints of sexual harassment. Women are also more likely to complain of sexual harassment in semi-skilled or unskilled jobs or in secretarial or clerical jobs (Petrocelli and Repa 1992). However, this data fails to capture sexual harassment that may occur but does not result in an official complaint.

SEXUAL HARASSMENT IN THE CLASSROOM

Sexual harassment does not occur only in the workplace. The American Association of University Women conducted a national survey of public school students in grades 8 through 11 and found that 83 percent of girls and 79 percent of boys report being sexually harassed (American Association of University Women 2001). In college, 62 percent of women and 61 percent of men report being sexually harassed (American Association of University Women 2001).

Sexual harassment in schools occurs often and early. Over one-quarter of students consider their experiences with sexual harassment to happen "often" and over one-third of students claim that their first experience with harassment occurred in elementary school. Most, commonly peers, not teachers, harass students. Only 7 percent of students report that their harassers are their teachers. Sexual harassment in schools is most likely to be perpetrated by peers in classrooms and hallways with unknowing teachers present.

The most common ways in which students are sexually harassed include having sexual rumors spread about them, having clothing removed in a sexual way, being called gay or lesbian, being forced into sexual acts other than kissing, or being watched as they shower or dress at school. Seventy-six percent of students experience nonphysical harassment, while 58 percent experience physical harassment.

Sexual harassment continues in college. At colleges, peers again are most often the perpetrators of harassment. University employees commit less than 10 percent of sexual harassment in college. College students seem to be aware that they are perpetrating harassing behaviors against their peers, with 51 percent of males and 31 percent of females admitting to sexually harassing someone in college.

Sexual harassment at colleges and universities between students and professors is a particularly sensitive subject. While students are old enough to consent to a sexual relationship with a professor, many colleges ban such relationships. Teachers and professors are in a position of power, and some argue that any relationship with a student, whether consensual or not, is inappropriate.

According to Billie Wright Dziech and Linda Weiner, professors use multiple ways to lure students into sexual relationships, from acting like a counselor or mother/father figure to being a confidant (Dzeich and Weiner 1992). Professors may also try to impress a student with their intellectual abilities or prey on a student's vulnerabilities and desires to succeed in school. Students should be aware of both peer and teacher/professor sexual harassment since both can have damaging consequences similar to those of sexual harassment in the workplace.

The effects of sexual harassment in schools or colleges can be upsetting for students, causing them to become self-conscious, embarrassed, angry, or afraid. Students may also find it difficult to pay attention in class, drop classes, skip school, or receive lower grades in classes. Psychological consequences, such as depression or anxiety, are also possible outcomes. Given the prevalence of sexual harassment in schools, it is easy to imagine how such negative and offensive behaviors continue as students graduate and enter the workplace.

TRENDS AND PREVENTION

As mentioned above, the EEOC receives approximately 15,000 sexual harassment complaints each year, of which about 15 percent are filed by males. It is important to realize that many cases of sexual harassment may go unreported, so this number may be grossly underestimating the pervasiveness of the problem. Even so, sexual harassment charges have been on the rise, almost tripling in the 1990s. In 1995, the EEOC received 10,532 complaints; the number rose to 15,497 in 2001. Recently, the number of complaints has been on a slight decline, reaching 12,679 in 2005 (see figure S.4).

Complaints filed by men have risen as well. In 1995, men made 9.9 percent of claims. Men's claims rose to 14.3 percent in 2005. Of course, women file the overwhelming majority of complaints, approximately 85 percent.

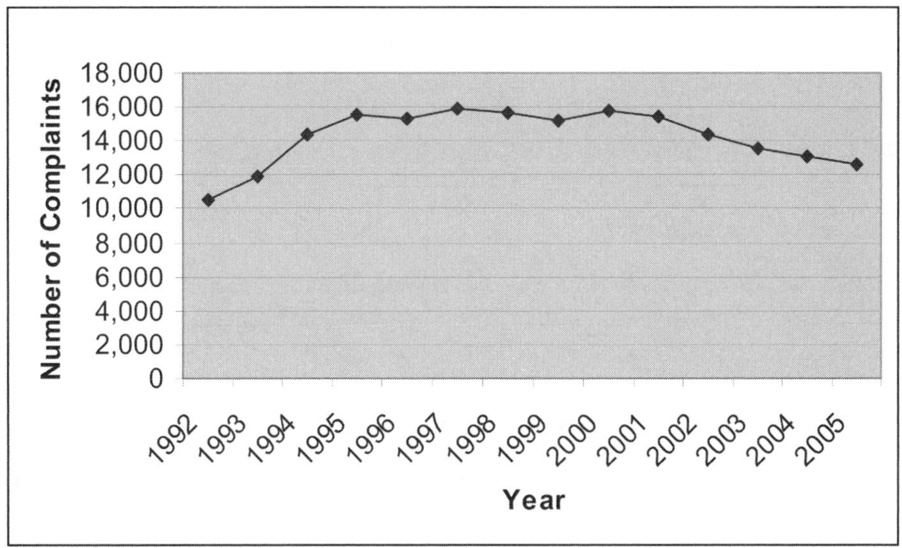

Figure S.4 EEOC sexual harassment complaints.

Source: Original data from the EEOC.

Businesses and other organizations have attempted to address issues of sexual harassment and eliminate the problem. The majority of businesses have specific policies related to sexual harassment that state a clear definition of harassment and detailing the disciplinary actions that are consequences of such harassment. Preventative measures are also taken.

SAMPLE SEXUAL HARASSMENT POLICY

[Company name]'s position is that sexual harassment is a form of misconduct that undermines the integrity of the employment relationship. All employees have the right to work in an environment free from all forms of discrimination and conduct that can be considered harassing, coercive, or disruptive, including sexual harassment. Anyone engaging in harassing conduct will be subject to discipline, ranging from a warning to termination.

What Is Sexual Harassment?

Sexual harassment is defined as any unwanted physical, verbal, or visual sexual advances, requests for sexual favors, and other sexually oriented conduct that is offensive or objectionable to the recipient, including, but not limited to epithets, derogatory or suggestive comments, slurs or gestures, and offensive posters, cartoons, pictures, or drawings.

When Is Conduct Unwelcome or Harassing?

Unwelcome sexual advances (either verbal or physical), requests for favors, and other verbal or physical conduct of a sexual nature constitute sexual harassment when:

- Submission to such conduct is either an explicit or implicit term or condition of employment (e.g., promotion, training, timekeeping or overtime assignments).
- Submission to or rejection of the conduct is used as a basis for making employment decisions (hiring, promotion, termination).
- The conduct has the purpose or effect of interfering with an individual's work performance or creating an intimidating, hostile, or offensive work environment.

What Is Not Sexual Harassment?

Sexual harassment does not refer to occasional compliments of a socially acceptable nature. It refers to behavior that is not welcome, that is personally offensive, that debilitates morale, and that therefore interferes with work effectiveness.

What Should You Do if You Are Sexually Harassed?

If you feel that you have been the recipient of sexually harassing behavior, report it immediately to the owner of [company name] or other supervisor. It is preferable to make a complaint in writing, but you can accompany or follow up your written complaint with a verbal complaint.

If your supervisor is the source of the harassing conduct, report the behavior to that person's supervisor or to the owner of [company name].

Your identity will be protected and you will not be retaliated against for making a complaint.

What Happens after a Complaint Is Made?

Within [number] of days after a written complaint is made, a supervisor, or other person designated by the owner, will investigate the complaint. The person will speak with possible witnesses and will speak with the person named in your complaint. Your anonymity will be protected to the extent possible.

Depending on the complexity of the investigation, you should be contacted within [number plus measure of time (e.g., four days, two weeks, one month)] about the status of your complaint and whether action is being taken.

Source: Adapted from CCH Business Owner's Toolkit. For further information, see www.toolkit.cch.com

---

Prevention is important to help remedy the problem of sexual harassment in workplaces. The first step in prevention is creating awareness of the problem. In addition to informing employees of sexual harassment policies, businesses can try to prevent sexual harassment by training supervisors and managers to be aware of sexual harassment, creating concrete internal procedures for sexual harassment claims, completing a workplace audit to identify any visual items or behaviors that could be offensive, and improving employees' awareness of sexual harassment through training (Rifkind and Harper 1993).

While companies work to prevent incidences of sexual harassment and courts further modify and define laws regarding sexual harassment, men and women in schools and the workplace need to be aware of the problem. While data try to estimate how prevalent sexual harassment is, many incidents go still unreported. Awareness is the first step to prevention. With increased awareness, men and women can better understand their rights and how to recognize unfair and illegal behaviors, protecting themselves and their jobs.

References

American Association of University Women. 2001. *Hostile Hallways: The AAUW Survey on Sexual Harassment in America's Schools.* Washington, DC: AAUW Educational Foundation.

American Association of University Women. 2006. *Drawing the Line: Sexual Harassment on Campus.* Washington, DC: AAUW Educational Foundation.

Avina, C., and W. O'Donohue. 2002. "Sexual Harassment and the PTSD: Is Sexual Harassment Diagnosable Trauma?" *Journal of Traumatic Stress* 15 (1): 69–75.

Berhdahl, J., V. Magley, and C. Waldo. 1996. "The Sexual Harassment of Men? Exploring the Concept with Theory and Data." *Psychology of Women Quarterly* 20 (4): 527–47.

Dzeich, B. W., and L. Weiner. 1992. *The Lecherous Professor: Sexual Harassment on Campus.* Chicago: University of Illinois Press.

Equal Employment Opportunity Commission (EEOC). Available at www.eeoc.gov.

Gutek, B. 1985. *Sex and the Workplace.* San Francisco: Jossey-Bass.

Koss, M. 1987. "Changed Lives: The Psychological Impact of Sexual Harassment." In *Ivory Power: Sexual Harassment on Campus,* edited by M. Paludi. Albany: State University of New York Press.

MacKinnon, Catharine A. 1979. *Sexual Harassment of Working Women: A Case of Sex Discrimination.* New Haven, CT: Yale University Press.

Merit Systems Protection Board. 1981. *Sexual Harassment in the Federal Workplace.* Washington, DC: Office of Merit Systems Review and Studies.

Petrocelli, W., and B. Repa. 1992. *Sexual Harassment on the Job.* Berkeley, CA: Nolo Press.

Rifkind, L., and L. Harper. 1993. *Sexual Harassment in the Workplace: Women and Men in Labor.* Dubuque, IA: Kendall/Hunt.

Tangri, S., and S. Hayes. 1997. "Theories of Sexual Harassment." In *Sexual Harassment: Theory, Research and Treatment,* edited by W. O'Donohue. Boston: Allyn and Bacon.

Further Reading: Gregory, Raymond. 2004. *Unwelcome and Unlawful: Sexual Harassment in the American Workplace.* Ithaca, NY: Cornell University Press; MacKinnon, Catharine A. 1979. *Sexual Harassment of Working Women: A Case of Sex Discrimination.* New Haven, CT: Yale University Press.

Anne E. McDaniel

SHAREHOLDER ACTIVISM AND THE BATTLE FOR CORPORATE CONTROL

McDonald's used to sell hamburgers and coffee in Styrofoam containers but they stopped. Home Depot's lumber bins used to include lumber sourced from tropical old growth forests. Many oil companies have agreed to publish information about their own greenhouse gas emissions and set targets for their reduction. Why did these changes come about? These may not be the decisions executives would prefer to make, but they were moved by the emerging power of their own shareholding owners. In this entry, we will examine how activist shareholders are increasingly influencing how firms are structured and what they do.

Shareholder activism has been a feature of the corporate decision-making landscape for over a century. Certainly, it became much more visible in the aftermath of the stock market crash of 1929 in the United States, which galvanized reform efforts both at the federal level (through the formation of the Securities and Exchange Commission) and, more relevant to our point here, increased engagement by shareholders to determine their rights with respect to management decisions. Though the activity subsided for a period, activist approaches reemerged in the 1970s and became a prominent feature of annual meetings for many large firms as they sought to respond to challenges to actions and investments that some shareholders deemed irresponsible, such as investments in South Africa; environmental issues; and, as corporate takeover activity increased, governance structures that protected managers at the expense of shareholders. Today, shareholders are active in critiquing executive compensation, corporate social responsibility issues, and perceived mismanagement of organizations.

WHY IS THERE POTENTIAL FOR CONFLICT?

The modern corporation is distinguished by its separation of management and ownership. Consider it this way: in an entrepreneurial venture, the owner of a firm is usually the top manager. Her decisions about how to run the company reflect her own objectives for success and profitability. Later, though, she may turn to outside sources for additional capital to finance expansion and growth. Often this is accomplished through selling a portion of the equity of the firm. Equity represents an ownership stake; the entrepreneur gives up control over some portion of the firm's ownership in exchange for capital. An excellent example of this at a small level is the way that venture capitalists become minority equity partners with high-tech start-up owners. In exchange for funding, the venture capitalists usually get some say in how the firm is operated and a share of firm profits.

These rights of control and profit sharing also apply in large corporations, but their effect is diluted. When firms go public and offer shares of the organization on the stock market, ownership can be distributed across thousands or even millions of investors. There are several effects that emerge from this. First, most investors have a very small portion of ownership. If you own shares in a firm or in a mutual fund, you are an owner of the firm but your share is only fractions of a percent. Therefore, the voice of the small investor is weak because power is related to the number of shares owned. Second, with so many investors, it is impractical if not impossible for the owners to directly manage the firm. Therefore, managers are hired to run the corporation on behalf of the shareholders. The top executives report to the board of directors, a set of representatives from and for the shareholders.

This separation of management and ownership can open the door to what are termed agency problems. Managers are supposed to work as agents of the owners and therefore should seek to maximize the returns or benefits for those owners. However, managers sometimes pursue their own interests even when they conflict with owner goals. For example, managers may seek to build up perks such as country club memberships or corporate planes or art collections. To the extent these are for the satisfaction of the managers and do not reward the shareholders, this is an agency problem. Shareholder activism is a way for owners to reassert control of the organization and to try to make sure that their rights are respected.

HOW IS A BATTLE FOUGHT?

Challenges to how a company is being run from an owner's perspective occur at the annual meeting of a publicly held firm's shareholders (though other challenges emerge often from outside the firm). The vehicle for conducting a challenge is a proxy statement. If you own stock in a firm or a mutual fund, you have undoubtedly received large envelopes from the firm or fund with notice of the annual meeting and proxy information. A signed proxy conveys legal authority to someone else to vote your shares. Historically, the board of directors

THE ADELPHIA COMMUNICATIONS SCANDAL

In March 2002, executives at Adelphia Communications revealed for the first that more than $2 billion in debt owed by the company and the Rigas family had been kept off the books. The company plunged into a financial crisis and share price dropped from over $20 dollars to 12 cents, ultimately forcing the company to file for bankruptcy protection. The Rigas family constituted the top executives of the firm and dominated the board of directors. Though the family was collectively the majority stockholder in the company, they were not the only owners and since the late 1980s had not only engaged in misstating earnings and subscriber levels but had also used the firm's assets for their own ends. The Rigas were charged by the Securities and Exchange Commission with fraud and racketeering charges and it was ultimately determined that the total loan value (apparently interest-free) had topped $3 billion.

Various sources have identified how the money was used. The company's jets were used to fly family members on a safari to Africa, and Timothy Rigas successfully prevented the expense from being recorded. John Rigas, the company founder, used about $13 million to build a golf course on land he owned. He also used $25 million to buy 3,600 acres across the road from his home so his view wouldn't be spoiled. The family purchased condominiums in Mexico, Colorado, and New York City, where John Rigas's daughter and her husband stayed rent-free, and $252 million of company funds was used to meet margin calls on stock purchases. According to the complaint, "After John J. Rigas racked up a personal debt of more than $66 million by early 2001, he was withdrawing so much money from the company for personal use that his son Timothy had to limit him to $1 million a month—which he duly withdrew for 12 months, even as public filings listed his annual compensation at less than $1.9 million" (Markon and Frank 2002).

This has been described as one of the largest investor frauds in U.S. history and is a clear example of how agents (even if they are also among the owners) can exploit their positions to direct firms assets as they see fit. Even though John and Timothy Rigas were convicted of fraud, Adelphia still faced a $715 million settlement with the SEC and shareholders lost virtually all their investment with the firm. Coming as this did on the heels of the Enron and WorldCom collapses, shareholder activists have used these incidents to push for greater transparency in corporate reporting and for more independent boards to provide better oversight of firm operations.

has sought the proxy (that is, if you sign and return the form, you are typically granting the board the right to vote the shares as they see fit). They usually seek authority to vote on who is elected to the board, executive compensation, and so on. More recently, parties other than the board have been using proxies to bring proposals up at the annual meeting for balloting. Not everyone can do this; the process is expensive and time consuming, and there are very formal rules that must be obeyed.

The Securities and Exchange Commission has codified how shareholders can bring resolutions forward. First, shareholders must own at least $2,000 worth of stock or 1 percent of the company shares and have held it for at least a year.

The length of the resolution is limited to 500 words, and the SEC has shown that they must be carefully chosen words, because there are numerous grounds for dismissal of the resolution. One of the most common is that that resolution addresses normal business operations such as general compensation, hiring, promotion, and termination of employees. As a rule, this business judgment is left to the discretion of management and is excluded from debate at annual meetings. Other grounds for dismissal include addressing a portion of the business that constitutes less than 5 percent of revenues or profits, essentially duplicates another resolution being introduced at the same meeting, addresses a personal claim or grievance, or would compel the firm to break local, state, or national law in adopting it (Securities and Exchange Commission 2001). For the specific steps in how to generate a shareholder proposal, see the SEC's "Final Rule: Amendments to Rules on Shareholder Proposals" (http://www.sec.gov/rules/final/34–40018.htm). Successful proposals are provided on the proxy form sent out to all shareholders. Proposals that come from activists rarely do well in the first pass, and in order to be eligible to be considered at subsequent meetings, the proposal must win 3 percent of shareholder votes, 6 percent on the second submission, and 10 percent on the third. This requires an active response from shareholders: proxy ballots that are not returned default to the board of directors' position on the proposal. Therefore, if the proxy ballots are not returned and the board and management oppose a resolution, those missing shares are counted as votes against the proposal.

WHO ARE THE ACTIVISTS?

Shareholder activists generally fall into two groups: institutional and individual investors. Institutional investors are usually financial entities such as pension funds, insurance companies, and mutual funds, and they often control a large number of shares. Individual investors are, as the name suggests, individuals who privately own company shares. Either can bring shareholder proposals before the company, but their objectives sometimes differ.

Institutional investors have become much more important in the investment community over the past 20 years. By 2003, these investors collectively controlled about 60 percent of the equity issued by U.S. firms in total and about 70 percent of the equity of the 1,000 largest U.S. firms (Conference Board 2005). Being this large, though, is a mixed blessing: while size does convey some power, it also limits what actions they can take. If individual investors are displeased with the management direction, they can "vote with their feet" (that is, sell their shares and leave). Institutional investors don't have that much latitude. They owe a fiduciary duty to their shareholders (which means they must act to benefit their shareholders financially) so they cannot as easily exit an ownership position. If a large investor decides to sell, this places many shares on the market. In economic terms, this would rapidly increase the supply so the price of the shares would drop, which would decrease the value of the sale and of the shares held by the institution's owners. Therefore, institutional investors are often very interested in active participation with management rather than exit to change how the firm is being run (Loring and Taylor 2006).

WHAT ARE THE OBJECTIVES OF SHAREHOLDER ACTIVISM?

Usually, the goals of activists are divided into two groups. Governance issues deal with how the corporation is actually operated. This is typically what institutional investors pursue, though individuals can and do as well. Proposals usually deal with eliminating defenses to takeover, executive compensation, and board structure. Social issues deal with the relationship between the firm and society and address how the firm should deal with problems in the environment (such as global warming or pollution), social justice (such as apartheid in South Africa or the use of child labor in manufacturing), or what they make. Here, activists may argue against making cigarettes or alcohol, military weapons, nuclear power, or certain types of pharmaceuticals. Typically, these issues are brought forward by individual investors rather than institutions, though recently, a number of very large institutions (with more than $2 trillion in assets) have signed on to the United Nations–sponsored "Principles for Responsible Investing," which address both governance and social issues (Environment News Service 2006). Here are some examples of the issues and why activists get involved.

TAKEOVER DEFENSES

Corporations are sometimes pursued for acquisition by other firms. This means that the acquirer wishes to purchase a controlling portion of the outstanding shares of the target firm. Usually, these are friendly acquisitions and the management, board, and shareholders of the target agree that the purchase is a good opportunity. Almost always, in order to convince shareholders to sell quickly, the acquirer has to offer a premium price for the shares (a premium being some money in excess of the current market value). Obviously, this is a benefit to the owners of the targeted firm. In some cases, though, management and the board want to resist the takeover because it would likely mean the loss of their positions and income. Therefore, particularly since the late 1980s, so-called poison pills have been developed to deter acquisition. Triggered by a hostile bid, the pill is a policy that often allows current shareholders to buy additional shares at a deeply discounted price. This inflates the number of shares on the market and dramatically increases the cost for the acquirer—and often ends the bid. Therefore, owners do not receive the benefit of the higher offer price for their shares, which can be considered an agency problem. Management and boards have defended the practice by arguing that shareholders usually don't have sufficient information to make a good judgment about the offer or that the offer actually undervalued the firm (Nicklaus 2005). While this view has historically been supported in court, recent developments indicate that lawsuits brought by shareholders in opposition to poison pills limit the power of management and boards to act on their own to deter acquisition. Moreover, the number of shareholder actions introduced in corporate annual meetings to eliminate or control these acquisition defenses has increased substantially, especially between 1995 and 2000 (Graves, Rehbein, and Waddcek 2001). Proposals for rescinding or eliminating these defensive measures come most often from institutional investors because of the lost potential value to their shareholders when a portfolio firm deploys the poison pill (Lindstrorm 2005).

EXECUTIVE COMPENSATION

Shareholder proposals to restrict or modify executive compensation have also increased dramatically. From almost no proposals in 1998 to well over 150 in both 2003 and 2004, shareholders are taking aim at pay, stock options, and the severance packages known as golden parachutes that executives have arranged. Sometimes the focus is on how the compensation is unrelated to the performance of the firm while in other cases it is just the sheer magnitude of compensation that arouses action. According to Forbes, compensation for the CEOs of the Fortune 500 climbed 54 percent for 2003 versus 2002 where compensation includes salary, stock options, and stock gains or the value from exercising stock options in the past year. Of these executives, 138 earned more than $10 million in 2003. By 2004, median CEO pay among the several hundred largest U.S. firms had increased by 25 percent over the prior year to about $14 million. For institutional investors, this is particularly alarming when the performance of the firm is not nearly as spectacular. For instance, a report from the Corporate Library, a corporate-governance research group, showed that over a period of five years, CEO compensation in 11 firms totaled $865 million when the firms lost over $640 billion in shareholder value. These firms included Lucent, Time Warner, Safeway, Pfizer, and Merck (Crook 2006).

Institutional investors are not alone, though: many individual investors protest such compensation, albeit on more philosophical grounds that emphasize inequities in pay. To put it another way, for every dollar the average worker earned in 2004, CEOs earned $431. This ratio has grown rapidly: in 1990, CEOs made about 107 times more than the average worker, while in 1982, the ratio was 42 to 1 (DeCarlo 2005).

Golden parachutes are packages that award substantial benefits in the case that a firm is acquired and the executive's employment terminated and may include severance pay, bonuses, and stock options. The objective of a package like this is to permit executives to more objectively assess the merit of an offer. Ideally, the parachute would insulate shareholders from executives acting to protect their jobs rather than acting in the owners' interests. However, the size of the packages and their connection to performance has come under fire. For instance, Safeway (a firm mentioned above in the Corporate Library report) was recently purchased by SuperValu Inc. Larry Johnston, CEO of Safeway, will receive $105.5 million when the acquisition closes, including payments for health care, relocation expenses, outplacement services, stock options, and over $12 million to pay the income tax on the package. Four other Safeway executives were also slated for severance packages over $10 million. Payouts like these (and there are larger examples), and in particular the practice of covering taxes, are often opposed by institutional investors, because they deplete firms' assets.

BOARD STRUCTURE

During the 1980s, many firms introduced classified boards of directors to resist takeover attempts. "Classified" means that instead of electing directors all at the same time, typically a third are elected each year and each director sits for a three-year term. From a defensive point of view, this structure means that in the event of a takeover attempt, the buying firm would be restricted in governing the target firm, since two-thirds of the directors after the next election would still be affiliated with prior management. Classified boards have come under fire from shareholders because they are viewed as less responsive to shareholder initiatives. Annual election may make the directors more accountable.

Declassifying boards is one of the most common and successful areas of shareholder activism, even though these resolutions are nonbinding. However, boards and executives are paying attention to these sentiments: among the Fortune 500 firms, the percentage with classified boards declined from 44 percent to 32 percent from 2002 to 2005.

SOCIAL ISSUES

If governance issues are usually the domain of institutional investors, the push to introduce resolutions that address social concerns is the domain of individual investors. Historically, these resolutions have not been very successful, with the notable exception of the groundswell of support for the withdrawal of operations in South Africa in the 1980s and 1990s. Often, firms are able to omit resolutions from the proxy statement on one of the grounds listed above and, sometimes, because the objective of the resolution is too ambitious and beyond the capacity of the firm (e.g., a resolution to stop global warming). More recently, though, activists have been making headway as firms respond to pressures along the corporate social responsibility front. That is, shareholders represent one of potentially several groups that can motivate firms to change practices. For example, Exxon Mobil has become much more sensitive to and cooperative with efforts to change how it is perceived in terms of social responsibility. This is in part due to the fact that the company is being outpaced by competitors such as British Petroleum, which has been much more active in establishing CSR credentials, and is also due to Exxon's attempts to overcome the public relations problems from the Valdez disaster in Alaska in 1989. By 2003, 12 outside proposals made it to the agenda of the annual meeting (Energy Intelligence Group 2003).

Along with this, organizations have become much more skilled at crafting and presenting resolutions. Probably the best-known organization is the Interfaith Center on Corporate Responsibility, which has been pursuing an activist agenda for over 25 years and has introduced hundreds of resolutions on topics such as opposition to genetically modified food, requests that firms monitor their supply networks for human rights violations, global warming, and challenges to firms involved in production of military products and those in media with violent games or movies. Other groups such as socially responsible investment firms (mutual funds with selection and omission screens for the firms included in the funds) have also become more skilled.

Finally, societies themselves can change, making the regulatory environment change as well. The SEC, for example, once ruled in the Cracker Barrel case that a resolution to challenge the company's employment discrimination based on sexual orientation could be omitted because the hiring practice fell under the "ordinary business" rule discussed above. Eventually, the SEC reconsidered this position: "From time to time, in light of experience dealing with proposals in specific subject areas, and reflecting changing societal views, the Division adjusts its view with respect to 'social policy' proposals involving ordinary business. . . . We are adopting our proposal to reverse the Cracker Barrel position" (Securities and Exchange Commission 1998).

WRAPPING UP: DOES SHAREHOLDER ACTIVISM MATTER?

It depends. Certainly, attempts to change corporate governance have been much more popular and successful in recent years, particularly with respect to declassifying boards and creating more independent boards. Executives, directors, and the courts are also more receptive to eliminating takeover defenses of dubious benefit to shareholders. The record on social activism is less clear cut. Historically, social issue resolutions have received much less support because the audience for the message is diverse and because nonvoted proxies are always aligned with management and the board, which often oppose such proposals. Nonetheless, social issues have made headway in several respects. As noted above, the internal shareholder resolution often reflects similar external efforts by others, and firms have become increasingly responsive. So, while this may mean that a resolution gets to the floor of the annual meeting, it is also one reason that resolutions may be omitted or withdrawn: management agrees to commence a conversation on the idea with stakeholders. This doesn't count as a win in terms of the resolution but it probably does to those who care about the issue. This increased attention to the stakeholder point of view doesn't show signs of slowing, and if for no other reason than enlightened self interest, corporations will likely be more attentive to shareholder activists in the future.

References

Conference Board. 2005. *U.S. Institutional Investors Boost Control of U.S. Equity Market Assets*. Available at www.conference-board.org/UTILITIES/pressDetail.cfm?press_ID=2726. Accessed June 18, 2006.

Crook, Clive. 2006. "Shameless Gougers." *National Journal* 38 (15): 16–17.

DeCarlo, Scott. 2005. "CEO compensation." *Forbes Magazine*. Available at http://www.forbes.com/2005/04/20/05ceoland.html. Accessed May 30, 2006.

Energy Intelligence Group. 2003. "Exxon's Peer Pressure." *Energy Compass,* November 13, p. 1.

Environment News Service. 2006. *World's Largest Investors Back Principles for Responsible Investment*. Available at http://www.ens-newswire.com/ens/apr2006/2006-04-28-01.asp. Accessed June 17, 2006.

Graves, Samuel B., Kathleen Rehbein, and Sandra Waddock. 2001. "Fad and Fashion in Shareholder Activism: The Landscape of Shareholder Resolutions, 1988–1998." *Business and Society Review* 106 (4): 293–314.

Lindstrom, Soren. 2005. "Shareholder Activism against Poison Pills: An Effective Antidote?" *Wall Street Lawyer* 9 (2): 17–19.

Loring, Jason M., and C. Keith Taylor. 2006. "Shareholder Activism: Directorial Responses to Investors' Attempts to Change the Corporate Governance Landscape." *Wake Forest Law Review* 41 (1): 321–40.

Markon, Jerry, and Robert Frank. 2002. "Adelphia Officials Are Arrested, Charged with 'Massive Fraud.'" *Wall Street Journal,* July 25.

Nicklaus, David. 2005. "The Wonder of the Poison Pill Is That It Exists at All." *St. Louis Post-Dispatch,* January 7.

Securities and Exchange Commission. 1998. *Final Rule: Amendments to Rules on Shareholder Proposals*. Available at http://www.sec.gov/rules/final/34–40018.htm.Accessed June 22, 2006.

Securities and Exchange Commission. 2001. *Division of Corporation Finance.* Staff Legal Bulletin No. 14. Available at http://www.sec.gov/interps/legal/cfslb14.htm. Accessed June 17, 2006.

Further Reading: Charkham, Jonathan, and Anne Simpson. 1999. *Fair Shares: The Future of Shareholder Power and Responsibility.* Oxford: Oxford University Press; Monks, Robert A. G. 1998. *The Emperor's Nightingale: Restoring the Integrity of the Corporation in the Age of Shareholder Activism.* New York: Wiley; Monks, Robert A. G. 2001. *The New Global Investors: How Shareowners Can Unlock Sustainable Prosperity Worldwide.* New York: Wiley; Rosenberg, Hilary. 1998. *A Traitor to His Class: Robert A .G. Monks and the Battle to Change Corporate America.* New York: Wiley.

Al Warner

SOCIAL SECURITY, MEDICARE, AND MEDICAID

Most of us are free to decide how we spend some portion of our income—whether to take a vacation trip, go to a restaurant, see a movie, or buy another CD. But we also have obligations. We must use part of our income to pay taxes, rent, credit card debt, and household bills.

The same is true for the U.S. government. Congress can decide how much to spend on national parks, environmental protection, scientific research, and foreign aid. But the government also has obligations, payments it must make. Entitlements are such obligations—payments that people are legally entitled to receive through programs like Social Security, Medicare, and Medicaid. Social Security provides pensions to the retired; Medicare, health insurance for the elderly; and Medicaid, medical benefits for the poor.

In 2005, the federal government spent over a trillion dollars on these three entitlement programs, around 42 percent of federal spending (Congressional Budget Office 2006). Over the next several decades, as the number of retirees increases and medical costs rise, these entitlements will consume a growing share of the nation's income, increasing to 64 percent of federal spending in 2030, and 73 percent in 2050 (Congressional Budget Office n.d.).

Many are alarmed by these predictions. They worry that unless something is done to control entitlements, they will become an excessive burden on future taxpayers. There is heated disagreement among politicians and the public as to what to do.

The debate over entitlements involves passionate emotions and clashing values:

- Are we a society where individuals look after themselves and are responsible for their choices, or is our society a family in which risks are shared and members take care of each other?
- Should workers decide how much to save for retirement, and how to invest their savings, or should the government make these decisions?
- Who should provide health insurance, private insurance companies or the government, or some combination of the two?

Let's look at the three main entitlement programs and the political battles that rage around them.

SOCIAL SECURITY

Social Security was founded in 1935 during the Great Depression, when a huge segment of the population barely had enough money to live (Aaron and Reischauer n.d.; Benavie n.d.; Kingson and Schulz n.d.; Shaviro n.d.). Its purpose was to provide a reliable retirement income to people over 65. Each month the government takes a certain percentage of workers' pay checks. This payroll tax funds Social Security. The idea behind the program was that workers would be required to contribute to their own retirement and, by doing so, would earn the right to their Social Security pension. To guarantee its long-term survival, the founders of Social Security made the program universal: everyone pays and everyone collects benefits.

Other government programs—such as food stamps and Medicaid—are means tested, which means that only those beneath a certain income qualify. Programs for the poor tend to receive weak support from the American public. Social Security, on the other hand, provides benefits for both the rich and the poor. President Franklin D. Roosevelt, talking privately to an advisor, explained his rationale for Social Security this way: "We put those payroll contributions there so as to give the contributors a legal, moral and political right to collect their pensions. . . . With those taxes in there, no damn politician can ever scrap my Social Security program" (Seidman n.d.).

Social Security is a social insurance program: workers pay premiums (payroll taxes) so that the government will be obligated to pay them benefits in the event that their income drops due to retirement or disability. The payroll tax rate is currently 6.2 percent of earnings for the employee, and 6.2 percent for the employer. The rate for the self-employed is 12.4 percent (Social Security and Medicare Board of Trustees n.d.).

Workers who have paid payroll taxes for 10 years or more are entitled to a Social Security pension when they retire. Spouses are also covered even if they've never worked. Benefits are based on a worker's average wage, an average based on the 35 years of highest earnings. Higher-income earners receive higher monthly benefits, but not proportionately so. That is, if you've paid twice the payroll taxes I have, you get higher benefits than I do, but not twice as high. This reflects the fact that the formula applied to your average wage, which determines your monthly benefit, is designed in such a way that Social Security also serves as an antipoverty program, redistributing income from the rich to the poor (Benavie n.d.).

Social Security has done more to eliminate poverty among the elderly than any other government program, including welfare. During the past 30 years, thanks largely to Social Security, the poverty rate among the elderly has dropped from three times that of the general population to about the same (Ball and Bethell n.d.).

Pensions for the retired are not the only benefit provided by Social Security; it also supports families who suffer the death or disability of a breadwinner. These benefits do not require extra premiums; they're covered by payroll taxes.

As of December 31, 2005, benefits were paid to a total of 48.4 million people, including 4 million children (www.ssa.gov/OACT/FACTS/fs 2005_12.html). This number included 33.5 million retired workers and their family members, 6.7 million survivors of deceased breadwinners, and 6.5 million disabled workers, along with 1.8 million of their dependents.

Social Security has other desirable features:

- The program is much more efficient than private insurance. The cost of administering Social Security is less than 1 percent of the benefits paid out, compared to 10 to 15 percent for most private insurance (Chen and Goss n.d.).
- Social Security payments are automatically protected against unexpected inflation (increases in the general price level). Private pensions do not protect against this risk. If the price level increased by 3 percent a year, the purchasing power of a fixed monthly benefit would be cut almost in half in 20 years. Thanks to the cost-of–living adjustment adopted by Congress in 1972, Social Security benefits retain their purchasing power throughout the life of the beneficiary.
- Unlike many private pension plans, Social Security is portable. It follows you from job to job.

AN IMPORTANT DATE FOR SOCIAL SECURITY—2017

Payroll taxes are credited to the OASDI (Old Age Survivors and Disability Insurance) Trust Fund. The U.S. Treasury draws on the Trust Fund to pay Social Security benefits. Every year that payroll taxes exceed benefits, the Treasury is required by law to borrow the excess taxes and spend them on congressionally authorized non–Social Security purposes. Each time the Treasury borrows these payroll taxes, it must deposit an IOU—a Treasury bond—in the Trust Fund to record its debt to Social Security. At the end of 2005, the Treasury bonds in the Trust Fund totaled almost $1.9 trillion, reflecting the amount the Treasury had borrowed from Social Security over the years.

The Treasury will continue borrowing from Social Security until 2017, at which time payroll taxes will begin falling short of benefits (Social Security and Medicare Board of Trustees n.d.). Starting that year, the Treasury will begin paying off its debt to Social Security as it chips in to help payroll taxes pay benefits. By 2040, the Treasury's debt will have been paid; that is, there will be no more Treasury bonds in the Trust Fund. At that point, Social Security benefits will fall by 30 percent unless Congress passes legislation to boost revenue.

Politicians and the media frequently warn that Social Security is headed for bankruptcy. Not true. The Social Security Trustees estimate that payroll tax revenues are adequate to pay all benefits until 2040 (Social Security and Medicare Board of Trustees n.d.). After that, payroll taxes will continue to roll in but will only cover an average of about 70 percent of benefits. So, Social Security will need more revenue over the long run if it's going to pay all benefits currently on the books. Is this a serious revenue shortfall? Not according to the experts. The trustees have stated that the long-run financial problem "can be solved by small gradual changes" (1999 report of the Social Security Trustees). (There is, however, an important date for Social Security coming up in the year 2017.)

What can Congress do to eliminate the long-run deficit in Social Security? The trustees estimate that revenue would equal benefits for the next 75 years—the long-run time frame used by actuaries—if the payroll tax rate were boosted by about 2 percent of earnings, that is, from 12.4 percent to 14.4 percent (1 percent on workers and 1 percent on employers; Benavie n.d.). No one proposes this as a major part of the solution, since polls show that Americans are against boosting the payroll tax by almost two to one (NPR/Kaiser/

CONFLICT OVER HOW TO ELIMINATE SOCIAL SECURITY DEFICIT

One proposal to eliminate the long-run shortfall of Social Security would be to lengthen the period for averaging wages, from 35 years to, for example, 38 (Benavie n.d.). That would reduce the average wage, hence benefits, since earnings for the years presently excluded are not as high as the 35-year average.

Supporters argue that most people work more than 35 years, so incorporating additional years would more accurately link benefits to career earnings. Opponents point out that the benefit reduction would weigh more heavily on women who stayed home to raise children. In addition, studies find that this proposal would cut benefits more for the poor than the rich (Baker and Weisbrot n.d.).

Another benefit-cutting recommendation would increase the normal retirement age faster than currently scheduled (Benavie n.d.). The rationale is that as life expectancy increases, so should the length of the work life. Opponents point out that just because people live longer doesn't mean they'll want to work longer or that they'll be able to find jobs. These critics also stress that workers who are engaged in physically demanding work may be forced to retire early. Finally, Congress has already enacted an increase in the normal retirement age—currently 66 but scheduled to reach 67 by 2022. Opponents of further increases argue that the repercussions of this increase should be evaluated before further changes are made.

Finally, means testing, that is, denying benefits to anyone above a certain income level, is recommended. To supporters it seems unfair that billionaires like Ross Perot and Bill Gates should get Social Security.

Opponents argue that enacting this proposal would discourage young people from saving by sending them the message that if they're savers they will be penalized by having their benefits cut (Report of the 1994–1996 Advisory Council on Social Security n.d.). Means testing also violates the political compact underlying Social Security—that paying Social Security taxes over a lifetime of work earns workers the right to a pension based on earnings when they retire (Aaron and Reischauer n.d.).

Kennedy Survey, May 20, 1999). There are a variety of proposals that have been offered by analysts and politicians to raise revenue or cut benefits, many of which are hotly contested (Benavie n.d.). For example, we could make more use of the income tax to supplement the payroll tax. Another possibility would be to raise the maximum earnings subject to the payroll tax more rapidly than currently scheduled. (As of 2005, income over $90,000 was not taxed.) This cap is scheduled to go up, but it could be raised faster; that would boost both revenue and benefits, but revenue would increase by more.

In recent years, the Republicans, led by President George W. Bush, along with a few Democrats, have campaigned for a radical restructuring of Social Security, namely, permitting workers to divert part of their payroll taxes from Social Security into personal retirement accounts, which could be invested in the stock market. The earnings on these accounts would replace a portion of Social Security benefits. This push to privatize is the major conflict over Social Security.

Supporters of privatization argue that Social Security must be overhauled because its rate of return is dismal. In response, experts point out that comparing the rate of return on Social Security with that of an investment portfolio is "comparing apples and oranges (Diamond n.d.). Social Security is not a portfolio; it's insurance, which provides benefits in the event that a particular problem (e.g., disability) or condition (e.g., retirement) occurs. Claiming Social Security's return is dismal is as meaningless as claiming that the return you get on your fire insurance premiums is dismal.

The main perceived benefit of partially privatizing Social Security is that all workers would be able to invest in the stock market, sharing in the profits that accrue as a result of our growing economy. In addition, workers would have some freedom in choosing what kind of assets to purchase for their personal retirement accounts. The expectation is that the workers' investment portfolios—containing a mix of stocks, corporate bonds, and government bonds—would earn more over the long run than would Social Security, where excess payroll taxes are invested only in lower-earning government bonds.

The main argument against privatization is that we would be trading in Social Security benefits that are computed and committed years in advance for an income that is linked to the gyrations of the stock market. The result would be a heightened uncertainty about our core retirement income. As the economist Alicia Munnell put it, "Uncertain outcomes may be appropriate for supplementary retirement benefits, but not for the basic guarantee" (Munnell n.d.).

Several costs would cut down the income earned from personal retirement accounts:

- Diverting payroll taxes into retirement accounts would deprive Social Security of those funds. Consequently, for several decades, workers would not only have to build up their own retirement accounts but would also have to pay the pensions of retired or near-retired workers who are not part of the new program.
- Shifting payroll taxes out of Social Security would result in a smaller pension as well as a reduction in Social Security benefits for families who lose income as a result of the death or disability of a breadwinner.

- The cost of administering personal retirement accounts would be significantly higher than the cost of administering Social Security.
- Privatization would require a new bureaucracy to transfer the taxes into personal retirement accounts, allocate the funds to selected investments, keep records of deposits and earnings, and provide information to employees and the government. The government would have to police the whole process, which would involve regulatory and enforcement costs.

Even if the stock market performs well over the next several decades, it's likely, as a result of these privatization costs, that many of our children would be hurt if they were allowed to replace Social Security benefits with personal retirement accounts.

The heart of the battle over privatization is not dollars-and-cents calculations, but the clash between the values of individual freedom and collective responsibility. The visions in conflict both have an honored place in American tradition. One sees a society in which individuals are responsible for their lives and are free to make their own financial decisions. Through this lens Social Security looks paternalistic; it taxes people's earnings and decides how much of a pension they will receive. As an aide to President George W. Bush expressed it this way: "Our goal is to provide a path to greater opportunity, more freedom, and more control for individuals over their own lives. That is what the personal account debate is fundamentally about" (Suellentrop 2005).

The philosophy embodied in Social Security is that society is a family responsible for its members. Risks are shared. The cost of caring for the elderly, the disabled, and the poor is spread over the entire society. The highest earners contribute the most and the less fortunate receive help.

Privatization has been rejected by most Democrats and, so far, by the majority of the public, who are reluctant to tamper with the most popular and successful domestic program in American history. As of the summer of 2006, the campaign to allow payroll taxes to be diverted into personal retirement accounts appears dead. Yet the passion of the privatizers remains very much alive, and the issue will surely be resurrected in the future (Benavie n.d.).

MEDICARE

Medicare is a federal health insurance program for people over 65 and for those who are disabled ("Medicare and You 2006"). Medicare Part A (Hospital Insurance) helps pay for inpatient care in hospitals or skilled nursing facilities. It also covers some hospice care and limited home health care after hospitalization. Everyone who is entitled to Social Security is entitled to Medicare Part A. They don't have to pay a premium (a monthly fee) for this insurance because they, or their spouse, paid Medicare taxes while they worked. The elderly or disabled who are not eligible for Social Security must pay a premium for these benefits, which was $393 per month in 2006. Part A is financed by a payroll tax on earnings that is paid by employees and their employers as well as the self-employed. The current Hospital Insurance tax rate is 1.45 percent of earnings for both workers and their employers. The self-employed pay the combined employer and employee tax rate of 2.90 percent.

Medicare Part B (Supplemental Medical Insurance) helps cover doctors' services and outpatient care. It also pays some medical services that Part A doesn't cover, such as physical therapy and limited home health care. Part B is voluntary, but nearly all seniors choose to enroll since it's such a good deal, far better than the private sector can afford. The reason it's so attractive is that the premium pays only about 25 percent of the costs ($88.50 a month in 2006), and income taxes pay the rest (Shaviro n.d.). Daniel Shaviro calls it a "Don Corleone offer," one that "you almost cannot refuse" (Shaviro n.d.). Part B also requires payment of a deductible each year ($124 in 2006) before Medicare pays its share.

Medicare recipients can go to any physician who accepts Medicare patients, or to any hospital, but they have to pay a copayment for a portion of most of the services they get (*Medicare and You 2006*).

Medicare was created in 1965 during the administration of President Lyndon Johnson. In 2003, President George W. Bush signed into law a prescription drug benefit called Part D, the biggest expansion since the program began. Here's how the new part works.

All 42 million Medicare beneficiaries are eligible. The drug benefit is provided by private insurance companies and is subsidized and regulated by the government. Those eligible need not sign up, but postponing enrollment involves a financial penalty. Deciding which plan to join is no easy matter since numerous plans covering different drugs with different premiums and copayments are available. Monthly premiums average $32 but can vary between less than $2 and more than $100. After a year, providers can pull out of Medicare, increase premiums, and change the drugs they cover. Beneficiaries can switch plans yearly. Low-income earners may be eligible for financial help. In addition to premiums, a person joining the Medicare drug plan is by law required to pay an annual deductible of $250, 25 percent of drug costs from $251 to $2,250, and 100 percent of the next $2,850 in expenses (*Medicare and You 2006*). Beyond that—$5,100 a year and more—Medicare will cover around 95 percent of drug costs. The $2,850 gap in the coverage between $2,250 and $5,100 has been called the "doughnut hole."

Experts predict that Medicare's future financial difficulties will be more severe than those confronting Social Security (Social Security and Medicare Board of Trustees n.d.; Pear 2004). Medicare's costs will more than triple as a fraction of the nation's income over the next four-and-a-half decades; specifically, the program will grow from the current 2.7 percent of national income to 5.5 percent in 2025, and to 8.6 percent in 2050 (Congressional Budget Office n.d.; Pear 2004). Will future generations be willing to shoulder the increases in tax rates needed to pay the medical costs of the elderly and disabled? If so, who will pay? If not, will these benefits become more strictly rationed, and if so, how? These are some of the issues that will be debated over the coming decades.

In spite of the financial worries over Medicare, the basic structure of Parts A and B is so well established and so popular that it's unlikely to be significantly altered. On the other hand, the new Medicare Part D, the prescription drug plan, is generating a great deal of criticism.

HOW TO COMPUTE GAINS OR LOSSES BY JOINING MEDICARE PART D

Joining Part D, regardless of the amount of your medical costs, requires an average premium of $32 a month, or $384 a year.

If your drug costs were $2,000 a year, joining the Medicare drug plan would require you to pay the following: the premium of $384 plus the deductible of $250 plus 25 percent of the costs from $251 to $2000, or $437.25, which sums to $1,071.25. So, joining the plan would save you $2,000 minus $1,071 (rounding off), or $929.

If your drug expenses were $5,000 a year, joining the plan would require you to pay $384 plus $250 plus 25 percent of the costs from 251 to 2250, or $500 (rounding off), plus 100 percent of the remaining costs up to $5,000 (this is part of the "doughnut hole"), or $2,749, which sums to $3,883. Joining would save you $5,000 minus $3,883, or $1,117.

If your drug costs were only $500 a year, joining would cost $384 plus $250 plus 25 percent of $500 minus $251, or $62 (rounding), which sums to $696. In this case, joining Part D would increase your drug costs by $196.

Compute the savings if your drug expenses were $10,000 a year. (Answer: $5,172)

First, it requires Medicare recipients to sort through dozens of options with radically different benefits and costs. Even the government admits to having made errors in explaining it (Pear 2005). A survey by the Government Accountability Office—the investigative arm of Congress—found that the government's customer service representatives provided correct information about Part D only 41 percent of the time (Krugman 2006)! As health policy expert Geraldine Dallek of Georgetown University put it, the program

> lacks the simplicity of a single Medicare drug benefit program. Yet it also lacks the virtues of a truly competitive market. Buying a prescription drug benefit isn't like buying a toaster or a pair of shoes. The legislation creates limited but baffling choices for ill-informed consumers unable to predict their needs, judge quality of service, or price shop effectively (Dallek 2003).

In most states, 40 prescription drug plans are available (Pear 2005). A study conducted for the Institute of Medicine concluded that the coverage and cost-sharing differences between these plans makes it unlikely that seniors will be able to make rational choices (Stateline.org n.d.).

Second, the doughnut hole causes out-of-pocket expenses to soar whenever an individual's annual drug costs rise above $2,250. At that point, some beneficiaries will be forced to cut back on even essential medications (Krugman 2005). One way to respond to this problem would have been for a recipient to buy supplemental insurance to cover the gap, but the law specifically prohibits that option (Krugman 2005; Pear 2005).

Finally, the total cost of providing drug benefits through private insurance is considerably higher than it would be for the government to provide these benefits directly. The cost of administering Parts A and B is a mere 2 percent of benefits. The administrative costs of private insurance plans, like Part D, are many times higher (Social Security and Medicare Board of Trustees n.d.; Ball and Bethell n.d.). The reason Medicare is more efficient is that it's universal and nonprofit. Consequently, it hasn't had to spend huge sums on sales, advertising, and management fees. Supporters of Part D argue that competition will bring down the administrative costs of private insurance companies. But competition can't work if consumers are unable to understand their choices (Dallek 2003). In fact, competition has not worked any such magic in the privatized Social Security programs of Great Britain or Chile Benavie n.d.; Levin 2003).

Adding further to the cost of Part D, the federal government is giving billions to insurance companies to induce them to provide a prescription drug benefit. Many of these companies had stopped offering Medicare services in recent years, disrupting care for over 2 million people (Shaviro n.d.; Dallek 2003). The government is also dispensing billions to corporations to maintain their drug benefits so they won't shift employees onto the Medicare program (Walsh 2006). Even so, the Congressional Budget Office has estimated that up to 25 percent of the 2.7 million retirees with existing drug coverage through a former employer will lose that coverage (Levin 2003).

Experts, as well as most Democrats, have been critical of the new Medicare drug plan. They argue that Medicare, since its inception, has been an effective, efficient, and universal vehicle for providing health care to seniors and the disabled. By contrast, Medicare Part D involves large administrative costs, requires subsidies to insurance companies and corporations, is no longer universal, and permits private health providers to drop out of Medicare at the end of each year (Dallek 2003).

But again, the key issue here is not financial. As with the abortive attempt to privatize Social Security, the debate over the new Medicare drug program reflects the ideological battle over entitlements. President George W. Bush, along with most Republicans, believes that individuals should have more freedom to make their own financial decisions and bear more of the responsibility for taking care of themselves. Part D reflects that philosophy. As the former Republican majority leader of the House of Representatives, Tom DeLay, put it, referring to Part D: "I'm very proud of that. We took Republican philosophy to the welfare state. We introduced competition, choice, personal responsibility, new health care methods that were not covered by Medicare" (Delay 2006).

Medicare Parts A and B are an expression of the opposite view. Workers are required to pay a tax for Part A, or induced by irresistible terms to join Part B, in exchange for government-funded medical benefits upon reaching 65 or becoming disabled (Shaviro n.d.). This struggle between individual freedom and collective responsibility will be with us for many generations to come.

MEDICAID

Medicaid was born in 1965 on the same day as Medicare. It's a joint federal/state program providing medical benefits for people with limited incomes and resources. Medicaid provides coverage for the following groups: children and their parents, the elderly, pregnant women, and the disabled (Kaiser Commission on Medicaid and the Uninsured 2004). Since programs for the poor are never popular, Medicaid was scarcely mentioned by President Lyndon Johnson in the bill-signing ceremony, where he focused almost entirely on Medicare (Stateline.org.n.d.). Yet Medicaid has become the largest public health-care program in the nation, serving 57 million people in 2005, as compared to 42 million for Medicare (Congressional Budget Office n.d.).

Apart from the fact that the two programs have similar names, they are very different. Medicare is a federal program, while Medicaid is actually 50 different programs designed and administered by each state under federal guidelines and with federal support. Unlike Medicare, Medicaid is means tested: to be eligible you have to be poor enough. The state programs are required to cover a broad range of services, such as physician and hospital care, nursing home care, and prescription drugs (Kaiser Commission 2004). Medicaid also fills in gaps in Medicare coverage for low-income seniors, such as prescription drugs and long-term care (Kaiser Commission 2004; Trite 2005).

There are also Medicaid services that are provided by some states and not others. For example, states have flexibility in determining what services are medically necessary for the mentally retarded who are in intermediate care facilities, or for those over 65 who are institutionalized. State programs may differ on the number of days a medical service can be provided or the number of prescriptions that can be filled in a specified time. Also, the income requirements for enrolling vary from state to state, so people who are eligible for Medicaid in one state may not be eligible in another (Pear 2004; Department of Health and Human Services 2005).

In addition to Medicaid, the federal government also contributes to a state-run health insurance program for children up to age 19 called SCHIP (State Children's Health Insurance Program) (Department of Health and Human Services 2005). In some states SCHIP is combined with Medicaid, and in some states it's separate. The purpose of the program is to cover children whose parents are too well off for Medicaid but too poor to afford private insurance. Most states provide coverage to families whose incomes are below 200 percent of the federal poverty level. (The 2005 federal poverty level for a family of four in the 48 contiguous states and Washington, D.C., is $19,350. In Alaska, it's $24,190, and in Hawaii $22,269. See www.atdn.org/access/poverty.html.)

The federal government matches a portion of states' Medicaid spending, using a formula to calculate how much to give each state. The richer the state is, the less it gets. The federal matching rate—the fraction of the state's Medicaid expenses covered by federal funds—is based on the state's per capita income and ranges between 50 and 80 percent. The federal government's share of Medicaid spending averages about 57 percent (Congressional Budget Office n.d.).

On average, states spend about 16 percent of their revenue on Medicaid, which is the second-largest item in their budget, exceeded only by elementary and secondary education. About 30 percent of the spending on Medicaid is directed to low-income children and their parents, while 70 percent goes to the disabled and the elderly (Kaiser Commission 2004).

Over the next several decades, Medicaid is expected to grow almost as rapidly as Medicare, from 1.5 percent of GDP in 2005 to 2.6 percent in 2025, and to 4.0 percent in 2050 (Congressional Budget Office n.d.).

Like the other entitlements, Medicaid is an emotional and divisive issue between Democrats and Republicans. As an example, consider the Deficit

Reduction Act, passed in February 2006 by a Republican-controlled House and Senate and signed by President George W. Bush. The ostensible purpose of the act, as its name indicates, was to reduce the huge budget deficits incurred under President Bush and predicted to last well into the future. (A budget deficit exists whenever the federal government spends more than it collects in taxes and is forced to borrow the difference.) Opposed by almost all Democrats, the act trimmed the deficit by hacking away at Medicaid, thus cutting health-care services for the poor by around $42 billion over the next decade (Parrott, Park, and Greenstein 2006; Kaiser Commission 2006; Kassner 2006). This budget saving will scarcely make a dent in the looming deficits; it's mere pocket change to a government that will spend an average of $3 trillion a year over the next 10 years. But to the impoverished, it could mean suffering or even death. The Senate passed the Deficit Reduction Act by a vote of 52 to 46, with 50 Republicans and only 2 Democrats voting aye, and 41 Democrats and 5 Republicans voting nay (U.S. Senate Web Site). Consider some of the provisions of the act.

All 57 million people on Medicaid must now show acceptable documentation to prove they are U.S. citizens. Not even those with severe physical or mental impairments, such as Alzheimer's disease, will be exempt (Parrott, Park, and Greenstein 2006). This provision was justified as a way to prevent illegal immigrants from getting benefits from Medicaid; but a recent study by the inspector general of the Department of Health and Human Services found no evidence to support the contention that illegal immigrants had enrolled in Medicaid (HHS Office of Inspector General 2005). The study concluded that this requirement will prevent millions of low-income citizens from receiving Medicaid. Data from a national survey found that 3 to 5million citizens—including 1.4 to 2.9 million children—enrolled in Medicaid may not have access to a birth certificate or a passport and as a result may lose their Medicaid coverage. In some cases, people may never have had a birth certificate or had their birth officially registered. This appears to be a particular problem with elderly African Americans, many of whom, because of racial discrimination and poverty, were not born in a hospital (Ku and Broaddus 2006).

Prior to the Deficit Reduction Act, states could not charge premiums to Medicaid beneficiaries and could only charge $3 for each service or medication, with children exempt. The act now requires beneficiaries, including 6 million children, to begin paying considerably more for Medicaid services (the upper limit on these cost increases is 5 percent of a family's income over a three-month period ; Parrott, Park, and Greenstein 2006):

- For beneficiaries with incomes of 100 to 150 percent of the poverty line, a co-payment of 10 percent of the cost of a needed medical service replaces a maximum fee of $3. So, a procedure costing $800 now requires a co-payment of $80 instead of a fee of $3.
- For beneficiaries with incomes above 150 percent of the poverty line, states may now charge premiums to participate in Medicaid as well as co-payments of up to 20 percent of the cost of a needed medical service.
- For beneficiaries below the poverty line, the $3 fee will now increase each year at a faster rate than the general price level.

According to the Congressional Budget Office, these increases in premiums and co-payments will likely cause many Medicaid beneficiaries to forego needed services and medications and to prevent some impoverished people from enrolling in Medicaid (Parrott, Park, and Greenstein 2006).

At the same time the federal government was reducing the budget deficit by squeezing Medicaid, President Bush and the Republicans were campaigning to make the tax cuts of 2001 and 2003 permanent. If these tax reductions, which mostly benefit the wealthy, were made permanent, the budget deficit would be increased by about $2.5 trillion over the next decade, swamping the deficit cuts of $14 billion over the next decade resulting from trimming Medicaid (Greestein, Freidman, and Aron-Dine 2005).

It appears that the Deficit Reduction Act was concerned with deficit reduction in name only. Its real goal was to shrink Medicaid, a program less popular with Republicans than Democrats—revealing once again a sharp difference in philosophy between our two major political parties over the issue of entitlements.

CONCLUSION

Ideological conflict is the gut issue in the battle over entitlements. On one side is the Republican philosophy, which focuses on the freedom of individuals to make their own decisions and assume the responsibility for taking care of themselves, rather than being limited by and dependent on the government. On the other side are those who emphasize the obligations of the government to empower its citizens and to care for the weak and the unfortunate. Bill Clinton summarized the Democratic philosophy this way: "We think the role of government should be to give people the tools to create the conditions to make the most of their lives. And we think everybody should have that chance" (Speech to the Democratic National Convertion, July 29, 2004).

This ideological split is reflected in the fight over privatizing Social Security. The issue is whether workers should be given the option of putting their payroll taxes into a personal retirement account instead of turning them over to the government. Under privatization, workers would have the freedom to invest a portion of their payroll taxes in the stock market and upon retirement they would have access to the assets that have accumulated in their portfolio. Under Social Security, the government invests payroll taxes only in Treasury bonds and uses a formula to determine the amount that pension workers receive when they retire. But the increase in freedom under privatization would be achieved at a cost: there would be a heightened uncertainty over the core income of retirees due to the gyrations of the stock market, and the major program for reducing poverty among the elderly would be downsized.

The same philosophical division exists for Medicare. Those favoring individual freedom and responsibility dislike the payroll tax funding Medicare Part A (Hospital Insurance). They would prefer to take care of themselves. Supporters of this insurance argue that without the tax, many would fail to save enough to provide health care for themselves when they reach 65. The freedom provided by the new Medicare drug prescription program to select a private insurance company comes at a steep price: namely, the confusion and uncertainty experienced by seniors when faced with the daunting task of making a rational choice from among dozens of companies with radical differences in costs and drug coverage.

As for Medicaid, many citizens dislike being taxed for the purpose of supporting others, many of whom they feel should be made to care for themselves. Others are inspired by the idea that we take care of each other, with the more fortunate helping the less fortunate.

Entitlements remain passionately controversial and always have been. While powerful forces detest them, they are also strongly supported by most Americans. The battle lines are drawn and the outcome will affect the nature of the society our children grow up in.

References

Aaron, Henry J., and Robert D. Reischauer. *Countdown to Reform.*

Baker, Dean, and Mark Weisbrot, *Social Security: The Phony Crisis,*.111–14.

Ball, Robert M., with Thomas N. Bethell. "A Framework for Considering Social Security Reform." In *Framing the Social Security Debate,* edited by R. D. Arnold, M. J. Graetz, and A. H. Munnell, p. 30.

Ball, Robert, with Thomas Bethell "Bridging the Centuries." In *Social Security in the 21st Century,* edited by Eric Kingson and James Schulz, p. 276.

Benavie, Arthur. *Social Security Under the Gun.*

Chen, Yung-Ping, and Stephen Goss. "Are Returns on Payroll Taxes Fair?" In *Social Security in the 21st Century,* edited by Eric Kingson and James Schulz, p. 77.

Congressional Budget Office. *The Long-Term Budget Outlook.* Table 1–1.

Congressional Budget Office. 2006. *Current Budget Projections.* March 3.

Dallek, Geraldine. 2003. "Thanks For the Medicare Muddle." *Washington Post,* December 7.

DeLay, Tom. 2006. Interview with Rush Limbaugh, April 5. Available at www.securingamerica.com/ccn/node/5394.

Department of Health and Human Services, Center for Medicare and Medicaid Services. *Medicaid At-a Glance 2005.*

Diamond, Peter A., ed. *Issues in Privatizing Social Security: Report of an Expert Panel of the National Academy of Social Insurance,* p. 17.

Greenstein, Robert, Joel Friedman, and Aviva Aron-Dine. 2005. "Two Tax Cuts Primarily Benefiting Millionaires Will Start Taking Effect on January 1." *Center on Budget and Policy Priorities,* December 28.

HHS Office of the Inspector General. 2005. *Self-Declaration of U.S. Citizenship Requirements for Medicaid.*

Kaiser Commission on Medicaid and the Uninsured. 2004. "The Continuing Medicaid Budget Challenge: State Medicaid Spending Growth and Cost Containment in Fiscal Years 2004 and 2005."

Kaiser Commission On Medicaid and the Uninsured. 2006. "Deficit Reduction Act of 2005: Implications for Medicaid."

Kassner, Enid. 2006. "Medicaid and Long-Term Services and Supports for Older People." *AARP Public Policy Institute.*

Kingson, Eric R., and James H. Schulz, eds. *Social Security in the 21st Century.*

Krugman, Paul. 2005. "The Deadly Doughnut." *New York Times,* November 11.

Krugman, Paul. 2006. "D for Debacle." *New York Times,* May 15.

Ku, Leighton, and Matt Broaddus. 2006. "New Requirement for Birth Certificates or Passports Could Threaten Medicaid Coverage for Vulnerable Beneficiaries: A State-By-State Analysis." *Center on Budget and Policy Priorities,* revised February 17.

Levin, Carl. 2003. *The Medicare Prescription Drug Improvement and Modernization Act of 2003 Conference Report.* November 23.

"Medicare and You, 2006." *The Official Government Handbook.*

Medicare and You 2006, Centers for Medicare and Medicaid Services, p. 23.

Munnell, Alicia. "Comment." In *Should the United Privatize Social Security,* by Henry Aaron and John Shoven, pp. 135–36.

Parrott, Sharon, Edwin Park, and Robert Greenstein. 2006. "Assessing the Effects of the Budget Conference Agreement on Low-income Families and Individuals." *Center on Budget and Policy Priorities,* pp. 2–3.

Pear, Robert. 2004. "Medicare System Worse—Big Drop in Funds/Bleak New Forecast: Health Plan Could Go Broke in 15 Year." *New York Times,* March 24.

Pear, Robert. 2004. "Medicare Overseers Expect Costs to Soar in Coming Decades." *New York Times,* March 24.

Pear, Robert. 2005. "As Deadline Nears, Sorting Out the Medicare Drug Plan." *New York Times,* October 11.

Report of the 1994–1996 Advisory Council on Social Security: Findings, Recommendations, and Statements, p. 7.

Seidman, Lawrence S. *Funding Social Security.* pp. 153–54.

Shaviro, Daniel. *Making Sense of Social Security Reform.*

Shaviro, Daniel. *Who Should Pay for Medicare?*

Social Security and Medicare Boards of Trustees. *A Summary of the 2005 Annual Reports.* Available at www.ssa.gov/OACT/TRSUM/trsummary.html.

Social Security and Medicare Boards of Trustees. *A Summary of the 2006 Annual Reports.* Available at www.ssa.gov/OACT/TRSUM/trsummary.html.

Stateline.org. *Medicaid—Cost and Complexity Tax Reform Efforts.*

Suellentrop, Chris. 2005. "George W. Bush. Philosopher King." *Slate.* January 17in www.slate.com

Tritz, Karen L. 2005. "Medicaid Expenditures, FY2002 and FY2003." *CRS Report for Congress,* updated February 15.

Walsh, Mary Williams. 2006. "U.S. to Pay Big Employers Billions Not to End Their Retiree Health Plans." *New York Times,* February 24; Levy, Clifford J. 2006. "The New Corporate Outsourcing." *New York Times,* January 29.

Further Reading: Benavie, Arthur. *Social Security Under the Gun*; Shaviro, Daniel. *Who Should Pay for Medicare?* Department of Health and Human Services, Center for Medicare and Medicaid Services. *Medicaid At-a Glance 2005.*

Arthur Benavie

STOCK MARKET PREDICTIONS

In the autumn of 1995, investors in the Magellan Fund of Fidelity Management & Research Company could look back on a remarkable record of performance: an average annual total return of 22.7 percent per year over the previous 15 years, which surpassed the return on the Standard & Poor's 500 Index by 7.77 percent per year. A simple example will help to explain these numbers: if you were an investor who spent $1,000 to purchase this mutual fund in 1980 and had held it for 15 years, by 1995, your investment would be worth $21,511!

Of special note was that the fund had delivered superior performance despite turnover in its management. The fund's long-standing and highly successful manager, Peter Lynch, retired in 1990. His replacement was Morris Smith, who retired in 1992. His replacement was Jeffrey Vinik. The financial press noted that all three managers "beat the market" during their tenure.

The successful story of Magellan Fund raised a question. Can somebody or anybody "beat the market" on a sustained basis? The answer seems to be a definite yes given the above-mentioned information. But not so fast! Let's first see what had happened to Magellan Fund after 1995.

Vinik retired on June 3, 1996. During his tenure, the Magellan Fund beat the S&P 500 by only 1.61 percent. Vinik was followed by Robert E. Stansky. In late 1996, Morningstar reduced Magellan's coveted five-star ranking to four stars. The fund's total return for 1996 was 11.26 percent below the return on the S&P 500 Index. Observers wondered whether this marked the end of the era of Magellan's supernormal performance.

Now what would be your answer to the question? Along with this question there are some other questions. Why do we want to predict the stock market? Can the stock market be predicted? What is the difference between predicting the stock market and beating the market? Let's see if there are some answers to these important questions.

WHY DO WE WANT TO PREDICT THE STOCK MARKET?

One of the most popular thoughts about investing in stocks is that in order to be successful, you must be able to predict the stock market's movements. Why do people assume this? Some falsely assume that stocks bounce around in the same range forever, and they therefore conclude they must predict movements in order to be able to sell at the top of the range and buy at the bottom of the range (the typical "buy low, sell high" notion). For others, the desire to predict is borne out of human nature, which puts a premium on certainty. We just love to know what will happen in advance in order to protect ourselves.

Financial analysts on Wall Street love to advance the cause of market predicting, because they are paid to predict these movements. For instance, nearly every retail brokerage firm has a chief economist or market strategist whose main responsibility is to predict the climate for stocks. A large number of books and advisory services that are sold focus almost exclusively on prediction of how the stock market in general will perform in the future.

There is no doubt that if someone could accurately predict the short-term fluctuations of the stock market, that person would become the richest in the world very easily. Even a simple prediction of the directions of the stock market movement can help one get rich: when you get up each and every morning for the rest of your life, make this prediction: "The market will be up/down today." If your prediction is up today, you will buy the market index at the opening and sell it at the close. If your prediction is down today, you will short sell the market index at the opening and buy it at the close. Even if your predictions are not 100 percent accurate, perhaps only 9 out of 10 times accurate, you will be richer than the stock market gurus.

So, why do we want to predict the stock market? If we could simply predict the directions of stock market movement, we could easily beat the market and become rich. However, is the market predictable?

CAN WE PREDICT THE STOCK MARKET? NO!

Over 30 years ago, Burton G. Malkiel of Princeton University maintained that stock prices follow a random walk and cannot systematically be predicted by stock market professionals (Malkiel 1973). Professor Malkiel suggested that throwing darts (or, more realistically, a towel) at the newspaper stock listings is as good a way as any to pick stocks and is likely to beat the predictions of most professional investment managers. Malkiel does suggest how those who insist on trying to beat the market might attempt to do so, but he indicates that they are unlikely to be successful.

Basically, Malkiel believed that no one (or virtually no one) can predict the stock market. Someone may want to disagree, because we hear the success stories all the time. Yes, in the short run, there are some stock market gurus who can earn extraordinary profits by spending time looking at charts and tables and trying to figure out what the trend of tomorrow's stock market will be. After all, you could buy a stock today and tomorrow a major discovery could be announced that would cause its stock price to increase significantly. Does that mean that you beat the market? Obviously not; it means that you are either very skillful or, more likely, very lucky. The question is, can you and enough other investors do this a sufficient number of times in the long run to earn abnormal profits? The story of Magellan Fund is a good example of this argument.

The concept described above is defined as the efficient market hypothesis, which is simply the idea that securities markets are efficient, and prices of securities reflect their economic value. In a perfectly efficient market, securities prices always immediately reflect all available information, and investors are not able to use available information to earn abnormal returns, because it is already impounded in prices. In other words, if the efficient market hypothesis holds true, you simply cannot predict the stock market and therefore beat the market.

There is evidence that proves that the stock market is efficient. The announcement of a takeover and the day's stock price reaction is a good example. It is well documented that when one company buys another, the stock price of the target company will go up on the date of the announcement of the takeover (Jensen and Ruback 1983). In the following, let's see whether we could earn some extra money following an AOL and Time Warner merger announcement.

On January 10, 2000, the wire services reported the proposed blockbuster merger of AOL and Time Warner. Though described as a merger of equals, AOL really acquired Time Warner. So, in this merger, AOL is the bidder firm, and Time Warner is the target firm. From that information, we can predict that on January 10, 2000, Time Warner's stock price will go up. On January 7, 2000 (one trading day before January 10, 2000, because January 10 is a Monday), Time Warner's stock was traded on the NYSE and closed at $64.75. If we knew that on Monday Time Warner will be acquired by AOL, we would definitely purchase Time Warner's stock on the previous Friday and earn enormous profits. But do we know that in advance? No, no one knows that on the previous Friday except for corporate insiders. Keep in mind that according to the U.S. Securities and Exchange Commission regulation, insiders are not allowed to trade.

So, we will have to wait until next Monday (January 10, 2000). Suppose you were an early bird and got up at 5 a.m. You also had a good habit of reading the Wall Street Journal when you had breakfast. You saw the news of the merger announcement and immediately realized that today the stock price of Time Warner would go up. You impatiently waited until 9:30 A.M. for the market opening and planned to purchase the stocks of Time Warner and then sold it later the same day. Can you earn abnormal profits? The answer is a definite no. Wonder why? Let's take a look at the stock price movement during these several days.

Figure S.5 shows that Time Warner's stock was closed at $64.75 at 4 P.M. on January 7, 2000. However, when the market reopens the next Monday, Time Warner's stock was open at $91 on the announcement date of the proposed merger. So, when you make your move on January 10, you are not the only person. There are a large number of investors who are constantly "playing the game." Both individuals and institutions follow the market closely on a daily basis, standing ready to buy or sell when they think it is appropriate. When these investors saw the news, they would make the same decision—that is, immediately purchase the stocks of Time Warner, expecting that its stock price would go up today. As a result, the high demand of Time Warner's stocks would drive the stock price up. So, when you started to make your move (at 9:30 A.M.), the stock price of Time Warner had already gone up and you were unable to make abnormal profits. The market in which investors adjust security prices very quickly to reflect random information coming into the market is called an efficient market, and if the market is efficient, you are unable to make abnormal profits.

CAN WE PREDICT THE STOCK MARKET? YES!

Having considered the type of evidence supporting market efficiency, we can now consider some market anomalies. By definition, an anomaly is an exception to a rule or model. Thus, these market anomalies are in contrast to what would be expected in a totally efficient market and constitute exceptions to market efficiency. To date, most of them have not been explained away, and until that happens, they remain anomalies or exceptions to market efficiency.

In last section, we mentioned that stock prices follow a "random walk" and there is no historical pattern on the stock price movements. However, several

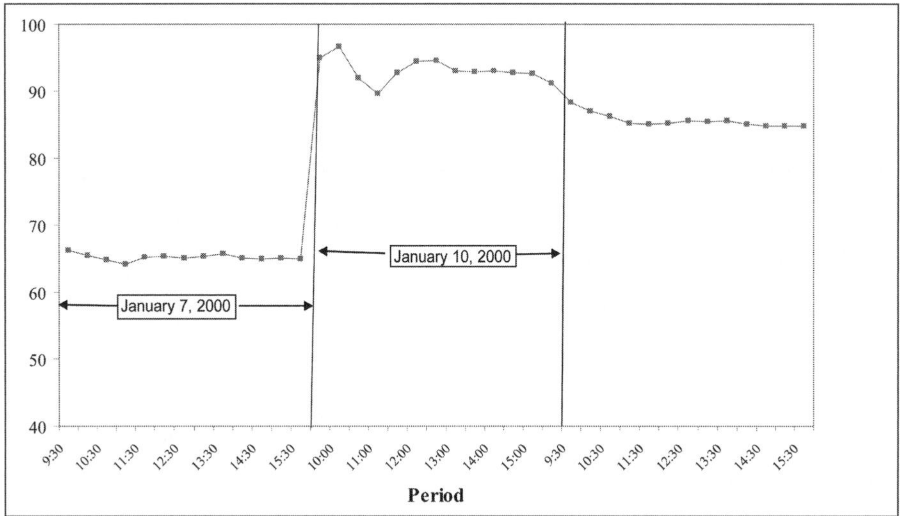

Figure S.5 Price pattern for Time Warner around merger announcement.
Source: Trade and Quote database.

studies in the past have suggested that seasonality exists in the stock market. Some of the seasonalities could simply be coincidences. For example, there is evidence that daily returns around new moons have been roughly double those around full moons. It seems difficult to believe that this is anything other than a chance relationship—fun to read about, but not a concern for serious investors or financial managers. But not all exceptions can be dismissed so easily. Among others, the so-called January effect is one of the most famous anomalies on market efficiency.

In 1983, Professor Keim found that small NYSE and Amex firms had abnormal returns over large stocks with data for 1963 to 1979 (Keim 1983). More interestingly, roughly half of the excess returns occurred in January, and more than half of the excess January returns occurred during the first five trading days of that month. The first trading day of the year showed a high small-firm premium for every year of the period studied. The strong performance in January by small-company stocks has become known as the January effect. Recent evidence on the January effect, as measured by the performance of the NASDAQ Composite Index for the month of January, is shown in Figure S.6.

This simple evidence, which makes no comparisons or other judgments, suggests that the January effect has continued to exist in recent years, at least in the sense of a solid January performance for these stocks. As the data indicates, there were only three negative years through January 2003.

The information about a possible January effect has been available for years and has been widely discussed in the press. If the market was really efficient and investors in later years had exploited this information (i.e., purchase small stocks

1985	112.7%	1995	0.4%
1986	3.3%	1996	0.7%
1987	112.4%	1997	6.9%
1988	4.3%	1998	3.1%
1989	5.2%	1999	14.2%
1990	–8.6%	2000	-3.2%
1991	110.8%	2001	12.2%
1992	5.8%	2002	–0.8%
1993	2.9%	2003	-1.1%
1994	3.1%		

Figure S.6 Recent evidence on January effect (1985–2003).
Source: Jones, Charles P. Investments. 9th ed. New York: Wiley.

WHAT IS A RANDOM WALK?

In his book A Random Walk Down Wall Street, published in 1973, Malkiel maintained that stock prices follow a random walk and cannot systematically be predicted by stock market professionals. Figure S.7 provides an explanation of what a random walk is.

In Figure S.7, the horizontal axis shows the return on the Standard & Poor 500 Index in one week, while the vertical axis shows the return in the following week. Each point in the chart represents a different week between January 1955 and April 2002. If a market rise one week tended to be followed by a rise the next week, the points in the chart would plot along an upward-sloping line. But you can see from the figure that there is no such tendency; the points are scattered randomly across the figure. In fact, prices appear to wander randomly, virtually equally likely to offer a high or low return on any particular day, regardless of what has occurred on previous days. This is the notion of the random walk of stock prices.

Random walk theory has important implications for technical analysts, who try to achieve superior returns by spotting and exploiting patterns in stock prices. This investing strategy may seem plausible on first sight. For example, you might hope to beat the market by buying stocks when they are on their way up and by selling them on their way down. Unfortunately, it turns out that such simple rules don't work. From the above figure, we can see that a large price rise in one period may be followed by a further rise in the next period, but it is just as likely to be followed by a fall. Therefore, random walk theory is a big blow to the technical analysts. If stock prices really follow a random walk, you cannot make money on a consistent basis by looking at historical trends of stock prices (since there is no trend), technical analysis does not work, and all these technicians should quit their jobs. Now do you see why efficient market hypothesis has not grabbed hold of the public's imagination?

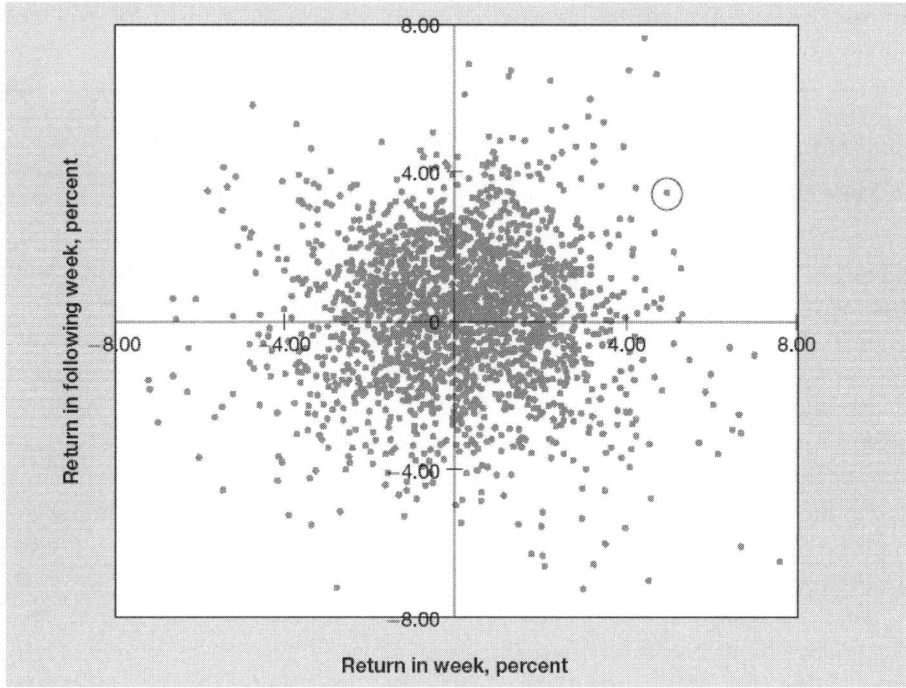

Figure S.7 Historical stock return on S&P index.

Source: Brealey, Richard A., Stewart C. Myers, and Alan J. Marcus. Fundamentals of Corporate Finance. 4th ed. Boston: McGraw-Hill Irwin.

during December and sell those stocks in January) to earn abnormal profits, prices of the small stocks would have reflected this public knowledge and then there would be no January effect in later years. But why does reality prove otherwise? The question arises, therefore, as to why a January effect would persist and recur again and again. Because the anomaly can be inexpensively exploited, its persistence provides counterevidence for the theory of efficient markets.

Another example that efficient market proponents feel uncomfortable explaining is the market bubble that burst in 2000, after which the stock market declined sharply over the next two years. During the dot-com boom of the late 1990s, stock prices rose to astronomical levels. The NASDAQ Composite Index rose 580 percent from the beginning of 1995 to its peak in March 2000 and then fell by nearly 80 percent. A strict interpretation of the efficient market hypothesis would say that a rational explanation should exist for what happened in the market in the late 1990s as stocks were bid up to higher and higher levels before ultimately collapsing. But most observers today argue that stock prices are open to speculative bubbles, where investors are caught up in a whirl of irrational exuberance. Now it may well be true that some of us are liable to become overexcited, but why don't professional investors bail out of the overpriced stocks?

Obviously the Internet bubble in 2000 is not in agreement with the efficient markets view.

WHY SHOULD WE CARE IF THE MARKET IS EFFICIENT?

Why should we as investors care if the market is efficient, an issue that has been debated vigorously by academics for many years? In an informationally efficient market, many traditional investing activities are suspect at best and useless at worst. Why? Because in a truly efficient market, it should be impossible to discriminate between a profitable investment and an unprofitable one, given currently available information. Yes, you can spend tons of time looking at charts and tables and doing research on the stock market, but your performance may not be better than that of investors who just pick up stocks they want to buy by throwing darts at the stock listings. Therefore, if you are interested in a job in the securities business, your expected probability of beating the market as a portfolio manager is small; furthermore, the value of the product of a typical security analyst may be very small.

The idea of an efficient market has generated tremendous controversy over the years, which continues today. This is not surprising in view of the enormous implications that an efficient market has for everyone concerned with securities. Some market participants' jobs and reputations are at stake, and they are not going to accept this concept readily. Think of the large number of highly paid portfolio managers of actively managed mutual funds as well as other institutional portfolios—how would you expect them to react to the notion that they are unlikely to add value because the market is efficient?

Whether or not the market is efficient is really important as well for individual investors. If an investor believes that the U.S. stock market is highly efficient and therefore active management by portfolio managers will not result in a better performance, such an investor should opt for a passive approach. This approach takes a long-term view on a buy-and-hold basis. The investor will buy stocks and plan to hold them for the long run or buy stocks with the intent of doing as well as a market index.

SUMMARY

We have been told both sides of the stories, and now the question is, So, is the stock market efficient? Can we predict the stock market movement?

There is a telling joke about two economists walking down Wall Street. They spot a $20 bill on the sidewalk. One starts to pick it up, but the other one says, "Don't bother; if the bill were real someone would have picked it up already." The lesson is clear. An extreme view on either side is probably unwarranted. On one hand, there is evidence of market efficiency; and on the other hand, there are enough anomalies to refute market efficiency. The conclusion is that it is not about whether the hypothesis is right or wrong. There must obviously be some level of efficiency in the markets. However, there exists enough evidence that suggests that the market is not perfectly efficient. The question should be, how efficient is it? It is not an all-or-nothing issue.

References

Jensen, Michael C., and Richard S. Ruback. 1983. "The Market for Corporate Control." *Journal of Financial Economics* 11:5–50.

Keim, Donald B. 1983. "Size-Related Anomalies and Stock Return Seasonality." *Journal of Financial Economics* 12:13–32.

Malkiel, Burton G. 1973. *A Random Walk Down Wall Street.* New York: Norton.

Further Reading: Greenblatt, Joel, and Andrew Tobias. 2005. *The Little Book that Beats the Market.* New York: John Wiley & Sons; Malkiel, Burton G. 1973. *A Random Walk Down Wall Street.* New York: Norton; Wyss, B. O'Neill. 2001. *Fundamentals of the Stock Market.* New York: McGraw-Hill.

Xin Zhao

STRATEGIC PLANNING

Strategic planning isn't dead, although it has undergone significant changes since its heyday in the 1960s and 1970s. After a period of dormancy when it fell out of favor during the 1980s, it has seen a resurgence since the mid-1990s as managers have recognized its usefulness in establishing a direction for their organizations when it can be made more flexible to respond to today's fast-paced environments.

DEFINITION

Strategic planning is the process of developing organization-wide goals or objectives and an approach to achieving them. This is a deceivingly simple definition, because in reality strategic planning requires leaders to consider virtually all factors relevant to an organization's circumstances—internally and externally—and how they should respond to them. Strategic planning is designed to establish the direction of an organization so that it can be moved toward a desirable future state, thereby achieving, maintaining, or enhancing its success.

THE HISTORY OF STRATEGY AND STRATEGIC PLANNING

Strategic planning establishes the foundation for strategic management, which is the application of forward-looking thinking and principles with an emphasis on an organization's big picture rather than its day-to-day activities and decisions. That leads to the fundamental question of what strategy is. To fully understand the importance and consequences of strategic planning, one must first understand the concept of strategy. At its core, strategy is concerned with two basic issues: where managers want their organizations to go and how they want them to get there. Although there are a number of technical definitions, strategy essentially boils down to the set of integrated competitive actions an organization undertakes in order to produce successful performance. To use a driving analogy, it is a roadmap for an organization; to employ a sports analogy, it is an organization's game plan. By definition, strategic situations and decisions involve the entire organization, influence its goals and objectives, affect its position relative to its rivals in the competitive environment, and are applied over some period of time so that they can be measured and evaluated.

Strategy and strategic planning are nothing new. In fact, their origins can be traced to the days of Greece in the fifth century B.C., where the word strategia was used to describe the ability to use available resources (manpower, weapons, and tactics) to wage and win military campaigns, and the title strategos, literally meaning "leader of the army," was bestowed upon its generals. It was a term reserved principally for military contexts until after World War II, when business enterprises started to appropriate military terminology to describe competitive activities and rival firms. During that period, strategic planning took root, first in those large business enterprises, and subsequently in smaller businesses, nonprofit organizations, and public entities.

Strategic planning today is a management tool, and as such, its sole purpose should be for an organization to improve itself and do a better job for its constituents and stakeholders, who share an interest in its performance. Strategic planning should help organizations focus their efforts and precious resources—time, people, and money—so that they work toward the same ends. There is nothing magical or mystical about strategic planning. It is the establishment of a path, based on a series of decisions and actions, that will shape and guide the organization with a focus on its future.

THE EVOLUTION OF STRATEGIC PLANNING

Strategic planning has undergone some dramatic changes since it was first widely used in the heady days of U.S. business in the 1960s and 1970s. Then, strategic planning was concerned with establishing abstract, cerebral stratagems to keep an organization ahead of its fairly predictable competitors. Large industrial companies established centralized strategic planning departments populated by planning specialists, largely isolated from the day-to-day grind of business and responsible only to top executives or perhaps even the board of directors. Elegant, broad strategic postures set the stage for the development of organization-wide initiatives designed to maintain an organization's position in its competitive environment. Such traditional approaches to strategic planning emphasized the formulation of strategies without much thought to the implementation of those strategies. Prospector companies pursued new ideas and stayed a step ahead of rivals in terms of their product and service offerings. Defender companies carved out large market shares and established cost barriers designed to thwart rivals and make it difficult for others to overcome if they attempted to enter their industries. Analyzer companies sought to establish and maintain a balance of the features that characterized prospectors and defenders, pursuing some new initiatives through technological innovation and market development, but simultaneously remaining focused on bread-and-butter product-market sets by striving for efficiency. Companies' strategic planning groups were largely isolated from daily operations and reported to senior executives. Strategy was concerned with cleverness rather than survival.

In the mid- to late 1980s, things changed. The nature of competition had been fundamentally and permanently altered, and the structure of entire industries underwent seismic shifts. Customers began to demand more and more for less and less and at higher levels of quality and service than ever before. Nimble new organizations arrived on the scene and with their closer attention to customer needs and service threatened the very existence of established incumbent organizations. The erosion of customer and employee loyalty threatened to overturn existing ways of doing business and governing organizations. Global competitors presented major challenges to established ways of conducting operations. In response, strategic planning became a mechanism used to play catch-up. Restructuring and downsizing replaced true strategic thinking as companies adopted more reactive responses to their new competitive realities. "Strategy" became a bad word and elicited suspicion, fear, and (sometimes) loathing. After all, it is hard to think strategically when others are nipping at your heels or eating your lunch.

Recently, however, the tide has turned once again, and organizations have reacquainted themselves with strategic planning. Managers and researchers agree that organizational strategy has reemerged as one of the most important management issues today. But the differences between the models of then and now are significant and clear. Strategic planning has evolved. Henry Mintzberg, a management scholar of tremendous influence, is perhaps the greatest critic of traditional strategic planning and the most vocal proponent of new approaches aimed at creating strategy. In The Rise and Fall of Strategic Planning, as well as a series of articles published in 1994, he made a number of suggestions to make strategic planning relevant again. First, he argued that to effect change, organizational leaders need to "unfreeze" their fundamental beliefs, seek new ones, then "refreeze" those beliefs (Mintzberg 1994a, b, c, d). He suggested that traditional strategic planning and its models were responsible for those frozen beliefs. His major criticism was not with strategic planning per se, but rather the flawed process that had become isolated from other activities in the organization; too conservative, favoring incrementalism at the expense of creativity, and inflexible. He faulted managers for their inability to mentally step outside the process and examine their situations more critically, instead of following lock-step established procedures. He also criticized the political activity that inevitably surrounds the strategic planning process and interferes with the generation of objective, value-free organizational goals.

In essence, Mintzberg stated that strategic planning had fallen out of favor because it failed to reflect strategic thinking, focusing instead on strategic programming—the implementation of already existing strategies with an emphasis on analyzing and manipulating numbers. He cautioned that such activity often works against truly strategic thinking, which should establish the direction for an organization to proceed. His views have been validated to a great extent in how organizations have modified their approaches to strategic planning during the past decade.

TRENDS IN CONTEMPORARY STRATEGIC PLANNING

The emergence of the information age, instant communication, and globalization has given rise to new ideas about strategic planning. Today's need for organizations to be faster, more flexible, and adept at handling increasing amounts of information with unparalleled accuracy and making wise decisions under time constraints is being mirrored in changes to the strategic planning process. Sustaining success is harder and harder to do, and it follows that the very factors that lead to earlier success might be those that restrain organizations from building on that success. Accordingly, contemporary strategic planning reflects that awareness as well.

Several trends typify contemporary strategic planning. First is the need for speed. Organizations that use strategic planning most effectively perform it quickly. They really don't have much choice; their environments and competitive situations are changing so rapidly that time lost in planning translates to plans that are not precisely targeted for maximum effectiveness. Traditional strategic planning was simply too slow a process.

Second is the increased popularity of shorter and less decorative strategic plans. Gone are the days when strategic plans resembled exquisitely detailed, carefully crafted, beautifully bound books suitable for display on executives' shelves.

Third is involving more people in the generation of strategic planning. This has occurred as the process itself has been viewed less as the exclusive domain of a nucleus of top executives. Of particular note is the ever-increasing participation of line managers—those with direct responsibility for the value that an organization creates, who must take the responsibility for implementing the strategic plan once it has been developed.

Fourth is increased frequency. Instead of making it an annual exercise, many organizations convene to review and revise their strategic plans on a quarterly or even monthly basis to ensure that they reflect their changing situations. As competitive environments become ever more dynamic and complex, they demand an immediate, thoughtful, and comprehensive planned response. Strategic planning therefore resembles more closely a combination of planned (rational) and emergent (adaptive) elements.

Fifth is an emphasis on implementation. Planners can no longer afford to devise strategic objectives that face an uncertain future in terms of their accomplishment, so they have incorporated serious consideration of implementation and execution issues into the planning process itself. These trends echo the advice offered by management scholar Kathleen Eisenhardt, whose research revealed that successful companies in fast-paced markets make fast, reasonably wise strategic decisions on a frequent basis, implement them efficiently, then adapt them as required (Eisenhardt 1997, 1999).

In order to accomplish those changes, most organizations have abandoned permanent (and usually insulated) strategic planning departments altogether. Instead, they convene the right people when necessary to plan or revisit existing plans. Many have eliminated the top-down approach completely, relying instead on decentralized groups of senior line managers and other members to conduct, or at least initiate, strategic planning. Those people, regardless of their level in the organization's hierarchy, have the advantage of interacting with the organization's environment and dealing with its competitive situation every day. They are uniquely able to detect subtle but important changes quickly and bring the proper information into the planning process. Ad hoc groups of people from various departments, called cross-functional teams, have largely replaced planning specialists, and organizations' partners—their customers and suppliers—are increasingly being asked to join the strategic planning process. In short, the process has become more democratic and open to diverse ideas.

To support the observation that strategic planning is on the rebound, one needs only to consider some recent strategic planning activity in the business world—Hewlett-Packard, Proctor and Gamble, Microsoft, Sears, and Electronic Data Systems—all of which illustrate the benefits of strategic planning, but with a difference—none of those companies use a central planning department or have a head of strategic planning, and that is because they cannot afford for the strategic planning process to become a centralized, isolated, and ultimately bureaucratic activity.

EXAMPLES OF STRATEGIC PLANNING

- Hewlett-Packard utilizes a planning process that requires its general managers to meet and interact with key customers and suppliers to identify, and sometimes create, new product and market opportunities.
- Procter and Gamble's recent strategic planning has incorporated more comprehensive sources of information, leading to a company-wide initiative aimed at low-price products, and resulting in soaring earnings.
- Microsoft, one of the most successful companies on the planet, has intensified its strategic planning and focused it directly on the Internet and Web-based software applications, developing internal capabilities and forging partnerships to compete more effectively in the age of information.
- Sears has undergone a renaissance led by CEO Arthur C. Martinez, who listened to his constituents and orchestrated a major strategic overhaul that centered on reestablishing the retailer's core business, renovating aging stores, and upgrading women's apparel, all to reconnect with customers who were familiar with Sears and had perhaps grown up in an era when Sears ruled the world of retailing but needed to be lured back.
- Electronic Data Systems routinely involves many of its employees at all levels and geographic regions in the strategic planning process, resulting in a more efficient organization that identifies opportunities more quickly and reacts more effectively to potentially threatening changes in its competitive environment.

THE STRATEGIC PLANNING PROCESS—AN EFFECTIVE MODEL

The following process model is presented to help managers who seek to realize the benefits of strategic planning. The model is based on four essential strategic questions:

- Where is our organization right now?
- Where do we want to take it?
- How will we get there?
- How will we determine whether we got there and how we did it?

Those questions form the framework for an effective strategic planning process, and the answers to those questions constitute the essence of the strategic plan. To organize and direct their strategic planning processes, many organizations use a sequential approach to developing an effective strategic plan based on the four questions. Although that model varies, it typically resembles the following:

1. Developing the Mission—the organization's present purpose, why the organization exists, whom it serves, what it contributes, and what makes it unique
2. Establishing Vision and Values—the organization's desired future state, reflecting what it wishes to become
3. Conducting a Comprehensive Situation Analysis—identifying the organization's strengths and weaknesses (internal factors over which it can exert control) as well as its opportunities and threats (external factors over which it has only limited control at best)
4. Generating Strategic Objectives—few in number, broad in scope, based on a sound understanding of the mission, with due regard for the situation analysis, to move the organization toward achieving its vision
5. Devising Tactical Goals—fairly specific actions that need to be accomplished to support each strategic objective and should be SMART (specific, measurable, aggressive, realistic, and time bound)
6. Crafting an Implementation Plan—a specific set of actions to achieve each tactical goal by assigning individual responsibility and deadlines that is used to initiate budgets and other strategy execution mechanisms (e.g., individual roles, reporting and coordinating relationships, communication channels, structures, and other necessary resources)
7. Initiating an Evaluation Schedule—with outcomes to be measured to determine whether the implementation plan is being accomplished
8. Enacting Control and Correction—to address anticipated gaps between expectations and actual results, focusing on the reasons for the discrepancy and what needs to be accomplished at certain milestones to get the strategic plan back on track

Several comments seem appropriate at this point. The terms "strategy" and "tactics" are often confused, or used interchangeably, but they describe two separate concepts. "Strategy" implies a set of moves on a grand scale, as opposed to "tactics," which are specific, detailed activities undertaken to achieve the strategy. Strategy and tactics can be mutually exclusive. Take, for example, the Japanese attack on Pearl Harbor, which was a tactical masterstroke (destruction, albeit temporarily, of the combat capability of the U.S. Pacific Fleet) but a strategic blunder of epic proportion (initiating the downfall of the empire). Strategies deal with the big picture of an organization, and tactics deal with specific actions.

Implementation has been demonstrated to be the weak link in most strategic initiatives, so it should be regarded as an integral component of the strategic planning process. If left as an afterthought, it will not receive the attention that it warrants. Control and correction are a normal and necessary part of any implementation effort, so it should involve constructive steering of organizational resources rather than non-constructive assignment of blame.

This bears repeating: implementation is always the weak link in strategy—always. It involves leading people who might not like what they need to do or may distrust management's motives. It explicitly deals with change, which many of us resist vigorously for reasons both real and imagined. It requires intense communication; careful coordination; sufficient time to be launched, evaluated, and modified; and usually a significant financial investment.

Implementation can, however, be accomplished more smoothly if its challenges are anticipated and dealt with directly. Implementation is facilitated greatly through active participation and open, honest communication. That is why so many contemporary organizations involve as many of their members as possible as early in the process as is practical. Obviously, full participation after the planning sessions are completed is essential, but enlightened managers know that involving the people who will be affected by a change in strategy early in the process pays dividends. The best formulated strategy is utterly useless if it cannot be executed. The only caveat that applies here is that existing structures, policies, procedures, and members' skills—those developed to support an earlier strategy—cannot be allowed to dictate or limit the new strategy. The challenges of implementation must be recognized, but they should never constrain consideration of all viable strategic alternatives.

IMPROVING THE LIKELIHOOD OF SUCCESSFUL STRATEGIC PLANNING

Although the strategic plan itself has been argued to be critically important, the process under which organizations create their strategic plans is often of equal importance. Organizations can learn a lot about themselves as managers and others do the necessary work that leads up to the formal process itself. New relationships can be established and misunderstandings resolved before, during, and after the strategic planning process.

Factors that can adversely affect strategic planning include:

- Power and politics
- Time constraints

- Inadequate accurate information about the external environment and/or internal resources and capabilities
- Generation of too few and insufficiently creative ideas
- Involving the wrong people
- Not involving enough people
- Inadequate preparation or insufficient analysis, leading to false assumptions and overuse of opinions rather than facts
- Lack of confidence in intuition and judgment (not to be confused with gut instinct)
- Situational complexity
- Uncertainty
- Overreliance on structure or rules

Organizations should identify those potential causes of problems prior to the strategic planning process and take action to address them. They will not go away of their own accord, and they will increase the odds of failure.

WHY CAN STRATEGIC PLANNING FAIL?

Failure of the process can generally be tracked back to failure of a single piece, because that is all that is required. The strategic planning process is a system that requires each stage to be built on the preceding stage. If the strategic plan is built on a shaky foundation (i.e., mission), strategic planning is very likely to fail. After all, if the organization's very reason for existence isn't solid, then how can it withstand the bumps and bruises that the strategic planning process itself will precipitate, let alone the slings and arrows of the competition?

If the situation assessment is not honest and open, the odds of failure increase. This is especially so when the organization's true weaknesses are misidentified and the threats in its environment are understated. If insufficient creativity is applied, it can fail. Remember, the strategic planning process may be one of the few times that managers can really think outside the box in any structured way, so they should be encouraged to do so.

Obviously, implementation is key. More good plans fail because they cannot be implemented and executed than for all other reasons combined. Each strategic implementation situation is unique and takes place in a different organizational and competitive context, so implementation is an art as much as a science. There is seldom one right way of implementing strategy, but there are many wrong ways—and most are recognized only in hindsight.

Finally, strategic planning can fail because people are just plain intimidated or reluctant to share their insights. This can be minimized through the use of an experienced facilitator from outside the organization to help guide the strategic planning process.

SUMMARY

Strategic planning is alive. A good strategic plan provides direction, establishes performance goals, specifies actions required to attain those goals, incorporates a sound analysis of the current situation, and is able to be implemented and evaluated. It is also able to be modified as the changing situation requires. Corrections are a normal and necessary part of the process, and only the most arrogant or misguided managers would fail to consider them. Organizations that plan strategically have more control over their destinies. There is plenty of evidence that the old adage "Failure to plan is planning to fail" might apply more today than ever.

References

Eisenhardt, Kathleen M. 1997. "Strategic Decisions and All That Jazz." *Business Strategy Review* 8 (3): 1–3.

Eisenhardt, Kathleen M. 1999. "Strategy as Strategic Decision Making." *Sloan Management Review* Spring: 65–72.

Mintzberg, Henry. 1994a. *The Rise and Fall of Strategic Planning: Reconceiving Roles for Planning, Plans, Planners.* New York: Free Press.

Mintzberg, Henry. 1994b. "Rethinking Strategic Planning Part I: Pitfalls and Fallacies." *Long Range Planning* 27 (3): 12–21.

Mintzberg, Henry. 1994c. "Rethinking Strategic Planning Part II: New Roles for Planners." *Long Range Planning* 27 (3): 22–30.

Mintzberg, Henry. 1994d. "The Fall and Rise of Strategic Planning." *Harvard Business Review* 72 (1): 107–14.

Further Reading: D'Aveni, Richard A. 1994. *Hypercompetition: Managing the Dynamics of Strategic Maneuvering.* New York: Free Press; Wilson, Ian. 1994. "Strategic Planning Isn't Dead—It Changed." *Long Range Planning* 27 (4): 12–24.

James F. Fairbank

SUPPLY CHAIN SECURITY AND TERRORISM

The supply chain of any product consists of all the businesses involved in moving that product from the raw material stage into the hands of the final consumer. In addition to the various manufacturers, suppliers, and retailers, it also includes transportation, storage, and distribution firms as well as the indirect resources such as finance, accounting, and information systems. All these companies—as well as the customer—are linked together to fulfill a customer's order.

One of the major themes dominating the recent thoughts of both supply chain managers and their suppliers has been the growing trend toward outsourcing and the use of international suppliers for raw materials, parts, and components. A second theme that has been dominating the thoughts of the same group as well as those of countries around the globe has been that of security from terrorist acts by individuals and groups. Unfortunately, the two themes are becoming more and more interrelated. This interrelationship has been underscored by the publicity surrounding the management and security control of ocean ports within the United States. A recent article in CIO Magazine suggested that the United States government will soon be requiring much more information on incoming foreign goods from firms that do business internationally. Specifically, the firms will need to provide information regarding not only the content of shipments prior to their arrival ashore but also the history of that content, points of origin, and routes of passage as well as who, specifically, has handled any shipments arriving in the United States from overseas. These requirements will undoubtedly increase the total costs of that material to the firm and also, since there is only a single true source of funds in any supply chain, to that source: the customer. Those costs are not just monetary in nature. They also include other aspects of a firm's competitive advantage and the customer's requirements, such as speed of delivery, flexibility, and reliability. These last costs can be significant when viewed in context with other recent business trends.

The move toward leaner production systems, such as those of Dell and Hewlett-Packard, where inventory levels are kept at a minimum, has meant lower costs with greater selection to the consumer. What it has also meant, however, is a supply chain that is much more vulnerable to interruption since even a short delay in the shipments of components or raw materials could mean the shutdown of an entire production facility.

These supply chain challenges are not limited to the links of seagoing ports alone. The other three major modes of transport—air, truck, and rail—and their distribution and transfer centers are all experiencing the same pressures. A recent article in Air Transport World describes the preliminary measures and costs being felt by European air freight companies. They include the millions of euros being spent for the new equipment and organizational changes needed to meet the new industry requirements. U.S. trucking and rail associations are also exerting preliminary efforts and have developed an Anti-Terrorist Action Plan. Every mode of transport and every transfer point involved in the supply chain is coming under scrutiny. At this point, however, no mode is receiving focused direction from the government in terms of concrete requirements or policies, which means that all security initiatives are either in the pilot study phase, sitting on a shelf, or awaiting development.

CURRENT INITIATIVES

C-TPAT Customs-Trade Partnership Against Terrorism

This is probably the best-known and most widely used initiative. It is a voluntary program, begun in November 2001, between private global organizations and the government. It is administered through the U.S. Department of Homeland Security by U.S. Customs and Border Protection. Currently, the program offers expedited customs handling for participants. In return, the participants provide Customs with information that indicates the company has performed security risk analysis on itself and its trading partners as well as ongoing best practices security measures. There are currently over 7,400 private participants. Further information can be obtained through the U.S. Customs Web site (www.cbp.gov).

ISPS Code and MTSA

The Maritime Transportation Security Act of 2002 (MTSA) is the U.S. response to the International Ship and Port Facility (ISPS) Code. ISPA is a 2002 code set out by the international maritime community delineating security requirements to be followed by all interested parties, including governments, shipping companies and port authorities. MTSA is the U.S. version that was passed in 2004. Both have three levels of security based on the perceived security threat.

ACE and ATDI

The Automated Commercial Environment is another U.S. Customs initiative. It is a trade processing system designed to provide the backbone of an Enterprise Resource Planning system for Customs that will enable it to monitor its own processes and transactions. Its impact here is that it will also be used to analyze such things as risk factors in targeting containers for inspection. As an additional module, Customs has also been looking at the Advance Trade Data Initiative, which will be the data collection interface with importers. It will require importers to submit all information regarding all shipments, such as the purchase order, ports through which the shipment has passed, final destination, and even where on the ship a particular container is located . This program may eventually become a requirement of C-TPAT.

CommerceGuard and RFID

CommerceGuard is a technology for securing cargo containers and is jointly held by GE Security, Mitsubishi Corporation, and Siemens Building Technologies. It consists of a relatively small devise that magnetically clamps across the door of a cargo container and monitors both the door and the contents. It can record when and how many times the door was opened, the temperature movement inside the container, and other information, as programmed. Visit www.gesecurity.com for additional information. Radio Frequency Identification (RFID) is a method of identifying unique items using radio waves. Though it is not a new technology, it gained attention recently when Wal-Mart required many of its vendors to apply RFID tags to their goods. Different RFID technology can be used in varying applications, including determining and recording the temperature, light, and sound environment through which it (and therefore its goods) has passed. Various associations and committees are still in the process of establishing standards for this technology. For the latest information on current research in this area specifically targeted to practical business applications, visit the RFID Research Center at Penn State-Behrend (http://www.ebizitpa.org/RFID).

The basic conflict faced by American businesses is the security of those goods entering the borders of the United States versus the cost of that security. The ramifications are twofold. First are the implications for competition: if a company can move its goods through security points and inspections faster and at a lower cost, then it has a competitive advantage. Second is the additional cost to the final consumer, who will ultimately bear the burden of the heightened security requirements.

This entry discusses the challenges associated with developing the necessary supply chain skills and infrastructure that will likely be needed in the future to minimize those costs. Specifically, it looks at these new heightened security requirements from the perspective of their effect on the two major components of supply chain management: the supply chain strategy and the supply chain structure, which includes the drivers of supply chain performance. These four drivers are facilities, inventory, transportation, and information. Finally, it will look at tactics to facilitate that security.

SUPPLY CHAIN STRATEGY

Stanford's Hau Lee has developed a highly respected framework for the strategic design of supply chains based on the variability, or risk, in both the demand for a product and the supply of raw materials, parts, and components to produce that product. As the variability of either dimension increases, the cost of designing and operating a supply chain increases, as does the complexity of managing it. Past terrorist attacks and threats have led to an emphasis on increased security, which, if randomly applied to incoming shipments, will increase the variability in acquiring upstream materials from suppliers. This variability may take the form of longer times waiting for inspections, the amount of time required for more thorough inspections, or even the availability of goods from certain points of origin.

The strategic design of the supply chain, based on demand variability, is to provide either efficiency through low cost or responsiveness through speed and flexibility. Either choice is affected by the time and cost created by added security.

The lowest-cost and least flexible chain is termed an efficient supply chain. At the opposite end of the spectrum is the agile supply chain. More and more, the two trends of increasing competition and a more demanding consumer are forcing companies to move their supply chains toward the agile. By definition, this supply chain strategy requires shorter lead times, higher customer service levels, greater flexibility, and the ability to handle supply uncertainty. All of this agility, of course, comes at a cost, as companies employing this strategy employ more expensive modes of transportation and maintain excess capacity to handle both supply and demand variation. While meeting the new specter of international terrorism will impose added costs, those on the agile end are more adapted to handle the variation.

Where the costs will have the most effect will be on the efficient supply chain. These chains operate on the basis of lowest cost created by very stable, and predictable, supply and demand. Staples, such as food items or standardized commodities that operate on a very low margin, fall into this category. Even a minimal increase in the cost of goods sold is felt immediately. Added variability in this supply chain strategy would be quickly translated into higher costs. The focus at both ends of the spectrum, then, will be to reduce the variability on either side of the supply chain in order to create and maintain a competitive advantage.

Finally, any supply chain strategy must include a contingency plan. The value of such a contingency plan was well illustrated by Dell during the West Coast dock strike of 2002. While other computer manufacturers were scrambling to find alternative sources for components that were being manufactured on the Pacific Rim, or sitting idle during the 10-day strike while their parts sat on idle ships, Dell was able to continue operating with just 72 hours of inventory. Dell did all this without a single delay in customer orders. It was able to do so because it had previously developed an internal management team designed to handle such situations, close ties to various suppliers, and access to alternative transportation sources.

A firm's strategy determines how the supply chain must be structured in order to achieve that strategy. The strategy selected will necessarily have a major impact on the cost of securing that supply chain.

SUPPLY CHAIN STRUCTURE AND DRIVERS

The drivers of supply chain performance are facilities, inventory, transportation, and information. How these are organized and positioned within the supply chain establishes the structure of the supply chain. An agile supply chain will generally have more decentralized facilities and a distributed, standardized inventory in order to provide the most flexibility and to be located as close to the customer as possible. It will use faster transportation, which will result in higher costs per item. Information systems must be more robust and complex. What this means in terms of security is a more complex system to oversee and protect.

Facilities are the physical locations (land and buildings) where product is created, manufactured, assembled, or stored. The more agile the supply chain is, the more facilities will be involved. The impact here will be both on the facilities themselves as well as the equipment necessary to meet the new security requirements. Part of this will likely be in the form of special RFID tags or other similar electronic monitoring devices such as GE's CommerceGuard , which are attached to the products or the containers in which the products are stored. This means that specialized equipment will need to be present in the facilities to read the product devices, which becomes part of the facility cost. Other facility costs will be those necessary to secure the physical property itself, such as fencing, security personnel, and alarm systems.

IN THE MEDIA

Recently, the History Channel aired a segment of its "Modern Marvels" series that focused on containers. They spent a good deal of air time describing today's supply chain security problems with shipping containers as well as one possible solution developed by General Electric called the Commerce Guard. The episode is likely to air again, but you may also purchase a copy of this episode for viewing at http://store.aetv.com.

Inventory consists of all raw materials, work in process, finished goods, and supplies held. There are four costs associated with inventory: holding or carrying cost, set-up or change-over costs, ordering costs (which includes shipping), and the cost of stock-outs (not having the product when the customer demands it). The strategy and structure of the supply chain affect these costs. Reducing inventory reduces the holding costs but increases ordering costs (since more frequent orders are needed to meet the same demand), and vice versa. The more facilities the chain employs, the more inventory is needed to stock each location, increasing both holding and ordering.

Security against terrorism will mean that the stores of inventory being held will need to be more closely guarded and monitored, increasing the holding costs. As closer monitoring, tagging, and information requirements for each shipment increase, so do the ordering costs. RFID tags, or other identification methods, will be added to the cost, as will the labor and equipment needed to apply and read them.

Although the cost of shipping is usually accounted for under inventory costs, there are several decisions involved with this driver. These include the mode of transportation (air, truck, rail, or water), routing, and the network design (e.g., use of direct shipping, warehouses, cross-docking, or postponement). Since every additional link in the supply chain may mean an added security step or check, companies may be inclined to move more toward direct shipping, bypassing the middlemen of warehouses, distributors, or even retailers. It may also mean an increasing use of third-party logistics (3PLs) companies so that a firm may hand off the responsibility for the security of a shipment to a company that specializes in logistics and is able to use economies of scale to absorb the additional costs of security.

Every security initiative under consideration at the current time will involve, at the very least, an increased requirement for information on the contents and history of all shipments entering or traversing the United States, whether this data will need to be supplied to U.S. Customs or another agency. These increased information requirements necessitate the need for new methods for collecting the data, more complex software to receive and organize it, and the hardware and peripherals on which to operate it. While the cost of RFID tags and the associated reader equipment is coming down, they still present a formidable outlay of capital, especially for smaller companies.

In addition, many of the initiatives currently considered involve the use of some type of tracking device attached to or inserted in each shipment. Some even call for identification of each item in that shipment. In either event, this would require reading equipment, as well as software that will provide an interface between the equipment and the company's internal information system.

All this information will not only need to be maintained by the company, but it will also have to be forwarded to the appropriate government (and possibly industry) body in the format dictated by that group. Unfortunately, that standard has yet to be established.

TACTICS

Tactics to address the impact of added security on the supply chain focuses on those two areas: strategy and drivers. Strategically, firms must understand that regardless of whether they consider their products to be functional or innovative, their supply chains will need to maintain a higher degree of flexibility to remain competitive. In the paranoid environment in which businesses now operate, it takes little to disrupt a supply chain. A terrorist attack is not even needed. Take, for example, the closing of Port Hueneme in Ventura County, California. This major port was closed for hours because dock workers found a threatening sentence scrawled on the interior bulkhead of a ship coming in from Guatemala. Since this is one of the largest ports in the United States in terms of fresh produce imports, such a shutdown had the potential to create major problems. The case of the Alameda Corridor illustrates that it is not just facilities themselves that pose a risk in the supply chain. Firms must be prepared for such events with alternative supply chain tactics that include having excess capacity in the drivers.

The drivers themselves must be more flexible and robust. Companies must have alternative transportation partners and modes, alternative facilities in terms of distribution or aggregation points, and alternative sources of inventory in terms of suppliers.

THE ALAMEDA CORRIDOR

The Alameda Corridor is a 20- mile-long multi-rail right-of-way that connects the ports of Los Angeles and Long Beach to the rest of the nation's rail lines. It was completed in 2002 at a cost of $2.4 billion. What is its significance for security in the supply chain? Consider this. Together, those two seaports handle more cargo traffic than any other port in the United States. Over one-third of all traffic entering or exiting those ports does so through the Alameda corridor. The heart of that throughway is a 10-mile-long trench that is 33 feet deep and 50 feet wide. A 30-foot by 50-foot trench might appear to be an easier target than the 7,500 acres that the Port of Los Angeles occupies. Also consider the fact that most of the other two-thirds of that cargo traffic is carried in 6.3 million containers per year on the highways in the Los Angeles area, most of which travels on a single freeway: the 710, Long Beach Freeway. A terrorist attack would not necessarily need to pinpoint a port itself. Crippling access to any point of aggregation for shipments to and from U.S. businesses would effectively serve to close the port itself, seriously affecting the economy. For more information on this vital artery in the U.S supply chain, access the Alameda Corridor Transportation Authority Web site (www.acta.org).

The form of the method will be in two areas: prevention and disaster recovery. Prevention will likely take the form of increased information requirements from companies about their shipments, increased inspections, and increased physical security requirements, such as monitoring and safety equipment. Exactly what prevention measure will be required will depend on the level of risk the company is willing, or able, to accept. How much it is willing to risk will be a corporate decision. How much it is able to risk will likely be a government or industry decision implemented by standards and regulations. Disaster recovery tactics will need to include preplanning efforts, a pre-designated and well-trained team, and flexibility and alternative driver capabilities.

The added prevention measures and maintaining this flexibility in terms of alternate sources of strategies and drivers will cost money. Companies will tend to avoid costs for threats that have not yet materialized because the added cost will, in the short run, put them at a competitive disadvantage. As Dell proved, however, in the dock strike of 2002, such upfront costs should be considered an investment that will pay dividends at a later time.

Somehow, these costs will filter down to the consumer. It is the price to be paid for maintaining the amount and breadth of products that the American consumer is used to having.

CONCLUSIONS

What is the final balance between security against terrorism and the price of that security? It is likely that the level of security will eventually be established either by government mandate or, even more likely, by voluntary industry standards. That level will be a determining factor in the cost to us, the consumer. It may also mean that smaller companies, those without the capital resources necessary to acquire and maintain the needed equipment and procedures, may lose their ability to operate in a global environment unless there are partnered with a larger company that has that capability. But what that level may finally be, if indeed it ever is final, is now unknown. What is known, however, is that one business axiom will still hold true. Whichever companies manage to achieve that level at the lowest cost will create a competitive advantage. Early adopters and experimenters may be able to develop a sustainable advantage if their lower costs enable them to increase their market share sufficiently.

Further Reading: Cook, Thomas. 2006. *Supply Chains Post 9/11.* New York: Springer-Verlag; Schniederjans, Marc J., Ashlyn M. Schniederjans, and Dara G. Schniederjans. 2005. *Outsourcing and Insourcing in an International Context.* Armonk, NY: M. E. Sharpe.

Peter B. Southard

T

TEAM-BASED CULTURES AND INDIVIDUAL REWARDS

Teams have become an essential competitive tool that enables companies to be responsive to the ever-changing business environment. One way that companies can sustain high-performing teams is to design and execute a well-thought-out reward system that allows for both individual and team recognition. However, many companies continue to implement individual reward systems that prove to be counterproductive to team-based environments. Why do organizations continue to implement individually based reward systems within team-based environments? How can companies design reward systems that support a team-based culture while at the same time recognizing the efforts on an individual level?

WHAT IS AN INDIVIDUAL REWARD SYSTEM?

Individual reward systems are based on the principles of scientific management, which emphasize a functional division of labor, hierarchical differentiation in authority, and direct standardization of work routines (Agarwal and Singh 1998).

Organizations have the ability to reward individuals in many ways. Financial rewards such as direct payments (salary) and indirect payment (benefits) are an effective reward for employees. From a nonfinancial perspective, individual rewards such as employee involvement, recognition, career development, and training opportunities are available to employees. Because they can vary both the kinds of rewards given and the reasons for which they give them, organizations can select from an almost infinite number of approaches to reward individuals.

WHAT IS A TEAM-BASED REWARD SYSTEM?

To provide a broader motivation plan than is offered by individually based plans, some companies opt for team-based reward systems. A team-based reward system is a system in which group members' reward is at least partly contingent on the performance of their group or team. Team rewards are intended to increase cohesiveness and cooperation within the group and to provide recognition based on the output of the team as whole. Team rewards are most effective when jobs are highly integrated (Cascio 2006).

When implementing team-based reward systems, managers must be aware of equity within the system. For plans such as this to be effective, team members should understand how team rewards are established and how performance and accountability will be evaluated as a unit. A failure to communicate this information could lead to a failed reward system and can defeat the intent of group effectiveness (Dulebohn and Martocchio 1998).

WHAT MAKES A REWARD SYSTEM EFFECTIVE?

Regardless of the type of reward system one implements, an effective reward system should be based on two widely accepted principles: increased motivation improves performance and recognition is a major factor in motivation. As a general guide, reward systems should follow four simple rules, as shown in Figure T.1.

DO ORGANIZATIONS WANT A TEAM CULTURE?

Organizations continue to rely on groups to perform critical functions that contribute to the overall competitiveness and viability of the company. An early study showed that over 50 percent of the 700 organizations studied were using teams and that over 40 percent had more than half of their employees working in groups (Osterman 1994). In 1995, ongoing research verified that this trend continues at a rapid pace (Heneman, Fisher, and Dixon 2001). In this study, 60 percent of the 313 organizations investigated claimed that they would increase or greatly increase their use of teams over the next decade while only 3 percent admitted that they would reduce or discontinue the use of teams. It is reasonable to believe that groups are, in fact, a vital and sustaining competitive tool in today's business environment. It appears evident that most organizations strive for high-performing teams that will allow them to be competitive. Companies with an effective team culture that is aligned with the business strategy are able to outperform companies that foster a culture of individualism that is out of sync with the team-oriented business strategy (Heneman, Fisher, and Dixon 2001).

WHAT IS THE ISSUE?

Now that we understand the difference in reward systems and the fact that most organizations strive for team cultures in order to provide a competitive

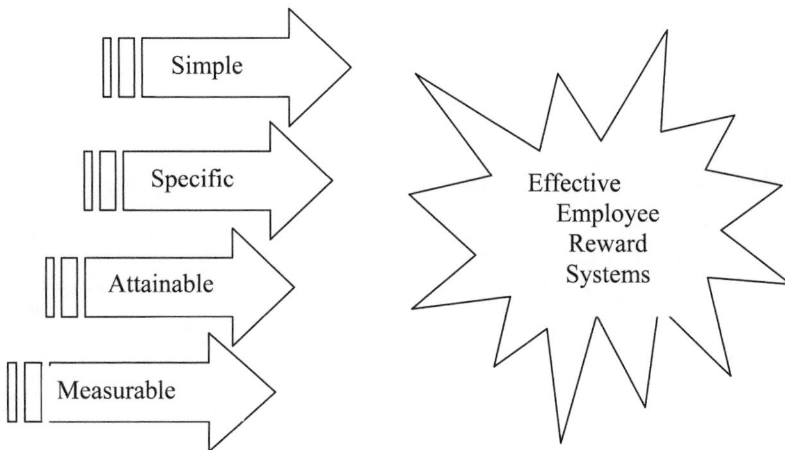

Be simple: The rules of the system should be brief, clear and understandable.

Be specific: Employees need to know exactly what they are to do.

Be attainable: Every employee should have a reasonable chance to gain something.

Be measurable: Objectives must be clearly stated so that all variables can be measured.

Figure T.1 Effective reward systems.

Source: Available at www.commerce.gov.

edge, we are faced with a critical dilemma. The issue is that although most organizations desire a team environment, many organizations implement reward systems that reinforce individual performance rather than team performance. This tactic is contradictory in nature and causes confusion for employees trying to understand the company's vision and their role within the organization. The use of team-based rewards has interested managers, but many hesitate to implement a team-based system because team rewards appear more complex and may have adverse effects on individual performance.

Rewards are one of the clearest ways that leaders can convey the intended organizational culture, or what they consider to be important. Individual behavior is influenced in large part by the way that individuals are measured, recognized, and rewarded. So when companies institute individually based reward systems, they send a message to employees that they should be focused on their performance as individuals. Yet most companies emphasize the importance of a team structure. Therefore, the concept is simple. If managers want employees to work together in teams, they must implement performance goals and reward systems that reward employees as team members. This strategy reinforces the desired culture and shows a clear connection between the employee's contribution and the overall goals of the company.[6] However, in many cases, this is not happening.

STAGES OF TEAM LIFE CYCLE AND TEAM REWARDS

In determining the rewards that are suitable for individuals within teams and for teams as a whole, four factors need to be considered (Gross 1995). These are:

1. Stages of team life cycle
2. Reward and recognition categories
3. Type of teams
4. Whether the company is part of the public, private, or not-for-profit sector
5. Culture of the team and organization

These factors need to be examined in order to establish the best combination of rewards at the most appropriate time.

WHY DO COMPANIES CHOOSE INDIVIDUALLY BASED REWARD SYSTEMS?

Given this information, we need to understand why an organization with a desire to be team oriented would chose to reward on an individual basis. By nature, individuals need to be motivated. People do not instinctively come to work, continue to work, or work hard for an organization without a purpose, intent, or motivation. The most widely accepted explanation for why people are motivated to work, perform, learn, and change is rooted in what psychologists call expectancy theory. Expectancy theory argues that people are mostly rational decision makers who think about their actions and act in ways that satisfy their needs and help them reach their goals. This theory supports the notion of individual reward systems due to the fact that individuals have unique needs and different factors motivate them. In many cases, individual reward systems appear to be more simplistic, direct, and easier to implement (Cacioppe 1999).

Barry Gerhart of the University of Wisconsin believes that the variance in individual performance is too substantial to be successful in a team reward system (Thornburg 1992). He believes that individuals should be recognized for the specific work they do. In this way, there is no ambiguity when it comes to accountability, contribution, and participation. The action and reward are clearer cut. This leads us the benefits or the pros and cons of each reward system as it exists in a team-based culture. Figure T.2 summarizes the pro and cons of team-based reward systems and individually based reward systems within a team-based culture.

Organizations implementing individual reward systems may feel that they are effective and see no reason to change, even if they foster a team-based management approach. As noted above, individual rewards are typically rewarded on a pay-for-performance basis. Such rewards have several implications. First, the criteria on which pay is based are clear and known by the employees. The employee understands that performance determines pay, and someone else's performance poses no complications to his or her pursuit of such a reward. Because the employee controls his or her own behavior, he or she has the ability to work well and achieve high performance levels and thus receive increases in pay (Gross 1995).

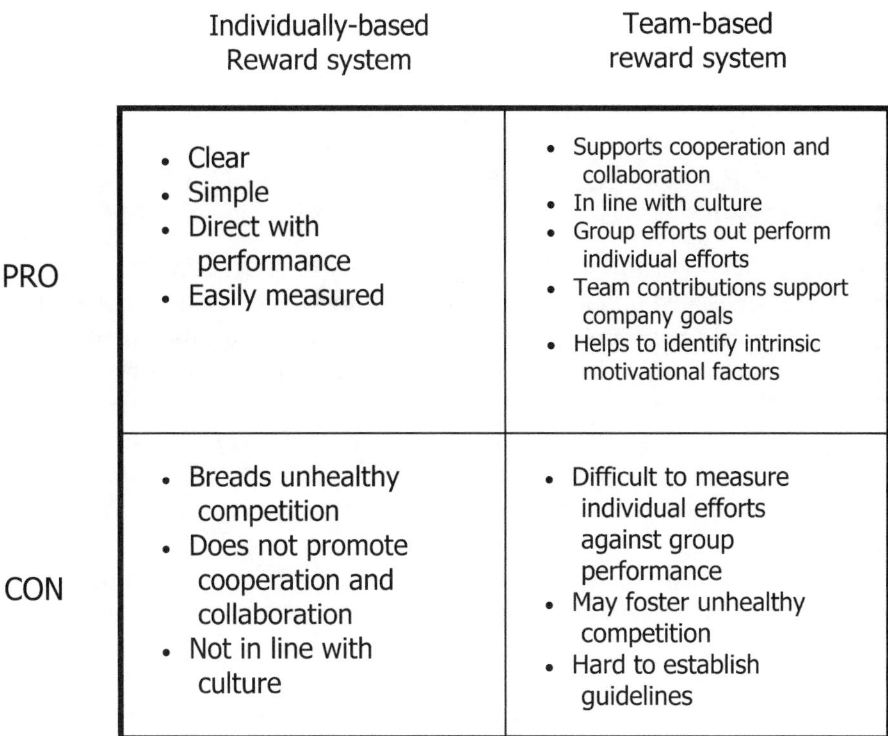

Figure T.2 Pros and cons of individual vs. team-based reward systems in a team-based culture.

The downfall of an individual reward system in a team-based culture is evident. Employees look for a clear connection between the goals and mission of the company and their specific job roles and responsibility. Contradictions in this relationship cause confusion and frustration on the part of the employee. The practice of individual reward systems can affect moral and can lead to lack of respect for leadership and company goals. In this way, the team factor loses much of its credibility. The team culture becomes a logo on the wall instead of an integrated practice within the company.

There are many reasons why managers need to support the implementation of team-based reward systems. The most fundamental reason is that the organization structure is team-based management. Also, team reward systems promote team productivity and increase cooperation among team members. Some organizations use team reward systems because they give employees an opportunity to see more directly the rewards for their hard work. Others continue to use more long-term reward systems in addition to team rewards, such as gain sharing and profit sharing (Cacioppe 1999).

However, this methodology of recognition and reward does not come without challenges, as noted in Figure T.2. So how can companies overcome some of the obvious challenges that accompany team-based reward systems?

WHAT ARE THE CHALLENGES OF INSTITUTING TEAM-BASED REWARD SYSTEMS?

The challenges of team-based reward systems are often explained in relation to theories of motivation. These challenges are relevant for many companies as they strive for team-based cultures. Several of the challenges are discussed below (Cacioppe 1999).

1. The difficulty that individual employees may have in seeing how their effort is translated into group performance, on which rewards are based. In other words, how are individual contribution and effort measured against the group performance? This may be especially significant for high achievers. When they are rewarded with the same reward and at the same level is lower-performing counterparts, they may become very frustrated and feel like they are being treated unfairly. This may reward underperformer and may cause these high achievers to lose motivation to perform at the group level.
2. There has been criticism of the ability of teams to maintain cooperation, and the type of reward system (individual, group, or both) has been found to have no effect on cooperation, mutual assistance, or job satisfaction.
3. Team-based rewards may create competition between teams, encouraging teams to focus on their own performance at the expense of other teams' performance. This may exist in cross-functional teams as well and may lead to a reluctance to share information or assist other teams. This is especially problematic when a team's work is highly integrated with that of others, as in the case of problem solving and continuous improvement initiatives.
4. A possible limitation or resistance of an organization to using team reward systems may be the fact that there are not clear, specific guidelines available for each organization to use that will ensure the effectiveness of team reward systems. There are many conditions under which team reward systems may succeed or fail, and the exact conditions under which team reward systems will be effective are unclear. There is a definite need for more research concerning the effectiveness of various implementation strategies or team reward systems. The majority of research at this time is focused on the basic characteristics of team reward systems, as opposed to individual rewards (Cacioppe 1999).

SEVERAL STRATEGIES EXIST FOR OVERCOMING THESE CHALLENGES

1. Establish clear guidelines and measurements for team performance and reward. This information should be clearly defined in a psychological contract and should detail measurement tools and related rewards for teams. All details of the plan should be discussed with the team members, and concerns or questions should be addressed.

2. Allow for team members to establish their own policy of reward and recognition. In this way, employees gain confidence in the system and gain a greater sense of comfort and accountability with the guidelines.
3. Institute a 360-degree performance evaluation or a team peer-review policy that allows team members to provide feedback on another team member's performance. Team members should be encouraged to provide constructive criticism on the team member's performance and should be guaranteed confidentiality by management.
4 Consider reward systems that recognize both the team performance as well as individual contributions. Many sports teams adopt this philosophy by awarding a most valuable player award. This system recognizes team efforts but also gives special attention to individual efforts within the team. Companies can also award individual efforts based on peer reviews or manager observations of the team activities. This process can award an employee of the month within a team or can recognize individual team performance on a specific team project.
5. Use clearly defined pay systems to blend individual and team efforts. In the example of professional sports cited previously, it may be possible and very effective to continue to reward individuals annually based on their yearly performance as well as reward the team with more short-term and immediate rewards. In this way, individuals may be eligible to receive merit pay increases each year because of individual effort, a team will receive team-based rewards that are allocated equally, and a gain-sharing program based on the entire organization's productivity can be used. In larger organizations, this approach may be very feasible and very helpful. Although it may not be possible to use this exact solution in a smaller organization, it may be in the organization's best interests to find a creative solution in which all three of these types or rewards may be used (Cacioppe 1999).

By implementing a blended reward and recognition system, organizations are able to maintain credibility within the system while at the same time fostering a healthy competitive environment. This approach attempts to maximize the team performance, cooperation, and collaboration as well as individual expertise and dedication. The dilemma arises when management must choose between cohesion in the team or maximizing team performance by choosing either a team-based or individually based reward system.

When implemented by themselves, individual rewards should be examined closely to determine to what degree they should be kept and how new performance standards and appraisals should be conducted. A specific set of measures should be used to evaluate the effectiveness of individual rewards as well as team rewards. Also, team leaders should examine the value of intrinsic motivation and how it will increase among team members as team reward systems are used.

Furthermore, it is generally agreed that when using a team reward system, it is important to reward individuals who go above and beyond. A system should be set up by which these individuals are rewarded for outstanding effort. However, according to Hitchcock and Willard, these individual rewards should never receive more attention than the team rewards. These rewards should also be a surprise (Gross 1995). The organization should never make public its intentions of rewarding outstanding performers, and these individual rewards should be presented to the individual in the form of a choice among a few things that he or she particularly enjoys (Cacioppe 1999).

SUMMARY

In order for reward and recognition programs to be effective they must reflect the desired culture of the organization. Therefore, if an organization has adopted a team-oriented culture, it should reward on the basis of team performance or it should use a blended approach that recognizes both team and individual efforts. By making the connection between the reward systems and the company mission, employees are able to see how their efforts and contribution support the company's vision. This is extremely relevant to the achievement of long-standing success and the overall credibility of the organization and its leaders.

On the other hand, contradiction between the desired culture and the reward and recognition program creates confusion for employees and disconnects them from the goals of the company. This feeling of disconnectedness can lead to lack of communication, job dissatisfaction, and employee turnover.

If implemented and used correctly, team reward systems have the potential to be an extremely helpful tool for organizations that are using a team-based system of management. There are many variables that must be analyzed and considered as the transition to team reward systems occurs. Team reward systems have great potential to grow and foster cohesiveness and cooperation within a team as well as enable the employees within an organization to find intrinsic motivation and self-fulfillment within the workplace. However, more research must be done on how best to implement and support team-based reward and recognition programs.

References

Agarwal, N., and P. Singh. 1998. "Organizational Rewards for a Changing Workplace: An Examination of Theory and Practice." *International Journal of Technology Management* 18 (5): 671–88.

Cacioppe, R. 1999. "Using Team-Individual Reward and Recognition Strategies to Drive Organizational Success." *Leadership and Organizational Development Journal* 20 (6): 322.

Cascio, W. F. 2006. *Managing Human Resources: Productivity, Quality of Work Life, Profits.* New York: McGraw-Hill & Irwin.

Coli, M. 1997. "Strategic Team Reward and Recognition Strategies at Motorola." In *The Best of Team Conference Proceedings,* 519–605. San Francisco: Linkage.

Dulebohn, J. H., and J. J. Martocchio. 1998. "The Role of Influence Tactics in Perceptions of Performance Evaluations' Fairness." *Academy of Management Journal* 42 (3): 288–304.

Gross, S. E. 1995. *Compensation for Teams: How to Design and Implement Team-Based Reward Programs.* New York: American Management Association.

Heneman, R. L., M. M. Fisher, and K. E. Dixon. 2001. "Reward and Organizational Systems Alignment: An Expert System." *Compensation and Benefits Review* 33 (6): 18–29.

Lawler, E. E., III. 1990. *Strategic Pay: Aligning Organizational Strategies and Pay System.* San Francisco: Jossey-Bass.

Osterman, P. 1994. "Supervision, Discretion, and Work Organization." *American Economic Review* 84 (2): 380–85.

Thornburg, L. 1992. "Training in a Changing World." *HR Magazine* 37 (8), 44–48.

Further Reading: Gross, S. E. 1997. "When Jobs Become Team Roles, What Do You Pay For?" *Compensation and Benefits Review* 29 (1), 48–52; Nelson, B., and D. R. Spitzer. 2002. *The 1001 Rewards and Recognition Fieldbook: The Complete Guide.* New York: Workman; Wingfield, B., and J. Berry. 2001. *Retaining Your Employees: Using Respect, Recognition, and Rewards for Positive Results.* Menlo Park, CA: Crisp Publications.

Janet M. Duck

TECHNOLOGICAL CONNECTIVITY

Let's define technology here as personal communications technology. It's not entirely new. At one time a more efficient postal system for delivering written letters was considered an improvement in personal communication. The telegraph and then the telephone were vast improvements. They changed business practices and personal lives, and they must have presented challenges as well as improvements. But the end of the twentieth and the beginning of the twenty-first centuries are presenting us with leaps in technologies of the kind that more and more conveniently connect us. They include PCs, laptops, cell phones, iPods, PDAs, and Blackberries. They connect us through phone calls, voicemail, e-mail, and instant messaging. In the future they will be merged, refined, and made still more convenient.

It stands to reason that these leaps in technology might strain our social and managerial abilities to make the best use of technology, to maximize the advantages and minimize the problems. Indeed, we are finding that many questions and debates have already been raised. Legislation, managerial decisions, and etiquette norms have begun to develop. We are today scratching the surface in dealing with these questions, while technology leaps forward into new opportunities and challenges.

This discussion will focus more on employees than on customers and more on the unintended consequences and problems than on the many obvious advantages of personal technology. It will address changes in personal lives and work lives, changes in our social interactions, and the resulting management challenges. Because so many problematic changes are gradual and not immediately apparent, we often fail to realize that they change work patterns and become management challenges. Some problems are harder to see and may not be apparent until ineffectiveness, inefficiency, and work problems have become obvious. Business managers can gain strategic advantage by being more proactive in solving problems before they develop into larger ones. Just as with other forms of technology in the past, those businesses that adopt these new technologies effectively will be more successful.

A FEW QUESTIONS THAT MIGHT NOT YET HAVE ANSWERS

- Should the use of cell phones and portable computers while driving be banned? State laws differ. Does it matter if the phones are hands-free? How about in theaters? Classes? Customer meetings?
- How long is too long to wait to answer voicemail, e-mail, or instant messaging? At what point will someone be offended that the message has not been answered or consider a coworker irresponsible? One hour? One week? Is it ever okay to be unreachable?
- What trumps what? With phone and computers at home, at work, and on one's person, which should one check most often? Which should be dealt with first when one has messages from a coworker, one's boss, a customer, a family member, and a friend? What are one's personal obligations?
- What's polite? Answering the cell call or IM during a face-to-face discussion with a friend about our relationship? During a meeting with a boss? While working with a customer?
- Should a company prescribe detailed technology etiquette for its employees?
- Is it okay for a company to contact its employees 24/7? Should a company be able to control an employee's calendar? If so, how many hours per day?
- Is it sufficient to schedule a business meeting or issue a policy directive by e-mail only if one is dealing with workers who receive 100 or more e-mails per day?
- If a company buys the technology and has provided the employee with it, is it okay for the company to monitor its use and location? (Courts are affirming the owner's right to monitor, for example, Internet use.) Would it be okay to insert GPS devices (global positioning systems, which show one's exact geographical location) in the employee's company cell phone or Blackberry, enabling 24/7 geographical tracking of the device (and anyone carrying it)?
- Companies have typically rewarded and promoted those who demonstrate not only good work skills but also give their time and commitment to the company. Should someone wanting to succeed in a rewarding career welcome a 24/7 technology connection to the company's activities?
- With such easy communications technology, should someone on vacation stay in touch with customers, bosses, and coworkers? How many hours per vacation day?

SOCIAL CHANGE—WILL TECHNOLOGY CREATE MORE SOCIAL CONNECTION OR MORE PERSONAL ISOLATION?

The answer is probably yes. Both. Is the person on a cell phone or using a laptop, Blackberry, or iPod while in a restaurant, in a car, on a park bench, or in a group crossing the street socially connected or personally isolated? The technology provides a world of connections—with those selected parties at the other end of the technology. But the person is isolated or "cocooned" from nearby diners, drivers, and walkers. There are obvious safety issues. The less obvious issues are questions of etiquette and civility in social interaction. When the person walking on the street says loudly, "Why did you cut me off?" or "Where did you get that fungus?" it may take the people around him an anxious moment to notice the cell phone hanging from his ear. Cell phone users often speak loudly, creating confusion and irritation. The likely reason is that the user is having trouble hearing due to poor reception and surrounding noise. The speaker's attention is intimately connected to a distant listener but isolated from those physically close. Norms for social interaction are changing, and new norms have not yet evolved.

THE INTERNET: THE GLOBAL CARNIVAL

It began as a way of linking researchers in government, business, medicine, and universities—highly educated, usually objective, professionally careful and responsible people who welcomed the opportunity to communicate easily with each other in a relatively private and protected (since few people had access to it) environment. The opportunities for even more effective communication and sharing of research and ideas created by the expansion of access to more high-level researchers were exciting. But as more people gained access, early users lamented that the quality of communications was declining and the discussions held via Internet were degenerating into less responsible chatting. That was before the general public came aboard. Then, as PCs became common fixtures in homes and everyone began to have access, the original vision dissipated, and the Internet became a public place.

There are obvious major differences between private, controlled places and public places. A wide range of different behaviors in free societies with freedom of expression make public places interesting, confusing, problematic, and even dangerous. As the Internet has become an immense public place, it has presented us with opportunities and problems we never before imagined. We will likely be working on the problems for generations to come.

Fragmentation of social networks is becoming possible on a scale never before imagined. Marketers are no longer limited directing one message at everyone, or four demographic age groups, or 104 psychographic groups, or nine-digit neighborhood zip codes. They can customize messages, in theory, to specific individuals—for example, to the guy on your street who reads Civil War novels, likes ragtime piano, eats lightly buttered popcorn, has a large dog, and carries over $10,000 in credit card debt. Once Wal-Mart and other corporations fully implement RFID (radio frequency identification device), the technology will not only make checkout and inventorying more efficient but also make possible the activation of a voice message at the end of the aisle asking, "Jennifer, did you forget your orange juice this week?" While some consumers will be irritated by the Big Brother aspect of this, others will be charmed by the stunning specificity, the personal appeal, and the sense of (virtual) connection with the entities at the other end of the technology.

Short of totally customized marketing are the development of more and more connections with small groups of others anywhere who share our interests. The Internet provides amazing opportunities to share extremely specific interests with others worldwide. It also provides additional opportunities for social fragmentation. We can delve into our own interests much more deeply. With more news channels and countless blogs, we can go to those with interests closest to our own to get information as well as attitudes and values that amplify our own. Our next-door neighbors and sometimes our friends (if they don't use the same sites) get differing information and attitudes. We don't necessarily share a common social experience. In fact, as the extent of our virtual connections increases, we probably share less and less with others geographically close to us.

What about solitude? The connection with others in the social networks we build—or allow to build—and the ease of maintaining contact with them change our lives in unprecedented ways. We need no longer be alone or out of touch. Or lonely. Or independent. Henry David Thoreau had to deliberately remove himself from the social network of the town to learn and enjoy the solitude of Walden Pond. Today he would have to be careful to leave his cell phone and laptop in town, lest innumerable virtual towns went with him into his cabin.

It is becoming more common to hear someone in a museum, on a forest trail, in a kayak, or at the Grand Canyon phoning a friend on a cell phone to immediately share their elation about the experience. These are opportunities to share experiences more closely with personal networks, but they may detract from the individual's assimilation of the raw experience. Every piece of technology has an off button. The question is whether the user has the wisdom, timing, and discipline to use it.

Is cyberspace a new gated community? Additional social fragmentation occurs with the overall differences between those who are connected and those who are not. Considerable social pressure to use technology heavily has built steadily over the two decades since the possession of home PCs became widely feasible. The perceived need for children to learn technology to get ahead quickly has become a genuine requirement for all schoolchildren. Some technological sophistication has become, in most workplaces, a necessity for hiring and promotion. Technological literacy is becoming a divider. Older workers and retirees may or may not eagerly participate. For that matter, many of those in younger generations may not be participating eagerly. In any case, the social pressure to be technologically savvy is pervasive and sometimes discriminatory. Meetings and parties are scheduled, and news and gossip are shared in the absence of paper or verbal discussion. Those who are out of these virtual social networks are out of it. Individual e-mails are free. The technology and monthly access are not. The poor must choose to put some of their limited funds into technological connection or stand outside the cyberworld.

FROM GUTENBERG TO JUNK MAIL

After the first printing press was invented, there were opportunities for expanded communication. The sheer physical effort of writing by hand any message one wanted to share had limited the communications. Now multiple copies were generated with relative ease. Anyone with a press had the opportunity to have a wide impact. As better and faster presses made the production of unlimited copies faster and cheaper, opportunities for communication exploded. But a new social role was needed: publishers and editors, who sorted through potential works for those by the most responsible, certified (presumably truthful) writers. In research and academia, writers must submit their articles, books, and manuscripts, and the journal or publishing house accepts those that meet their standards. However, today almost anyone can be published—on the Internet. Similarly, with the recent profusion of paper and printing, individuals have a significant task in separating junk mail from mail they may actually want to open. The reader's job has shifted from trying to understand what recognized authorities are saying to searching, sorting, and wondering what to believe.

CAN CONNECTIONS MAKE US LESS INDEPENDENT?

Do the comforting connections we have with others have the unintended consequence of making us less self-sufficient and more dependent? Do we become less effective as decision makers? A husband picking up a few things at the grocery store can call his wife to ask, "Should I get the 14-oz. can of tomato paste or two of the 8-oz. cans?" The question is self-protective (from a hassle later) but probably unnecessary. A coworker e-mails the entire project team ("It's only one click") to ask whether the pie charts in the proposal should be one-and-a-half or two inches in diameter. Most don't care, but once the question is asked, they feel the need to respond responsibly. And if the responses are mixed, another round or two of e-mail discussions may be necessary to ensure consensus on a decision the original party is paid to make. Personal accountability is sometimes uncomfortable. Getting in touch with everyone is easy and self-protective and is considered sociable. In some ways technological connection reduces mistakes and contributes to efficiency. In other ways it may enable dependent behaviors that have immeasurable costs to efficiency.

PERSONAL CHALLENGES IN ADOPTING TECHNOLOGY—CONTROLLING THE CONNECTIONS

For the most part, we don't have the time or inclination to think through every aspect of adopting new technology. We get the new technology—or are given it by an employer—because it's now available and sparkles with new advantages. "I can send pictures with my cell phone." "I can work from the beach on Fridays." The unintended consequences are often not immediately apparent. The stress of having more places to collect voicemail, e-mail, and advertising messages may only become apparent later. The obligations to meet the higher expectations of more people in our networks will rise gradually. There may be no clearly defined points at which we will consciously say, "No more messages!" So while we think we're making decisions to acquire one more piece of cool technology, we might be deciding to make further lifestyle changes that we only partly understand or control.

To simplify, let's suppose there are three basic approaches: the eager adopter, the Luddite, and those somewhere in between.

- The eager adopter takes genuine interest in each new technology, enjoys learning to use it, aggressively pursues new uses, awaits the next jump in technology, and adopts technology as a hobby and maybe as a business.
- With today's technologies, the Luddite—an old name for those who hated all machinery and in the early industrial eras demonstrated against and even destroyed machines, rejecting the social and lifestyle changes associated with them—might have a TV and a telephone but would not have a computer, cell phone, PDA, or iPod and would consistently resent the business and social changes resulting from them. Luddites are becoming generally unhireable and unpromotable and may willingly give up evolving social networks.
- As-needed adopters are neither eager adopters nor Luddites. They tend to adopt some new technology when it has a clear appeal to them or becomes a job requirement or a social expectation. They may delay adopting a form of technology until the second or third version or generation has come out, because by then it is better debugged, has wider compatibility or standardization, and is more affordable.

The as-needed adopters are the in-betweeners and the bulk of the society of consumers and employees. If we are among them, we will spend much of our lives trying to decide what is really needed or beneficial. We have opportunities to make more conscious decisions consistent with our lifestyle preferences. We do have some career control over the industries, companies, and jobs we work in. As employees, we can be less-than-eager adopters, encouraging the company and our colleagues to respect our preferences. Our own behaviors and positions on issues play a role in the establishment of new social and workplace norms.

Most as-needed adopters will sooner or later seek to manage our own use of technology even if that takes social courage. We can choose to be unconnected or less connected by using the off button or by delaying responses, but we then need to manage the consequences. Some things to consider:

- Go to Walden Pond when you can get away with it. Think of not being connected as a personal luxury that is often legitimate on evenings, weekends, and vacations.
- Write your own usage rules. Instead of waiting for rules and reminders to turn off your cell phone (e.g. in theaters and classrooms), remind yourself to turn it off whenever you should not be distracted or distracting. This might means while driving, while you are in a meeting, or as a face-to-face

conversation turns serious (a new kind of compliment or an affirmation of undivided attention).

- Think civility. Especially in places where distracting behavior is undesirable, control your own distractions.
- Manage others' expectations about your responsiveness to messages, fielding the social pressure with civil but unapologetic explanations.
- Remain aware of how much fragmentation your own preferred networks represent. Know which are mainstream and which are esoteric.
- Remain aware of the number and types of new social networks you build through technological connections. Keep accurate records of numbers and addresses.
- Monitor your connection-induced stress levels, observing their ups and downs and evaluating the importance and urgency of messages.

BUSINESS CHALLENGES IN HANDLING TECHNOLOGICAL CONNECTIONS

It is obvious that any business needs to be as technologically advanced as possible in accomplishing its business mission. Businesses can use technology to increase efficiencies and reduce costs. They can use technology to improve products and services. They can use technology to gain strategic advantage over competitors or to achieve breakthroughs to new services. All of this has been true of technology in general and is equally true of the personal communications technology discussed here. Any business should regularly ask how it can improve connections with customers and among employees. And any business should beware of unintended consequences and the preferences of employees and customers.

CHALLENGES WITH EMPLOYEE CONNECTIONS

It is not so obvious that businesses can get hurt by some unintended consequences of quickly adopting each new technological opportunity. Business managers spend most of their attention managing work processes and relationships. Those processes and relationships change, sometimes gradually and imperceptibly, as interpersonal connections change. While increased connections (e.g., e-mail) offer much efficiency, better teamwork, and off-site working opportunities, they also can change relationships and the nature of jobs. Managers should be alert to changes and, while respecting the preferences of customers and employees, restructure work processes for the effectiveness of the organization. Here are some problems to watch for:

- Office gossip and politicking. If you can see people whispering and snickering by the water cooler, you might surmise that their discussions are not work related, but you have a good idea about how much time at the office is spent. While conversation like this is inevitable and sometimes necessary, too much can be wasteful and can erode an effective company culture. But e-mail is an easy channel for water cooler talk, is invisible, and is always a click away from another screen image. So, it can easily increase the wasting of time and the development of an underground culture possibly antagonistic to the company culture, sometimes to harmful levels.

- Off-loading. Sometimes the efficiency in technology is gained not by the company but by the individual benefiting from more free time at work. Consider the administrative assistant who is happy that the boss is now fully computer literate and can handle her own e-mail and do her own typing. The boss has more to do. Hard copy junk mail and junk memos may still be sorted through by the assistant, but sorting external and internal e-mail spam is now the boss's job. While the boss's connectedness through e-mail with activities in the organization may happily increase, the hourly or daily burden of e-mail can become crushing. Meanwhile, unless work responsibilities are redefined, the assistant has more time to e-mail or IM friends and associates and to shop for patio furniture or place orders with QVC. Job responsibilities should be redefined regularly as work patterns shift.
- Off-loading. If you're face to face or on the phone with someone and you ask him or her about something, the problem is that you might get an answer immediately, which puts the ball in your court. But if you can leave a voicemail or e-mail, you can, at least temporarily, relax until he or she answers. And if it takes a long time for the person to answer, it's that person's fault because the ball was in his or her court. This is especially convenient if you're just trying to "clear your desk" before lunch, at the end of the workday, or on a Friday afternoon.
- Overkill distribution. The inconvenience and costs of copying and distributing hard copy memos sometimes exert an intelligent discipline on distribution, limiting the need to read the memo to those who should read it. But the free and convenient distribution of e-mail—just click on "All Corp. users" or "All Dept. X"—puts the message before many who don't need to read it. The e-mail is free, but the (small) cost in time and energy for each person who trashes it as internal spam adds up quickly. Most organizations wait until they have already become frustrated with the volume of internal spam to encourage disciplined distribution.
- Cover-yourself memos. Again, e-mail makes it easier to guard oneself against all contingencies or complaints. A wide distribution list and the informality of e-mail tempts one to let everyone in the organization know that two weeks from Thursday three spaces in the parking lost will be closed for painting or that a software conversion between 3 and 5 A.M. may slow the system. Then, if anyone happens to complain, the response—"Didn't you read your e-mail?"—forces them to shift blame to themselves.
- Appropriate communications channels. Communication channels like phoning, face-to-face meetings, formal memos, and e-mail vary in their ability to convey information and nuances of meaning effectively. For certain kinds of information, a written record is important. But if discussion is beneficial, an interactive channel is better than an exchange of written

messages. Hearing the voice and seeing facial expressions and body language make face-to-face meetings the best channel for discussion and phone calls the second best. Voicemail still carries some nuances. But e-mail, especially given its speed and informality and the different writing style used, is sometimes misunderstood. Misunderstandings of meaning or nuance can be costly in terms of work relationships. So, on those occasions when discussion or nuances are important, one of the richer communication channels is needed.

- Dependencies within teams. With unlimited technology connections, virtual team meetings are possible anytime, regardless of where everyone is geographically. This has huge advantages in consensus building and flexible off-site working. It may have the unintended consequence of reducing self-sufficiency and responsibility. The example above of a team member consulting with the whole team about the diameter of pie charts demonstrates both the impulse to cover oneself and the tendency to become dependent at the expense of team members' time and attention.
- Dependencies between managers and subordinates. With unlimited technological connections, employees, for the same reasons as those mentioned above, may cover themselves frequently and resist self-initiatives. At the same time, managers who have trouble confidently delegating may welcome the unlimited consultation, creating codependency.
- Reactive management. Managers in some businesses complain of a growing phenomenon: inundation by technological messages (i.e., calls, voicemail, IMs, e-mails) to the point that all their time is spent responding to messages. Their management activity, for good and bad, becomes on the fly and reactive. They risk leaving no time or energy for proactive, reflective, long-range, or strategic thinking, not to mention personal time and energy. Growing numbers of CEOs, who have the career status to get away with it, are arranging times to go to Walden Pond or at least leave their laptops, PDAs, and Blackberries, taking only a cell phone with a private number while they talk with major customers, investors, or other key executives. This practice may become more popular and respected at all organizational levels.
- Inattention or "collective ADHD." Effective multitasking is possible only when each of the tasks involved requires only partial and fleeting attention. Hence the concern and controversy over using a cell phone while driving, which periodically and unpredictably requires one's immediate full attention. The temptation for most of us, however, is to imagine that if we seem to be getting away with two things at once, we can add a third, or that when the primary task requires full attention, we will have no trouble snapping to it. We may even be attracted to the go-go style and the busyness and super-competency it suggests. The reality is that we can inadvertently miss key points or nuances and miss those moments when one task needs to be focused on. Some organizations develop rules for meetings, defining how much personal technology will be allowed.

- Office space in a virtual world. Off-site working provides business opportunities for a mobile, flexible, and agile workforce, and it's popular with employees. It also creates opportunities for efficiencies in "unloading space and re-thinking what's left" (*Business Week*, July 3, 2006, p.100). If up to 40 percent of the workforce in a company is not physically in the office on a given day (and the percentage will grow as more professionals "go Bedouin" or "location-agnostic"), then the company will have opportunities to reduce and reconfigure space. Someone feeling trapped in his cube will likely resent the Bedouin whose office with a window sits empty across the hall. Resentment of off-site workers and the abrasion of work relationships create new management challenges in the virtual world.

How should businesses meet these new management challenges? By consciously and regularly reevaluating work processes and relationships, they can restructure not only office spaces but job responsibilities, maintaining both more flexible. They can define expectations and etiquette in the use of technology and then train employees, redefining and retraining as needed. They can gracefully point out unintended consequences like dependencies and off-loading practices. And, they can respect the privacy, personal time, and life choices of employees, inviting them to discuss and clarify how they do their best work.

CHALLENGES WITH CUSTOMER CONNECTIONS

Customers are people too. Like employees, they differ. Some are eager adopters; some are Luddites; most are in between, trying to manage their responses to a changing society. They may be, after all, those employees of one organization now doing business with another. They may even feel comfortable with technological efficiencies in their own organization but see them as offensive efficiencies in another.

Some customers like a computerized phone receptionist with a large menu of options or many layers of "drilling down" to the appropriate party. Some don't. The computerized receptionist is highly efficient, reducing the number of calls bounced around among a reduced staff. It is also, to some, highly offensive, reducing the number of calls because of frustrated hang-ups. A customer's conclusion that a company's system has difficulty dealing with certain questions or complaints is not good for business. And a customer's suspicion that the system design signals the company's unwillingness to listen is sometimes the end of the business connection.

Some customers forgive a store clerk who takes phone calls while physically present customers wait. Some don't. Some expect Web sites to be full of ads, tease, and spin or to be untended. They expect complex site navigation, outdated links, poor response times, and differing service levels. Some don't. Some willingly share personal information at a checkout or on a Web site. Others don't. Or they do, but they'd rather not. Technology is creating countless new opportunities for customer connection. Businesses are jumping at these opportunities. It is also creating countless new opportunities for failure. Smart businesses will avoid these or fix them quickly, gaining strategic advantage over those who don't.

Age-old wisdom about connections with customers applies even more to today's technological connections. Showing honesty, establishing trust, listening, and providing options for different customer preferences will likely reach new higher standards as businesses realize their strategic advantages. Expectations about technological development rise quickly, and customers will come to expect superior connections with businesses as soon as the best businesses do it.

Most business activity in a sophisticated economy is based, at some level, on trust. The more distant the connection, the greater the need for trust. "The very nature of e-commerce demands more trust than has ever existed in our business transactions. We trust that everyone will honor pledges made with simply a click" (Jennings 2002).

Ethical interactivity (connection) with customers and the empowerment of customers and their choices may create new high business standards. "Paying close attention to the ethical aspects of the use of web-based technologies in marketing might constitute a differentiating force for proactive firms. . . . The ethical sensitivity of a consumer could even become a segmentation criterion" (Gauzente and Ranchhod 2001). With looming privacy concerns, for example, most customers feel more secure and empowered if a business keeps them informed about any data collected and how it's used, gives them the options of agreeing or not agreeing to allow the company to use it, gives them access to it, and gives them a contact person if they don't like it.

Similarly respectful connections with customers can be established for informational messages, suggestions, and advertisements. Acknowledging that customers differ and empowering them to choose the forms of connections used respects the personal challenges they have in managing their own lives in a changing society.

See also: Telecommuting and the Virtual Workplace

References

Gauzente, Claire, and Ashok Ranchhod. 2001. "Ethical Marketing for Competitive Advantage on the Internet." *Academy of Marketing Science Review* 10 [Online].

Jennings, Marianne M. 2002. "Ethics in Cyberspace." *Biz Ed,* January/February, pp. 18–23.

Newsweek. 2006. May 15.

Further Reading: Rothfeder, Jeffrey. 2004. "Privacy in the Age of Transparency." *Strategy and Business,* Spring, pp. 99–103; Sultan, Fareena, and Hussain A. Mooraj. 2001. "Designing a Trust-Based E-Business Strategy." *Marketing Management,* 10 (4): 40–45.

Philip K. Iobst

TELECOMMUTING AND THE VIRTUAL WORKPLACE

Mary Barton, who works for a local nonprofit organization in marketing, recently began to work at home three days a week. She feels that working from her home office saves her time and provides a more relaxed work environment. In addition, she has more time to devote to her special-needs child, as she is not spending as much time traveling to and from work, which takes 40 minute each way. Mary also feels a greater sense of flexibility since she can spend time with her husband and other children in a stress-free environment where she can work at the times when she is most productive. She is confident in her ability to multitask her work in conjunction with household tasks. Mary is experiencing a phenomenon that has grown over the past 20 years, and most significantly over the past 6 years, called telecommuting.

The term "telecommuting" was coined in 1975 during a study conducted at the University of Southern California. Telecommuting was originally an organizational method intended to alleviate the growing problems of transportation in large urban areas. The idea, as developed by Jack Nilles, would allow for certain employees to work from home or other locations rather than travel to the office (Nilles 1975).

Since its inception, the idea of telecommuting has grown significantly in concept and scope. Telecommuting, which is currently defined as employees working from home one or more days a week during typical business hours, has become a small component of the large umbrella concept of Telework.

Telework, a broader concept developed in Europe, allows for the use of technology to change the standard approach to work, where employees report to a specific company office or location with other employees and complete the tasks assigned. Telework is the next level of telecommuting that enables employees to work at any time or place to complete their assigned tasks or responsibilities. Telework includes telecommuting; the use of virtual or mobile offices; technology use in hotels, on- or offshore, in satellite offices, and telework centers; or even locating the office in the customer's place of business. Telework, "with the help of information technology, allows for the movement of the work to wherever the worker chooses rather than moving the workers to the work" (Nilles 1998). Thus, the composition of the telework pool, as well as the various categories of teleworkers, is rather broad.

The employed teleworker, like the traditional worker, is one who has a contract of employment that specifies the home as his or her worksite alone or in addition to the location of the organization. Mary Barton is an example of the employee with a telework agreement in her contract. She works from home and the office. Unlike the unofficial teleworker, who just takes extra work home for which he or she is are not paid, employed teleworkers earn their salary for the time they spend working from home or elsewhere as required.

Many companies like AT&T, IBM, and Sun Microsystems provide multiple options for employees to telework. Forty-six percent of Sun Microsystems' workforce chooses what they call open work practice, which allows employees to choose whether they work from home, satellite offices, or a telecenter, or the option of hoteling based on the type of work they do (Richert and Rush 2006). A satellite office is a completely equipped office that the company strategically locates in settings closer to employees' homes that employees can easily reach, and at which they can reserve space to work one or more days a week. These offices reduce employee commute times and help reduce traffic congestion. A telecenter is similar to a satellite office, but employees from more than one company share the space. These centers are usually owned and operated independently; companies utilizing the space and services pay a fee for daily use by their employees. In contrast, hoteling is a unique concept that allows employees to come to the company location but share office space on a stop-in basis with other employees. Employees can provide an advanced reservation for the space or just stop in to use a cubicle equipped with the standard office technology they need to do their jobs on an as-needed basis or a predetermined day of the week.

In contrast to the formal or employed teleworker is the informal or the freelance teleworker. Informal teleworkers are individuals who might have an agreement with their supervisors to work from home for reasons they deem compelling without a formal contract or approval of the company. This may occur if the employee needs to care for a sick child or avoid a major traffic holdup or does not want to spread flu germs to the other employees, or for other reasons. This informal practice is more common than one would think. The concept of the freelance teleworker is one that has been around for decades. A contract teleworker such as a freelance writer is an informal teleworker who normally works at home but will go to the contract organization if requested.

The entrepreneurial teleworker is one who runs his or her own business but without the brick and mortar. In his book Free Agent Nation: The Future of Working for Yourself, Daniel Pink discusses the swift movement toward self-employment in our country and across the world. He states that over 20 million Americans are now self-employed, while around one in ten works for a large well-known corporation (Pink 2002). Pink supports the notion of the entrepreneurial teleworker, as he contends a new definition of employment has developed as millions of individuals become "free agents" with skills to offer to those who have opportunities or needs. They work out of their homes or have virtual offices employing the technology needed for success.

In April 2006, a group of five acquaintances convened to discuss starting their own business. The consulting business they wished to develop, Global Strategies and Solutions, would provide services in the areas of business strategy, marketing, and information technology. The members of this newly formed company, who were spread over the East Coast and Midwest, faced the dilemma of where to locate the business, as they did not want to limit their customer base geographically. After some research and discussion, the partners determined that a physical location was not immediately necessary or financially feasible, although they wanted to have one address for the company letterhead and business cards. To solve the problem, Global Strategies and Solutions found a virtual office space, provided for them at a limited cost in a large metropolitan area on the East Coast. Additionally, the team of partners identified a Web-based technology that would allow them to communicate with each other, share schedules and files online, and conduct virtual meetings. In the first two months of business, the group has collaboratively obtained a significant number of projects and clients with all partners working at their home offices and growing the business on a networked basis. This is an example of the entrepreneurial teleworker.

WHO IS PARTICIPATING IN TELEWORK?

Corporate America has participated extensively in telework over the past few years. According to the Society for Human Resource Management's 2005 benefits survey, 33 percent of U.S. companies offer a shorter work week, 56 percent provide flextime, and 37 percent allow telecommuting (Telework Coalitions 2006). In March 2006, the Telework Coalition conducted a benchmarking study to determine the best practices of organizations participating in a comprehensive telework program for at least ten years or more and to look at how their programs have evolved. Thirteen companies with over 137,000 employees participating in some form of telework program participated. This alone shows the growth in telework programs across corporations globally. The study's primary findings indicate that most organizations participating in a telework program are driven by cost savings, and much of that comes with a reduction in their real estate holdings. Additionally, many organizations are finding their telework program enhances their ability to recruit and retain highly qualified individuals who are interested in a flexible schedule and may be located globally. Another factor important to the participating organization is the ability to continue operations in the face of disaster. Many companies found that after events such as September 11 or Hurricane Katrina, employees who teleworked were able quickly to resume their work duties from other locations. A significant concern was the organizations' ability to copete successfully in a global market. Thus, the majority of participants feel teleworking is vital to ensuring the stability and success of their business or organization overall (Telework Coalitions 2006).

BENEFITS OF TELEWORK

Telework offers numerous and significant returns to three different groups who have varying perspectives on the advantages. The employee, the employer, and the economic society as a whole experience both positive and negative affects. Most research to date emphasizes the positive returns. There are numerous benefits to the employee teleworker, such as more time with families, less time spent traveling to and from the office, less stress. However, the benefits to organizations are also rich. These benefits translate to significant cost savings, competitive advantage, and retention plans. Organizations implementing telework programs are finding new ways to accomplish their objectives and experience success for their organization in a global economy. The continuous growth in the availability and reduced cost of technology supports the organizations' ability to implement a telework program, while changes in society connected to the emergence of the global market and the cost of transportation, as well as societal and family constraints, demonstrate the fact that telework is here to stay. The question is, to what degree?

EMPLOYEE BENEFITS

There are numerous benefits to employee telework. Most common is the time more readily available to the family and the flexibility one has in how one spends such time. Teleworkers can see more of their family and participate in family and household responsibilities such as the children's sporting events, shopping, cleaning, and dinner preparation.

Flexibility and time for family is commonly perceived as the most significant employee benefit of telework. However, most teleworkers also find great benefit in work opportunities that cover a broader geographical area. They are not confined to jobs within reasonable travel distance to their homes and they appreciate reduced travel time and costs as a primary motivation and benefit. Telework supporters argue that most teleworkers have used at least part of what was previously travel time to get more work done, in contrast to the perception that such time is misused for personal reasons, such as sleeping late.

Another important benefit for the many teleworkers is the ability to provide service to their community because they have more time available. The contribution to one's community has great rewards with few time constraints. Mary is an active member of the PTA and is able to participate as a board member of the local YMCA. She would not have as much time to participate in such activities if she did not have the flexibility to telework.

EMPLOYER BENEFITS

As previously stated , telework can be useful in establishing a more efficient business approach by decreasing overhead costs, reducing the need for additional office and parking space, helping employees balance the demands of work and family, complying with state and local environmental requirements and disaster preparedness, as well as obtaining and retaining valuable employees.

The study conducted by the Telework Coalition found that employer participants realized an annual average savings of $3,000 to $10,000 per employee, which was related to real estate holdings (two of the participating companies indicated a real estate–related savings of close to $200 million).

Organizations permitting employees to work from home usually pay a one-time cost to install the needed technology at the employee's home or in telecenters. These costs cover Internet and phone connections, computer, printer, fax, software, and the like. However, this means the organization does not need as much office space or real estate, which provides significant savings over time.

Many organizations feel telework helps to reduce problems with punctuality and attendance. Teleworkers do not have to worry about the traffic jams or blizzards that may affect their ability to arrive at work on time. They are likely to ignore colds or body aches and work comfortably at home if they do not have to drive to the office. If their child has a doctor's appointment, they are not as likely to take the day off, but only the time needed for the appointment.

Employers have greater opportunity to hire employees who are more qualified if they implement a telework program. Telework is a trump card they may use in recruitment and retention. Mary Barton, the marketing employee the nonprofit organization (which are typically lower paying), would look for another job if she did not have the flexibility she needs. With the organizational dilemma of finding and retaining good people, telework may help open doors to talented individuals with physical disabilities or personal circumstances that require greater flexibility or may help organizations keep employees who must move due to a spouse's job change. Additionally, employees who take a career break can continue working part time and remain current in their field and organizational practices. Employees who take maternity or paternity leave can continue to carry out some of their work while on leave and remain current on procedures and issues within the organization as well.

Employers may use telework as a trade-off for employee pay. Like Mary, many employees live in housing areas outside city limits and have a considerable drive to work. The cost in time, gas, auto depreciation and maintenance, eating out, and business clothing is substantial. These accumulated expenses cost employees thousands of dollars annually. An employer may be able to use the cost savings as a negotiation chip in hiring and retaining employees.

Numerous employers participating in a telework program have reported a productivity increase of up to 40 percent, a number that is confirmed by both teleworkers and managers; however, long-term productivity studies are few. In addition, some studies find that successful telework programs improve employee motivation. Employees are said to respond well to the trust and confidence demonstrated by the employer through the implementation of telework programs and the acceptance of independent work styles.

Two other benefits of telework to the employer are enhanced customer service and disaster preparedness. Through telework, employees may offer customer services outside the typical working hours each day or week without overtime costs or the need for additional staff. The effects of a natural disaster such as Hurricane Katrina, or a terrorist attack such as September 11, can be devastating to a company without proper resources to handle such an event. Some experts recommend that organizations be well prepared for such events by setting up a telework system as part of their disaster recovery plan. This will enable employees to work at home if there are environmental or safety issues preventing them from going into the office. If the United States experiences the bird flu or another pandemic, organizations that do not have a telework program will experience a significant increase in absenteeism and reduced productivity. Many employees will not work if they are ill or may be caring for sick relatives.

SOCIAL ECONOMIC BENEFITS

Telecommuting is an issue regarded as significant to the problem of increased population and traffic. As the study of this has evolved, researchers have begun to see telework as a way to resolve many of these problems in the overall global economy. Traffic reduction has been an economic benefit of telework. There are fewer people driving during defined rush hour traffic, which reduces congestion, gasoline consumption, and stress. With teleworkers generating a reduction in total car travel, there has been a noticeable decrease in pollution. In some states such as California and Georgia, there are legislation and programs designed to encourage telework programs in order to help reduce traffic congestion and pollution. These states have gone so far as to provide significant tax relief to organizations that provide telework programs for their employees. The federal government has satellite work offices outside the district limits of Washington, D.C., to give teleworkers access to technology and office assistance without commuting in Washington.

Another benefit is the potential reduction in unemployment that telework offers. Telework may provide skilled individuals who are unemployed with work opportunities in other countries. Additionally, those who have disabilities that make it difficult to travel to work or who work a nine-to-five job may have specialized skills to offer an organization and may become more self-sufficient and less dependent on government-subsidized programs. These and other benefits can enhance the case for telework. Many corporations that want to compete globally and have a significant number of knowledge workers can benefit from the implementation of a telework program as well as provide regional and national economic benefits.

LIMITATIONS OF TELEWORK

While telework programs offer many benefits, there are also many limitations. Telework is not for all organizations and employees. Teleworkers must be disciplined and trustworthy. They must know when to separate their work and home responsibilities. They must have a clear understanding of how to use technology and how it can benefit the company and the particular responsibilities of each individual. The Web-based application Global Strategies and Solutions plans to implement to facilitate online communication and collaboration requires initial set-up, training, and support in order to realize the full benefits of the technology both at the individual and company levels. Additionally, all partners must fully embrace and use the technology in order for it to function as intended. Home-based telework will not work for everyone. Those who are not self-motivated or have a distracting home environment may need the guidance and discipline provided by set office hours in a managed site. Fred, a partner in the consulting firm, is used to an eight-to-five office job. He may have difficulty being productive from home with five children in the house. Even those with high motivation may find it difficult focusing on important tasks with multiple distractions. A telecenter approach might be most appropriate for this situation.

Many say the fad of telecommuting will diminish. A number of researchers feel that the growth of teleworkers, which was around 12 percent in 2005, will decrease considerably by 2008 (Margulius 2006). According to the Bureau of Labor Statistics, there has been a decline in the number of teleworkers employed by corporations (Bureau of Labor Statistics 2005). In a survey conducted in May 2001, the number of teleworkers was 17.1 percent, whereas the same study conducted in May of 2004 found the number of teleworkers to be 16.2. The number of self-employed workers increased from 30.2 percent self-employed in May 2001 to 33.7 percent in May 2004. In addition, some recent studies have found that employees might not be as productive as originally determined. CareerBuilder.com recently conducted a poll of 2,450 teleworkers who shed some light on the limitations of telework. Twenty-five percent of the respondents admitted they spend less than one hour on work when home, 53 percent stated they work for less than three hours from the home office, and 14 percent suggested that they work a full eight-hour day. When asked what prevented them from working a full day, 22 percent indicated their children distracted them, while 39 percent conduct personal business, run errands, or clean the house and 15 percent watch TV and/or sleep (Butler 2006).

Laguerre states that although there are employee benefits, telework creates a sense of distance or disconnect between employees within a company (Laguerre 2005). They are missing the personal interaction and communication with co-workers, the ability to quickly get an answer to a question or work through a problem with the help of others with needed expertise. Teleworkers also miss promotional opportunities and even the personal milestones of other employees. Employees need to have a sense that they are of value to the organization and other employees. A social disconnect among team members who are working on the same project can reduce productivity and cause employees to feel less creative. With that said, new employees entering the workforce may receive greater benefit from working in a conventional office setting, which allows them to develop their social skills, contacts, and relationships with mentors.

Bailey and Kurland contend that unlike full-time teleworkers, employees who telework part time do not experience social disconnect or feelings of isolation (Bailey and Kurland 2002). Although there is a great deal of research evaluating the impact of telework on the individual employee, they emphasize the need for a comprehensive review of the impact telework has on the organization, how employees telework, and how best to implement varying levels of telework for appropriate job functions within an organization. Telework can be a failure at any organization that does not think through and plan for the development of a clearly defined program.

AT&T has been quite successful in its implementation of a telework program, according to Roitz and Jackson (Roitz and Jackson 2006). With a globally dispersed workforce of over 40,000, 71 percent are involved in some form of telework and more than half have given up corporate office space. Although the nature of work performed by AT&T employees is conducive to a prevalent telework force, there are obstacles preventing 100 percent of the workforce from becoming teleworkers. The obstacles defined by Roitz and Jackson are the same as those regularly identified by teleworkers in other organizations: they include reduced visibility, the need for human interaction, and a feeling of isolation or loneliness. Additionally, management style, and a lack of adequate broadband connection at home were variables identified as problems. Some companies have cultures that have not adapted to the flexibility fundamental to managing telework.

For employees, working at home or on their own outside the office may create a greater sense of self-efficacy or autonomy. Such feelings can negatively affect the hierarchical relationship between management and employee, thus making it difficult for the management process to occur. Managers need training in remote management skills and must develop confidence in their ability to manage teleworkers, as there is a surely an identified set of skills that will assist in that challenge. Clearly defined policies and procedures outlining expectations and requirements of the teleworker and the organization are necessary. In addition, corporate support for the program and management is important to building the confidence of the telesupervisor or manager.

The benefit of telework to the employer may mean some additional cost to the employee. The transfer of costs to the worker includes the additional use of utilities. Research shows that although telecommuters saved money on the reduced cost of gas, food, clothing, and the like, the savings were offset by the increased costs for energy in their homes. That is, the cost of heat, air conditioning, running the computer, and phone use increased.

Security is of concern to many organizations with telework programs. Employees have access to corporate equipment and knowledge and may not use either ethically. The employer most often provides all the equipment. With this comes the need to address technical support and physical security, as employees have access to corporate networks and maintain company equipment in their home. As telework programs grow, so too does the need to keep the resources of the organization secure (Messmer 2006). Health-care organizations such as hospitals are implementing telework programs so doctors have access to office information from home and medical information can be transcribed remotely. These organizations must ensure strict IT security to ensure privacy, information safety, and adherence to the law.

Although telecommuting offers many advantages to both the employee and employer, there are many issues that an organization should consider before implementing the process. Telecommuters must be disciplined, motivated, and able to work independently, and organizations must have strict policies and a clear system of evaluation.

See also: Technological Connectivity

References

Bailey, Diane E., and Nancy B. Kurland. 2002. "A Review of Telework Research: Findings, New Directions, and Lessons for the Study of Modern Work." *Journal of Organizational Behavior* 23 (4): 383.

Bureau of Labor Statistics. 2005. *Work at Home Summary.* Available at http://www.bls.gov/news.release/homey.nr0.htm. Accessed June 18, 2006. b

Butler, Kelley M. 2006. "Phoning It In: Survey Results Report Productivity Lag Among Teleworkers." *Employee Benefit News,* March, p. 1.

Laguerre, Michel S. 2005. *The Digital City.* Basingstoke, UK: Palgrave MacMillian

Margulius, D. 2006. "Telecommuting Gets More Elusive." *InfoWorld* 28 (6): 18.

Messmer, E. 2006. "Telecommuting, Security Concerns Grow." *Network World* 23 (16): 43.

Nilles J. M. 1975. "Telecommunications and Organizational Decentralization." *IEEE Transactions on Communications* 23 (10): 1142–47.

Nilles, J. 1998. *Managing Telework: Strategies for Managing the Virtual Workforce.* New York: Wiley.

Pink, D. 2002. *Free Agent Nation: The Future of Working for Yourself.* New York: Warner Business Books.

Richert, E., and D. Rush. 2006. "Sun Microsystems Case Study: Where Technology Enables Flexibility." *Workspan* 49 (2: 24.

Roitz, J., and E. Jackson. 2006. "AT&T Adds Business Continuity to the Long List of Telework's Advantages." *Journal of Organizational Excellence* 14 (6). Available at www.interscience.wiley.com.

Telework Coalitions. 2006. *Telework Benchmarking Study: Best Practices for Large-Scale Implementation in Public and Private Sector Organizations.* Washington, DC: Author.

Further Reading: Nilles, J. 1998. *Managing Telework: Strategies for Managing the Virtual Workforce.* New York: Wiley; Pink, D. 2002. *Free Agent Nation: The Future of Working for Yourself.* New York: Warner Business Books.

Kathleen J. Noce

TRADE SURPLUSES AND DEFICITS

Trade is the basis of much of the economic activity we see around us. The majority of our day-to-day activity involves trade. Examples abound—going to the grocery store and trading cash for food and even the act of obtaining cash by trading our time and effort for it. And we regularly account for the result of all this trading with quarterly readings on the pace of economic activity in our nation. But in those reports, one category of trade is singled out. Trade with "foreigners" is highlighted, and measured separately.

WHAT'S SO SPECIAL ABOUT FOREIGN TRADE?

Essentially, we trade because doing so makes us better off. One of the first lessons we learn in economics is that we are not all equally proficient at the same things. For example, one person may be a better cook and the other a better carpenter. Individually, one would be ill fed but well housed and the other well fed but ill housed. By trading services, each could—in theory, at least—be both well housed and fed. The added benefits from trading make both better off.

So trading is good because people trade only when it makes them better off (otherwise they don't trade). And we recognize the benefits of trade and economic activity within our borders. Every third month, when the latest report on the gross domestic product of the U.S. economy is released, the nightly news blares the rate of growth over the airwaves. Politicians take credit or pass blame. Stock traders rejoice or moan. Bond traders take notice. A big increase in GDP suggests that trade among Americans has increased, translating into stronger economic growth and cause for celebration.

But a big increase in trade with foreign interests is often met with far less enthusiasm. On the face of it, the reason isn't apparent. After all, we only trade with others—domestic or foreign—if it makes us better off. This activity gives U.S. consumers more products from which to choose and products that are—in some cases—less expensive. The same is true for foreign buyers of our goods and services. An increase in trade with foreign interests should be good news. So why not view it that way? Well, probably because if we simply buy more things from foreigners than we sell to them (as is usually the case), our measured economic activity tends to shrink. And lower measured economic activity in our economy is generally frowned upon.

In contrast, if we as a nation trade more with foreigners by selling them more than we buy from them, then more trade with foreigners is viewed as good because it raises measured economic activity in the United States.

So we generally view trade with other Americans as nearly always good but trade with foreigners as only good if we sell more to them than we buy from them. In other words, trade isn't always viewed as good even though both parties voluntarily engage in it, which presumably makes each better off.

SURPLUSES, DEFICITS, AND BALANCE

As was mentioned earlier, a lot of trade takes place each day, both among domestic residents and with foreigners. On the foreign trade front, domestic residents typically both trade their dollars for foreign goods and services (buy) and receive dollars from foreigners for U.S.-made goods and services (sell). If we buy more than we sell we are said to have a trade deficit. If selling outweighs buying, a trade (or current account) surplus emerges. When buying and selling perfectly match one another, this results in a trade balance.

If voluntary trade makes parties better off, why separate foreign trade in the economic accounting and why distinguish between deficits, surpluses, and balance? In a nutshell, trade with foreign interests is often viewed as having a dark side, in that sending more dollars abroad than we receive (a deficit) means some of our domestic consumer demands are met by foreign firms, which causes a drag on demand facing U.S. firms and reduces the demand for workers in the United States. Of course, consumers are made better off in that they have a broader array of goods from which to select. This benefit to consumers is widely recognized but typically is not publicized as a precisely measured benefit. Far more publicity is garnered by the estimated size and presumed costs imposed on U.S. citizens from trade deficits. A second concern is how long our economy can sustain trade deficits. Under the assumption that deficits create a drag on our economy, how much of a drag is required to slow the economy substantially? Let's address each of these questions in turn.

HOW BIG ARE TRADE DEFICITS?

Our trade balance is measured as the net difference between the dollar value of the goods and services we buy from abroad (imports) compared to the dollar value of goods and services we sell abroad (exports). In late 2006, our exports were averaging just over $120 billion per month at a seasonally adjusted annual rate. Imports at that time were nearly $190 billion a month.

In Figure T.3, it is clear that the value of both our imports and exports is typically rising over time. This is not surprising given the diverse nature of goods produced in the United States, the prominence of our currency, and our well-developed infrastructure, which makes the physical transportation of goods (and services) relatively easy. But with the value of imports rising faster than exports, our trade sector is increasingly in deficit, to the tune of $64 billion per month, or roughly $700 billion a year, according the most recent reports.

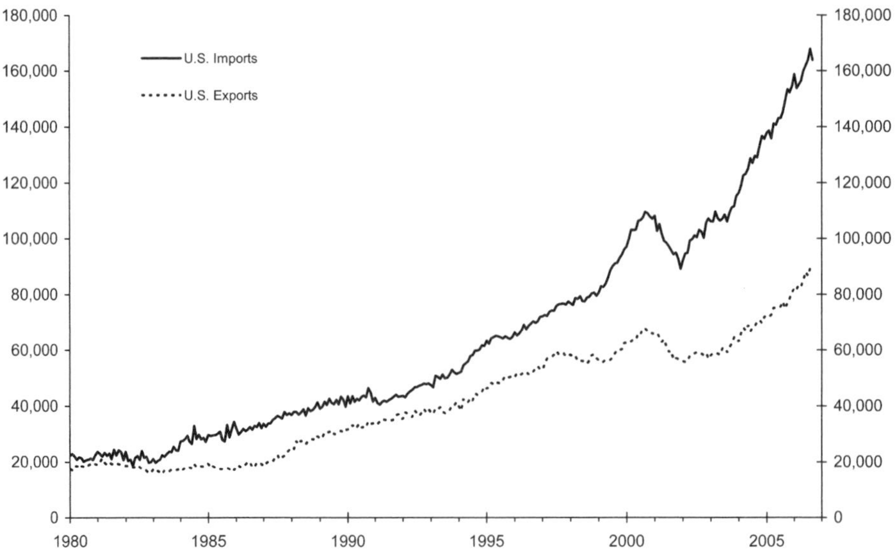

Figure T.3 U.S. imports and exports.

Source: U.S. Department of Commerce. Available at www.commerce.gov.

With rare exceptions, the United States has experienced trade deficits since the 1970s, as shown in Figure T.4. In recent years, these deficits have grown relatively large, in 2006 reaching around 6 percent of our nation's economy as measured by GDP. The current deficit is several times larger than it was just a few years ago and—if sustained—is cause for concern. But the recent bulge partly reflects soaring prices of imported oil, and if those prices moderate over time, so too will the size of the deficit. Of course, the current situation has spurred discussion over the drag these large trade deficits could potentially exert on the U.S. economy and the long-term consequences of this drag.

In part, deficits' impact on the economy depends on their causes. Since exports and imports—the two components of the trade balance—are measured in U.S. dollars, changes in the value of the dollar compared to the value of other currencies can affect the deficit's size. As 2006 drew to a close, the dollar's value had fallen compared to the values of the currencies of our major trading partners. This made the price of U.S.-produced goods relatively more attractive than the prices of foreign goods. Initially, a decreasing value of the dollar can widen the measured trade gap, as foreigners pay relatively less for our goods and we pay more for their goods. This can occur especially when the volumes of the goods traded changes little. Over time, however, the increasingly attractive prices of U.S. goods would be expected to stimulate demand for our products, pushing up our export volume and trimming the trade gap.

Another reason the U.S. trade deficit may be widening is that relatively strong economic growth in the United States has created demand for imported goods. As incomes in our nation have strengthened, consumers have responded by ramping up spending, including spending on foreign-produced goods.

Figure T.4 U.S. trade balance.

Source: U.S. Department of Commerce. Available at www.commerce.gov.

HAS DOMESTIC ECONOMIC ACTIVITY BEEN HARMED BY TRADE DEFICITS?

It is very difficult to assess whether trade deficits have affected our economy in a precise fashion (recall the earlier discussion of the arithmetic of consumer benefits, for example). However, data from U.S. labor markets and trade accounts do not make a compelling case for a strong near-term relationship between a rise in deficits and a drag on U.S. economic activity—at least through the labor market channel. Since 1980, for example, our trade deficit has grown markedly but has not trimmed domestic production enough to persistently raise our unemployment rate. As shown in Figure T.5, there have been fluctuations in our unemployment rate since 1980, but the periods of large increases have been tied to recessions that were largely independent of trade. The recessions in the early 1980s occurred because the Federal Reserve sent interest rates sharply higher to fight the severe inflationary pressures that had built up during the late 1970s. In the early 1990s, a recession occurred after the real estate and stock markets unwound following run-ups in activity in each. In the early part of this decade, a recession followed a reversal of the sharp increases in stock market prices in the preceding years.

In fact, these recessionary episodes aside, the unemployment rate has trended lower throughout the period, with the tightest labor markets often occurring during times when trade deficits were on the rise. From this perspective, it is not at all obvious that running a trade deficit has led to the loss of jobs and higher unemployment in the overall economy.

This is not to suggest, however, that trade deficits have had no impact on jobs in the United States. With the expanded global market in recent years, not only

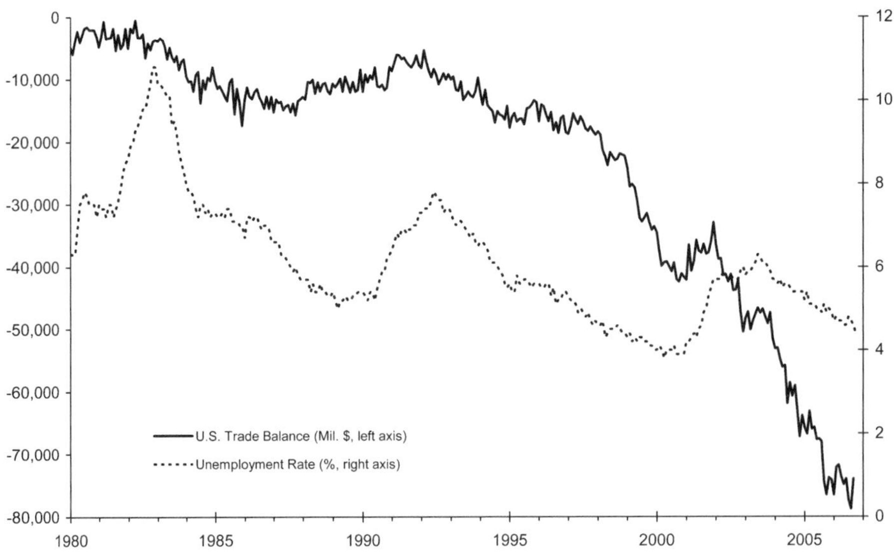

Figure T.5 U.S. trade balance and unemployment rate.

Source: U.S. Department of Commerce. Available at www.commerce.gov.

have global trade volumes increased, but the location of global production has been more dynamic. That is, firms have increasingly shifted their production among countries in an ongoing effort to contain costs and to match the location of production to that of emerging market demand. Through these channels, individual job categories in the United States have been affected. Jobs have declined in industries like textiles, for example, but have risen in other categories. This is textbook comparative advantage at work—with foreign producers making more of the world's fabric, American producers can develop more pharmaceuticals.

WHAT DO TRADE BALANCE FIGURES TELL US?

Broadly speaking, they tell us very little, really. While trade figures imply that the United States consumes more than it produces, this interpretation isn't so important, on balance. First, with well-functioning international financial markets, trade between nations has many implications that influence both the benefits and costs of the trade activity. The measures of trade flows (as imperfect as they are) are just one part of the story. Also important are the financial flows that result from the trade transactions.

When a domestic purchaser buys a good or service produced abroad, the purchase is an import. In this setting, the disposition of the dollars received by the foreign producer is important in determining the impact of the transaction on the U.S. economy. A foreign producer has several options with the acquired dollars: to hold them (an interest free loan to the U.S. government), exchange them for U.S. dollars on the foreign exchange markets (adding to the supply of dollars and pressuring the dollar lower), or invest them in dollar-denominated assets like a U.S. Treasury security or a factory in the United States.

In the first instance, we would like the foreign supplier to stuff its mattress with—or, better yet, burn—the dollars they receive. This way, we would get the goods or services from them and would provide in exchange only paper bills (which cost our country little to print). By either destroying or otherwise not spending the dollar bills, foreign claims to U.S. goods or assets are relinquished. But this isn't likely to occur very frequently because trading of this type is not in spirit mutually beneficial to both parties. More likely, the foreign holders of dollars could delay spending or investing those dollars—while they hold the dollars, they earn no interest on them—effectively providing an interest-free loan to us.

In the second case, dollars received by foreign producers are exchanged for their home currency. With a trade surplus (from their perspective, since if we have a deficit, they must have a surplus), they receive a greater amount of dollars than we receive of their currency. To equate the currency amounts on the foreign exchange market, the value of the dollar must fall relative to the value of the foreign currency. This makes goods and services priced in dollars more affordable, driving up the quantity of those goods demanded on international markets. But a falling dollar may jeopardize inflows of foreign capital into the United States and make dollar-denominated investments less attractive—but that's a story for another time.

In the third option, the foreign producer accumulates dollars to purchase assets valued in U.S. dollars. Toyota, Honda, and many foreign-based computer firms have large production facilities in the United States, for example, though most are invested in financial instruments. This is good because these businesses create investment, tax revenues, and jobs here. But foreign investment in the United States leaves some uncomfortable. In the late 1980s, Japanese firms were purchasing farmland in the United States, which led to debate about the impact on our economy. More recently, some concerns continue to be voiced about who receives the profits on the investments. With global stock markets, we need not be too concerned. If a U.S. citizen wants the profits from a large foreign corporation, then stock in that company—and a share in its profits—is available for purchase.

In addition, in today's world economy, firms in the United States sometimes have operations overseas. Imagine for a moment that a furniture producer in the United States decides to open a factory in China. To open the plant, the U.S. firm buys enough Chinese yuan (the Chinese currency) to enable it to build the plant. But the output is shipped to the United States (a foreign import that tends to add to our trade deficit) and the profits are dollars, part of which the firm retains in the United States and part of which are converted to yuan to cover the continuing operating expenses of the plant. In this case, the trade gap has widened, but the Chinese have not substantially increased their claims to U.S. assets in the future.

Is this kind of activity important? Well, in a word, yes. If we receive goods today and exchange only paper dollars, that's one thing. But if those paper dollars can potentially be redeemed for goods or factories or real estate in the United States at some future date, then that's another story, and we are a debtor nation,

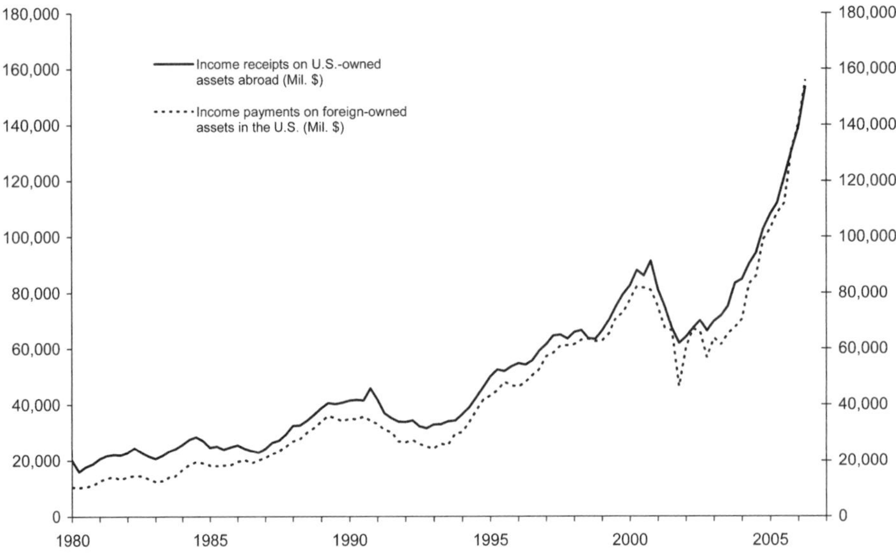

Figure T.6 U.S. international financial payments.

Source: U.S. Department of Commerce. Available at www.commerce.gov.

meaning we owe more money to foreigners than they owe us. Now, much of the money we owe them is in the form of Treasury securities. They bought them and we will have to redeem them one day. But is being a debtor nation so bad? As with many other aspects of trade and international finance, the answer is not crystal clear. One way to gauge our net position as a debtor nation is simply to look at the income we as a nation earn on assets we own abroad compared to the payments we make to foreign entities that own assets in the United States. Figure T.6 shows that our payments to foreigners have soared in recent years. But the chart also shows that our payments from them have kept pace. In fact, the chart suggests relatively little reason to lie awake at night worrying about our status as a debtor nation.

WHAT ABOUT FUTURE GENERATIONS?

Much of the discussion here has focused on near-term implications of our trade position. But critics point out that the impacts of today's trade actions may affect future generations. The argument is that trade deficits occur when our society consumes more that it produces. This behavior, if left unchecked, will eventually leave the nation with large unpaid bills for the goods and services consumed. This is like dining out excessively on your credit card. These critics correctly note that to eventually pay off the debt, the country will have to sell off some assets, leaving the next generation with fewer assets and potentially reducing their ability to produce goods and services.

This argument is plausible, and probably correct if sizeable trade deficits persist over a long period. But it is far from a foregone conclusion. For one thing, the trade deficit may moderate if energy prices fall or if the dollar falls in value. But there is another consideration. Just as running up a credit card balance sometimes makes sense, so does running a trade deficit. Imagine that some large nations are ramping up production but still have a lot of underutilized capacity. For a time, the goods produced in these nations may be a bargain. In this case, taking advantage of the sale prices may be worth reducing your asset holdings temporarily. Later, when assets are cheaper relative to consumer goods, the logical choice could be to accumulate capital goods relative to consumer goods.

SUMMARY

This entry began by asking what all the fuss concerning foreign trade is about. If trade with your neighbor is good, isn't trade with your neighboring nation also good? The answer to this and other trade-related questions—unfortunately—is not clear cut. While most agree that trade with other nations has many substantial benefits for the United States, measuring these benefits is difficult. In addition, many people are comfortable with trade as long as the value of our exports exceeds that of our imports—a trade surplus.

But aside from a surplus, our trade position with other nations often elicits mixed feelings. These feelings turn to concern as the trade balance moves deeper into deficit territory. Such a movement has occurred in recent years. But the widening of the trade deficit has not exhibited especially troubling effects on our economy. Economic growth in the United States has been relatively strong in recent years and our labor markets—aside from recessionary fluctuations—have remained generally tight. There are no signals yet that trade deficits are costing Americans jobs in the aggregate. In fact, labor markets were arguably becoming too tight in late 2006, as labor cost pressures emerged and complaints of worker shortage were being heard.

In addition, concerns that trade deficits lead to outsized foreign ownership of U.S. assets and debt may also be a bit overblown. More of our assets are in foreign hands, but so too are we holding many foreign assets. On balance, our earnings from those assets are about matching the interest and payments we make to foreign holders of U.S. assets.

In fact, as long as foreign interests want to hold more U.S. dollars, we can buy goods from abroad and foreign interests can get the dollars they want to hold. We want their goods and they want our dollars. Their use of those dollars can have somewhat differing impacts on our economy, but no bad impacts appear to be occurring. And we need to remember that consumers reap large benefits when we buy goods and services from foreign firms. But we can also increase trade deficits when our dollars flow to companies located abroad that are owned by U.S. parent firms. Such arrangements can offer these firms flexibility and profitability while containing the outflow of dollars that concerns some.

The bottom line may be that it doesn't matter so much with whom we trade. The real issue may be whether we are consuming more than we are producing. If we, as a society, consume more than we produce, we will eventually have to draw down our wealth to pay for the excess consumption. Whether we transfer that wealth to another nation or to someone in our nation, the bottom line is that future generations will have a lower stock of capital, and that could, under some circumstances, constrain their ability to produce goods and services in the future. But this is not to suggest we are at or near that point. It is not obvious that we are consuming substantial amounts of our capital base or seed corn. In addition, eating some seed corn today may be reasonable if some categories of goods and services currently are a bargain that is not expected to persist. So one possibility is to refocus the discussion to worry more about whether we, as a society, are properly balancing our consumption and savings—and worry less about where production is located.

Further Reading: Eisner, Robert. 1997. *The Great Deficit Scares: The Federal Budget, Trade, and Social Security.* New York: Twentieth Century Foundation; Preeg, Ernest H. 2000. *The Trade Deficit, the Dollar, and the National Interest.* Indianapolis: Hudson Institute.

Raymond Owens

U

UNIVERSAL HEALTH CARE

Health-care systems have occupied a place in society for centuries. A prevailing question throughout history has been how health care should be financed—publicly or privately. Most industrialized countries favor some form of national health-care service model. Under these models, universal health-care coverage is, at least in part, publicly financed.

The United States has an entrepreneurial model of health care in which insurance is either provided by an employer or is purchased on an individual basis with health-care providers. It exists largely in the private sector. The recent controversy in the United States centers on whether the current system is successful at providing health care to its citizens and whether the health system puts employers at a competitive disadvantage in terms of global competition because employers are expected to finance health coverage.

Businesses across the United States have been feeling the pinch of rising health-care costs. America's large automakers in Detroit are currently dealing with increasing costs. For example, GM reported that $1,500 for each vehicle manufactured goes toward health-care costs (Associated Press 2006).

According to the U.S. Census Bureau, more than 45 million people had no coverage in 2005, which was a 13 percent increase from the 39.8 million uninsured in 2000. This increase in the number of people who are uninsured is precipitated by the decrease in employer-provided health-care coverage, which decreased from 69 percent of employers in 2000 to only 60 percent in 2005 (Chua 2006).

The biannual PNC Economic Outlook Survey conducted in January and February 2006 surveyed 1,041 owners of small and mid-size businesses and senior decision makers across the United States and found that 57 percent are likely to

Table U.1

	United States	United Kingdom	Germany	France	Japan	Canada
Life expectancy at birth (2006 est.)	77.85	78.54	78.80	79.73	81.25	80.22
Infant mortality rate (deaths per 1,000 live births, 2006 est.)	6.43	5.08	4.12	4.21	3.24	4.69

Source: Available at http://www.cia.gov

reduce their employees' health-care coverage in the future. The problems are not going away, and corporate America may cut benefits further as it attempts to stay competitive and profitable.

Many proponents believe the health-care system in the United States, in which the private sector provides and finances the majority of health care, is the best. Indeed, free-market theorists predict that an industry operated with no government intervention encourages innovation and advancement. This theory suggests that the United States, which spends more on health care than any other nation, would be the healthiest. However, this is not true when one compares leading health indicators such as life expectancy and infant mortality among other industrialized countries that provide a universal health-care system (see Table U.1).

The health-care indicators above seem to suggest the overall health of U.S. citizens is worse than that of citizens of other industrialized countries. Unlike the United States, these countries have some form of universal health coverage for all citizens. The tables at the side of the page showing life expectancy at birth and infant mortality rates offer a larger comparison of life expectancy and infant mortality among additional countries. Note that the United States trails the Organization for Economic Cooperation and Development averages in both statistics.

LIFE EXPECTANCY AT BIRTH, 2003

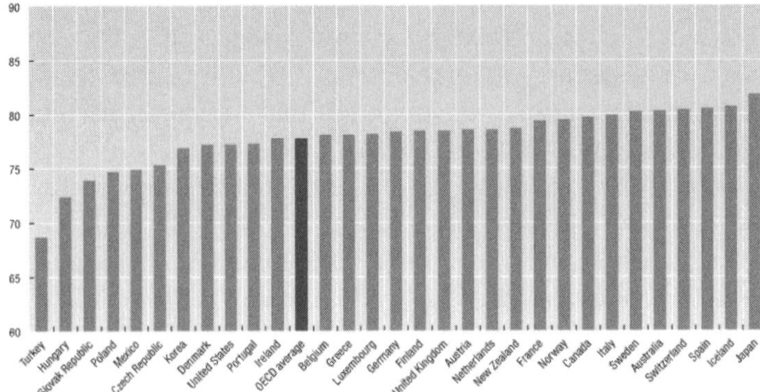

Figure U.1

INFANT MORTALITY, 2003

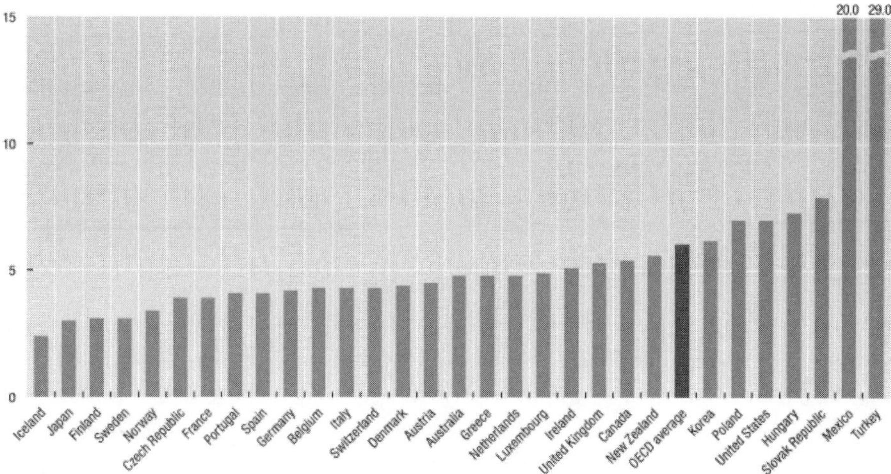

Figure U.2

In the past century, there have been six attempts to implement some kind of a universal health insurance program. These attempts suggest that there has always been support for the idea of a universal health-care system, however, not enough to implement any of the proposals.

ADVANTAGES OF A UNIVERSAL HEALTH-CARE SYSTEM

Several interests would be served with the implementation of a universal health plan. The 45 million Americans who currently have no health care would be able to get and afford the care they need. In addition, U.S. employers would be relieved of the primary duty of providing and paying for health care. Finally, it is believed that the entire U.S. economy would benefit from a universal health system with a healthier workforce and less spent on health care, although no one knows to what extent.

The United States has experienced exponential increases in health-care costs over the past few decades. Health insurance costs have placed a burden on many employers in both the public and private sectors. In 1999, U.S. employers represented 58 percent of the spending on private health insurance (Upshaw and Deal 2002). Historically, employers have shouldered most of the responsibility. These escalating costs have put U.S. companies at a strategic disadvantage against its global competitors, especially those competitors who operate in countries that have a universal health-care program where health costs are contained.

Recent trends show that employers who provide insurance have migrated toward plans that have deductibles, co-payments, and higher out-of-pocket expense limits. Employers are requiring their employees to expend a greater portion of total health-care costs via premium contributions, deductibles, and out-of-pocket expenses. This action shifts more of the health-care costs to the employee.

FAILED ATTEMPTS TO IMPLEMENT A UNIVERSAL HEALTH-CARE SYSTEM IN THE UNITED STATES

There have been several attempts in the past century to change the health care in the United States from a fee-for-service health-care system to a universal health-care system. All attempts, dating from 1912 right up to 1993 with President Clinton, have been vetoed unanimously. No president, presidential candidate, or interest group has been able to win enough votes to implement a truly universal health-care system.

1912–1920

There were several interest groups formed during this period to advocate universal health care. The Standard Bill, which applied to all manual workers and others earning less than $1,200 a year, was created to provide benefits consisting of medical aid, sick pay, maternity benefits, and death benefits. The bill was unsuccessful because many groups were opposed to it. Physicians feared that they would not be able to set their own fees, and businesses felt that they could provide their employees with better insurance themselves. The bill never got enough votes to get any farther than the state level.

The Roosevelt Administration

President Franklin Roosevelt lobbied heavily for a universal health-care system during his term. He was also very focused on what we know today as Social Security. He designated the Committee on Economic Security in 1934 to develop Social Security and a national health-care system. This was the federal government's first attempt to institute universal health care.

Employers were still opposed to the idea of universal health care because of the freeze on wages during World War II. The freeze did not apply to health benefits, which therefore allowed employers to recruit new employees with richer health-care packages. If the United States had changed over to a universal health-care system, employers would have lost this recruiting tool. Physicians, the AMA, and the emerging health insurance industry were also against a universal system.

President Roosevelt submitted his Social Security bill in 1935 but was opposed unanimously by all parts of Congress. After seeing the extent of the opposition to universal health care, he decided to cut the health insurance portion from his idea of an old age insurance program.

The Truman Administration

President Harry Truman tried to follow up on Roosevelt's push for a universal health-care system. It was difficult to get supporters for a universal system because of the cold war. The AMA was so opposed to President Truman's plan that they spent over $5 million denouncing his proposal. This helped to form America's current negative perception of universal health care. American society began to regard the implementation of a universal health-care system in the United States as one step toward communism. Physicians and laborers also felt that if a universal system was implemented, it would lower the quality of health care that people received. The bill went to Congress as part of President Truman's Fair Deal. It failed because Truman could not rally enough support to gain the majority of votes.

The Nixon Administration

As president, Nixon reintroduced the idea of a national health-care system. Due to the rising costs of health care, he spent most of his efforts trying to pass a plan for national health insurance. Nixon's program was designed to help the working poor and the unemployed. This plan required employers to pay 65 percent of employees' health costs. Any employee not covered by the employer mandate would be covered by the Assisted Health Insurance Program, a system of co-payments and deductibles. Republicans thought the plan was too expensive, and Democrats felt it was not expensive enough. There was not enough support from either party to gain enough votes to implement this plan.

The Carter Administration

Carter originally drafted a bill that would gradually phase in a universal health-care system. Senator Ted Kennedy felt that the plan wasn't good enough, so he countered President Carter's proposal by creating the Heath Care for All Americans Act. This plan was to guarantee health care for everyone. Carter countered by introducing his HealthCare plan, which didn't guarantee everyone universal health care but provided a large role for private insurance firms.

Eventually they decided to create a combination plan. This plan would be a merger of the HealthCare and Health Care for All Americans plans. However, the bill died in its early stages. The lack of support during Presidents Carter's term was largely influenced by the events around the world, such as the Watergate scandal and the Vietnam War. President Carter's main focus became restoring American pride and unifying a divided nation.

The Clinton Administration

Rising health-care costs in the 1990s again created a need for a revision in the current health care system. It was President Clinton who tried to make health care a top priority for the American people. Clinton's health-care proposal provided rich benefits for the working middle class, emphasized preventive care, and cut the financial burdens of a universal health-care system.

Clinton tried to bind the health reform plan to the budget reconciliation bill, but several key senators blocked this move. Clinton further alienated potential supporters by pledging to veto any bill that did not provide universal coverage. However, there was not enough support among the American people to pass any proposal. There were still many special interest groups, such as the American Medical Association and small businesses, that opposed the system.

Currently, more than 45 million Americans lack any form of health insurance, and many more are underinsured, meaning that they have insurance but lack adequate financial protection from health-care costs. Another angle from which the health-care issue can be viewed is a review of personal bankruptcy filings in 2005. A study showed that 46.2 percent of applicants cited a medical cause as the reason they were filing for protection. However, only 32.6 percent of applicants who cited medical costs as the reason were uninsured (Chua 2006). Even Americans with health insurance, when faced with deductibles, co-insurance, uncovered procedures, and out-of-pocket expenses, are finding it hard to afford health services.

PUBLIC AND PRIVATE EXPENDITURE ON HEALTH, 2003

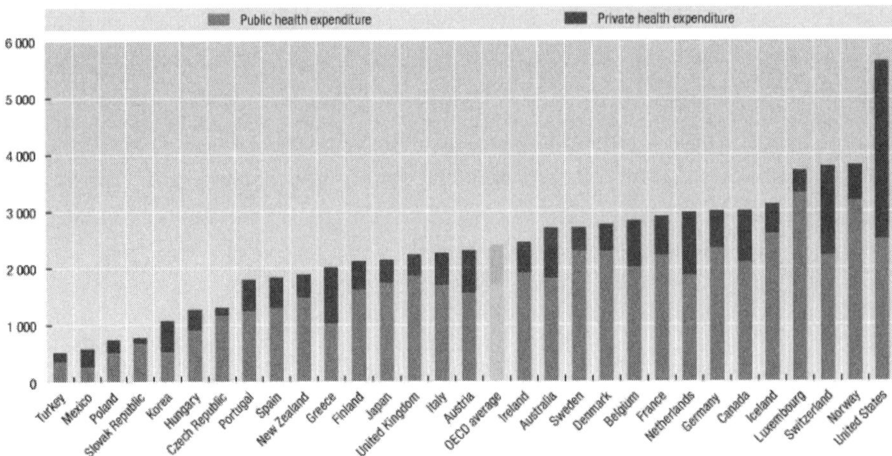

Figure U.3

Source: Organization for Economic Cooperation and Development. Available at www.oecd.org

Wages and benefits, including health insurance costs, are a cost of production, which is built into the costs of products and services. Since businesses in other industrialized countries are not responsible for financing the costs of health insurance for their employees, American companies either experience lower profit margins or must sell more expensive products.

If employers are relieved of the majority of the financial burden of health care, they could focus more on their core competencies, which would allow them to be more competitive. The removal of health-care expenses from a business's costs of production would improve the cost position of American products and services globally. In addition, employers who currently do not offer insurance or offer inadequate health coverage would be able to recruit more qualified employees. Health care is an important benefit to employees. If the United States had a universal health plan, there would be no differentiation among the health-care packages offered by domestic employers. Also, high-quality international employee candidates could be recruited since their health insurance would be guaranteed similar to what is available in other industrialized countries.

Making health-care access universal has also been shown to improve a nation's overall health, making it more efficient and profitable. A study by the Institute of Medicine documented several hidden costs of uninsurance (Institute of Medicine 2003). It reported that Americans without insurance cost the economy between $65 and $130 billion annually due to diminished health and shorter life spans. The Institute of Medicine estimates that the uninsured have an excess annual mortality rate of 25 percent. Fewer years of participation in the workforce translates to lost contributions to the economy.

WHY LEGISLATION HAS NOT BEEN ENACTED

Congress has repeatedly failed to pass legislation for a universal health-care system. If they haven't been able to enact legislation, then why haven't they been voted out of their positions? A possible reason is that the majority of the population is opposed to universal health coverage.

There are several explanations for why this may be true. One explanation is that many citizens incorrectly believe that the United States has the best health-care system in the world. It has been established that the United States ranks poorly relative to other industrialized nations in health care. The United States' infant mortality rates and life expectancy are below OECD averages. In addition, over 45 million people don't have coverage, an issue that countries with universal health coverage don't face. Surprisingly, the United States has the best-trained health-care providers and the best medical infrastructure and spends more than any other country in total on health care.

Another common opinion is that universal health care is too expensive. The United States spends at least 40 percent more per capita on health care than any other country with universal health care. Americans now pay a total of $1.2 trillion for health-care insurance and services (Faux 2006). The savings from a universal health-care system would provide coverage for less money. A study by the state of Massachusetts showed that universal health care would save approximately $1–2 billion per year of total medical expenses in the state (Battista 2006). The real issue is how to reshuffle the cost burden to finance the new system.

A final belief of many Americans is that universal health coverage would result in government control and intrusion. This implies that there would be less freedom of choice and options. However, unlike the current system, which requires people to see providers on the insurer's panel to obtain medical benefits, universal health-care systems throughout the world give consumers a choice of health-care providers. Fees and benefits would be decided by a board similar to a public trust that would represent consumers, providers, and business and government interests.

In addition, it reported that children who are uninsured are more likely to suffer delays in development affecting their future earnings potential. Lack of insurance also contributes to higher costs to public programs like Medicare, Social Security Disability Insurance, and the criminal justice system. The uninsured often don't get the preventive and chronic disease care they need early and are only treated after a disease has developed to an advanced stage, when costs are higher. Those who are uninsured also have less effective control of contagious diseases because they are not able to afford vaccinations and preventive care (Institute of Medicine 2003).

In 2005, Emory economist Dr. Kenneth Thorpe published an important report for the National Coalition for Health Care. The National Coalition for Health Care is a nonpartisan coalition of businesses, health care providers, unions, and other groups interested in improving the health-care system. Dr. Thorpe reports that creating a publicly financed universal plan would save the U.S. economy $1.1 trillion over 10 years. This is three times the savings of an employer-employee mandated program in which individuals are required to obtain a certain level of health benefits either through their employer or through some other mechanism (Thorpe 2005).

INCREASES IN HEALTH INSURANCE PREMIUMS COMPARED TO OTHER INDICATORS, 1998–2005

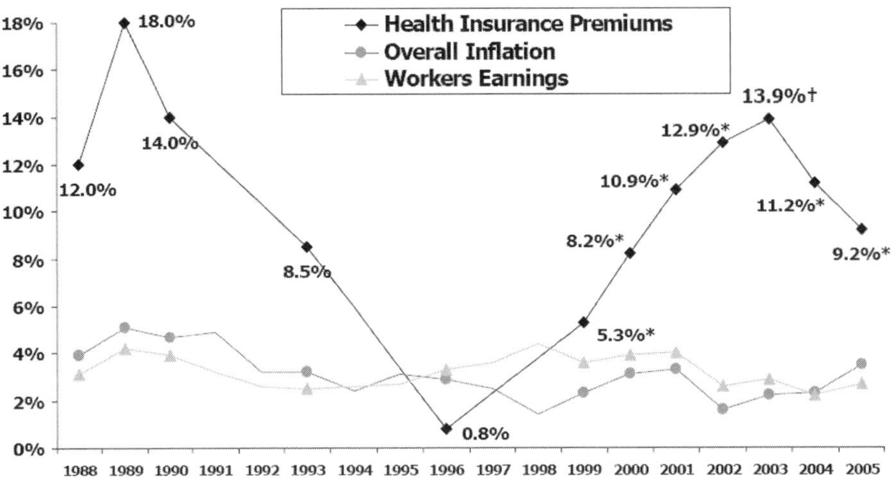

Figure U.4 Increases in health insurance premiums compared to other indicators (1998–2005).

* Estimate is statistically different from the previous year shown at $p < 0.05$. No statistical tests were conducted for years prior to 1999.

† Estimate is statistically different from the previous year shown at $p < 0.1$. No statistical tests were conducted for years prior to 1999.

Note: Data on premium increases reflect the cost of health insurance premiums for a family of four.

Source: Survey of Employer-Sponsored Health Benefits. 1999–2005; KMPG Survey of Employer-Sponsored Benefits. 1993, 1996; The Health Insurance Association of America. 1988, 1989, 1990. Bureau of Labor Statistics, Consumer Price Index (U.S. City Average of Annual Inflation (April to April. 1988–2005; Bureau of Labor Statistics, Seasonally Adjusted Data from the Current Employment Statistics Survey (April to April) 1988–2005.

Thorpe's study suggests that in order to meet these savings projections, the universal health plan would need to institute significant changes, including safeguards to reduce inappropriate clinical practice variation, computerized physician order entry, and centralization of certain administrative duties.

CONCERNS AND ROADBLOCKS TO A UNIVERSAL HEALTH-CARE SYSTEM

There are concerns regarding the implementation of a universal health-care system in the United States. The first, and largest, is how it will be paid for. One option for financing this change, which was discussed in the *International Journal of Health Services* in 1999, would be to increase the federal personal income tax by about 7 percent, or about $731 per year for the average middle-income household. The percent taxed to each individual would likely be progressive, just like the current federal income tax, which means that the greater your income, the more you pay in federal taxes. Individuals whose health insurance is already provided by their employer would be against the tax increase because it would decrease their final take-home pay. Although an employer would save money by not having to provide health care for employees, it is unlikely that the employer would pass these cost savings on to employees through increased wages (Rasell 1999). This issue must be addressed when a plan is developed.

A second concern is that people who work hard to keep themselves healthy would be paying for a service that they would rarely use. Those with healthier lifestyles would be providing coverage for people who do not take the time or effort to take care of themselves. In other words, "Costs would be redistributed from the sick to the healthy" (Rasell 1999). Many individuals would be paying higher taxes but would not be seeing any benefits. There would be no financial incentive for people to hold themselves personally responsible for their own well-being because others would be paying the bill. Scott McPherson states in his commentary about government-provided health care titled "Feeding Obesity": "The government subsidizes people's poor lifestyle choices" (McPheron 2004).

Another concern is that only procedures that are considered medically necessary would be covered. This means that even though people would be paying higher taxes to cover the universal system, they may have higher out-of-pocket expenses than they had with a private health-care system. One possible solution to this potential problem would be regionalization of specialized surgeries and tests. Although offering only one facility to provide the service for a given area would minimize the cost to the government, any transportation costs associated with traveling to a regional facility would not be covered under the system. This would make it more difficult for lower-income families to get specialized care because they could not afford the added expense of traveling to those locations.

Perhaps the most important concern associated with implementing a universal health-care system is that in all nations where there has been a national health-care system for a number of years, there is a shortage of services. Many of the industrialized nations providing health care through a universal system are experiencing the problems regarding availability of services. For example, in Great Britain over one million people are on a waiting list to receive needed health care. Because there is no personal accountability with regard to costs, people overuse the covered services, which makes it harder to access them when it is truly necessary.

Another important roadblock to implementing a universal health-care system is the issue of what will happen to the private health insurance industry. Switching to a single-payer system would "eliminate the jobs of hundreds of thousands of people who currently perform billing, advertising, eligibility determination, and other superfluous tasks" (Himmelstein and Woolhandler 2003). These administrative operations, currently managed by large insurance providers, would be handled by a government department. In a system that would mean less revenues and profits, insurance providers, pharmaceutical manufacturers, and physician associations like the American Medical Association have the most to lose. Therefore, in addition to the fear of losing these jobs, there is the issue of large insurance providers and pharmaceutical manufacturers in the industry exerting their influence against such a program through lobbying and campaign contributions.

CONCLUSION

There are many advantages and disadvantages of a universal health-care system. There is no one answer or view that can resolve the universal health-care debate. In light of increasing health-care costs and a rising uninsured population, the United States will need to move toward some form of a universal health-care system. This system would help make businesses more competitive in the global economy and provide needed health care to all citizens. The implementation and scope will be the challenge.

See also: Drug (Prescription) Costs; Health Care Costs; Social Security, Medicare, and Medicaid

References

Associated Press and Local State Wire. 2006. "GM to Slash Jobs, Close More Plants." *MSNBC.* Available at http://msnbc.msn.com/id/8129876/from/RL.2. Accessed June 18, 2006.

Battista, James Coleman. 2006. "Jurisdiction, Institutional Structure, and Committee Representativeness." *Political Research Quarterly,* 59: 47–56.

Chua, Kao-Ping, 2006. *The Case for Universal Health Insurance.* Available at http://www.amsa.org/uhc/CaseForUHC.pdf#search = %22The%20Case%20for%20Universal%20Health%22. Accessed June 20, 2006.

Faux, Jeff. 2006. *What Kind of American Dream Do We Want?* Available at http://www.ourfuture.org/projects/next_agenda/ch1_2.cfm. Accessed July 2, 2006.

Himmelstein, David U., and Steffie Woolhandler. 2003. "National Health Insurance or Incremental Reform: Aim High, or at Our Feet?" *American Journal of Public Health* 93 (1): 102–5.

Institute of Medicine. 2003. *Hidden Costs: Value Lost.* Washington DC: National Academies Press.

Institute of Medicine. 2003. *A Shared Destiny: Community Effects of Uninsurance.* Washington, DC: National Academies Press.

McPheron, Scott. 2004. "Feeding Obesity." The Future of Freedom Foundation. Available at www.fff.org. Accessed June 19, 2006.

Rasell, Edith, 1999. "An Equitable Way to Pay for Universal Coverage." *International Journal of Health Services* 29 (1): 179–88.

Thorpe, K. 2005. *Impacts of Health Care Reform: Projections of Costs and Savings.* Washington, DC: National Coalition on Health Care.

Upshaw, V. M., and K. M. Deal. 2002. "The United States of America." In *World Health Systems: Challenges and Perspectives,* edited by B. Fried and L. Gaydos. Chicago: Health Administration Press.

Further Reading: Anderson, Ronald M., Thomas H. Rice, and Gerald F. Kominski, 2001. *Changing the U.S. Health Care System: Key Issues in Health Services Policy and Management.* 2nd ed. San Francisco: Jossey-Bass; Fried, Bruce, and Laura Gaydos, eds. 2002. *World Health Systems: Challenges and Perspectives.* Chicago: Health Administration Press; Quadagno, Jill. 2005. *One Nation, Uninsured: Why the U.S. Has No National Health Insurance.* Oxford: Oxford University Press.

Keith Farrell, Mandy Knepper, Melissa Silka, Umer Pervez, and Melinda Przybyszewski

V

VIOLENCE IN THE WORKPLACE

When most people hear the words "workplace violence," they think of a mentally disturbed gunman shooting coworkers in anger to exact revenge for unfair treatment. What they don't realize is that beyond the highly publicized workplace homicides, there is widespread violence in many organizations that involves such things as sexual harassment, intimidation, bullying, verbal abuse, sabotage, fighting, vandalism, and assaults, and that these forms of workplace violence are much more prevalent than the homicides that receive most media attention.

Such workplace violence is not new but is a continuing problem in the United States and other countries. In the United States alone, nearly 1,000 deaths and more than 1.5 million incidents of nonfatal injuries each year are attributable to violence in the workplace. While most of the media attention focuses on fatalities (particularly shootings), there are a number of different kinds of violence in the workplace that are having a significant impact on workers, and on society in general.

The definitions of workplace violence are many and varied, but most experts agree that violence in the workplace includes verbal threats, threatening behavior, and/or physical assault. Health and safety executives define workplace violence as "any incident in which a person is abused, threatened or assaulted in circumstances relating to their work" (Hainsworth 2002).

Experts have identified four basic types of workplace violence:

1. Violence by strangers who have no legitimate business relationship to the workplace (for example, entering the workplace to commit a robbery)

U.S. WORKPLACE STATISTICS (2003)

Violence at work	*Number of victims*
Murder	631
Physical attacks	2 million
Threats	6 million
Verbal harassment or bullying	16 million

Fatalities

According to the U.S. Bureau of Labor Statistics, workplace homicides increased at a faster rate than any other cause of worker fatalities in 2003. A total of 631 people were killed, of whom 81 percent were female. The majority of homicides were shootings (487) and stabbings (58). In total, 5,559 people died from job-related injuries in the United States in 2003.

The Costs of Workplace Violence

The annual cost in the United States for violence and associated stress is estimated to be $13.5 billion in medical costs and about two million days of work missed by 500,000 workers (Grossman 2002).

2. Violence by customers (current or former) or clients (patients, prisoners, students, passengers, etc.), usually against those who provide direct service to the public
3. Violence by current or former coworkers (employees, supervisors, managers, etc.), who often seek revenge for perceived unfair treatment
4. Violence by an assailant who confronts an individual with whom an outside personal relationship exists (for example, a man entering the workplace and assaulting his ex-wife; Lipscomb etal. 2002)

The negative effects of workplace violence for employers are that it can include lower employee morale, lower productivity, higher turnover, negative publicity, lawsuits for not protecting employees, and medical and other health-care costs for victims. For employees, the costs of workplace violence (beyond death, of course) can include stress-related illnesses, diminished productivity, sickness absences, and lost wages. Because of these negative outcomes, it seems clear that employers should cultivate a healthy workplace climate—one that discourages violence and aggression.

The primary controversy, however, concerns how to prevent such workplace violence or at least minimize it. Different approaches have been suggested and prompt the following questions: Are current prevention programs working? Are there other things that organizations could be doing? Will organizational efforts at prevention never work, meaning that violence in the workplace is inevitable? If so, should employees be allowed to carry guns to the workplace so they can protect themselves?

THE BENEFITS OF CURRENT PREVENTION PROGRAMS

The National Institute for Occupational Safety and Health, the Occupational Safety and Health Administration, and other government agencies have issued guidelines for preventing workplace violence. These agencies and most experts concerned with workplace violence recommend that organizations adopt a multifaceted prevention program that includes a written policy, training for managers and employees, new employee background screening, adoption of a zero tolerance policy, and better security measures for the workplace itself.

A thorough written policy should define harassment (i.e., workplace violence of all kinds), specify how to report it, explain how complaints will be investigated, and describe the consequences for infractions. Including such a policy in the employee handbook is also believed to go a long way in protecting the organization from legal liability in the event of workplace violence.

Training should make supervisors and employees aware of company policy and help them understand all its components. Training can also help employees and managers develop skills in conflict resolution, effective communication, and dispute resolution. In addition, supervisors can be trained to recognize signs of a troubled employee so that they may intervene before an incident occurs. Early intervention is one way to reduce the potential for workplace violence. Managers can also be trained to recognize symptoms of abuse, such as depression or frequent absences.

Safety education programs can be implemented to make employees aware of company safety policies and employee support services. Organizations can also provide seminars and educational materials about ways to maximize workplace safety (Coco 1998). In addition, organizations can conduct thorough preemployment screening. Prospective employees should also be warned that background investigations will be conducted, and that applicants will be required to sign a waiver to allow the company to access criminal, employment, military, financial, and other appropriate records.

Many experts argue that any effective prevention program must include a zero tolerance policy. In fact, a recent Occupational Safety and Health Administration publication recommends that violence prevention programs "create and disseminate a clear policy of zero tolerance for workplace violence, verbal and nonverbal threats and related actions" (U.S. Department of Labor Occupational Health and Safety Administration 1994). A zero tolerance policy means that organizations will not tolerate any violence or aggression in the workplace and that employees will be subject to disciplinary actions—including dismissal for severe violations—if they engage in any such dysfunctional behavior. Most experts agree that zero tolerance policies are necessary to help guide employee behaviors and let employees know that violence will not be tolerated in the workplace.

Physical security programs to protect employees can also be implemented. These programs can include methods such as monitoring systems (e.g., cameras, video, e-mail), limited-access key cards, strict visitor sign-in policies, and security guards.

There is anecdotal evidence that each of these measures is effective in reducing or preventing workplace violence. The experts—health and safety officials, violence prevention consultants, risk management specialists, and legal experts—all seem to agree that organizations need comprehensive workplace violence prevention programs that foster an organizational culture that doesn't tolerate violence in any form and is proactive in identifying acts of violence and precursors to violence. Many organizations report that implementing various violence prevention policies and programs leads to a reduction in violence and a healthier climate throughout the organization.

U.S. WORKPLACE HOMICIDES BY PROFESSION (2003)

Profession	Homicides
Sales and related occupations	182
Protective service occupations	95
Transportation and material moving	83
Management	64
Food preparation and serving related	41
Office and administrative support	37
Installation, maintenance, and repair	27
Production occupations	27
Construction and extraction	17
Personal care and service	11
Building grounds, cleaning, and maintenance	10
Farming, fishing, and forestry	9
Health-care practitioners and technical workers	6
Health-care support occupations	6
Supervisors, production workers	6
Business and financial operations	4
Community and social services	3
Unspecified	3

Source: Bureau of Labor Statistics. Available at www.bls.gov. Accessed September 5, 2006.

THE SHORTCOMINGS OF VIOLENCE PREVENTION PROGRAMS

One of the problems with violence prevention in the workplace is that, for all the recommendations made by the experts, not all organizations take their advice. Research has shown that many organizations have engaged in numerous violence prevention efforts, but some are sorely lacking.

In a 2000 survey released by the Risk and Insurance Management Society and the American Society of Safety Engineers, 70 percent of 299 risk managers and safety professionals reported that their organizations lack a formal risk assessment of potential violence in the workplace. And while 62 percent said their organizations have a written workplace violence policy, only 24 percent said their organizations offer worker training in identifying warning signs of violent behavior (Katz 2000).

Patricia Biles, coordinator of the workplace violence program at the Occupational Safety and Health Administration, says that about two-thirds of companies in the United States don't have any violence protection program. But, for those that do, it's not enough to have a written program if managers are not trained and companies do not take steps to ensure that it works. Furthermore, if training is limited to making managers and employees aware of the policy, little, if any, behavioral change will be achieved within the organization. Training needs to include skill development and recognition of potential problems and emphasize behavioral change.

For example, many experts claim that there are always warning signs before physical aggression occurs in the workplace, and data indicate that training employees and managers to identify cues does reduce workplace physical aggression. The founders of one threat management and risk assessment firm that specializes in workplace violence prevention and training state that most acts of workplace violence are preceded by verbal threats and/or offhanded remarks to friends and colleagues that reveal sinister intentions. However, when managers and employees are not trained to recognize such behavior and there is no system in place to capture this information and report it to the appropriate individuals, there is no way to intervene and contain these potential threats before they develop into workplace violence.

Consultants claim that employees who receive training and are informed about who and what to look for, and how to report it discreetly, can pinpoint employees displaying a propensity toward violence. In addition, they identify the typical perpetrators of workplace violence as men between 25 and 40 who can't handle stress, exhibit manipulative behavior, and are constantly complaining. They say that the people who meet these criteria and also exhibit what they call red-flag factors—such as making verbal threats, exploding in verbal outbursts, harboring grudges, and disrespecting the relationship between employees and supervisors—can be identified by trained employees so management can intervene and prevent further aggression or violence (Viollis and Kane 2005).

Further evidence that not all organizations are doing all they can to prevent workplace violence was provided by a workplace violence survey conducted by the Society of Human Resource Management in 2004 of 270 human resource professionals across the United States. The survey revealed that organizations use several prevention methods: 80 percent checked employees' references, and 80 percent had a physical security program that controlled access to buildings, but only 32 percent provided employee training on conflict resolution, and merely 32 percent provided training on the organization's workplace violence policy. It also showed that larger organizations tend to do twice as much training on workplace violence policies as small organizations, but only 41 percent of larger organizations are doing it. The survey also indicated that about half of all organizations had zero tolerance policies (including immediate termination) concerning threats of violence.

Some other studies found that good hiring practices and violence training were among the most popular violence prevention techniques. In addition, many organizations are engaged in physical security efforts, such as limiting access to buildings.

In addition to simply not doing some of the recommended violence prevention activities, some organizations have violence prevention practices but aren't implementing them properly. Zero tolerance is a prime example of this. For many organizations, having a zero tolerance policy seems to be primarily intended to reduce employer liability when violence occurs. They believe that simply having the policy on the books means that they are less likely to be held responsible for workplace violence in their organization and consequently will avoid the costs associated with that liability. The problem with this position is that enforcement of the policy is often automatic and too stringent and doesn't take into consideration the specifics of the situation. This may have effects that are contrary to the intentions of the policy. For example, an employer terminates an employee who violates the violence policy without taking into account the circumstances. The employee may perceive the termination as unfair and a violation of her rights. Such feelings could actually escalate into violence—exactly what a zero tolerance policy is supposed prevent (Lucero and Allen 2006).

The key to this dilemma is for managers to understand that a zero tolerance policy does not mean that any employee who violates the policy will be terminated without consideration for the circumstances. Rather, zero tolerance enforcement means that every incident will be taken seriously and investigated completely and fairly, and that discipline will be imposed if it is determined that the rule was violated. Furthermore, it means that the discipline will be fair and commensurate with the crime.

Security measures are another area where many organizations are falling short in their prevention programs. Since many violent acts in the workplace are committed by ex-employees, it isn't enough simply to have security measures for employees. Security systems must prevent ex-employees and outsiders from having access to the workplace. This means that security guards must screen everyone carefully and be especially vigilant when an ex-employee attempts to enter the workplace. Likewise, if there is any cause for concern, then codes for limited-access key cards must be changed so that only approved personnel may enter the workplace.

In the security arena, the passage of some new state gun laws has created quite a controversy. These new laws allow people to use deadly force to protect themselves and their property without fear of prosecution. A person could use any manner of force, including deadly force, against someone whom he fears will cause death or bodily harm. The legislation also provides immunity from civil suits and criminal prosecution for shooters who had reason to believe the use of deadly force was necessary ("A New Wave of Gun Laws" 2006). Florida's law permits employees to keep loaded guns in their cars on company property. It also is the first of its kind to impose felony charges against employers who ban guns on company premises.

The National Rifle Association has been sponsoring these bills, which it calls Stand Your Ground, and intends to get similar legislation introduced in all 50 states. While the National Rifle Association says such laws will increase safety by creating a viable deterrent to violence and crime, employers contend that having guns close to the workplace will increase the danger of violence, particularly in situations that are already tense, such as firings or other disciplinary actions.

Employers also have concerns about higher security costs and the negative impact on company morale of such laws. With the passage of these bills, employers will have to ramp up security measures. To make sure employees don't bring guns into the workplace itself, organizations will need to install metal detectors and hire additional staff to oversee them. It will also necessitate more thorough background checks. The presence of guns in parking lots next to work sites also creates a heightened concern for safety at workplaces where there are flammable materials, such as chemical plants.

Many employers believe that the new gun laws will have a negative impact on company culture. Having metal detectors and more stringent security may make employees feel like the company doesn't trust them. In addition, employers believe that many employees won't want to work in environments where guns are nearby. Likewise, the new laws may require managers who have to discipline or dismiss an employee to change their processes to defuse a potentially volatile situation. Only time will tell whether employers' worries about these new laws are justified. But with over 20 states now looking at new gun laws similar to Florida's, we will soon be able to measure the impact on the workplace by looking at changes in workplace violence, employer costs, and employee morale in those states where the legislation is adopted.

Experts continue to provide prescriptions for programs to prevent workplace violence, but there is little data that show the effectiveness of these prevention activities. Most of the data come from case studies that chronicle a single organization's program and the self-reported success of some of its prevention tactics. There is a great need for more research to be conducted on a large number of organizations to assess the effectiveness of different workplace violence prevention programs in different settings, and with different kinds of employees. Until that data is available, employers may just have to listen to the experts and have faith in their recommendations.

See also: Sexual Harassment

References

Coco, M. 1998. "The New War Zone: The Workplace." *Advanced Management Journal* 63:15–20.

Grossman, R. J. 2002. "Bulletproof Practices." *HR Magazine* 47:34–43.

Hainsworth, Karen. 2002. "Office Hours: Violence at Work: Each Year Increasing Numbers of Us Are Assaulted While Doing Our Job. Are People Becoming More Aggressive, and If So, What Can We Do to Protect?" *The Guardian,* April, p. 2.

Katz, D. M. 2000. "Study Finds Lag in Violence Prevention." *National Underwriter* 9:9.

Lipscomb, Jane, Barbara Silverstein, Thomas Slavin, Eileen Cody, and Lynn Jenkins. 2002. "Perspectives on Legal Strategies to Prevent Workplace Violence." *Journal of Law, Medicine & Ethics* (30) 3: 166–72.

Lucero, Margaret, and Robert Allen. 2006. "Implementing Zero Tolerance Policies: Balancing Strict Enforcement with Fair Treatment." *SAM Advanced Management Journal* 71 (1): 35–41.

"A New Wave of Gun Laws." 2006. *State Legislatures* 32 (4): 10.

U.S. Department of Labor Occupational Health and Safety Administration. 1994. *Guidelines for Preventing Workplace Violence for Health Care and Social Service Workers*. Available at www.osha.gov/publications/osha3148.pdf.p. Accessed September 5, 2006.

Viollis, Paul, and Doug Kane. 2005. "At-Risk Terminations: Protecting Employees, Preventing Disaster." *Risk Management Magazine* 52 (5): 28–33.

Further Reading: Geffner, Robert, Mark Braverman, Joseph Galasso, and Janessa Marsh. 2005. *Aggression in Organizations: Violence, Abuse, and Harassment at Work and in Schools*. Binghamton, NY: Hayworth Press.

Randy C. Brown

W

WAR AND THE ECONOMY

The link between war and the economy is an ancient one. More than 2,000 years ago, Cicero observed, "*Nervo belli, pecuniam infinitam*"—the sinews of war are money in abundance (Cicero 2003)—and war has often been viewed as an avenue to economic prosperity. A leading economic history textbook has a chapter entitled "The 'Prosperity' of Wartime" (Hughes and Cain 2003), and World War II has become the standard explanation for the end of the Great Depression: "It has long been an article of faith that the Second World War brought an end to the long depression of the thirties" (Smiley 1994). In his Pulitzer Prize–winning history of the era, David M. Kennedy notes that "the war compelled government spending on an unexampled scale, capital was unshackled, and the economy energized." He concludes: "Ordinary Americans . . . had never had it so good" (Kennedy 1999).

Despite the unambiguous tone of these observations, opinions on war's impact on the economy are hardly unanimous. The great Austrian economist Ludwig von Mises attacked the very notion of wartime prosperity: "War prosperity is like the prosperity that an earthquake or a plague brings" (Higgs 1992). While economists and historians may debate the point, generals seem less divided. Douglas MacArthur emphasized war's "utter destruction," and William Tecumseh Sherman famously said of war that "it is all hell" (MacArthur 1951). Tellingly, neither emphasized war's prosperity.

What is the supposed link between war and economic prosperity? How might a war lead to prosperity? Why did Von Mises equate wartime prosperity with that of a natural disaster?

THE AMERICAN CIVIL WAR: WHAT WAS IT WORTH?

Calculating the cost of war presents economists and historians with a challenge. There are the direct costs—largely government expenditures on material—which are easy enough to track, but there are also indirect costs, which, although just as important in an economic sense, are less easily quantified. Take for example the lost economic production that results from a war-related death. We do not know exactly how much output the dead individual would have contributed to the economy over the course of his or her life; neither do we know exactly what the present market value of that worker's future output would be. After all, the value of a dollar today is not the same as the value of a dollar 10 or 20 years from now. However, because the fact that a topic is difficult does not mean would should avoid it. Economists regularly estimate the future productivity of individuals—for example, those injured or killed in automobile accidents—and they calculate the value today of future income streams, which also happens to be the foundation of the thriving business in annuities. If one applies these techniques to the estimation of the direct and indirect costs of war, some interesting figures emerge.

During the Civil War, the United States government directly spent $1.8 billion, while the Confederate states spent $1.0 billion (in 1860 dollars). Estimates of the indirect costs of the war are in the neighborhood of $1.6 billion for the United States and $2.3 billion for the Confederacy (Goldin 1973). Thus the combined costs of the war were $6.7 billion ($3.4 billion for the North and $3.3 billion in the South). With a total U.S. population of roughly 35 million, it follows that the war cost about $50 per person per year, during its four years.

To put these figures into perspective, consider that the cost of purchasing the freedom of the entire slave stock in 1860 would have been $2.7 billion, or about 40 percent of the war's actual cost. Financed by the issue of 30-year U.S. treasury bonds at 6 percent interest, this option would have cost the northern population $9.66 in taxes per person per year. Indeed, depending on which groups were taxed to pay off the bonds, the payments would have been considerably less than this. Given that annual income per person at the time was around $200 dollars, the tax rate would have been less than 5 percent—a fraction of the current average federal income tax rate today. Perhaps somewhat paradoxically, these figures seem to confirm Ulysses S. Grant's observation that "There never was a time when, in my opinion, some way could not be found to prevent the drawing of the sword" (WestPoint Graduates against the War n.d.).

Cost of Immediate Emancipation in 1860 (Atack and Passell 1994)

Cost per Person per Year for 30 Years

Total Cost	*All Persons*	*All Free Persons*	*Northerners*
$2.7 (billion)	$6.30	$7.25	$9.66

Of course, calculations such as these distort the fact that the fundamental economic condition of war is not its average cost or benefit but rather its distributional effect, or, as one economic historian put it: "The economic benefits of the Civil War were bestowed upon those who were able to take advantage of the changes it generated [not the least of whom were the emancipated slaves], while its costs were most heavily born by those who suffered and died on its fields of glory" (Craig 1996).

WHAT IS WAR PROSPERITY?

The standard economic indicator for the performance of any economy is gross domestic product—"the total value of all final goods and services produced for the marketplace during a given year within a nation's borders" (Lieberman and Hall 2005). It follows from this definition that GDP is the sum of various types of expenditures on goods and services, including private personal consumption expenditures, investment, expenditures on exports minus those on imports, and government expenditures. In any economy at any point in time, it is possible, perhaps even likely, that there are some productive resources (e.g., land, labor, or capital) that are unemployed or at least underemployed. As war approaches or is unleashed, governments employ their coercive powers to facilitate military operations. Men are conscripted to fight, capital is directed toward the production of war materiel, and so forth. Thus, government expenditures tend to increase, sometimes dramatically, during wartime, and since those expenditures are mathematically a component of the GDP, it typically increases during war.

To see this phenomenon in practice, consider Figure W.1. It shows an index of real (i.e., inflation-adjusted) GDP for the U.S. economy before, during, and after U.S. involvement in two twentieth-century wars: World War II (1941–1945) and the Korean War (1950–1953). Using the year before the United States entered each war as the base year, in which GDP = 100, the figure illustrates how the economy took off during the war years, and how it leveled off as the war ended. Clearly, from this indicator, one would be justified in referring to the prosperity associated with these wars.

If government spending during wartime leads to prosperity, then shouldn't government spending during peacetime lead to prosperity? In short, why isn't more government spending always a good thing? In order to answer those

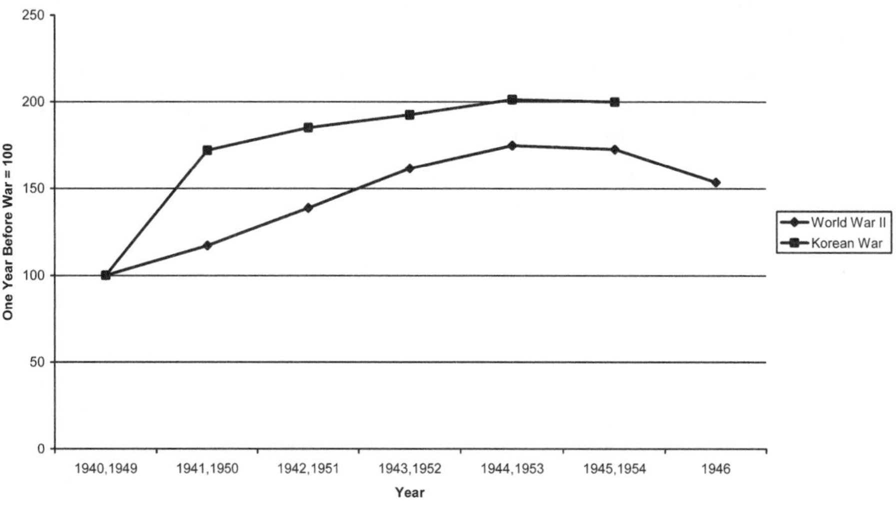

Figure W.1 Wartime prosperity: Economic output (real GDP): Before, during, and after World War II and the Korean War.

Source: U.S. Department of Commerce. Available at www.commerce.gov.

questions, we must consider where the government obtains the money it spends during wartime or peacetime. Governments obtain funds from three sources. They can raise the money via taxation; they can borrow the money, which is just future taxation; and/or they can print more money, which just leads to inflation and is a form of taxation. (Since printing money depreciates the value of money, inflation is a form of taxation on those holding money.) So, in the end, all government spending is financed one way or the other through taxation. Typically, governments turn to some combination of all three revenue sources, especially during wartime.

Once we recognize that government spending is just taxation, then we can see why it does not in general lead to prosperity. If governments fight wars with tax dollars, and if they obtain the tax dollars from consumers, then it follows that a dollar of taxation going to government spending and increasing GDP will simply be taken from a dollar of private personal consumer spending, which would in turn decrease GDP.

It does not always work like this, dollar for dollar, for at least two reasons. First, with respect to borrowing, recall from above that GDP represents the value of current expenditures. Government borrowing is future taxation, and the decrease in consumer spending might not show up immediately. Thus GDP goes up today and is reduced at some time in the future. This is just robbing Peter tomorrow to pay Paul today. As a general policy, government borrowing might or might not be good for the economy—depending on how the borrowed funds are expended—but the exigencies of war are such that governments often do not worry about the future consequences of borrowing.

Secondly, war changes the economy in other ways that would offset the decrease in consumption resulting from taxation. For example, one of the most common forms of taxation during war is the conscription or drafting of soldiers who pay the tax with their labor. Historically, soldiers were not paid a market wage, which is why conscription is a regular companion of war. The difference between what conscripted soldiers are paid and what they would have to be paid in order to get them to volunteer represents a measure of the soldiers' tax burden. When a soldier goes to war, he (historically, conscripts tend to be men) leaves the civilian labor force, which tends to reduce his family's consumption, but often women (and children and the elderly), who might otherwise have been employed in nonmarket pursuits, replace men in the labor force. Thus, economic activity, as measured in GDP, would now include the government spending on the soldier and the consumption generated by the women who replaced soldiers in the labor force. Rosie the Riveter, of World War II fame, is the classic example of this phenomenon. Since Rosie's prewar nonmarket activity in the household was not counted as a component of GDP—riveting is; preparing dinner, changing diapers, and cleaning the house are not—when her work is added to the government's increased wartime spending, GDP increases, just as it did during World War II.

This then is wartime prosperity. Unemployed or underemployed resources, or resources formerly employed in nonmarket activity, are put to work by government's wartime spending—usually spurred by increased borrowing—as companies obtain government contracts individuals who formally did not contribute to GDP now do so (like Rosie the Riveter); and many who did contribute to GDP in the private sector are now contributing in the government sector, albeit as conscripted soldiers. Prosperity, at least as measured by GDP, follows. Why then have some of the leading figures in economics and economic history questioned the concept of wartime prosperity?

IS WAR A HUMAN-MADE DISASTER?

The comparison of war to a natural disaster is common, because both seem to create prosperity. It is not uncommon for certain types of economic activity to pick up following a natural disaster. For example, in the wake of a hurricane, roofing contractors expect to see an increase in the demand for their services, as they are called upon to repair damage to homes resulting from falling trees. Indeed, consider the whole series of related economic activities. A tree service might be called to remove the tree, the family might stay in a hotel until the roof is repaired, painters might repair internal water damage, and so forth. None of these particular expenditures would have been made by the family in the absence of the hurricane. Multiplying these and other costs incurred from damage by the number of households affected by the hurricane would yield an aggregate measure of the value of services rendered following the storm. Thus, one might conclude that the storm itself yielded the resulting prosperity.

The fundamental problem with this observation is that it assumes that the families in our example would have neither spent nor saved the monies they expended as a direct result of the storm. Perhaps they would have purchased a new automobile, a purchase that will now be postponed. Perhaps they would have stayed in a hotel on vacation, a trip that will now be canceled. In these cases, all the hurricane did was redirect the families' spending from something they had planned or hoped to purchase (i.e., a new car or a vacation) to something they would not have wanted in the absence of the storm (i.e., a new roof and a stay at the hotel down the road).

What if a family had merely taken money out of the bank to pay for the new roof and hotel visit—money that they were in fact saving for a rainy day? They could still purchase the car and vacation with other funds. Would these monies not be better spent on a new roof than just sitting in the bank? The answer is no, because the bank does not just sit on the money that is deposited there; it turns around and loans that money for productive economic activity. If people take loanable funds out of banks to pay for new roofs that they would not have needed in the absence of a hurricane—that is, if they reduce the supply of loanable funds—then the banks increase their interest rates in order to induce other people to make new deposits. This increase in interest rates in turn reduces the number of loans taken.

Well, then why not just borrow the money from the bank? Because as people borrow money to repair the storm damage, they increase the demand for loanable funds, which in turn increases interest rates and reduces the number of loans taken. Thus, as a result of the hurricane, economic activity is redirected—from new cars and vacations to new roofs—and less economic activity occurs as upward pressure is placed on interest rates. Neither of these effects is good for the economy.

War has the same two negative effects on the economy. The opportunity cost of war is never zero. A dollar spent on a weapon, a shell, or a uniform is a dollar coercively extracted through taxation or borrowed, which again is merely future taxation, and therefore not spent on some other activity. If consumers were better off purchasing a shell rather than an automobile, they would demand shells during peacetime, rather than cars or houses or education for their children. So the forced substitution of war production for private consumption cannot be understood generally as making people better off.

As for borrowing, recall that one of the most common of war's effects on the economy is an increase in the demand for credit, as countries borrow to finance the construction of their war machines. This increases the demand for credit, which increases interest rates, which tends to drive down or crowd out private investment. So we again see governments' wartime expenditures simply replacing private expenditures. Since people generally prefer to borrow money for a home, automobile, or education rather than a plane that might get shot down over enemy territory, it is difficult to argue that the increase in government spending improves people's financial situations.

As for printing money and generating inflation to finance the war, if this were good for the economy (and it is not), then we would expect to see governments doing this during peacetime as well. Although in recent decades there has been some peacetime high inflation, it is not perceived to be a positive factor for the economy, and anything more than a little inflation is generally greeted unfavorably by lenders and consumers (and voters; woe to the president running for reelection during periods of rampant inflation, such as Jimmy Carter.)

Of course, war, just like a natural disaster, redirects economic activity. Suppliers of weapons and uniforms will see an increase in the demand for their products relative to other goods and services—just as roofers see an increase in the demand for their services after hurricanes. Those who see their taxes increase, now and in the future, are among the groups whose resources are directed toward military suppliers, but the group most likely to bear a disproportionate share of the tax burden is the soldiers who pay with their labor, especially those who ultimately pay with their lives. The death of soldier is a tragedy to his or her family. For the economy it represents the loss of all of his or her future economic output.

What then does this tell us about the persistent metaphor of wartime prosperity? The main thing is that the manner in which standard economic measures of well-being, such as GDP, are constructed biases them upwards during wartime. The substitution of market for nonmarket activity increases GDP, but it does not mean people are necessarily better off. In addition, the substitution of spending today in return for consumption tomorrow might be good public policy, but it should not be confused with prosperity in any conventional sense of the word.

MEASURING WARTIME PROSPERITY

Are people better off economically as a result of wars? How do we calculate economic well-being? The great Scottish philosopher and economist Adam Smith had an answer. According to Smith, "Consumption is the sole end and purpose of all production" (Smith 1976). Typically, personal consumption expenditures are the largest component of a country's total economic output, as measured by gross domestic product. So, looking at what happens to consumption expenditures during wartime is a good place to begin in answering questions about the link between wars and economic prosperity.

The table below contains an index of personal consumption expenditures, adjusted for inflation, between 1939 and 1945—the years coinciding with World War II (although the United States did not formally enter the war until after Pearl Harbor in December 1941, war production had begun to accelerate in 1939). The figures in column 1 are based on U.S. Commerce Department data and show a 23.4 percent increase during the war. This would correspond with an average annual compounded rate of growth of 3.6 percent, which was quite robust at the time, considering that during the previous decade the country had weathered the Great Depression. When comparing the war years to the Great Depression, it is not surprising that many U.S. citizens, remembered the war as an era of economic prosperity, at least those citizens who were not in Bastogne or on Guadalcanal.

Estimates of Real Personal Consumption Expenditures (1939–1945)

Year	Commerce	Adjusted
1939	100.0	100.0
1940	104.6	104.2
1941	110.5	108.7
1942	109.8	104.2
1943	112.4	101.9
1944	115.9	102.0
1945	123.4	106.8

Source: Higgs, Robert. 1992. "Wartime Prosperity? A Reassessment of the U.S Economy in the 1940s." Journal of Economic History 52:41–60.

However, the measurement of consumption expenditures is not without controversy. For one thing, there was tremendous inflation during the war—inflation that was accompanied by government-mandated price controls. Thus the official prices used to adjust for this inflation do not necessarily account for the true inflation rate as reflected in, for example, black-market or illegal prices. The figures in column 2 of the table, which adjust personal consumption expenditures during the war, were calculated using an alternative set of inflation-adjusted prices. Here we see that consumption increased by only 6.8 percent over the course of the war, a rate of growth that did not even keep up with population growth. Thus, during the so-called wartime prosperity, real average consumption per person actually fell. This is not what one typically associates with prosperity. As is often the case in economics, the devil is in the details, and the details are in the numbers.

WINNERS AND LOSERS

From our discussion above, it appears that rather than enriching an economy, war simply changes it. Holding other things constant, war represents a net transfer of resources from taxpayers (including soldiers) to suppliers of war materiel (companies), and from borrowers (again, future taxpayers) to holders of savings (specifically, buyers of government bonds). Of course, in war, other things are not constant. In particular, our discussion to this point has said nothing about winners and losers. The destruction wrought by war can nearly completely devastate an area. After the destruction of Carthage in 146 B.C., the Romans supposedly sowed salt in the earth so that the Carthaginians would never rise again. Byzantium never recovered from the Fourth Crusade. Hiroshima was turned into ash. Neither the Carthaginians nor the Byzantines nor the Japanese spoke of wartime prosperity.

There is one way in which the economy can emerge a winner from war. This is if war is engaged in to remove a threat to the country and make the economy more secure. Households and businesses will be more reluctant to make important and needed investments in the economy if they fear the country won't exist, or at least will be severely damaged, in the future. In this case, a war to remove the threat and increase the likelihood of a peaceful future can ultimately improve long-run economic prosperity. The cold war's triumph of capitalism over communism offers a good recent example of this type of benefit, perhaps justifying, in economic terms at least, the war's tremendous cost in lives and treasure.

Ultimately, however, war is more than an economic activity. Clemenceau's admonition that war is too important to be left to generals applies here; it is too important to be left to economists as well. For those who see war as the alternative to annihilation, a blip in real GDP is of little importance. Winning at almost any cost is what matters.

References

Atack, Jeremy, and Peter Passell. 1994. *A New Economic View of American History.* 2nd ed. New York: Norton, p. 359.

Marcus Tullius Cicero. 2003. *The Fifth Philippic.* Cambridge: Cambridge University Press.

Craig, Lee A. 1996. "Industry, Agriculture, and the Economy During the Civil War." In *The American Civil War: A Handbook of Literature and Research,* edited by Steven E. Woodworth. Westport, CT: Greenwood Press.

Goldin, Claudia. 1973. "The Economics of Emancipation." *Journal of Economic History* 33:66–85; Goldin, Claudia, and Frank D. Lewis. 1975. "The Economic Cost of the American Civil War: Estimates and Implications." *Journal of Economic History* 35:304–9.

Higgs, Robert. 1992. "Wartime Prosperity? A Reassessment of the U.S Economy in the 1940s." *Journal of Economic History* 52:41–60.

Hughes, Jonathan, and Louis P. Cain. 2003. *American Economic History.* 6th ed. Boston: Addison Wesley.

Kennedy, David M. 1999. *Freedom from Fear: The American People in Depression and War, 1929–1945.* New York: Oxford University Press, p. 376 and p. 786.

Lieberman, Marc, and Robert E. Hall. 2005. *Introduction to Economics.* 2nd ed. Mason, OH: South-Western.

MacArthur, Douglas. 1951. *Farewell Address to Congress.* Available at http://www.americanrhetoric.com/speeches/douglasmacarthurfarewelladdress; Lewis, Lloyd. [1932]. 1993. *Sherman: Fighting Prophet.* Reprint, Lincoln: University of Nebraska Press.

Smiley, Gene. 1994. *The American Economy in the Twentieth Century.* Cincinnati, OH: South-Western, p. 197.

Smith, Adam. [1776]. 1976. *An Inquiry into the Nature and Causes of the Wealth of Nations.* Vol. 2. Indianapolis, IN: Liberty Classics, p. 179.

West Point Graduates Against the War. (n.d.). *Wise Words from Old Grads.* Available at http://www.westpointgradsagainstthewar.org/wise_words_from_old_grads.htm

Lee A. Craig

WHISTLE-BLOWERS

Whistle-blowing means reporting an organization's illegal or unethical activities. The reporting may be internal—to someone with higher responsibility in the organization—or external—to a government agency or the media. The whistle-blower is typically an employee who has become aware of activities that are not widely known.

Whistle-blowing has received more and more attention over the last several decades as government regulation—of the environment, worker safety, employer responsibilities, discrimination, and harassment—has increased. As regulation has increased, the business sector has complained that strict regulation with a command-and-control style of enforcement makes companies less efficient and less competitive globally, thus hurting the economy. They say meeting unnecessary requirements costs companies and costs the government to enforce too strictly. Companies say they can more effectively meet the spirit of the regulations if they do it their way. They prefer a "voluntary compliance" approach, and regulations have been moving in this direction. This approach has economic advantages, but it depends on companies having the best of intentions and the ability to self-police. When companies fall short of this ideal, whistle-blowers become essential in preserving the goals of the democratic society that created the legislation. Whistle-blowers are the insiders who risk their own comfort to speak out for the goals of the larger society.

Much of the most recent attention has focused on financial reporting activities in which corporations violated accounting rules and practices to misrepresent their financial conditions or overcompensate some key employees. Countless individuals employed by these corporations or their auditing firms faced the dilemma of whether to participate in questionable or fraudulent activities, look the other way, or blow the whistle. The wave of corporate scandals at the turn of this century involved dozens of major corporations embroiled in much-publicized scandals and hundreds more with questionable practices. Because inaccurate or inadequate financial information harms investors, and because a growing percentage of the general public is investing in the stock market, these corporate scandals created a strong sentiment in favor of increased regulation with tighter rules and reporting requirements for publicly traded companies.

When the Sarbanes-Oxley Act was passed in 2002, it included, along with tighter reporting requirements, a section (301) mandating the establishment of whistle-blower hotlines within corporations and a section (806) on how companies should respond without retaliation. The intent is to create corporate cultures in which employee participation in making responsible changes is encouraged and, if that fails, to make external whistle-blowing possible without corporate retaliation.

Sherron Watkins, a corporate accounting executive with Enron, blew the whistle on Enron, the seventh-largest corporation in the United States at the time. The spectacular and highly publicized downfall of Enron brought Watkins hero status, and she was named Time's person of the year. She admits her experience was bizarre and considers herself now unemployable in a normal corporate job. But she considers herself fortunate and says she has no regrets. Her advice to others: "Look out for yourself. Find the safety net of another job and leave before you say anything. Also, don't do it alone. Then you can't be dismissed as one lone voice. But be ready to lose your job" (*Business Week*, June12, 2006, p.98).

There is much debate about the requirements of the Sarbanes-Oxley Act. Corporations often chafe at increased regulation, and many find it odd to be encouraging behavior that they see as damaging and disloyal. On the other hand, there are opportunities for corporations to be more responsible without losing competitiveness and to maintain a fair and open work environment. Will the Sarbanes-Oxley Act work as intended? Will whistle-blowing increase? Will employees feel more free to blow the whistle internally and, if necessary, externally? How should employees handle dilemmas about whether to blow the whistle or not?

On the face of it, the question of whether or not to blow the whistle is a relatively simple moral matter. When we see something wrong and we can't change it, we must report it. It turns out, however, that in many cases the question becomes a serious ethical dilemma with arguments on both sides. Also, while we might imagine that these dilemmas happen only to a few people or will happen only a few times in our work lives and that the incidents are dramatic, in fact, most people witness events that are questionable in their workplaces. Most people repeatedly face the whistle-blowing dilemma. While major whistle-blowing might be all too rare, whistle-blowing dilemmas are common and widespread.

What then are these dilemmas? What kinds of arguments can be made on each side? What forces—social, legal, economic, and personal—come into play in how individuals handle these dilemmas? What are the pros and cons of becoming a whistle-blower?

REASONS WE MIGHT RESIST BLOWING THE WHISTLE

- There are very strong cultural norms against "ratting" or "snitching" on others within our social group. Groups often have secrets. Secrets within families, within cliques, within classes, within fraternities, and within companies often strengthen these groups. We see early in life the consequences of a "snitch" breaking the bonds within a group and suffering social rejection, isolation, or even expulsion from the group. Blowing the whistle on our own company or group might seem similar, and we might fear similar rejection or ostracism.

- Sometimes groups have negative feelings about someone or some organization with authority over the group. Children resist snitching to a parent or teacher. Gangs evade authority, such as the police. Taxpayers foster an industry committed to paying the Internal Revenue Service the absolute minimum tax. In general, the greater the emotional distance from an authority, the stronger is the social bond against that authority. In contrast to a company for which one feels some loyalty, a remote governmental regulatory agency, for example, might seem more an enemy than a friend.
- Companies have opportunities to create strong bonds with employees. The economic bond—the paycheck and benefits—is the first and often the strongest. A job title and the activities associated with it become part of our identities. Especially in higher managerial jobs and in technical and professional jobs, our pride and our sense of identity are related to the job. Workplaces also create and sustain cultures that provide friendships and a social network. These are all threatened by the prospect of blowing the whistle on the company. Workers become, to varying degrees, dependent on their employers. Companies and the workplaces they create engender loyalty to the company. The potential whistle-blower must consider the impact of overriding that loyalty.
- Since it is sometimes true that whistles are blown by whiners who complain about everything, a potential whistle-blower must consider whether he or she is just whining. This may well be a defense that the company takes, and if the individual feels it might be true or that it might be perceived as true, even by the courts, then it may be a reason to resist formally blowing the whistle.
- We might discover something in a company's practices that seems unfair or possibly illegal but decide that it is a small issue compared to the overall mission of the company or organization. We might tell ourselves that in the overall scheme of things, the good this organization contributes outweighs the minor unfairness.
- We might look at an issue but then dismiss it because we know or we surmise or we decide to believe that everyone does it. In competitive industries, companies compete aggressively. Everyone tries to get an edge. Effective competitors in sports try to get away with everything the referees allow, regardless of the formal rules of the sport. This is the way the game is played. If our company treats its customers, employees, suppliers, or investors in ethically questionable ways, we might assume that competitors are the same or worse. The organization we work for is not perfect, but it's better than the competition. So, given all the reasons for playing along, why blow the whistle?

- We might feel that if we as employees or managers don't carry out questionable practices, the company will simply put someone else into our positions. Thus if our objective in blowing the whistle is to change the company's behavior, it will only work if it is fully successful. If we doubt that it will fully succeed, we might decide to play along and collect the paycheck instead.
- If we share in the profits of the company—through stock, stock options, or higher wages—we may feel that the company's success is our success. Profit-sharing plans are designed to reward all of us for the company's success and to keep all employees engaged in improving the profits. They also encourage us to share in the company's defensiveness against threats, including the threat of whistle-blowing to parties outside the company.
- We might feel that we are already sliding full speed down a slippery slope, and it's too late to start getting moralistic. If we have worked for the company for years and have already contributed our efforts to practices that are questionable, we might ask, "Why now?" We might even worry that if this whole mess becomes public, we ourselves might be sharing the blame.

REASONS TO BLOW THE WHISTLE

We might argue that most of us do not join a company with the attitude that it will be the thing that comes first in our thinking and first in our lives. Even if we are happy to have a job with the company, even if we may eventually develop strong loyalty and dependency with the company, it is not our primary loyalty. Our stronger commitments should be to ourselves as responsible and moral individuals, to our families and friends, to our churches or other affiliations that support our values and principles, and to our country and the laws and principles it tries to maintain. As responsible individuals, our primary loyalties should be to sustain the fairest conditions for the society we share. As citizens, our loyalty should be to the good of the whole society and to the strength of a fair nation.

- So, as individuals we should not compromise our own moral values just to make a company a little more profitable.
- As citizens we owe it to our society to be a watchdog against behavior that harms the society. Loyalty should never be to the company first. With a swing in regulatory style toward voluntary compliance by companies, insider watchdogs must be relied on to blow the whistle when necessary.
- If we work for a company that does business on a local level, we should value the welfare of our friends and neighbors above the profits of the company. If we work for a company operating nationally or globally, we should place our citizenship and our shared humanity above the company's success. Companies come and go. Most last for one or two generations at most. Few last for more than 50 years, even major corporations. But communities and nations have more permanence.

- We might respect the founders and leaders of our company, but we respect them for their contributions to the social good, not for their ability to squeeze out exceptional profits, especially if those profits come at the expense of others. Their leadership value is that they provide goods and services valued by customers and a fair return to investors. Their value is not in any personal greed through which they aspire to more personal wealth than they deserve. If we see company activities that appear to be driven by greed, we don't respect the leadership enough to not blow the whistle.
- If we see the leadership of an organization as close associates and even friends, we are reluctant to blow the whistle against them. But, as is often the case, especially in large corporations, if we see the leadership as remote from us, they might be the authority against which many of us feel rebellious. We might see them as more remote from us than the friendly folks in the local state attorney general's office.
- "Snitching" or "ratting" does not easily produce the same rejection or ostracism when it is done not by an individual but by a group. Collective whistle-blowing is easier. It depends, of course, on coworkers agreeing that something is wrong, that change is possible, and that the change is worth the risks involved in whistle-blowing.
- If we are competent employees and have been recognized as such in performance reviews, we have a better position from which to blow the whistle. A classic company defense is that the whistle-blower is incompetent. Also, if we do not have the reputation as a whiner or disgruntled employee, we are better prepared for those common charges as well.
- The slippery slope effect—we've already participated in questionable practices—is not unstoppable. If we are already involved, we can still refuse to go further or to go to a next level. The insidious thing about a slippery slope is that it may be bottomless, and the speed of descent keeps increasing. If we're sledding down an increasingly slippery slope, the time to bail out and get some snow in our faces is better sooner than later. So the slippery slope need not be an excuse for not blowing the whistle.
- We might be especially offended by questionable company behaviors if they are related to a cause we have a particular interest in. If, for example, we have strong feelings about environmental responsibility and we discover that the company is harming the environment in violation of Environmental Protection Agency standards, we are probably more willing to blow the whistle.
- If we are personally affected by questionable company behaviors, we are probably more willing. If, for example, we ourselves are the subject of illegal discrimination or harassment, we have strong reasons to seek change to the hostile work environment.

WHAT MIGHT HAPPEN IF WE BLOW THE WHISTLE?

It is possible that things will go well. Blowing a whistle internally may be lauded by colleagues, some of whom will corroborate and support us. Superiors and the company leaders may be respectful and even thankful that difficulties were reported, and they may quickly fix the problem. There may be no retaliation and resentment or changes in personal relationships. The whistle-blower may even get a raise or promotion.

It is also possible that the company will react defensively, especially if the whistle is blown externally to the company. Company leaders may quickly take the position that the company is innocent, or at least that the activity is not illegal and that other companies do the same thing. They may retaliate by changing the whistle-blower's job responsibilities, making the argument that the person is apparently not happy or comfortable with his or her current responsibilities. They may even move the whistle-blower's office to that space down the hall and around the corner next to the utility room. The employee may be isolated from former job activities and fellow workers. Since common defenses are that the whistle-blower is incompetent or a disgruntled employee or is mentally unstable and a chronic complainer, these actions and other retaliatory measures may become a self-fulfilling prophecy. It is not uncommon for whistle-blowers who were previously competent, stable, and satisfied in their jobs to become less competent with new responsibilities, more and more disgruntled as duties and relationships change, and emotionally troubled by isolation and resentment from fellow workers. They may take emotional stress home with them, harming personal relationships and creating more isolation and self-doubt. By the time the charges of disgruntlement or mental instability are made in court, if it goes that far, they are sometimes truer than they were initially.

HOW CAN WE RESOLVE A DILEMMA AND DECIDE WHAT'S RIGHT FOR US?

Sages, philosophers, and religious leaders have developed many approaches, even systems, for thinking through ethical dilemmas. But often the conclusion reached by one approach is countered by that of another approach. Two different people may even get two different answers to the same dilemma from the same approach. Dilemmas are by definition the hard cases, the cases with pros and cons on each side of the question. Though most of us are not ethicists, we use at least portions of various ethical systems, and these sometimes make us comfortable with our decisions.

One of the popular approaches to ethical dilemmas is the disclosure rule (Steiner and Steiner 2006). sometimes called the New York Times rule. While it never dictates a conclusion, it gives us another perspective from which to evaluate the issues and may be especially helpful in whistle-blowing dilemmas. It asks us how we would feel if the action we're considering (e.g., blowing the whistle on a company we work for) were to become a major media story tomorrow. How would we feel and how would others feel about us when the story broke? How would our family, friends, neighbors, colleagues, and investors feel? How would we feel about their reactions? Could we answer for what we did and feel comfortable in our own skin?

POTENTIAL STAGES IN WHISTLE-BLOWING

If we are thinking seriously about blowing the whistle, it is helpful to think through the potential process or order of events. The experience will probably not be an orderly process and will be full of surprises, but we will handle it better if we prepare for it the best we can. Here are some likely stages:

- Suspicion of illegality or lack of ethics. We become consciously aware that something might be wrong. We wonder whether there is evidence or documentation.
- Questioning—even mild or casual—of colleagues and perhaps managers about what is going on. We might also be wondering whether the activity is ethically questionable or, in fact, illegal.
- Confirmation (or partial confirmation) that there is or is not a legal or ethical issue. We might find that something seemed wrong but that there was a good explanation for it or that it might be legal but seems ethically questionable. Or we may discover that it is indeed a problem, and we are confronted with the whistle-blowing dilemma.
- Weighing the dilemma. Should we go along and get along or get ready to blow the whistle? Does the leadership know about the issue? Is it likely that they want to behave ethically and will welcome constructive criticism? Are we already implicated in this and are we sliding down the slippery slope? Are we ready for possible financial and emotional consequences? Are we ourselves just generally disgruntled employees who are looking for one more thing to whine about? Could we handle the publicity if this mess blows up?
- Preparing. Find evidence and documentation if possible, even though most courts are currently not requiring that the whistle-blower prove an allegation, only that they have a good faith belief that a violation occurred. Find others who can be trusted and will be supportive. Keep private documentation on all activities (not on the company computer), noting changes in assignments, in treatment, and in the attitudes of management, supervisors, and coworkers. Perhaps confide privately to friends outside the company who can provide emotional support in the future if necessary.
- Deciding whom to tell first. Is internal whistle-blowing realistic? Is there a working hotline to trustworthy parties? Is management likely to react responsibly? Are there company policies encouraging participation and discouraging retaliation? Does management appear to "walk the talk"? If internal routes are unrealistic, or if they have negative results, there is a next decision point: whether to blow the whistle externally.
- Whistle-blowing externally. Begin inquiring at government agencies (federal, state, or local) about which is most appropriate for the issue in question. While any agency may have drawbacks (e.g., nonresponsiveness, potential lack of confidentiality), careful inquiries should lead you to an appropriate one. Consider:
    - The state attorney general's office
    - The inspector general's office

- Regulatory agencies related to the issue, such as the Environmental Protection Agency, the Occupational Safety and Health Administration, or the Securities and Exchange Commission
- Congress or state legislative offices
- Advocacy groups

Consider whether the issue is one the media would be interested in and whether the impact of a media story would be desirable. Going to the media is considered by many to be the most disloyal act and the most potentially embarrassing to the organization. It usually provokes the most severe retaliation. Research and choose a reporter carefully, knowing what he or she will and will not be able to do.

Consider finding a lawyer with experience in the issue. Contact advocacy groups, unions, the National Lawyers Guild, or the American Bar Association for suggestions. Ask them about their experience in whistle-blowing, employment law, or wrongful discharge. Summarize the story, get time and financial commitments, and check for conflicts of interest.

WHAT SHOULD COMPANIES BE DOING?

The Sarbanes-Oxley Act concerns financial reporting and applies to publicly traded corporations. It contains provisions protecting whistle-blowers. Other (nonpublic) companies would be smart to follow the same requirements regarding whistle-blowing. Many requirements of governmental agencies, especially those dealing with employment law, apply to companies with 50 or more employees. But smaller companies would be smart to follow similar principles. Many successful companies have found that strong and meaningful corporate ethics programs tend to foster a culture with more productive employees, more responsible investors, and more satisfied customers. These ethics programs, whether they address environmental issues, accurate financial reporting, customer relationships, community responsibilities, or employee rules and behaviors, all have some of the same features:

- Written policies, appropriately distributed and displayed, in understandable language
- Leadership commitment and example—if company leaders do not talk about issues and then "walk the talk," no one takes them seriously
- Training and retraining of everyone, especially supervisors and managers, who may be most closely involved with employees when issues arise
- Hotlines that are easily accessible, placed high in the organization structure, and administered with credible confidentiality, as well as open-door policies at all management levels
- Response procedures that follow up effectively, generate changes as needed, and avoid any retaliatory measures

If more and more companies come to understand that by welcoming internal whistle-blowing they can create valuable changes and get efficiency gains, then some of the current risks for whistle-blowers could decrease. External whistle-blowing, however, will remain a personally risky but socially important phenomenon.

See also: Employee Loyalty and Engagement; Ethics in Business at the Individual Level

References

Steiner, George A., and John F. Steiner. 2006. *Business, Government, and Society.* 11th ed. Chicago: McGraw-Hill/Irwin.

Further Reading: Blowing the Whistle. (n.d.). *Tip of the Day.* Available at www.whistleblowing.org/Tips.htm; Kohn, Stephen M., Michael D. Kohn, and David K. Colapinto. 2004. *Whistleblower Law: A Guide to Corporate Legal Protections and Procedures.* Westport, CT: Praeger; Richardson, John E., ed. *Business Ethics, Annual Editions 06/07.* Guilford, CT: McGraw-Hill/Dushkin; Schwartz, Mimi, with Sherron Watkins. 2003. *Power Failure: The Inside Story of the Collapse of Enron.* New York: Random House.

Philip K. Iobst

WHOLESALE BUYING CONTROL BY BIG-BOX RETAILERS

Over the last few years retailing has become more and more concentrated in fewer and fewer big-box retailers such as Wal-Mart. Concern has grown at the same time that this concentration might create a situation where these retailers are able to force their suppliers to provide pricing lower than what would emerge in an open and freely competitive market. In legal language, this is called monopsony when one is referring to the case of a single buyer, or oligopsony when the case is one of a few buyers acting together. Monopsony is effectively the mirror image of monopoly: equal but opposite. It is a situation where the buyer controls the market using buyer power, instead of the seller controlling the market by monopolizing resources. There are two principal issues concerning monopsony. First is the question of whether or not the big-box retailers actually have gained sufficient buyer power to force price concessions from their suppliers. Second is whether this market control could have a negative impact on consumers across the board.

The problem of monopsony is not new. In 1949, the U.S. government filed suit against the Great Atlantic and Pacific Tea Company when it was ruled that they had violated antitrust laws by using their extreme market control to force suppliers to provide price concessions. More recently lawsuits have been filed against buyers of food products such as blueberries, tobacco, and meat. Similar lawsuits have also been filed in the health-care industry, the paper industry, and e-commerce.[1] In all these cases, the concern is whether the purchaser in the supply chain has gained sufficient buyer power to force the seller to offer a lower price than would be expected in a free market. This reduction in price forces the supplier to lower its output to compensate for the loss in revenue. The reason the supplier produces less is because with a reduced price, the point at which the supplier's marginal costs equal its marginal revenues is reached at a lower production volume. As a result the supplier has no incentive to produce larger quantities. The lower production volumes mean that they reduce their consumption of raw materials over the long run. The long-term impact on society is a net reduction in efficiency and a shift of wealth from the producer to the consumer in what is then referred to as a monopsony market. With this concept in mind, it is useful to consider how a buyer might gain sufficient power to be able to induce these conditions (i.e., reduction of supplier revenue and downturn in societal efficiency) and whether or not big-box retailers are in a position to establish such monopsony control.

In order to do this, we must consider the definition of buyer power: buyer power is one of the five competitive forces identified by Porter as shaping competition in industry. The other four competitive forces are supplier power, the threat of new entrants into the industry, the threat of substitute goods or services, and industry rivalry. Porter also identifies seven factors that lead to the possession of substantial buyer power by a buyer or buyer group in an industry. We will consider each of these factors in turn relative to big-box retailers.

BUYER POWER AND BIG-BOX RETAILERS

The critical question in understanding monospsony is whether or not a retailer (or any buyer) has sufficient power to demand (or extort, as some would put it) price concessions beyond the ordinary from any supplier. Buyer power in its simplest form can be called the relative incentive relationship between a buyer and a seller. If, for example, a buyer has little reason to stick with a particular supplier, but that supplier has many powerful reasons to want (or need) to keep that buyer as a customer, the buyer has a strong hand, or what is called a powerful buyer position. Porter discusses seven ways buyers might gain power over their suppliers.

The first is the volume that the buyer purchases. Large-volume purchasers, like the big-box retailers, represent a large percentage of the production for suppliers. It becomes critical to the supplier to maintain the large order volume with the buyer so that output remains at a high level. In other words, a supplier has a great incentive to continue to sell to the big-box retailer, while the buyer has little or no incentive to buy from any given supplier. Small firms or firms that have very high fixed costs are extremely sensitive to this form of power. By their very nature, the big-box retailers deal in large volumes, so they clearly have the ability to amass buyer power via this mechanism.

Second, Porter predicts that buyers gain power if the products they purchase are undifferentiated or standardized. Big-box retailers base their success on low prices; they are competing directly on price, never on differentiation. This means that consumers are coming to their stores searching for lower prices on standard items. Since the products sold in their stores are standardized, the retailers have several potential sources for their supply of product. Purchasing from one supplier or another has no differentiating value, because these suppliers are essentially providing identical products.

Porter maintains that the buyer is more likely to spend more effort searching for lower-cost alternatives if the products represent a large percentage of the buyer's cost than if those products represent a small percentage of the buyer's costs. In the case of big-box retailers, the products sold represent the largest total portion of their overall cost. For example, Wal-Mart in particular is known for aggressively reducing operating costs, which leaves the cost of inventory the largest percentage of the company's overall cost breakdown. This results in a reduced incentive for the buyer to purchase products except on a price basis. The increased desire to find a lower-cost supplier supersedes other factors such as service. The effect is an increase in the buyer power of big-box retailers relative to their suppliers.

Another contributor to buyer power is the great incentive a buyer has to search for lower prices if they have low profit margins. This low profit margin practically defines the big-box or deep-discount retailers. As such, they are constantly searching for lower-cost goods even if the difference between their current supplier and the alternate supplier is marginal. Only a supplier with a low-cost strategy can motivate them to do business. Suppliers are thus forced to maintain the very lowest price they can bear if they want to continue to do business with the deep-discount retailer, and once again, we see that most of the incentive to continue the relationship is on the side of the supplier.

Porter also predicts that the quality of the goods also play a role in the relative strength of the buyer versus the supplier in the big-box retail market segment. As noted above, the products that are typically provided to the consumer in this retail segment tend to be uniform or undifferentiated from one another. Since the goods are uniform, the products' levels of quality tend to be uniform. The result is that suppliers cannot create a competitive advantage for themselves by offering superior product quality. Once an acceptable level of quality is achieved, there is no reason for the buyer to search for superior goods at higher prices. Good enough is good enough.

Suppliers may mitigate the buyer's power if their goods or services save the buyer money. Since buyers tend to be price insensitive when purchasing highly profitable items, they are not motivated to find alternative sources. However, since big-box retailers offer the consumer products that may be found in many places, their only competitive advantage is that they are offering products at a lower cost to the consumer. The consequence is that the buyer is not gaining significant profits by utilizing any particular supplier, so any supplier will serve. Once again, we see that all the motivation for the sale rests with the supplier.

The last of Michael Porter's factors that generate buyer power is the threat that the buyer might back integrate into the supplier's industry. This threat exists only if there is a creditable opportunity for the buyer to begin producing the product it is buying. For example, it is possible that an automotive producer could manufacture components that it currently purchases from suppliers. This source of buyer power is the only one of Porter's seven that does not have a bearing on the buyer-supplier relationship in the deep-discount retail arena.

Given the differences in the capabilities of manufacturing and retail sales, it is highly unlikely that a retailer would begin to manufacture products.

When we consider the big-box retailers and their suppliers in the context of buyer power overall, several points become abundantly clear. The retailers are highly motivated to find alternative suppliers. Low profits, product inventories that represent a high net percentage of total costs, standardized goods, a lack of relationship between sales and the quality of the goods purchased, and a lack of significant cost savings generated from any particular supplier's products all result in no incentive for the big-box retailer to do business with a given supplier. In fact, these factors act as incentives for the buyer to seek out alternative suppliers. Conversely, the fact that these retailers purchase in large volumes makes suppliers highly motivated to maintain a contract despite any demand placed on them by their buyers. The existence of buyer power, even in extreme cases, does not in and of itself create a monopsony. It is necessary for the buyer to have sufficient control of the market to impose price controls. If it doesn't have control of the market, suppliers will simply seek an alternative buyer. It is also necessary for economic rents, the premium a producer receives for manufacturing one product instead of another, to be present on the supply side of the relationship. Without the motivation of economic rents, suppliers would merely exit the market when faced with price-control efforts and produce other merchandise.

MONOPSONY AND THE CONSUMER

Antitrust legislation aimed at eliminating monopolies has a long and well-established history. Legal action against oil companies, steel companies, railroads and other industry giants during the nineteenth century broke large corporate monopolies into smaller competing firms. More recently, Microsoft faced antitrust legislation brought of the widespread perception that it had a monopoly with its Windows operating system. Contrary to widely held belief, antitrust legislation is not aimed purely at preventing the monopolist or, as in our discussion, a monopsony from overpricing goods. In fact, the Standard Oil trust lowered the price of a barrel of oil from 58 cents to 8 cents around the turn of the nineteenth century, and in a similar manner the monopoly power of U.S. Steel significantly lowered prices in the steel industry during the same time period. The end result in both cases was that the actions of these monopolists actually lowered prices in these industries to the benefit of society. These examples highlight the fact that antitrust legislation actually has a deeper and more important economic motivation than simple price control. This is not to say that monopolies and monopsonies could not and have not increased prices above free-market levels given the opportunity. Rather, it establishes only that the situation is more complex than it seems on its face and that price-protection manipulation, in and of itself, is not the only goal of antitrust legislation.

Another side of antitrust legislation is its effort to protect the public against the accumulation of too much power by any single element in the economy. This could theoretically lead to a net reduction of social welfare in the economy. Too much centralized power could result in a reduction of productivity and inappropriate and inefficient utilization of resources, thus resulting in a lower net social good. This could happen if one firm or group of firms could prevent prices from achieving the equilibrium level at which they would normally balance in an openly competitive market place. Such an artificially fixed price could reduce productivity in the market. The aim would be for a monopolist or monopsonist to derive an artificially high profitability at the expense of the rest of society. Concerns relative to monopsony are symmetrical to those of monopoly in that the exploitation results in the same type of waste, but the manipulation is being initiated by a buyer in the supply chain instead of a supplier. Hence, it suggests the image of the mirror.

One of the dangers of a market controlled by a monopsony is that firms that might normally enter the market and improve the efficient use of resources do not enter due to the artificially controlled prices and lower competition, which leads to poor utilization of resources. With reduced competition, development stagnates, new products are not developed, and existing processes are not refined, and the result is that consumers are deprived of development options. These customers must then absorb the waste of missed opportunity to progress in the form of reduced values. Fair market profits that would normally be distributed equitably throughout the industry based on free-market forces are usurped by the controlling faction. Suppliers are forced to produce at a level below which they would normally have produced had the industry been allowed to come to economic equilibrium. In turn, those suppliers do not make purchases of raw materials or pay fair wages. The result is that the economy is repressed and society as a whole is not as productive as it could be. Now that we have this basic understanding of why monopsony might represent some kind of a threat economically and how buyer power can lead to a monopsony situation, the question for consideration is: Has the recent advent of big-box retailers created a monopsony condition?

BIG-BOX RETAILERS AND MONOPSONY

The heart of the monopsony problem is not one of whether or not the potential exists for the development of a monopsony. It does. The structure of the system that the big-box retailers have developed is one marked by its ability to accrue buyer power, which can then be used to develop a monopsony environment. Nor is the debate one of whether or not the law should be applied to a monopsony in is the same manner that it is applied to a monopoly. It should and has been in the case of the A&P. The real question is: Where is the division between a firm aggressively seeking to legitimately lower prices and excessively manipulating suppliers? That line of demarcation has not yet been established, and this creates a highly complex problem. Many economists have viewed the potential for lower pricing in the retail industry as beneficial to consumers until it reaches the point where producers stop innovation, lower production levels, or flee the market completely because of their inability to be profitable. Concern over the problem is growing exponentially.

In 2001, Bloom and Perry examined suppliers to Wal-Mart in an effort to evaluate the impact Wal-Mart's buyer power might have on its suppliers. They could not reach any conclusions. On one hand, they found that some suppliers, in particular, suppliers holding a large share of their markets, perform well as suppliers to Wal-Mart. Conversely, suppliers that hold a small market share in their segment do not perform well as suppliers to Wal-Mart. This might be an indication that suppliers that do not depend on Wal-Mart for a large portion of their sales are more immune to its power and that market share is a crucial factor in the equation.

Boulding and Staelin determined that firms with high market shares gain no extra benefits from their position except in cases where they have a powerful position relative to their suppliers. This implies that Wal-Mart, with its large market share and a high level of power, is in a position to reap added benefits from its position in the retail industry. This is also consistent with Cool and Henderson's finding that buyer power was a better explanation than supplier power for seller profitability. While these factors point to some potential metrics for monopsony situations, they do not allow for other compounding factors that might influence firm success, such as greater productivity.

In the A&P case, the A&P was found guilty because it allegedly used its buying power to force suppliers to lower prices to the A&P and thereby was able to lower its prices to consumers. It was then able to force competitors out of business, which increased its market share. Ironically enough, today antitrust researchers feel that the case was incorrectly decided because A&P did not collude to control pricing but rather only took advantage of technical innovations that provided gains in efficiency by using what has become the common practice of privately labeling products for sale in their stores. In others words, according to this reevaluation, A&P was effectively taking first-mover advantage of technical innovations that would eventually be available to all competitors and did not collude to control markets. While there may be differing evaluations of this 1949 case relative to when buyer power transcends legitimate competition and develops into a monopsony, one point seems crystal clear: collusion with other members of the supply chain is strictly forbidden.

At the turn of this century, the courts ruled that Toys "R" Us had illegally used its power in an attempt to inhibit its suppliers from supplying its competitors. This is similar to the finding in 1912 that the Terminal R. R. Association could use its power for increasing profits but it could not collude to preserve its power. The findings in these two cases almost a century apart provide what might be considered a guide for this discussion. Firms may use buyer power to enhance their profitability but not to preserve and/or to protect their position of power.

Recently the chairman of Wal-Mart Stores Inc. discussed some of the implications of buyer power relative to his company and its supply chain. A consideration of some of his positions is enlightening. Initially, Walton clearly stated that the overriding policy of Wal-Mart is to offer everyday low prices. He noted that this policy is responsible for the growth of Wal-Mart. The motivation to find low-cost products to offer at low prices is consistent with great buyer power. Walton discussed the fact that his firm makes great efforts to reduce operating costs. This is also consistent with the powerful buyer profile. Regarding the adaptation of new technologies to reduce operating costs, Walton pointed out that Wal-Mart required its top 100 suppliers to be radio frequency identification compliant by 2005. This is an interesting statement because at the time, it was only a supposition on the part of Wal-Mart that this technology would enhance efficiency, not an established fact. Suppliers were expected to absorb the costs based not on scientific evidence, but on home-based speculation that the technology would lower operating costs for Wal-Mart.

He pointed out that some of Wal-Mart's suppliers are very successful as a result of dealing with Wal-Mart. This fact is aligned with Bloom and Perry's findings that some suppliers, given the correct conditions, are successful while dealing with a powerful buyer. At the same time, it in no way refutes their position that a relationship with power buyers is not be successful for others.

In terms of lowering operating costs, Walton offered further examples. He noted that the assembly of bicycles came at a cost to Wal-Mart and explained that his firm went to the bicycle manufacturers and had them reengineer their products so that the bicycles that came to them were mostly preassembled. This represents an interesting incongruity in the Wal-Mart supply chain. Generally, cooperation in a supply chain aims at lowering overall costs so that all members benefit. On the surface, this example indicates that the sole beneficiary of preassembled bicycles was Wal-Mart, while their suppliers absorbed the cost of reengineering.

Yet another example offered by Walton of working with the company's suppliers was that of small gas grill manufacturers, who were approached to reengineer their products to enable the end user to assemble the product in less time. This example raises a truly interesting question: Why weren't larger gas grill manufacturers approached with the same request? Or had they been asked and refused to act on the request? If so, their refusal prompted Wal-Mart to exert their buyer power and search for alternative (i.e., smaller) suppliers. If the larger manufacturers of gas grills declined to reengineer their product for Wal-Mart, it is highly likely that they declined because they did not feel concern over the potential loss of the Wal-Mart business. Conversely, the smaller manufacturers would have been more influenced by the threat of losing business.

Another example of Wal-Mart's buyer power is related by Fishman. In this example a supplier was asked to provide an arbitrarily sized product at a price unrelated to the economic supply or demand for the product. The supplier complied but after time realized that it was cannibalizing its other product lines at great cost to the company. This fact was taken to the executives at Wal-Mart, and a request was made to raise the price on the product so that it would be more in line with other products in the segment. Wal-Mart's stance was typical of a powerful buyer dealing with a supplier. Wal-Mart affirmed that it would take its business elsewhere. While not illegal, this is a typical example of the type of moral situation that has developed with powerful big-box suppliers.

The use of buyer power is neither illegal nor unethical. It may create concerns for suppliers doing business with powerful buyers, but it is part of doing business. However, if buyer power is used to maintain the buyer's power in the form of a monopsony then it is not simply a part of normal business. Eventually in this case, it is assumed that the government will take action in its role to protect the common good and dissipate the monopsony. The question is largely one of degree, and only time will provide answers.

References

Blair, R. D., and J. L. Harrison. 1993. *Monopsony: Antitrust Law and Economics.* Princeton, NJ: Princeton University Press. Bloom, P., and V. Perry. 2001. "Retailer Power and Supplier Welfare: The Case of Walmart." Journal of Retailing, 77: 379–96.

Boulding, William, and Richard Staelin. 1995. Identifying Generalizable Effects of Strategic Actions on Firm Performance: The Case of Demand-Side Returns to R&D Spending." *Marketing Science* 14, no. 3 (special issue): G222–36.

Cool, Karen, and James Henderson. 1998. "Power and Firm Profitability in Supply Chains: French Manufacturing Industry in 1993." *Strategic Management Journal* 19, no. 10: 909.

Fishman, Charles. 2006. *The Wal-Mart Effect.* New York: Penguin.

Further Reading: Blair, R. D., and J. L. Harrison. 1993. *Monopsony: Antitrust Law and Economics.* Princeton, NJ: Princeton University Press; Porter, M. E. 1980. *Competitive Strategy.* New York: Free Press.

Eric C. Jackson

WORKAHOLISM

Barry and Shankar are both first-line supervisors at Newline Manufacturing Company. They often go to lunch together and use that opportunity to air their frustration about dealing with subordinate employees. Today Barry is talking about one of the production teams in his section. "I think the members of this team are all smart and capable of more, so it's irritating to see their numbers come in as only satisfactory. Of the five people, Jeff does the work of three, and the rest of the team is barely filling in around that. If they all worked like Jeff, they'd be the top team in production every quarter."

From Barry's comments, how would you interpret the situation with this team? One possibility is that the other members are not as smart or capable, and that both his ability and his willingness to make up the difference so that the team meets its goals each quarter do indeed make Jeff the better employee. Another possibility is that the other team members are capable—they would do more if they needed to, but they have learned that Jeff will step forward if they show any hesitation. They get paid the same and are not working as hard.

Consider a third possibility. Maybe the team would like to do more but Jeff gets in the way. Perhaps they would like to cross-train on different functions, as recommended, but Jeff can't tolerate anyone doing it differently from how he would, as he is convinced they cannot or will not do it as well. If Jeff keeps a tight hold on important information, the others have no chance to demonstrate their abilities. By now, they would be tired of fighting Jeff over the work and have learned that the most peaceful resolution is just to stand aside and let Jeff run the show.

If this third possibility is an accurate description of what it happening, this would be an indication that Jeff is a workaholic.

WHAT DOES IT MEAN TO BE A WORKAHOLIC?

An article in the popular magazine Psychology Today provided an overview of the problem of workaholism, asserting that workaholics are unable to delegate effectively, have a high need for control, and often allow (if not encourage) crises to develop (Goodman 2006). A good crisis offers the opportunity for the workaholic to step in and be the hero. This gives a temporary boost to self-esteem and elicits support from the company and boss for doing extra work, an important factor that allows the workaholic to deny there is anything wrong with the extra time and effort he or she is devoting to the job.

Overall, workaholism is a pattern of excess work that parallels addictions of other types—substance abuse and other behaviors like gambling (Porter 2005). Identity becomes attached to the job or the workplace, so that all life satisfaction is sought through that activity. Other sources of satisfaction, like family and friends, are sacrificed when necessary to support the work. Deterioration of personal health and well-being are often ignored in favor of working more. Some people receive a wake-up call from health issues or their children's comments about the parent not being around. Others, however, jump right back into the job after heart attacks or divorces and other family disruptions.

When work is clearly causing problems in other facets of life, and the individual continues to choose work as the top priority, this is addictive behavior. In addition, this need for more and more work is an internal drive of the individual; it is not simply a response to demands in the workplace. Those external demands may be very real, but they are not the real cause—only a convenient excuse for the workaholic's behavior.

WHAT ABOUT WORK-LIFE BALANCE?

Other entries in this volume provide information about the demands of the workplace and the challenges of work-life balance, such as the extra demands of dual-earner households, the career impact of the "mommy track," and trends in telecommuting. It's well recognized that the work-life conflict is bidirectional. Work issues can leak over into what should be personal time, and personal issues intrude on work time. Workaholics give priority to work, so it is a one-way interference.

Workaholics may bring information to the job about personal problems that are resulting from what they refer to as the heavy demands of the job as a means of emphasizing the sacrifice they are making. They may even occasionally feel some genuine guilt about what they are doing to family and friends, but they continue to choose work. Therefore, the true imbalance is unidirectional.

Some people like having clear boundaries between work and personal life. They want to give full effort to work while on the job but then walk out the door at quitting time and leave work concerns behind. Others are not looking for this strict segmentation; they enjoy life as a more integrated combination where the boundaries are comparatively blurred. They may take work home to do after the children are in bed and, conversely, expect to answer personal phone calls and e-mail while at the office. The choice between segmentation and integration is not a distinguishing factor in identifying workaholism, only whether or not some attention to other interests is actively maintained.

A workaholic is not likely to seek out companies with family-friendly policies that support work-life balance or, if working in one, not likely to take advantage of the policies offered. It's much more common for a workaholic to seek out situations that encourage, or even require, working long hours and always being on call.

As in the opening story about Jeff, managers often choose not to look beyond the surface appearance and reward workaholic behavior that is, in fact, detrimental to overall performance of the unit. Faced with an over-controlling workaholic, coworkers have to adjust in some way. Jeff's coworkers stepped back, let him take over increasing amounts of the work, and lived with the fact that their managers thought Jeff to be the superior employee. They might also have tried to fight fire with fire and become more like Jeff.

The situation is more intense when workaholics are the bosses. They impose perfectionist standards that can never be satisfactorily met but provide an unending supply of reasons to work more and more. Their subordinates may find they have to adopt workaholic behaviors to keep their jobs. Ultimately, the culture of the organizations shifts so that workaholism is the norm (Shaef and Fassel 1988). Even if the company has family-friendly policies in place, people facing a culture of workaholism know that it would damage their career prospects to make use of those policies.

WHO ARE THE WORKAHOLICS?

Although workaholism is internal to the individual, there is a great deal of societal support for working to excess, and individuals develop in the presence of those societal influences. In the United States, the national culture developed from the principles of the early European settlers. They had left a system in which the aristocratic elite were able to live completely idle lives of leisure, supported by the work of others. In their new country, they held a strong belief that everyone must work and that each individual must benefit from their own work (McElroy 1999). This set the groundwork. Work is good. Therefore, more work is better?

As the country developed, many popular stories, like those by Horatio Alger, featured a rags-to-riches theme. Characters would achieve new heights through their hard work and diligence. In such a land of opportunity, those willing to work harder and longer were applauded as being exemplary. The nation's founding values included equal opportunity along a belief that those willing to do more deserve greater wealth and social position. The message does make it sound like more is better, and no one stopped to define when it goes to an unhealthy extreme.

The history of the United States offers one explanation of social support for excess work, but workaholism is not unique to the United States. Japan's struggle with the issue of karoshi, death by overwork, is well known. Widows of karoshi victims are increasingly suing to receive death benefits, and the government has established guidelines for determining when excess work might be considered the cause of an employee's death. In China, overwork death is called guolaosi, and in Korea gwarose. In Germany this is referred to as Arbeitssucht, or work craze, which they consider comparable to drug craze, purchase craze, and problems with alcohol. In the Czeck Republic, the word zavislost refers to work addiction. A recent business publication in Brazil highlighted the problem of workaholism (Correa 2002). It seems that the phenomenon exists and is receiving increased attention in many parts of the world.

Just as workaholics are found in many countries around the world, they are found in settings other than the workplace. The stereotype of the male workaholic was based on a world in which the man was breadwinner and the woman stayed at home to care for the children. Yet women found ways to indulge their workaholic tendencies with various social commitments—parent-teacher organizations and other school-related projects, charitable foundations, community development projects, and the entertainment responsibilities in support of their husbands' career ambitions.

Now that a high percentage of women have moved into the paid workforce, these tendencies are more readily recognized as the same workaholism displayed by men. Whereas in the past, the man could use the good breadwinner excuse for working more and more, a female workaholic can always use the added difficulties of making it in a man's world to explain her extra time. This is not to say that a man's need to provide for his family and the challenges a woman faces in the workplace are not real. Rather, it is to point out that neither situation has a defined boundary of when enough is enough. When an individual is unable to set his or her own boundaries, these realities become handy excuses for neglecting other important things in life.

Workaholism is not reserved for white-collar jobs, although that is the image that people typically have. People at any organizational level and in any type of job might be workaholics, but in some situations it is easier to disguise the behavior than in others. When a factory assembler takes on a second job, the tendency is to view that as an economic decision. In contrast, an accountant has the option to spend twice as much time as colleagues on a work project, but the pay doesn't change. Either of these people might be a workaholic. The accountant is better suited to most people's idea of workaholism because that extension of time on the job seems more at the employee's discretion.

In today's working world, technology provides enhanced opportunities to keep working all the time. It also implies a certain responsibility to be working all the time. Global operations mean having various workers on the job 24 hours a day. Sending e-mail between the United States to Australia means a lag of a full day for response, unless someone is willing to be on the job at night. In heightened competition, a full day can be too long to wait for revised numbers or the okay to move ahead with a project. So, while e-mail eliminates the need to synchronize a phone call time, it doesn't eliminate the need to work outside of normally prescribed office hours.

Nowadays, a small handheld device can serve as a phone, an e-mail device, and a link to office files. This device fits into a pocket or purse or clips easily into a case on one's belt. This offers freedom from staying at the office at all hours. It also tethers one to the workplace at all times. All these connections make it easier for a workaholic to stay involved with work in the evening, over weekends, or while on vacation. It's not uncommon now to see people checking e-mail during social gatherings or at church. As this becomes the norm, it gets more and more difficult to identify who might be checking on a legitimately critical situation versus a person indulging in workaholic behavior.

People who work routinely with technology might be particularly susceptible to developing workaholic habits. When the job itself is based on computer operations, the level and speed of work are somewhat adaptable to individuals' preferences. This helps draw them into a state of attention on that focus to the exclusion of outside interference. It becomes increasingly easy to lose track of time and miss outside cues to shift one's attention. Many people have experienced this with computer games or when doing a Web search in which one piece of information branches off into another topic and then another—suddenly, hours have passed unnoticed.

People with a high need for control might also prefer to work with the logic and predictability of their computers rather than the seeming irrationality of human coworkers. Computers also offer the means to rework indefinitely to a higher level of perfectionist standards. Overall, jobs focused on technology might be particularly desirable spot for a workaholic. Among those whose initial pattern was less extreme, the conditions in these jobs might encourage work habits that, once accepted and encouraged, become an addictive pattern of workaholism.

ARE WE DOOMED?

It may sound as if there is no escape. When people are born into a society that places high value on hard work, the pace of the world and business requirements are accelerating, and the technology intended to help further enables excess, can there be a safe harbor from workaholism? Some companies have taken action in recent years to make sure there are options. Of all the companies with family-friendly policies for work-life balance, some put extra effort into making sure they are used appropriately. One way they do this is to publicize examples of high-ranking executives taking time for family events and other personal interests. Creating the expectation that these policies are to be used also serves to highlight workaholics who refuse to take advantage of them. Dealing with workaholism begins with recognition of the problem.

Responsiveness is key to being competitive in business. Everyone learned the quality messages during the 1980s, and in the 1990s quickness became the competitive edge. Now, customers not only want quality and fast turnaround to their requests, but they also want rapid customized changes as they redefine their needs. None of these things can be accomplished by operating out of massive policy and procedure manuals. Employees must work together to serve the customer, operating from a foundation of mutual trust rather than policy adherence. Workaholics, due to their controlling nature, do not develop trusting relationships. When it is necessary to maintain control, they will withhold information or change facts to protect their own situation. They are not be trustworthy and do not trust others.

Another way in which organizations combat workaholism is by paying attention to stress and stress-related illness. Because the workaholic places work above attention to personal needs, he or she is vulnerable to illness. Further, workaholics cause a great deal of stress among coworkers and subordinates. In addition to the trust issues just discussed, workaholics have an inclination toward perfectionism (to ensure an ongoing supply of more work to do) and may be in denial about causing any of the interpersonal difficulties in the workplace. They also allow crisis situations to continue. Others are often forced to accommodate these behaviors, even though they can see that many of the problems could be avoided or alleviated. Their frustration and anxiety become persistent stress. Companies that have stress reduction programs in place have a much better chance of uncovering the true nature of the problems. They can help employees cope or identify alternatives and, again, this attention highlights the workaholic person at the center of the situation and offers a chance to deal with the source of the stress rather than only treating the symptoms.

As companies strive to cut costs, many emphasize managing for results rather than activity. Employees are being held accountable for outcomes. Workaholics generate a lot of activity, but do they get results? Many times they do succeed on the standard metrics for measuring performance. Many times they do not but have a long list of excuses, which usually involve the failings of others to live up to the workaholic's high standards and having to cover too much of the work personally (as in the case of Jeff). To the extent that results indicators match well with the workaholic's addiction to excess work activity, both may happen. However, as with any addiction, when the two don't align well, more work will win out. Workaholics are not trying to be as efficient as possible, only to have lots of work to do.

Moving forward, increasing numbers of companies are concerned with values-based management. This effort involves establishing a clear set of company values that serve as the foundation for all employee decisions and actions. For example, companies that value strong families formulate family-friendly policies such as flex-time or on-site child care. True values-based management also means that they will not only have these policies but also actively enforce them.

Increased attention to the issue of workaholism may also develop as a result of lawsuits or the threat of legal action for detrimental effects of excess work. In recent years, people have held companies liable for health problems from smoking. Individuals have attempted to hold the fast-food business liable for obesity and related health problems. It is not hard to imagine that individuals (workaholics and others employees, as well as other interested parties) will begin to sue for the damages of excess work if companies do not take actions to show they are not requiring this of their workers. Just as the widows in Japan are suing for karoshi, it is likely that families will soon test the idea in U.S. courts. Companies looking for a defense against these actions should begin now to look at how they define job requirements and to identify employees who put them at risk.

IS THE MESSAGE HERE NOT TO WORK HARD?

There are many legitimate reasons to work very hard at one's job. Special projects may require intense focus for a specific period of time. However, these are specified for a limited time, after which a more reasonable workload is expected. Many jobs have these fluctuations, but a workaholic makes sure the next special project (or a crisis if no project can be found) is beginning before the workload for the current one begins to ease. Not everyone who works hard is a workaholic, and special projects, when there is some relief of the ending point, are a legitimate reason for some excess work.

In addition, there are bona fide crisis situations. Events that could not have been avoided occur or work exceeds the amount expected, regardless of precautions that have been taken. We see this at a regional and national level with extreme weather conditions, such as floods and hurricanes, and acts of terrorism. Companies respond to these and other internal crises by having people work more and at an accelerated pace. At these times, everyone hopes that those in a position to help will contribute as needed. When the crisis conditions begin to subside, however, people would normally seek a return to their normal work routines and be happy for the relief.

Another frequent justification for excess work is the early career stages in many professions. This is a time when the individual is striving to get established, to gain visibility, and to create a reputation of achievement. Lawyers and accountants want to make partner, college professors want to get tenure, physicians must survive their residency, and so on. The trick is to decide when this is no longer necessary and to remember all the other interests that have been ignored and are worth investing time in. People with high ambitions nearly always experience one or more stages at which excess work may well be necessary. This is not necessarily a problem, as long as there are periods of attention to other life interests.

Physically and mentally, people adapt to a certain level of stimulation. When excess work becomes the dominant pattern, there can be very real and serious withdrawal symptoms that occur when one moves to a lower level. The stories about executives who die of a heart attack when they finally break away from the office for a real vacation are not entirely myth. Feeling some anxiety over the idea of not going to work or not calling in twice a day while away are signs of a problem.

So, yes, it is okay to work very hard—even to excess for a specific reason and a limited period of time. Those who willingly back away when the reason is gone and the time has ended are not workaholics. Even they might feel some pangs of separation anxiety, but non-workaholics know the value of working through that to a life that involves more than work.

IS THERE A CONCLUSION?

For individual workers, the concluding thought would simply be a reminder to guard against sacrificing everything else in favor of work. Set aside some time to cut the tether of technological connectivity. Learn to prioritize and recognize the things that just don't need to be perfect. Decide who you most trust in your life; when they say work is taking over, listen and seriously consider the validity of their observations.

For managers in the workplace, the concluding recommendation is to look past surface-level appearance of high activity and question the assumption that people in the office on Saturday or in the evening are the more devoted employees. A person who consistently works on Saturday will soon begin to set work aside for the weekend, and the routine continues as habit more than as need. In contrast, a person who wants to be home for dinner each night and to attend the children's soccer games and swim meets on Saturday will work as efficiently as possible to protect that time. If both are getting their jobs done, who is the better worker?

When individuals are truly striving for work-life balance, and managers are looking beyond face time (visible presence in the workplace) to determine who gets rewarded in pay and promotion, those with the addictive pattern of workaholism are easy to spot. While this at first seems like a personal decision, it has ramifications that reach beyond that specific individual. The workaholic may say, "This is my chosen life and it is no one else's concern," but a different story often comes from family and friends. Additionally, as highlighted here, the patterns of interaction between the workaholic and others in the workplace are a hindrance to potential higher performance.

The addiction to work, sometimes called a clean addiction, leads to many of the same problems as other addictive behaviors and should be taken seriously for the good of both the individual and the organization.

References

Correa, C. 2002. "Procura-Se Atleta Corporativo." *Exame,* pp. 32–45. Available at http://portalexame.abril.com.br.

Goodman, B. 2006. "A Field Guide to the Workaholic." *Psychology Today.* Available at http://www.psychologytoday.com/articles/index.php?term=pto-20060518–000002. Accessed June 12, 2006.

McElroy, J. H. 1999. *American Beliefs.* Chicago: Ivan R. Dee.

Porter, G. 2005. "Workaholism." In *Work Family Encyclopedia.* Available at http://wfnetwork.bc.edu/. Accessed July 5, 2006.

Shaef, A. W., and D. Fassel. 1988. *The Addictive Organization.* San Francisco: Harper.

Further Reading: Beder, S. 2000. *Selling the Work Ethic.* Carlton North, Victoria: Scribe Publications; Ciulla, J. B. 2000. *The Work Life: The Promise and Betrayal of Modern Work.* New York: Times Books/Random House; Fassel, D. 1990. *Working Ourselves to Death: The High Cost of Workaholism and the Rewards of Recovery.* New York: HarperCollins;

Fraser, J. A. 2001. *White-Collar Sweatshop: The Deterioration of Work and Its Rewards in Corporate America.* New York: Norton; Killinger, B. 1991. *Workaholics: The Respectable Addicts.* New York: Simon & Schuster; Kofodimos, J. 1993. *Balancing Act: How Managers Can Integrate Successful Careers and Fulfilling Personal Lives.* San Francisco: Jossey-Bass; O'Neil, J. R. 1993. *The Paradox of Success: When Winning at Work Means Losing at Life.* New York: Putnam; Robinson, B. E. 1989. *Work Addiction.* Deerfield Beach, FL: Health Communications; Robinson, B. E. 1998. *Chained to the Desk: A Guidebook for Workaholics, Their Partners and Children, and the Clinicians Who Treat Them.* New York: New York University Press; Schor, J. 1993. *The Overworked American: The Unexpected Decline of Leisure.* New York: Basic Books.

Gayle Porter

GENERAL BIBLIOGRAPHY

Anderson, Ronald M., Thomas H. Rice, and Gerald F. Kominski, *Changing the U.S. Health Care System: Key Issues in Health Services Policy and Management.* 2nd ed. San Francisco: Jossey-Bass, 2001.

Anderson, Terry H. *The Pursuit of Fairness: A History of Affirmative Action.* New York: Oxford University Press, 2004.

Bass, Bernard M. *Leadership and Performance beyond Expectations.* New York: Basic Books, 1985.

Batra, R. *The Myth of Free Trade: The Pooring of America.* New York: Touchstone, 1996.

Beckwith, F., and T. Jones, eds. *Affirmative Action: Social Justice or Reverse Discrimination?* Amherst, NY: Prometheus Books, 1997.

Blair, R. D., and J. L. Harrison. *Monopsony: Antitrust Law and Economics.* Princeton, NJ: Princeton University Press, 1993.

Blau, Francine, Marianne Ferber, and Anne Winkler. *The Economics of Women, Men, and Work.* Upper Saddle River, NJ: Prentice Hall, 1998.

Borjas, George J. *Friends or Strangers: The Impact of Immigrants on the U.S. Economy.* New York: Basic Books, 1990.

Burton, G. Malkiel. *A Random Walk Down Wall Street.* New York: W. W. Norton, 1973.

Cappelli, Peter. *The New Deal at Work: Managing the Market Driven Workforce.* Boston: Harvard Business School Press, 1999.

Charkham, Jonathan, and Anne Simpson. *Fair Shares: The Future of Shareholder Power and Responsibility.* Oxford: Oxford University Press, 1999.

Clotfelter, Charles T., and Philip J. Cook. *Selling Hope: State Lotteries in America.* Cambridge, MA: Harvard University Press, 1989.

Conger, Jay A., R. N. Kanungo, and associates. *Charismatic Leadership: The Elusive Factor in Organizational Effectiveness.* San Francisco: Jossey-Bass, 1988.

Congressional Research Service. *China's Currency: Economic Issues and Options for U.S. Trade Policy.* CRS Report for Congress. Washington, DC: Library of Congress, April 18, 2006.

Cook, Thoms. *Supply Chains Post 9/11.* New York: Springer, 2006.

Coontz, Stephanie. *Marriage, a History.* New York: Viking, 2005.

Cronin, Anne M. *Advertising Myths.* London: Routledge, 2004.

Cross, Gary. *An All Consuming Society: Why Commercialism Won in Modern America.* New York: Columbia University Press, 2001.

Crystal, Graef S. *In Search of Excess: The Overcompensation of American Executives.* New York: W. W. Norton, 1991.

Curry, G., and C. West, eds. *The Affirmative Action Debate.* New York: Perseus Books, 1996.

Danziger, Pamela N. *Why People Buy Things They Don't Need.* New York: Paramount Market, 2002.

D'Aveni, Richard A. *Hypercompetition: Managing the Dynamics of Strategic Maneuvering.* New York: Free Press, 1994.

Deal, Terrence E., and Allan A. Kennedy. *The New Corporate Cultures: Revitalizing the Workplace after Downsizing, Mergers and Reengineering.* New York: Perseus, 1999.

Dychtwald, Maddy. *Cycles: How We Will Live, Work, and Buy.* New York: Free Press, 2003.

Ellig, Bruce R. *The Complete Guide to Executive Compensation.* New York: McGraw-Hill, 2002.

Federal Trade Commission. *Investigation of Gasoline Price Manipulation and Post-Katrina Gasoline Price Increases.* Washington, DC: Federal Trade Commission, 2006.

Fried, Bruce, and Laura Gaydos, eds. *World Health Systems: Challenges and Perspectives.* Chicago: Health Administration Press, 2002.

Funabashhi, Yoichi. *Managing the Dollar: From the Plaza to the Louvre.* 2nd ed. Washington, DC: Institute for International Economics, 1989.

Geffner, Robert, Mark Braverman, Joseph Galasso, and Janessa Marsh. *Aggression in Organizations: Violence, Abuse, and Harassment at Work and in Schools.* Binghamton, NY: Haworth Maltreatment and Trauma, 2004.

Gratzer, David. *The Cure: How Capitalism Can Save American Health Care.* New York: Encounter Books, 2006.

Greenblatt, Joel, and Andrew Tobias. *The Little Book That Beats the Market.* New York: John Wiley, 2005.

Gregory, Raymond. *Unwelcome and Unlawful: Sexual Harassment in the American Workplace.* Ithaca, NY: Cornell University Press, 2004.

Greider, Katharine. *The Big Fix: How the Pharmaceutical Industry Rips Off American Consumers.* New York: Public Affairs, 2003.

Grogan, Sarah. *Body Image.* New York: Routledge Press, 2007.

Hanuskek, Eric A. "School Resources and Student Performance." In *The Effect of School Resources on Student Achievement and Adult Success,* ed. Gary Burtless. Washington, DC: Brookings Institution Press, 1996.

Hewlett, Sylvia A., Carolyn B. Luce, P. Shiller, and Sandra Southwell. *The Hidden Brain Drain: Off-Ramps and On-Ramps in Womens' Careers.* Research Report 9491. Cambridge, MA: Harvard Business Review, March 2005.

Hoffer, Jeffrey A., Joey F. George, and Joseph S. Valacich. *Modern Systems Analysis and Design*. Upper Saddle River, NJ: Prentice Hall, 2005.

Irwin, D. A. *Free Trade Under Fire*. 2nd ed. Princeton, NJ: Princeton University Press, 2002.

Kamentz, Anya. *Generation Debt: Why Now Is a Terrible Time to Be Young*. New York: Riverhead Books, 2006.

Kang, Lawler. *Passion at Work: How to Find Work You Love and Live the Time of Your Life*. Upper Saddle River, NJ: Prentice Hall, 2005.

Katznelson, I. *When Affirmative Action Was White: An Untold History of Racial Inequality in Twentieth Century America*. New York: W. W. Norton, 2005.

Kilbourne, Jean. *Deadly Persuasion: Why Women and Girls Must Fight the Addictive Power of Advertising*. New York: Free Press, 1999.

———. *Can't Buy My Love: How Advertising Changes the Way We Think and Feel*. New York: Simon and Schuster, 2000.

Kohn, Stephen M., Michael D. Kohn, and David K. Colapinto. *Whistleblower Law: A Guide to Corporate Legal Protections and Procedures*. Westport, CT: Praeger, 2004.

Lee, Dwight R., and Richard B. McKenzie. *Getting Rich in America*. New York: HarperCollins, 1999.

Leonard, Gregory K., and Lauren J. Stiroh, eds. *Economic Approaches to Intellectual Property Policy, Litigation, and Management*. White Plains, NY: National Economic Research Associate, 2005.

Lindsey, Brick, and Daniel Ikenson. *Anti Dumping 101: The Devilish Details of Unfair Trade Law*. Trade Policy Analysis 20. Washington, DC: Cato Institute, November 2002.

Lomborg, Bjorn. *The Skeptical Environmentalist*. Cambridge: Cambridge University Press, 2001.

MacKinnon, Catharine. *Sexual Harassment of Working Women: A Case of Sex Discrimination*. New Haven, CT: Yale University Press, 1979.

Manning, Robert D. *Credit Card Nation*. New York: Perseus, 2000.

McKinnell, Hank. *A Call to Action: Taking Back Healthcare for Future Generations*. New York: McGraw-Hill, 2005.

McNeal, James U. *The Kids' Market: Myths and Realities*. Ithaca, NY: Paramount Market, 1999.

Mitchell, William C. *Beyond Politics: Markets, Welfare, and the Failure of Bureaucracy*. Boulder, CO: Westview Press, 1994.

Monks, Robert A. G. *The Emperor's Nightingale: Restoring the Integrity of the Corporation in the Age of Shareholder Activism*. New York: John Wiley, 1998.

———. *The New Global Investors: How Shareowners Can Unlock Sustainable Prosperity Worldwide*. New York: John Wiley, 2001.

Morgan, Carol M., and Doran J. Levy. *Segmenting the Mature Market*. Ithaca, NY: American Demographics Books, 1996.

Murphy, Evelyn, and E. J. Graff. *Getting Even: Why Women Don't Get Paid Like Men—and What to Do about It*. New York: Simon and Schuster, 2005.

Murray, Charles. *Losing Ground*. New York: Basic Books, 1984.

Neef, D. *E-Procurement: From Strategy to Implementation*. Upper Saddle River, NJ: Prentice Hall, 2001.

Nelson, B., and D. R. Spitzer. *The 1001 Rewards and Recognition Fieldbook: The Complete Guide.* New York: Workman, 2002.

Nilles, J. *Managing Telework: Strategies for Managing the Virtual Workforce.* New York: John Wiley, 1998.

Oates, W. E. *The RFF Reader in Environmental and Resource Policy.* 2nd ed. Washington, DC: RFF Press, 2005.

Pearce, John A., II. "The Company Mission As a Strategic Goal." *Sloan Management Review,* Spring 1982, 15–24.

Pink, D. *Free Agent Nation: The Future of Working for Yourself.* New York: Warner Business Books, 2002.

Porter, G. "Workaholism." In *Work Family Encyclopedia.* Boston: Sloan Foundation Work and Family Research Network, 2005. http://wfnetwork.bc.edu/.

Quadagno, Jill. *One Nation, Uninsured: Why the U.S. Has No National Health Insurance.* Oxford: Oxford University Press, 2005.

Richardson, John E., ed. *Business Ethics, Annual Editions.* New York: McGraw-Hill/Dushkin, 2007.

Schiffman, Leon G., and Leslie Lazar Kanuk. *Consumer Behavior.* 9th ed. Upper Saddle River, NJ: Pearson Education, 2007.

Schmidt, F. L., D. O. Ones, and J. E. Hunter. "Personnel Selection." *Annual Review of Psychology* 43 (1992): 627–70.

Schwartz, Mimi, and Sherron Watkins. *Power Failure: The Inside Story of the Collapse of Enron.* New York: Random House, 2003.

Scoble, R., and S. Israel. *Naked Conversations.* New York: John Wiley, 1996.

Segrave, Kerry. *Age Discrimination by Employers.* Jefferson, NC: McFarland, 2001.

Shaviro, Daniel N. *Corporate Tax Shelters in a Global Economy.* Washington, DC: AEI Press, 2004.

Steinhorn, Leonard. *The Greater Generation: In Defense of the Baby Boom Legacy.* New York: St. Martin's Press, 2006.

Stith, A. *Breaking the Glass Ceiling: Sexism and Racism in Corporate America: The Myths, Realities, and the Solutions.* Toronto: Warwick, 1998.

Sullivan, Teresa A., Elizabeth Warren, and Jay Westbrook. *The Fragile Middle Class.* New Haven, CT: Yale University Press, 2001.

Tells, Gerard J. *Effective Advertising.* Thousand Oaks, CA: Sage, 2003.

Trevino, Linda K., and Michael E. Brown. "Managing to Be Ethical: Debunking Five Business Ethics Myths." *Academy of Management Executive* 18 (2004): 69–83.

Trevino, Linda K., and K. A. Nelson. *Managing Business Ethics: Straight Talk about How to Do It Right.* Hoboken, NJ: John Wiley, 2003.

Verville, Jacques, and Alannah Halingten. *Acquiring Enterprise Software.* Upper Saddle River, NJ: Prentice Hall, 2001.

Vogel, David. *The Market for Virtue: The Potential Limits of Corporate Social Responsibility.* Washington, DC: Brookings Institution Press, 2005.

Walsh, David. *Selling Out America's Children: How America Puts Profits before Values and What Parents Can Do.* Minneapolis, MN: Fairview Press, 1995.

Watson, Charles E. *Managing with Integrity: Lessons from America's CEOs.* Westport, CT: Praeger, 1990.

———. *How Honesty Pays: Restoring Integrity to the Workplace.* Westport, CT: Praeger, 2005.

Wattenberg, Ben J. *Fewer: How the New Demography of Depopulation Will Shape Our Future.* Chicago: Ivan R. Dee, 2004.

Wilson, Ian. "Strategic Planning Isn't Dead—It Changed." *Long Range Planning* 27 (1994): 12–24.

Woodward, Bob. *Maestro: Greenspan's Fed and the American Boom.* New York: Simon and Schuster, 2000.

ABOUT THE EDITORS AND CONTRIBUTORS

Michael L. Walden is a William Neal Reynolds Distinguished Professor in the Department of Agricultural and Resource Economics at North Carolina State University. Holder of a PhD from Cornell University, Walden's career spans 30 years and includes publication of seven books and hundreds of articles as well as service on dozens of commissions and study groups. Additionally, Walden writes a regular newspaper column and produces daily radio programs, for which he has won national awards.

Peg Thoms, PhD, is a professor of management and director of the MBA program at the Black School of Business, Penn State Erie, The Behrend College. She is the author of numerous books and articles on leadership and human resources management. In addition, she has 16 years of management experience.

Carl R. Anderson, CPA, MBA, Penn State Erie, The Behrend College, is the vice president of finance at High Pressure Equipment Company and an adjunct faculty member at Edinboro University of Pennsylvania. His areas of expertise are financial and cost management.

Arthur Benavie is a professor emeritus of economics at the University of North Carolina at Chapel Hill. With a PhD from the University of Michigan, he received several teaching awards and published widely. He is the author of two recent books on Social Security and the federal deficit.

Michael E. Brown, PhD, is an assistant professor of management in the Sam and Irene Black School of Business at Penn State Erie. His research interests are positive approaches to leadership with a focus on ethical leadership.

Randy C. Brown, MA, is a lecturer in management and finance at the Black School of Business, Penn State Erie, The Behrend College. His areas of expertise are strategic management and human resources. He is also a real estate investor and has over 25 years of experience in the commercial real estate industry.

William Castellano, MS, Rutgers University, is a doctoral student in industrial relations and human resources at Rutgers University School of Management and Labor Relations. Castellano has over 20 years of management experience. His areas of expertise include human resource management and the management of contract human capital and strategic partnerships.

Jason A. Checque, Esq., practices law in Erie, Pennsylvania. He is a student in the MBA program at the Black School of Business, Penn State Erie, The Behrend College. He received his law degree from Duquesne University School of Law.

Lee A. Craig is an alumni distinguished undergraduate professor of economics at North Carolina State University, where he has taught for almost two decades. A noted economic historian, Craig has written on such diverse topics as the history of public pensions, the impact of mechanical refrigeration on nutrition, and the European economy.

John D. Crane, BS, Penn State Erie, The Behrend College, is an insurance management trainee with Bankers Life and Causality Company. He is also a psychological and marketing researcher at Penn State, with expertise in the effects of marketing endeavors on vulnerable populations and cultural socialization influences on individuals' behavior.

Ashutosh Deshmukh, PhD, is a professor of accounting and management information systems at the Black School of Business, Penn State Erie, The Behrend College. He specializes in accounting information systems and auditing and has published extensively in these areas.

Janet M. Duck, PhD, is a faculty member in the Management Division for the MBA program at the School of Graduate and Professional Studies, Penn State Great Valley. Her areas of expertise are virtual team dynamics, collaboration in online learning, and group efficacy.

Edward W. Erickson is a professor emeritus of economics at North Carolina State University, where he taught for over 35 years. Predating the energy crises of the 1970s, he earned a PhD from Vanderbilt University and wrote his dissertation on the oil market. He then became an internationally recognized expert on energy and oil and published and consulted on these topics throughout his career.

James F. Fairbank, PhD, is an associate professor of management at the Black School of Business, Penn State Erie, The Behrend College. Prior to his academic career, he was an officer in the U.S. Navy and a manager of technical business development in public and private companies.

Keith C. Farrell, CPA, MBA, Penn State Erie, The Behrend College, is the accounting manager at Reed Manufacturing Company. His areas of expertise are financial accounting, cost management, and corporate taxation.

Robert M. Fearn, a professor emeritus of economics at North Carolina State University, earned a PhD from the University of Chicago and focused his teaching, research, and writing on the operation of labor markets. Prior to his academic career, he worked as a specialist on the former Soviet Union's economy for the U.S. Central Intelligence Agency.

Thomas Grennes is a professor of economics at North Carolina State University, where he has taught students for 40 years. His research specialties are international trade and monetary economics. He has published books and academic articles and has been a guest lecturer in eastern Europe.

Jeanne M. Hogarth is program manager in the Division of Consumer and Community Affairs at the Federal Reserve Board. She has had a long career in education, including as a high school teacher and an associate professor at Cornell University. Her PhD is from Cornell University, and she has published widely on consumer economics and personal finance.

Ying Hong, with an MS in industrial/organizational psychology from Saint Mary's University, is a doctoral candidate in human resource management at the School of Management and Labor Relations, Rutgers University. Her expertise is human resource management and customer service outcomes.

John M. Hood is president of the John Locke Foundation, a public policy think tank in North Carolina. A graduate of the University of North Carolina–Chapel Hill's School of Journalism, Hood is a syndicated columnist whose articles have appeared in such publications as *Reader's Digest,* the *Wall Street Journal,* and the *National Review.* He has also authored three books.

Dale M. Hoover is professor emeritus of agricultural and resource economics and economics at North Carolina State University, where he taught from 1959 to 1995. His fields of expertise include education policy, rural labor markets, farm programs, and income support programs.

David N. Hyman has been a professor of economics at North Carolina State University for over 35 years. He earned his PhD from Princeton University. He is the author of several popular college-level economics textbooks and served on the staff of the President's Council of Economic Advisors during the Reagan administration.

Philip K. Iobst, PhD, is a lecturer in management with a teaching interest in business ethics at the Black School of Business, Penn State Erie, The Behrend College. He spent 20 years in corporate executive positions in manufacturing, insurance, and health care. He also does management and strategy consulting with many nonprofit organizations.

Eric C. Jackson, PhD, is an assistant professor of management at the Black School of Business, Penn State Erie, The Behrend College. He worked in the chemical industry from 1982 to 1998 as a manager in engineering, production, and research.

James H. Johnson Jr. is the William R. Kenan Jr. Distinguished Professor of Entrepreneurship and director of the Urban Investment Strategies Center at the University of North Carolina at Chapel Hill. His PhD is from Michigan State University, and his research interests include community economic development and the effects of demographic change on the workplace. Johnson is frequently quoted in the national media, including *USA Today* and National Public Radio.

Kerry A. King, PhD, is an assistant professor of economics at the Black School of Business, Penn State Erie, The Behrend College. Her areas of expertise are managerial and public economics.

Amanda Knepper, MBA, Penn State Erie, The Behrend College, is an accountant.

Brandon Kramer, MBA, Penn State Erie, The Behrend College, is a territory manager for Kos Pharmaceuticals. His areas of expertise are health care management and pharmaceutical sales.

John S. Lapp is an alumni distinguished undergraduate professor of economics at North Carolina State University, where he has taught for over 30 years. His PhD is from Princeton University, and his research and publications have concentrated on inflation, interest rates, the Federal Reserve, and monetary policy.

David Lepak, PhD, is an associate professor of human resource management and director of the doctoral program at the School of Management and Labor Relations, Rutgers University. His research interests include the strategic management of human capital and managing the contingent workforce.

Kenneth Louie, PhD, is an associate professor of economics and chair of the International Business Program at the Black School of Business, Penn State Erie, The Behrend College. His areas of expertise are international economics and the economics of labor markets.

Phylis M. Mansfield, PhD, is an associate professor of marketing at the Black School of Business, Penn State Erie, The Behrend College. She is the author of several book chapters and articles on consumer complaint resolution, service quality, and social issues and ethics in marketing. In addition, she has 20 years of corporate marketing experience.

Steve Margolis is professor of economics at North Carolina State University. With a PhD from the University of California–Los Angeles, his research has focused on issues related to industrial organization, including questions of antitrust, networks, and brand names. Dr. Margolis has also consulted for major corporations.

Anne E. McDaniel, MA, Ohio State University, is a doctoral student in sociology at Ohio State. Her areas of expertise include comparative research in gender and educational stratification.

Robert J. Nelson, MEd, is a lecturer in management information systems and computer science at the Black School of Business, Penn State Erie, The Behrend College. His areas of expertise are systems analysis and enterprise-wide information systems. In addition, he has over 25 years of information technology experience.

Kathleen J. Noce, PhD, is a lecturer of management information systems at the Black School of Business, Penn State Erie, The Behrend College. She is the director of Partnership-Erie, an outreach center providing Web site and technical assistance to nonprofit organizations. In addition, she has over 25 years of experience in the area of information technology and systems implementation in industry and education.

Raymond Owens is a research economist at the Federal Reserve Bank of Richmond. He holds academic degrees from Virginia Tech, and he tracks the national and regional economies for the bank. A frequent public speaker, Owens has also written papers on credit issues, real estate markets, and economic development incentives.

Diane H. Parente, PhD, is associate professor of management at the Black School of Business, Penn State Erie, The Behrend College. She is a second-career academic and the author of numerous articles mostly concerning interdisciplinary solutions to business issues. She is a frequent speaker on strategy, online education, and project management.

Allan M. Parnell is vice president of the Cedar Grove Institute for Sustainable Communities. He received his PhD degree in sociology from the University of North Carolina at Chapel Hill and has served as a research associate at the National Academy of Sciences and on the sociology faculty at Duke University.

E. C. Pasour Jr. is a professor emeritus of agricultural and resource economics at North Carolina State University. With a PhD from Michigan State University, Pasour is the author of two books and numerous articles, primarily on the agricultural economy and market economics. He received a Freedom's Foundation Leavey Award for Excellence in Private Enterprise Education in 1988.

Douglas K. Pearce is professor of economics and department head at North Carolina State University. His PhD is from the University of Wisconsin–Madison, and his research concentration is on monetary economics. He has published in recognized journals such as the *Journal of Macroeconomics,* the *Southern Economic Review,* and *Economic Inquiry.* He has also worked for the Federal Reserve Bank of Kansas City.

Umer Pervez, MBA, Penn State Erie, The Behrend College.

Daniel J. Phaneuf is an associate professor of agricultural and resource economics at North Carolina State University and director of the Center for Environmental and Resource Economics Policy. His PhD is from Iowa State University, and his teaching and research are directed toward environmental and resource issues such as pollution control and valuing unpriced natural amenities.

Mary Beth Pinto, PhD, is an associate professor of marketing and director of the Center for Credit and Consumer Research at the Black School of Business, Penn State Erie, The Behrend College. She is the author of numerous articles on consumer behavior, health care marketing, and advertising.

Gayle Porter, PhD, is a member of the management faculty at the Rutgers University School of Business in Camden, New Jersey. She has published more than 30 book chapters and articles on workaholism, collaborative work, and other topics related to employee performance and development. Porter previously worked in industry for 20 years.

Melinda Przybyszewski, MBA, Penn State Erie, The Behrend College, works for Stearns Promotional Services, Inc. Her areas of expertise are accounting and budgeting.

Mitch Renkow is professor in the Department of Agricultural and Resource Economics at North Carolina State University. With a PhD from that same institution, his teaching and research focus on economic development and regional economics. He also conducts programs for public audiences on issues related to governmental costs and budgets and benefits and costs from rapid residential growth.

Benjamin Russo is an associate professor of economics at the University of North Carolina at Charlotte. He earned his PhD from the University of Iowa and has become a nationally recognized expert on public finance, including tax reform and the relative merits of alternative types of taxes. He has served on state-level commissions and has published in prestigious journals.

Paul W. Schneider, MBA, Penn State Erie, The Behrend College, plans to pursue a PhD in management. He has numerous regional publications and professional organization memberships and specializes in communications.

John J. Seater is professor of economics at North Carolina State University. With a PhD from Brown University, he has also worked at the Federal Reserve Bank of Philadelphia. Both his teaching and research are in the areas of macroeconomics and monetary economics, and his journal publications include articles on impacts of budget deficits, movements in interest rates, and the response of household spending to changes in income.

Melissa Silka, MBA, Penn State Erie, The Behrend College. Professional in the insurance industry.

John Silvia is chief economist for Wachovia Corporation. He holds a PhD from Northeastern University, and prior to joining Wachovia, he worked for Kemper Funds and in positions at the U.S. Congress. Silvia sits on several boards and advisory groups, including the Economic Development Board for the State of North Carolina and the National Association of Business Economics, and has been president of the Charlotte Economics Club.

Dawn M. Slokan, MBA, Penn State Erie, The Behrend College, is the director of finance for Cathedral Preparatory School. Her areas of expertise include finance, accounting, management, and human resources.

James F. Smith is chief economist for Parsec Financial Management and professor of practice at the Institute for the Economy and the Future at Western Carolina University. Dr. Smith held prior positions at the University of North Carolina–Chapel Hill, the National Association of REALTORS, Sears, Robuck and Co., Union Carbide Corporation, and others. Named one of the most accurate economic forecasters by the *Wall Street Journal,* Smith has a PhD from Southern Methodist University.

Rebecca A. Smith, MBA, Penn State Erie, The Behrend College, is a lead buyer on the Strategic Sourcing Team at the Transportation Division of General Electric. Her areas of expertise are supply chain and operations management.

Peter B. Southard, PhD, is an assistant professor of management at the Black School of Business, Penn State Erie, The Behrend College. His expertise is in supply chain management, operations planning and control systems, and information systems. His management experience includes banking and the U.S. Department of Agriculture.

James A. Stanford, MBA, Penn State Erie, The Behrend College, has areas of expertise including Web site design, server-side scripting, and rich application development using PHP.

William M. Sturkey, MA, African American Studies Department, University of Wisconsin–Madison, is a PhD student in history. His area of expertise is the post–World War II history of African Americans.

Alfred G. Warner, PhD, is an associate professor of management at the Black School of Business, Penn State Erie, The Behrend College. His research interests are in strategic responses to innovation as well as the evolution of the institutional background of business.

Charles E. Watson is professor of management at Miami University (Ohio). A former manager with wide business experience, he is the author of over two dozen articles and eight books in management, including *Managing with Integrity* (Praeger, 1991; a Book-of-the-Month Club selection) and *How Honesty Pays* (Praeger, 2005).

Walter J. Wessels is a professor of economics at North Carolina State University. A nationally recognized expert on the labor market, his PhD is from the University of Chicago, and he has been teaching for over 30 years. His recent research and publications have dealt with the impact of unions and consequences for raising the minimum wage.

Xin Zhao, PhD, is an assistant professor of finance at the Black School of Business, Penn State Erie, The Behrend College. Her areas of expertise are market microstructure, IPOs, and investments.

INDEX